SOCIETY AND EXCHANGE IN NIAS

OXFORD STUDIES IN SOCIAL AND CULTURAL ANTHROPOLOGY

Oxford Studies in Social and Cultural Anthropology represents the work of authors, new and established, which will set the criteria of excellence in ethnographic description and innovation in analysis. The series serves as an essential source of information about the world and the discipline.

SOCIETY AND EXCHANGE
IN NIAS

ANDREW BEATTY

CLARENDON PRESS · OXFORD
1992

Oxford University Press, Walton Street, Oxford OX2 6DP

Oxford New York Toronto
Delhi Bombay Calcutta Madras Karachi
Petaling Jaya Singapore Hong Kong Tokyo
Nairobi Dar es Salaam Cape Town
Melbourne Auckland

and associated companies in
Berlin Ibadan

Oxford is a trade mark of Oxford University Press

Published in the United States
by Oxford University Press, New York

British Library Cataloguing in Publication Data
Data available

Library of Congress Cataloging in Publication Data
Beatty, Andrew.
Society and exchange in Nias / Andrew Beatty.
p. cm. — (Oxford studies in social and cultural
anthropology)
Includes bibliographical references and index.
1. Ceremonial exchange—Indonesia—Nias Island. 2. Rites and
ceremonies—Indonesia—Nias Island. 3. Kinship—Indonesia—Nias
Island. 4. Marriage customs and rites—Indonesia—Nias Island.
5. Nias Island (Indonesia)—Social life and customs. [1. Nias
Island (Indonesia)—Politics and government.] I. Title.
II. Series.
GN635.I65B43 1992 392'.09598—dc20 91–30711
ISBN 0–19–827865–9

Typeset by Hope Services (Abingdon) Ltd.
Printed and bound in
Great Britain by Biddles Ltd.,
Guildford and King's Lynn

For Mercedes

ACKNOWLEDGEMENTS

The research for this book was funded by a grant from the Economic and Social Research Council, and also by awards from Wolfson College, Oxford, and the Radcliffe-Brown Memorial Fund. The revision for publication was completed with the help of a Postdoctoral Fellowship from the British Academy. To all of these institutions I am grateful.

I would also like to thank the following institutions in Indonesia: Lembaga Ilmu Pengetahuan in Jakarta and Universitas Sumatera Utara in Medan, which co-ordinated the research project; Kantor Bupati Nias, Kantor Polisi Gunung Sitoli, and Kantor Camat Gomo, all of which were helpful in processing permits.

I would like to express my sincere gratitude to Dr R. H. Barnes, my supervisor at Oxford from 1983 to 1989, for his teaching and advice, for his unfailing support, and for many invaluable criticisms and comments. I have also learned much from the example of his work. My doctoral examiners, Professor Rodney Needham and Dr C. W. Watson, gave the thesis a careful reading and their suggestions have helped greatly in turning it into a book.

My wife, Mercedes, has shared in every aspect of the research from the very beginning. Her suggestions and criticisms have been crucial in the writing of the book; above all I thank her for sharing fieldwork with me.

Many people gave us their friendship and support in Nias. The Catholic Mission in Gunung Sitoli, Teluk Dalam, and Hilialawa, provided encouragement and friendship. My sincere thanks go to Father Johannes Hämmerle and the Fathers of the mission. The neighbouring chiefs, Ama Gazulo, Ama Da'oruzu, Ama Da'aro'ö, Ama Gatina, and Ama Rosa forgave my choice of Sifalagö Susua and were always courteous and helpful. To our hosts for the best part of two years, the people of Sifalagö, I express my profound gratitude and affection. My principal informant was Ama Huku (Farongo Ata'u'ö) who was both a fine teacher and a friend. Many others spent hours explaining the finer points of custom or offered simple companionship; but among special friends must be counted the following: the late chief of Sifalagö Ama Wati'asa (Fandru Humönö) and his wife Ina Setia, Ama Gamböta, Ama and Ina

Duho'aro, Ama Asamina, Ama and Ina Dahonogö, Ama Yumina, Wa'ö Laia, Ina Wogati, Ama Yarma, Ama Saya, Ama Da'orisi, Ama Firman, Ina Ato, Ina Ruti, Ama and Ina Damari, Ama Surya, Ama Yamo, Sökhiniwa'ö Laia, Ama and Ina Yerlina, Ama Ya'atulö, Ina Tinu, Ama Gati, Ama Hukumaera, Ama and Ina Siti, Ama Uzia, Ama and Ina Wati.

Chapter 3 of this book appeared in slightly shorter form in *Man* (1990), 454–71, under the title 'Asymmetric Alliance in Nias, Indonesia'. I am grateful to the editor and the Royal Anthropological Institute of Great Britain and Ireland for permission to reproduce this material. Chapters 9 and 10 are a greatly expanded version of 'Ovasa: Feasts of Merit in Nias', which appeared in *Bijdragen tot de Taal-, Land- en Volkenkunde* (1991). I thank the editors for permission to use this material here.

A.B.

CONTENTS

PLATES

between pp. 178 and 179

FIGURES

TABLES

RELATIONSHIP NOTATION

Standard abbreviations are used for kin types as follows:

F	father	H	husband
M	mother	W	wife
P	parent	E	spouse
B	brother	e	elder
Z	sister	y	younger
G	sibling	m	middle[1]
S	son	ms	man speaking
D	daughter	ws	woman speaking
C	child	F_2W	father's second wife

[1] i.e. one of a set of siblings between the eldest and youngest, irrespective of age relative to Ego.

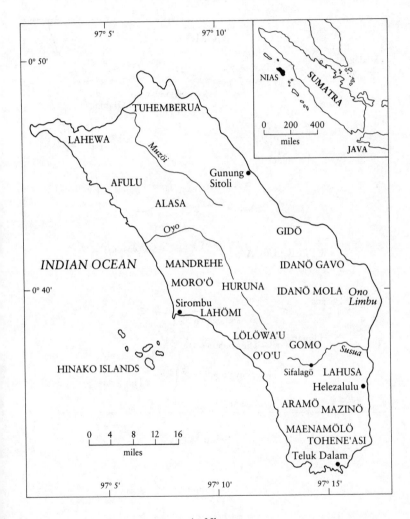

1. Nias

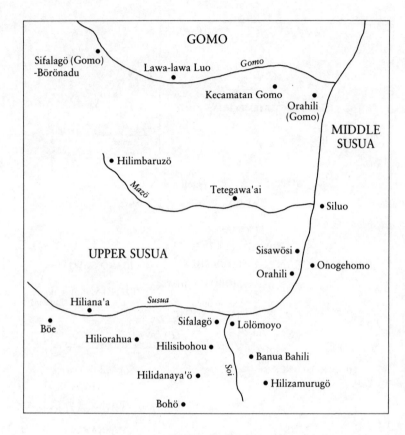

GOMO

Sifalagö (Gomo)
-Börönadu

Lawa-lawa Luo

Gomo

Kecamatan Gomo

Orahili
(Gomo)

MIDDLE
SUSUA

Hilimbaruzö

Mazö

Tetegawa'ai

Siluo

UPPER SUSUA

Sisawösi

Onogehomo

Orahili

Hiliana'a

Susua

Böe

Hiliorahua

Sifalagö

Lölömoyo

Hilisibohou

Soi

Banua Bahili

Hilidanaya'ö

Hilizamurugö

Bohö

2. Susua valley

Introduction

This book is about the relation between marriage alliance, social stratification, and ceremonial exchange in central Nias. The same complex of institutions has been analysed before in a number of societies of Southeast Asia, from highland Burma to eastern Indonesia, usually with an emphasis on one or other feature. The present study is intended to be both an ethnographic analysis and a contribution to theoretical discussions in that tradition.

The natural focus of a study of exchange and social organization in Nias is the feast of merit, in which the values of marriage alliance and social status are given equal prominence. The order of chapters therefore leads up to an analysis of the *ovasa* feast. However, the general approach is to consider the topic from every angle in order to build up a multifaceted interpretation of Nias social organization. To this end, the pragmatic aspects of exchange and rank are considered alongside symbolism and principles of order. Different modalities of gift-exchange are identified at different structural levels and the underlying principles are related to specific features of social structure. But I am as much concerned with the mundane interests of particular exchange partners as with abstract principles, and I explore in detail the politics of ceremonial exchange, concentrating on the links between prestige, rank, and power. Values and moral concepts are analysed using case histories and oral traditions as evidence, and the morality of gift-exchange is a focus of interest.

The first two chapters provide background information on the village community and local descent groups, leading into an analysis of marriage alliance which is intended to place Nias within a wider comparative framework. A brief account of the relationship terminology and chapters on marriage and bridewealth complete the first half of the book.

Chapter 8 explores concepts of measurement—a distinctive preoccupation in Nias and one which is central to the practice and symbolism of exchange. This leads into a long description of feasts of merit which shows the place of alliance in the sphere of political organization. Chapter 10 is devoted to rank and prestige and their relation to feasting.

1 Background

Nias is the largest of the chain of islands off the west coast of Sumatra. It has an area of 5,450 sq. km. and is located between 0°30′ and 1°30′ N. and 97° and 98° E. To the south are the Batu Islands, which were colonized by south Niasans some 200 years ago. The interior of Nias consists of forested hills up to 866 m. high interlaced with rivers and streams which are prone to regular flooding. With 200–250 rainy days annually there are no distinct wet or dry seasons, though rain is heaviest from October to December. The central and southern regions are thickly populated, with substantial villages and temporary field houses scattered among the hills.

Modern Nias is a *kabupaten* ('regency') of the North Sumatra province of Indonesia. Its 13 *kecamatan* ('administrative districts') contain an average of 50 villages each. In 1985 government statistics put the population at over 531,000 (including 22,583 in the Batu Islands) with an average density of 94.5 per sq. km.

The only major town in Nias is Gunung Sitoli, which has regular maritime commercial links with Sumatra, and is the principal market for cash crops and the source of imported goods. There is a small tourist industry in the south. Coastal dwellers (mainly Muslim) practise fishing from outrigger canoes. The vast majority of the population is engaged in agriculture and pig farming. Sweet potatoes, cassava, and rice are the staple crops, cultivated in swiddens and gardens mostly by traditional methods (no plough, draught animals, or fertilizers are used). Wet-rice farming is restricted by hilly terrain and low technology. Cash crops include coffee, raw rubber, cloves, patchouli oil, and copra. Little primary forest remains, and there is a serious shortage of land.

There are few roads on the island outside the north-east. A trunk road 120 km. long, connecting Gunung Sitoli with the southern port Teluk Dalam, was built only a few years ago over a derelict track but is frequently impassable. The journey once took me 24 hours, though this was possibly a record. There are no motor roads to the interior districts of Gomo and Lahusa. The field location is about 20 km. from the trunk road in the heart of the Upper Susua valley.

The word 'Nias' is probably a corruption of the indigenous name for the island, *tanö niha* ('land of the people'). While all men of whatever ethnic group are *niha*, the inhabitants of Nias refer to themselves as *ono niha* ('natives of Nias'), in contrast to other Indonesians, who are *dava*. Used adjectivally, the word *niha* always means Niasan. Thus the Nias language is *li niha*; traditional Nias houses are *omo niha*.

2 Outline of Nias History

The origin of the Nias people is unknown. Culturally there are similarities with the Batak, Toraja, Ngaju Dayak, and peoples of eastern Indonesia; but more precise links cannot as yet be postulated. The language belongs to the Western Malayo-Polynesian branch of the Austronesian language family. Further research is needed to establish a subgrouping of Nias with other related languages, but attempts have been made to link it with Mentawai and Toba Batak (Nothofer 1984).

Attempts to date the settlement of Nias have mostly relied on the evidence of myths and genealogies, which go back thirty to forty generations (Marschall 1976: 75; Rappard 1909: 512). All sources agree that the first probable reference to Nias or a similarly named island is in the *Akhbar al-Sin wa 'l-Hind*, dated AD 851 but probably a century older according to a recent commentary (Tibbetts 1979: 6). Other Arabic sources, from the thirteenth century, indicate the relative antiquity of the slave trade with Nias (Schröder 1917: 698; Tibbetts 1979: 57). We can conclude that the culture of Nias which we know today was probably established in essence well before genealogical time begins.

Regional differences in dialect, culture, and architecture have posed a problem for scholars. There is an island-wide myth of origin from the centre of Nias, and clan pedigrees, though varying in length, all ultimately connect up with a few tribal progenitors. The great cultural variation in Nias cannot therefore easily be explained by a theory of separate waves of migration to the island, and there is no conclusive theory as to how the variations arose.

By the time the Dutch East India Company (VOC) began to take an interest in Nias in the 1660s, Aceh in north Sumatra was regularly importing slaves on a large scale (Lombard 1967: 94). The traders brought gold, the supreme prestige object in Nias, needed for bridewealth and feasts of merit. By exploiting the unquenchable demand for gold and the incessant feuding among chiefs, the Acehnese were able to continue trading despite European opposition (Moor 1837). Fear of slavers gave the VOC an entry and accounts for the trade and protection pacts they procured with coastal chiefs (reproduced in Schröder 1917). The slave trade led to the depopulation of large areas of the north and was not brought under control until early in the twentieth century. Probably the militarization of Nias society was due to the violence and anarchy created by this trade, rather than to head-hunting, as is usually assumed (see Moor 1837). In 1840 the port of north-east Nias, Gunung Sitoli, was garrisoned. In 1857 the whole island came nominally under Dutch control, but a full-scale conquest was impracticable while the Aceh War occupied Dutch military resources during the last quarter of the century (Ricklefs 1981: 135–8). Nias remained marginal to colonial interests until the change in policy towards the Outer Islands, which led to its complete conquest in 1906.

Traders from Sumatra, some of whom settled in the port of Gunung Sitoli, brought Islam to many coastal areas. Christianity was introduced by German Protestant missionaries of the Rheinisch Missionsgesellschaft (RMG) in 1865, its geographical spread coinciding with colonial domination. However, it made little progress until traditional social structure and ideology were broken down by missionary and government interference, paving the way for a wholesale rejection of tradition. From around 1915 a series of apocalyptic conversion movements swept across the island from the heavily missionized north-east (Müller 1931). By 1930 half the population had been converted. The character of Christianity in Nias today and its relation to traditional culture owe much to this period which has come to be known as the Great Repentance. Although the missionaries generally welcomed the movement and saw it themselves in apocalyptic terms, they lost spiritual authority to its charismatic native leaders and prophets (Müller-Krüger 1968: 284). After the Second World War, the RMG missionaries had to compete with nativistic schisms as well as the newly arrived Roman Catholic missionaries (ibid. 285). The war of faiths since the Great Repentance has been minutely documented and would repay further anthropological study (see Kayser 1976 and Schekatz 1969).

The result of a century of missionary activity is a hybrid folk

Christianity which emphasizes a prohibitive and Old Testament relation between God and men, leaving the traditional scheme of values and the ethos of social life in many ways unchanged. Of course, the prohibition of institutions such as slavery, head-hunting, ancestor worship, and all pagan rituals has left a vastly changed culture. I have endeavoured to describe the culture as it is rather than to write 'salvage anthropology'. Nevertheless, the past needs to be taken into account in an interpretation of the present, especially since Niasans have a strong sense of history and of the weight of tradition. The middle-aged and old men who exercise authority have lived through these changes and remain close to the past.

Post-Independence Nias has seen some economic development, an expansion of the administrative capital, and an increasing centralization of power away from the villages. There is a marked difference between the deculturation of the north-east and the rest of the island.

3 Field Research

In March and April 1986 I toured the south and centre of the island, with guides, in search of an interesting location. I had no special requirements except that the village should not be too dispersed and that it should have a traditional (as opposed to government-appointed) chief. Of the three culturally distinct areas which scholars, since Schröder, have been accustomed to call north, centre, and south, the 'centre'—actually well to the south—is least well known. As the mythical place of origin of the Nias people and the least influenced by outsiders, it seemed the obvious choice for an ethnographic study. It is also the last area in Nias where feasts of merit are still regularly staged.

Sifalagö is the largest village in the Susua valley, the furthest from the road, the most traditional, and also the most beautiful. We arrived in the village on the day of a spectacular wedding and having visited most of the villages in Gomo and canvassed opinion widely I was sure that this was the right place. The chief, who died near the end of my stay, was the last of an illustrious line and a man of great achievements and formidable character. The village is also the last in central Nias to have an *omo sebua* (a chief's house), which is a powerful symbol of tradition and a focus of local pride. My wife

Mercedes and I were fortunate to be able to live in it for the whole of our stay.

Due to delays in processing my permit I was not able to begin fieldwork until late June 1986; my wife joined me in September and we remained in Sifalagö until April 1987, when we were obliged to leave during the national elections. The renewal of permits took four months in Jakarta. We returned to the field in August and I remained there until the end of July 1988—my wife had returned to Oxford in January to continue her studies. The total period in the field was about twenty months out of two years in Nias.

Although I already knew Indonesian from previous visits to the country, field research was conducted almost entirely in the Nias language, which I had begun to learn in Nias before I could start fieldwork. Niasans are magnificent orators and listening to them was one of the great joys of fieldwork. Naturally the quality of data obtained in the first and second periods of research was very different.

4 Sources

Nias is one of the most extensively described islands in Indonesia. I refer to only a fraction of the literature in this book—a policy determined both by constraints of space and the scope of the topic. Full bibliographies have been published by Suzuki (1958) and Roth (1985). The primary source for any scholar is Schröder's massive encyclopaedic study (1917), which is strong on detail and hard facts, but often misleading in its theorizing ('here we find the pyramid builders in origin'). The unpublished colonial reports of the 1920s and 1930s, now housed in the Korn Collection at the KITLV library in Leiden, form an essential supplement to Schröder's investigation of district federations. Complementing the colonial emphasis on social institutions and customary law is the missionary literature on Nias religion and Steinhart's superb collection of texts from the Batu Islands (1934, 1937, 1954).

Nias studies were given a new impetus by Suzuki's Leiden thesis (1959) which reconsidered the data from a structuralist point of view. Several recent works have taken Suzuki's interpretation as their point of departure. Surprisingly, no fieldwork had been done prior to that of Wolfgang Marschall in 1973. His engaging study of life in a south Nias village placed the ethnography on a new footing and showed that fresh insights could be derived by an application of anthropological methods (Marschall 1976). It was largely with a similar hope that my own fieldwork was undertaken, and I believe that most of what I have to say in this book is original, both in the material presented and (as far as the two are separable) in its interpretation.

Mention must also be made of Father Johannes Hämmerle, who continues to perform an outstanding service both to the Nias people and to scholars generally in his recording of traditional culture. His latest work is a compendium of oral traditions from south Nias (1986). Bamböwö La'iya, a Niasan from Botohili in the south, has written a useful study of kinship in his home village (La'iya 1980).

Comparative references to other parts of Indonesia and elsewhere are restricted to those which advance the analysis; they could easily have been added to had space permitted. References to eastern Indonesia are prominent simply because models of social organization developed for that region have a particular relevance to Nias ethnography, besides having an unusual and exemplary analytical clarity.

5 A Note on the Nias Language

The language has at least three dialects, corresponding to the cultural areas—north, centre, and south. Recent studies by Indonesian linguists identify as many as five dialects (Halawa et al. 1983). The major linguistic boundary is between the south and the rest of the island. (The Batu Islanders speak the southern dialect.) The Bible was translated by Sundermann in 1905 into the northern (Laraga) dialect and this has become the 'standard' form in vernacular publications. Indonesian, the language of government bureaucracy and education, is not widely known among ordinary villagers.

Sundermann's dictionary (1905a) has not been superseded; and for the learner there is no rival to Fries's grammatical primer (1915), outdated though it is. In this book I have adopted some of the orthographic conventions of previous scholars and of works published in Niasan in the interests of uniformity and readability (see Halawa et al. 1983: ch. 2). The midback unrounded vowel is rendered 'ö'; /dʒ/ is spelt 'z'; /tʃ/ is spelt 'c' (as in Indonesian). A voiced bilabial fricative /β/, which is written 'w' in Dutch sources, is given here as 'v' to distinguish it from /w/. The glottal stop is indicated by an apostrophe, e.g. *su'a*.

All syllables are open; there is no *VC or *CVC form. Niasans themselves contrast this peculiarity with Indonesian and claim that it makes their language mellifluous and sonorous (which is true) as well as easy to learn (untrue). A grammatical feature which will be noticed by the reader is the modification of the beginning of certain words according to position in a phrase. Some of these changes can be attributed to phonotactics; others are a form of inflection. The main changes are rendered in the orthography as follows:

In the modified form, vowels are preceded by 'n' or 'g' (e.g. *ama* → *nama*; *ulö* → *gulö*); 'b' → 'mb'; 'd' → 'ndr' (*döfi* → *ndröfi*); 'f' → 'v'; 'k' → 'g'; 's' → 'z'; 't' → 'd'.

The northern /t/ becomes /tʃ/ in the central dialect (e.g. N. *tua*, C. *cua*, grandfather); and /d/ following a vowel becomes /dʒ/ (N. *adu*, C. *azu*, idol).

PART I

The Social Matrix

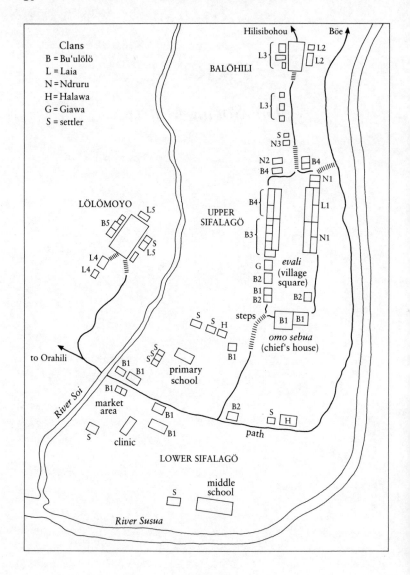

FIG. 1.1. Village plan of Sifalagö Susua

1
The Village

The villages of the Susua valley in central Nias are mostly buried in its thickly wooded hills; their seclusion, a legacy of the warlike past, reflects the cohesion of the community and suspicion of its neighbours. The tendency towards exclusiveness which equates Niasan with human (*niha*) to the neglect of other men is found also in the analogy between village, homeland, and cosmos, as if each village were a world unto itself. In fact, its self-sufficiency is breached by the exchange of brides, and the to and fro of festive invitations, as well as by petty trade in town goods.

Except on market-days, travellers hardly ever pass through the village square, preferring to skirt the main settlement and follow the course of the river on their way to buy a pig or reclaim a debt elsewhere. Though the fortified walls and guarded approaches of the old days have gone, the village remains aloof and unwelcoming, suspicious of strangers. Its tall houses present to the visitor a grim exterior; and the faces which appear at their latticed windows can see but cannot easily be seen.

The monumental style of Nias architecture, which Heine-Geldern (1972: 311) counts with 'the best that has ever been achieved in architectonic art outside of high civilizations', is calculated to create an impression of power. The stone-paved plaza, the arena of daily life and gargantuan feasts, has a gloomy grandeur which does not diminish with familiarity. Heroic narratives celebrate its rows of megaliths, its broad flagstones spattered red with betel juice and worn smooth by the feet of generations; and towering over all, the chief's house, raised on immense columns and casting a shadow over the end of the square. For all that, it is a scene of stark poverty: naked children with swollen bellies, skinny dogs, pigs rooting in the dirt, and an air of decrepitude and decay.

For most of the inhabitants, this hilltop settlement framed in stone and wood, with its surrounding fields and gardens, is the familiar world. In other villages one has affines and kinswomen who have married out, but contacts are generally limited to special occasions—visiting the sick, debt-collecting, feasts, and weddings. Village life is inward-looking and there is little curiosity about what goes on elsewhere. Corresponding to this narrowness of range there is a depth of history which gives an added dimension to social relations. In a setting in which genealogies reach back into mythical time, every important encounter or event is seen as part of a larger unfolding of history, connecting up with ancient feuds and alliances, illustrating family character, expiating past sins, and creating new social patterns out of the old. The poverty and shabbiness of the present is all too evident to people, but the glory of the past is something of which they are powerfully aware, and it gives their lives, in their own eyes, a significance and dignity which transcends their material circumstances.

This historical richness and social complexity contrasts with a sparseness of ritual and barrenness of symbol. A sense of a wider order, the sense of the whole which religion gives, is lost. Christianity has added a new perspective to ordinary life, but at the same time, as an alien and partially incorporated creed, it has fragmented experience; it does not permeate social life in the way of the old religion. It would be wrong, therefore, to begin this account with the myths of origin. If we want to understand Nias society as it is and not as it was, we must begin with the mundane reality of the village. Having understood the village as a historical entity and as a field of social relations, we can then appreciate the significance of the bonds of marriage alliance which intrude on its integrity, and the political ambitions which demand a wider audience for their realization.

1   The Modern Village

In the modern Indonesian state Sifalagö Susua is an administrative *desa* ('village cluster') consisting of seven hamlets or settlements scattered over a wide area of the Upper Susua. Official statistics put the total population in 1985 at 2,486, comprising a total of 487 *rumah tangga* ('nuclear families', defined in the census as house-holds). As such it is the largest of the 33 *desa* in Gomo district (*kecamatan*). The smallest, Ambukha, has only 197 inhabitants. However, these figures do not have much significance except in the minds of tax gatherers and statisticians, as the *desa* exists primarily as an administrative fiction. Some *desa* correspond to traditional village clusters. Others, like Sifalagö Susua, contain some hamlets which have little traditional connection with each other and whose links today are limited to official ones maintained by village officers.

In so far as I discuss 'the village' or 'village cluster' of Sifalagö in this book I am concerned only with those hamlets linked by history, common clanship, co-residence, and marriage alliance. Included in this category are Sifalagö (the capital), Balöhili, and Lölömoyo. My exclusion of the other settlements of the *desa* (Hilidanaya'ö, Banua Bahili, Hilizamurugö, Hilisibohou) is not a quest for traditional organization in disregard of modernity; it corresponds to the sociological rather than bureaucratic map of the area. Likewise, the descriptive isolation of a central cluster of hamlets is not an analytical convenience: though they were only welded into a village under a single chief in Dutch times, their development from the time of legendary first settlement has been linked, and members of these interrelated hamlets have long regarded themselves as fellow-villagers (*ono mbanua*). In contrast, Hilizamurugö, a large and dispersed settlement over an hour's walk from Sifalagö, was founded as late as three generations ago by fugitives from an internecine feud in Orahili village. The founders were granted protection by Sifalagö. Later raids drove them south to Aramö where they remained until colonial times, when they were able to repossess their land. Under Dutch and subsequent Indonesian administrations Hilizamurugö was governed from Sifalagö. Now it has its own *kepala dusun* ('ward/hamlet head') subservient to the *kepala desa* ('administrative village headman'). Banua Bahili was also founded by an offshoot of a lineage in Orahili in pre-colonial times. Due to the distance from Sifalagö and the lack of any traditional ties there is little contact between these hamlets and the 'capital' hamlet except on official government business and on market-days, when all the surrounding villages converge on Sifalagö.

Two other settlements are in a different category, deriving originally from Sifalagö. Although I did not include them in my household survey, I knew some of their inhabitants quite well. One of them, a master of oral tradition named Ama Gamböta, was among my best informants. His hamlet, Hilidanaya'ö, which is an hour from Sifalagö, was settled by a lineage of the Bu'ulölö clan about five generations ago. This lineage was forced to flee Sifalagö after a murder carried out on a fellow-clansman in revenge for adultery. Under Dutch rule part of the settlement was forcibly relocated in Sifalagö, but moved back to its land after Independence. It maintains some ties with Sifalagö but these are necessarily limited due to the distance, and visits are no more frequent than are those of members of other neighbouring villages. Its residents no longer own any land in Sifalagö.

The second offshoot of Sifalagö is Hilisibohou, a dispersed pioneer settlement inhabited by a single lineage of the Ndruru clan which moved there from Sifalagö after the war. Its inhabitants visit Sifalagö only on market-day and Sunday on the way to church. Sifalagö shares a church with Orahili, so attendance is not in itself an activity which enhances village solidarity.

On the basis of these considerations I excluded these outlying settlements from my household and genealogical survey and con-centrated on the central cluster comprising Sifalagö (upper and lower), Balöhili, and Lölömoyo. The survey was intended to be an exhaustive collection of basic data from a universe defined by sociological criteria, not a sample of the largely fictional entity which is the administrative village. Table 1.1 gives a summary of the residential composition of the village cluster. (A breakdown by local lineages is found in Appendix 1.) A large proportion of villagers (38%) live in field huts at a distance from their native hamlet. A rough distinction can be made between those hut-dwellers who maintain regular contact with a house in the village (which perhaps belongs to an agnate or is shared by a lineage segment) and those who have moved away on a permanent basis and who retain only nominal attachment to the village. In the government census all these hut-dwellers are included as members of the *desa*. However, over a hundred of them live in the wilds of Amoroa between Sifalagö and So'onogeu (Hilisimaetanö) in south Nias. It is with this latter village that they have more regular contact than with Sifalagö. Having made the gruelling four-hour journey there through forest and river to check for myself, I feel quite justified in regarding Amoroa and similar exile settlements as socially outside the village cluster under study. Many other natives of Sifalagö have built permanent or semi-permanent homes one or two hours away by forest path. Like their fellow-clansmen and affines in other villages, their visits to Sifalagö are confined to weddings, funerals, and feasts of merit. But for many villagers a spell of a few years in a field hut is only an interlude in their lives; in fact most residents have at one time or another spent a few years in the wilderness.

Niasans make a distinction between permanent houses (*omo*), temporary huts (*ose*), and semi-permanent field houses *(halama)*. In Table 1.1, for the sake of convenience I have adapted this useful threefold classification of buildings to my distinction between (1) residents, (2) hut-dwellers who remain actively a part of the village, and (3) those who can be regarded as exiles. In practice, there is a scale of attachment to/separation from the village; moreover, many of the remotest huts may be termed *ose*, and nearer ones *halama*. This does not detract from the usefulness (and sociological reality) of the distinction represented in the table.

Certain differences between the hamlets are immediately obvious. Lower Sifalagö differs from the rest in that all its inhabitants, except for a lone widow, are permanent residents. There is approximately one household per house in this hamlet, as one would expect given that over half of households are those of occupational settlers accompanied by only their immediate families. Correspondingly these inhabitants enjoy a higher standard of living.[1]

Little more than one-third of the largest hamlet, upper Sifalagö, actually resides permanently in the village. Many of the largest Bu'ulölö lineage, which is short of land near Sifalagö, moved between six and fifteen years ago to Amoroa and cleared new fields. Balöhili is still comparatively rich in land and has a greater proportion of permanent residents.

Lower Sifalagö has come into existence in the last twenty years. It is referred to as 'the market' (*ona*) or simply 'Sifalagö down there'. The site is a plain about 100 yards below the upper hamlet and outside the former village gate. It was here that the mission built a primary school in the 1920s. It now contains the government primary school (Sekolah Dasar) with accommodation for its four teachers, and a private middle school (SMP Swasta) maintained by individual subscription and staffed by young men of the village who have completed senior school (SMA or equivalent) in Gunung Sitoli (only two village girls have ever graduated from SMA). The nearest government middle school is in the district capital, Gomo, four hours away. Almost all children resident in the village, and a

---

[1] Settlers found in the rest of the village are of a traditional kind: uxorilocal sons-in-law or descendants of fugitives.

TABLE 1.1 Residential composition of the village cluster, 1986

Hamlet	Population[a]	Resident population[b]	Houses[c]	Households[d]	Resident households[e]	ose(%)[f]	halama(%)[g]
Lower Sifalagö	117	116	19	20	19	0.8	0
Upper Sifalagö	307	127	22	61	26	20	38
Balöhili	138	99	11	23	15	10	18
Lölömoyo[h]	77	53	9	14	8	29	3
TOTAL	639	395	61	118	68	—	—

Notes: The total number of individuals counted as *ose* dwellers is 99 (15%); the total for *halama* is 99 (15%); the total for *halama* is 145 (23%). The three categories of residence cannot easily be applied to hamlets excluded from my household survey. As dispersed offshoot settlements they lack a clear nucleus of permanent houses. The 18 households of Hilisibohou, for example, are scattered over a wide area, some of them occupying temporary huts, others in half-concrete houses which were formerly huts.

a Total (notional) population of each hamlet, based on who is counted to be a member, whether they are residents or hut-dwellers.
b Number of permanent residents in each hamlet.
c This figure refers to separate self-contained accommodation, whether a single undivided house, or an apartment in a larger building. More than one household (with a maximum of nine in my survey) may be attached, with varying degrees of commitment and differing sharing arrangements, to a house/apartment.
d Unit of production and consumption consisting usually of parents, children, and other dependents (e.g. widowed mother). A few households are based on the joint family of brothers with their wives, sons, and sons' families.
e Households residing permanently in the hamlet.
f Percentage of notional hamlet population living in temporary (*ose*) huts with a genuine attachment to a house in the hamlet.
g Percentage of notional hamlet population living permanently away in field houses (*halama*), with only a nominal attachment to a house and to the hamlet.
h The low percentage of *halama*-dwellers from Lölömoyo is due to the fact that I included several households in the *ose* category which are actually marginal.

large proportion of those living in field huts, attend primary school. By the time they have finished they have the elements of literacy and know a few words of Indonesian, mostly in the form of patriotic songs. Those few who complete middle school have an elementary grasp of the national language and can recite the five principles of the state ideology. SMA graduates, with experience of town life and access to the mass media, are generally fluent in Indonesian. It is recognized by villagers that the education available in the village is of little practical use and is of a lower standard than that offered by schools in town. However, the example of the few who complete their education and obtain government jobs encourages many in their hope that their children will secure a better living through education.

A polyclinic (Puskesmas), with a resident government paramedic dispenses, for purchase, all-purpose injections and some rudimentary first aid to Sifalagö and neighbouring villages. The major health problems of the population—malaria, cholera epidemics, and an infant mortality rate which I estimate at 40–50 per cent—are untreated. According to the paramedic only six couples in the hamlets I surveyed practise birth control.

In the same section of the village the market is located. Formerly the nearest weekly market (dating from colonial times) was in Helezalulu near the east coast, three hours' walk away. In 1971, shortly after the clinic was built, a market was opened in Sifalagö. Every Thursday lower Sifalagö is packed with market-goers from all the villages in the Upper Susua valley between Böe and Orahili. The rest of the week lower Sifalagö is quiet. Markets are held in two other villages on alternate days.

The market provides pots and pans, cloth, kerosene for lamps, tobacco, trinkets, etc. Half a dozen villagers of Sifalagö run stalls as a sideline to farming. The rest of the stalls are operated by people from neighbouring villages who rent a space. Some market-goers sell a little surplus betel or fruit for pin-money. Before the rice harvest there is a shortage and imported rice from Sumatra is sold by outside dealers, middlemen who live in villages near the trunk road. There is a lively trade in pigs beside the river Soi. Several pigs are bought by dealers from other villages and butchered on the spot for sale by the kilo. Ten years ago patchouli was introduced and now many enterprising young men plant this and sell the oil to outside dealers. There are no other cash crops produced on a significant scale. Unlike exchanges outside the market system, all dealings are transacted in cash.

Slightly more than half of the households in lower Sifalagö are those of settlers, who make their living out of the schools, market, or clinic. The other houses belong to villagers who run market stalls or who had moved there before the market was opened. In 1980 the village chief built a concrete house next to the market and moved down there from his traditional chief's house (*omo sebua*) in upper Sifalagö. This move, incidentally, made the division between his traditional and modern functions clearer. Meetings on traditional matters are usually held in the *omo sebua*, while visiting government officials are entertained down below in the modern house. Health, education, commerce, and state government are therefore located in the artificial community of lower Sifalagö, with its preponderance of settlers and periodic invasions of outsiders. Religion, the remaining component of modern Indonesia, is represented by a Protestant priest, another outsider, who is housed on a slope between upper and lower Sifalagö. The village (at least the central cluster of hamlets) shares a church with Orahili on its common border, built in 1957.

Thus the modern world is neatly confined physically and symbolically to a single area, though of course its influence is felt throughout the village. The half dozen occupational settlers have little contact with the upper hamlets and rarely set foot in them. It is the chief's lineage which spans this spatial and symbolic divide, having learned how to benefit from both old and new systems. Open to the outside, where the old hamlets are closed, the new settlement is nevertheless in some respects a world of its own, where people have more money, disdain manual labour, and have different manners. In itself, this isolation of one hamlet from another is nothing new; it merely gains a different rationale. Although the central hamlets are only a few minutes apart, it is surprising how little circulation there is among them. On Sundays (when work is prohibited by the Church) and on market-day, people wander from house to house socializing; otherwise one visits another hamlet only with a definite purpose in view. Generally, patterns of association remain traditional, based on ties of kinship and co-residence. Households with affinal links in two hamlets serve an important function as channels of communication in the village community as a whole.

2 The Traditional Village

This brings me to the question of what constitutes a traditional settlement. Village-cluster and hamlet alike are called *banua*, a word which also means 'sky' and 'heavens'. As in several Indonesian societies, the village is conceived to be on earth as it is in heaven (or vice versa). *Banua yawa* ('sky above') is strictly speaking the firmament, rather than the upper world where the gods reside, which is called Teteholi Ana'a. However, the analogy between these two realms—the heavenly and the earthly village—is explicit in mythology.

The traditional settlement is centred on a paved rectangular plaza called *evali* or, in poetic parallelism, *olayama* ('ceremonial dancing ground'). At one end, usually on an eminence and facing upstream, stands the house of the chiefly line, the *omo sebua* ('great house'). Along the sides (*bele nomo*), houses are ranged close together. In front of some of the houses stand megaliths (*behu*), unhewn columns erected at feasts of merit in pagan times.

Traditional Nias houses are among the finest in Southeast Asia and I cannot attempt to do justice to the subject here.[2] Raised on piles, like Toraja and Batak houses, they have soaring roofs double the height of the house itself, with projecting eaves hooding the façade. An *omo sebua* differs from an ordinary house (*omo niha*) in size rather than form. The chief's house in Sifalagö, the last of its kind in central Nias, stands 20 m. high, erected on massive columns 150 cm. in circumference. The interior of houses is light and airy with a large public front room (*tavolo*) separated from a private back area where the kitchen and bedrooms are located. In some houses the rear section has separate apartments for its constituent families.

Once crowded with ancestor figures, the traditional house is now bare and there is little or no furniture.[3] A bench runs along the inner front wall, built like a broad step into the structure of the façade. During gatherings the elders sit along it in a row, with their knees drawn up under tattered sarongs, like birds of prey roosting. From

---

[2] Good descriptions are found in Feldman 1979 and Viaro 1980.

[3] The missionary Noll (1930) claims that he once removed over 2,000 'idols' from the house of a Christian convert in the north. Kramer (1890) saw houses collapse under their weight.

their perch they can turn to survey the square through the window slats or to spit betel juice down on to the stones. A chief usually sits in the centre of the bench with his back resting on the central pillar, commanding the wide space before him. Women and children shuffle about on the floor, and lesser men squat on their haunches during the elders' speeches with upturned faces. When they get up they creep about to maintain the distinction of levels. The bedrooms are dark and musty, containing only a mat and a few heirlooms kept under lock and key. In contrast, the back area, which usually incorporates a big wood-framed hearth, is homely and intimate, furnished with an array of hunting instruments, bamboo water tubes, winnowing trays, fishing nets, half-woven mats, and coconut-shell ladles—all hanging from the walls or beams, with sometimes a row of pig's jaws over the lintel.

The houses surrounding the square in Sifalagö appear very old, but everything is prematurely aged in the dampness and heat. The large lineage houses on either side were built in the 1950s but have already acquired an encrusted weathered look, like venerable hulks drawn up on a shore. The outer planking rapidly becomes white and mottled with mildew. The massive pink boles of *afoa* wood on which the structure stands grow a soft greenish skin. But while the materials require periodic renewal, the basic design is unchanging, and a house may go through several incarnations from the time of its ancestral founding.

In a traditional settlement one end of the plaza is usually left open; the other, which is closed off by a house, is called *samalöi* ('that which ends', from *balö*, 'end'). The open end is the *hörö nevali* ('eye/end of the square'), where the graveyard (*nelu*) was often situated; in verse, passage beyond this point means death:

> *Sikoli ba nasi, sara wawa ba mangawuli*
> *Sikoli ba hörö nevali sagötö tanö lö fasae*
>
> Who travels over the sea returns in a month
> Who sojourns at the end of the village square
> is seen no more on this earth.

In Sifalagö the graveyard was to one side, in an area now left vacant, thus within the bounds of the village. Bodies were put to rot on platforms until the bones were clean, when, if the deceased was a man of rank, his spirit could be despatched to the upper world.

The present form of the village has evolved over many generations, and older men sometimes confusingly refer to features which have long ago disappeared, such as the graveyard and the former village gate, which still retain a topographical significance. The megaliths which fringe the square provide a map of the past and a roll-call of the village heroes. In the iconoclastic zeal following conversion to Christianity, a number of stone monuments were smashed or toppled. Most of them were immovable (proving what everyone knew, that men of the past were stronger), and in these more moderate times they remain a source of local pride. But the more perishable emblems of paganism, such as the village shrine, have gone. The *osali nazu* ('sacred house of idols') was a roofed shelter containing wooden statues of the village warrior heroes and guardian spirits. In Sifalagö it was located on top of a walled and paved embankment (*öli dao*) which formerly spanned the square about half-way up. In northern Nias the word *osali* referred to a council house used for village meetings and rituals. In the south this was called *bale* (a word which means 'stone paving' in the central dialect). There is no recollection of there ever having been a council house in central Nias, at least in the Susua valley. Village gatherings have always been held in the chief's house, which is big enough to hold a hundred dancers. The only other major change in the architecture of the village is the disappearance of the village gate, *bava göli* ('mouth of the fence'), which once stood next to the chief's house. Nowadays, in place of the narrow stone-framed entrance piercing a picket fence there is a rough flight of steps giving on to the square. The stones of the former gateway now serve as seats, with a panorama of the river below, and are a favourite place to sharpen a machete on one's way to the forest.

Along the centre of the square is a path which divides the village spatially into two. There is no term for this division and no evidence of a corresponding social divide. The fact that two lineages now face each other across it is fortuitous—in former times the arrangement was different. Likewise there is no fixed designation of right and left sides; indeed I rarely heard these terms used for spatial orientation. Usually one says simply *möi sa* or *tanö sa* ('to the side'). The important cardinal points are upstream (*raya*) and downstream (*yöu*). These words are in constant use. One never says 'he is at the house of Ama Yuni' without adding 'upstream' or 'downstream', even if the house is next door. I once heard a man tell a child who was trying to open a door to push the sliding peg 'downstream' (we should have said: 'to the left'). Villages along the Susua valley are always identified as upstream or downstream, as are particular fields and trees. Southerners are called *niha raya*, 'upstream people', northerners *niha yöu*. This is an idiomatic borrowing of the directions, since in fact the rivers of the centre flow east–west. As to the symbolic evaluation of this opposition, upstream lies the source or upper-course (*ulu*) which is associated with origins and things superior or sacred. Nobles in south Nias are *siulu* ('those at the source'). Downstream is the sea and the horizon (*amasulöna danö*, 'changing of the earth [with the sky]') inhabited by monsters and evil spirits.[4]

A second pair of directions of less significance is given by sunrise (*atumbukha luo*) and sunset (*aekhula luo*). One must not build a house facing the rising sun because illness and death will strike the house, just as the sun's rays penetrate it. North and south are both *talinga* ('ear'), that is, to one side or the other when one is facing east or west. These terms are rarely used, and practical directions are nearly always topographic.

Sifalagö and Balöhili are both oriented upstream–downstream, which happens to correspond nearly with the west–east axis. I was told that it was the former axis which determined the orientation when the settlements were founded. Lölömoyo, which also has a traditional layout, is roughly parallel with the river Soi. There are no other traditional sites intact in the area so I cannot say whether this orientation was always followed.

As elsewhere in Indonesia (Barnes 1974: 68; Forth 1981: 32), in constructing the house, vertical beams are placed in the direction in which the wood grew, i.e. with the root at the bottom. It is said to be the direction in which all living things grow. Horizontal pieces, e.g. floorboards, are laid with the root end towards the front of the house. The upswept beam-ends (*eve*) projecting from the façade, which Europeans have likened to ship's prows, are actually the buttress roots (*lali*) of certain species of hardwood. These roots grow from near the base of the tree above ground and are selected for their perfect curves. Pieces parallel with the façade are laid with the root end (*börö*) pointing downstream. The top or crown end (*hogu*) must point upstream to the source of the river. In principle

[4] Orientation and spatial symbolism in south Nias villages are along broadly similar lines (Marschall 1976: 67–8).

one sleeps head upstream; only the dead are laid out in the reverse direction. Actual sleeping arrangements show no particular attention to this principle.

Particular parts of the village are named according to some prominent characteristic or simply after the descent group which occupies the place, or its founder. The spot where the chief's house stands is called *Tuhe gafoa* ('Stump of the *afoa*'), after a great tree which was felled there. Beyond the lower gate a plot is reserved for the priest's house in the former 'Place of torture' (*Naha vakao*). No disrespect attaches to this position, though it is a little outside the *evali* and the stream of village life. Upstream is *Sotödömbawi* ('Has a pig's heart'), named after the shape of the hillock. Beyond this is *Ono Ndruru*, where a branch of the Ndruru clan lives.

Sifalagö and Lölömoyo are impressive traditional settlements with many fine houses. Balöhili, too, once had an *omo sebua*, a lineage house with nine separate apartments. But when it burned down forty-five years ago there were no resources to rebuild it. The present hamlet consists of small houses 'in the Indonesian style' (*omo ndrava*).

3   A Brief History of the Settlements

For an explanation of the present disposition of local descent groups in the village we must turn briefly to settlement history, as recorded in oral tradition. The area around Sifalagö was inhabited by ancestors of the present villagers several generations before a village of that name existed. The Bu'ulölö clan founded Sifalagö but the Laia claim to have preceded them in the area. Occasionally one hears a veteran of one clan refer disparagingly to the other as *sanofa* ('recent arrivals', 'incomers'), meaning they settled in Sifalagö 'only' seven or eight generations ago. The story of first settlement is told by the Bu'ulölö as follows.

The three major clans of Sifalagö descend from three brothers— in birth order, Laia, Ndruru, and Bu'ulölö. Their ancestor had migrated from Sifalagö Gomo, the sacred point of origin, to Lölöwa'u in the west, and from there to Börönövö at the source of the Susua. One day when sacrificing to the ancestors, Laia and Ndruru asked their younger brother, 'Where's your contribution?' Bu'ulölö could not reply. He owned nothing: no wife, no pigs, no gold. He left in shame to seek his fortune elsewhere. He measured the river Susua from source to mouth on the east coast, and at the half-way mark, where Sifalagö now stands, he built his hut and lived by hunting. Laia and Ndruru came looking for him and tried to persuade him to return, but he preferred to stay and cultivate a field there. He was ashamed not to be able to sacrifice a pig to their ancestors and refused to return. Piqued by his stubbornness they said, 'If you're so strong, avenge the murder of our grandfather.' In return, Laia, the eldest son, would give Bu'ulölö half of his pigs, and Ndruru would give him half of his gold. Bu'ulölö asked, 'How will I recognize the killer?' They told him, 'He lives on his own in a hovel in Mazinö, naked and half-blind, crouched over his fire, and he has a crooked nail.' Bu'ulölö went to Mazinö and found out where the killer lived. It was evening; people were returning from the fields; the fireflies were out. Bu'ulölö entered the dark hut and asked for an ember. As the old man handed it to him Bu'ulölö cut off his head. He brought it back to his brothers and claimed his reward. With the gold and pigs he was able to marry. Henceforth they regarded him as their elder (sa'a) and the successor to their father.

This story, which appears to be a charter of ultimogeniture, is told only by the Bu'ulölö. It is airily dismissed by present-day Laia, who point out that most of the land now owned by Bu'ulölö was obtained from them over the generations, so how can they be the 'newcomers'? In the Laia version of events, while the Bu'ulölö clan was still in Börönövö a Laia pioneer named Yawagavöni had founded Orahili and claimed the land upstream of it, including the present site of Sifalagö. When the Bu'ulölö settled there later, they obtained land piece by piece in the form of bridewealth gifts and in payment of debts. The most recent transfer was in colonial times, when the chief (a Bu'ulölö) obtained the lower plain, where the schoolhouse stands, from Orahili in settlement of debt.

Aside from competing claims of priority, it is generally agreed that it was a member of the Bu'ulölö clan, Fanedanu, who built the hamlet of Sifalagö in its present form some ten generations ago and gave it a name: Sifalagöniha (as it then was), glossed as *sifaondra niha* ('where men come together'). This turned out to be an apt title for a settlement composed of several clans, in contrast to the neighbouring villages of Böe and Orahili which were exclusively Laia. However, Sifalagö did not then include the Laia hamlet of Balöhili and those further afield, as it now does. Those who 'came together' were two Bu'ulölö lineages—the Ono Ziba'a and Ono Goyo. The Ndruru occupied a settlement across the river Susua until they were relocated in the square by the Dutch. The different clan groups occupying adjacent hamlets intermarried and lived side by side as rivals but allies, each led by its own senior men. The Bu'ulölö achieved mastery over a united village comprising all the hamlets when the Dutch introduced the official position of village chief.

About four generations after the founding of Sifalagö there was a struggle for power between the two Bu'ulölö lineages which had important consequences for the history of the village. Gavölö, leading man of the Ono Ziba'a lineage, lived in a small house on the right of the square (now occupied by the Ndruru). He did not bother to cultivate much land and lived mainly off the tribute of his wife-takers. He was a 'hard man'. The Ono Goyo, a rival lineage of the same clan, had their *omo sebua* on the hillock where the present chief's house now stands. One day they were down at the river building a dam. They needed leaves to plug gaps in the stones and started to help themselves from Gavölö's gardens. He was watching from his rear window, and when he saw them cutting down his banana leaves he shouted down to them that they were killing the trees. They answered with insults, so he took his spear and sword and his long hide shield, and went down alone to confront them. (His brother Halu was a coward and remained in the house.) For a long time he managed to hold out, parrying their stones with the shield, but was finally overwhelmed. To finish him off, Bagowahö picked up a boulder and dropped it on his head, breaking the jaw. But Gavölö was still breathing, so they washed him and brought him up to Halu, half-dead. There was no one around in the village strong enough to avenge the defeat. Unable to speak, he pointed in the direction of Orahili, downstream, where his son Lölömatua was living with his in-laws. When Lölömatua arrived, he was horrified to find his dying father closeted in the dark windowless bedroom for shame at his injury. He called together the agnates and the affines from Orahili and killed a pig before his father died. Then he sent a messenger to the Ono Goyo with this ultimatum: 'Their presence here is an insult to me. Let them go or be wiped out. They have three lineage houses: let them take their livestock but leave all the gold. Their houses are mine. I do not want to see their faces here longer.' The Ono Goyo fled to Aramö. More than a generation later, some of them returned to the area and sought the protection of a third Bu'ulölö lineage in Hilidanaya'ö, accepting wives from them—which involved a nominal change of clan—and becoming dependents. Around 1930 they were able to resettle Lölömoyo, only a stone's throw from their old location, and resume an uneasy truce with the dominant lineage. The circumstances of this tale—the fighting of fellow-clansmen and the anomalous endogamous alliances which ensured the survival of the losers—make it a controversial subject even today.

The settlement history of the other hamlets can be dealt with briefly. All the Laia lineages of Sifalagö (with the exception of the Ono Zilagö'ö who came three generations ago as fugitives from Siluo) stem from Tuvulani of Orahili. Tuvulani was the son of a second wife. Rather like Bu'ulölö in the story above, he was deprived of his share of the inheritance by his elder brothers, but he outwitted and eventually surpassed them in wealth. In both stories the disinheriting of the youngest son and his outmigration are idealized as a moral victory.

Two of the sons of Tuvulani founded Balöhili seven generations ago; descendants of a third son settled Hilizamurugö about three generations ago; descendants of a fourth and fifth settled Lölömoyo. Of the lineages stemming from these brothers, only those of Balöhili have retained their historical continuity and corporate integrity as political and territorial groups. The boundaries and membership of the other lineages have been subject to the comings and goings of lineage segments in search of land or escaping from feuds with Orahili. In the case of Lölömoyo, the history of flight and resettlement has resulted in the fact that the present inhabitants own only the land on which their houses stand, that is the *banua* itself. All the surrounding land belongs to a Bu'ulölö lineage of Sifalagö (B3–B4). The inhabitants are therefore obliged to borrow from the Bu'ulölö of Sifalagö and others or to cultivate remote ancestral plots—a situation which deprives them of a powerful independent voice in village affairs.

In outlining the residential pattern and its history I have had to postpone a definition of descent groups, which have appeared in this chapter in the form of territorial, political groups. This is a simplification; in reality, descent is adapted to different purposes and materializes at different structural levels according to context. The nature of descent is considered further in the next chapter.

4   The Village Scene

I have described the form and composition of the village, the setting of social life examined in the following chapters. But the description would not be complete without giving the reader some sense of the ebb and flow of activity to be observed on the square any day, the pattern of movement which makes the village a living reality instead of merely a historical concretion.

Daily life in a Nias village has a rhythm and routine dictated almost entirely by the arduous business of growing, getting, and preparing food. Activity begins in the first glimmerings before dawn when 'the trunks of the trees show white'. Women kindle fires to boil sweet potatoes while men move about in the half-light of the yard seeing to the pigs or chopping wood. The mingled stench of fresh pig dung and woodsmoke fills the air. Unless the river is high and turbid after rain, men go down to bathe, with their small children behind them carrying bamboo water containers. After a tasteless but filling meal, the women leave for the fields with one or two children in tow (the others go to school) while men occupy themselves with small tasks, or lean idly against the window slats in melancholy silence, staring down at the *evali*. There is no hurry to be off, and men's tasks are irregular and more varied than those of women. If there is heavy work to be done in the fields they accompany their wives. Babies are either slung on the mother's hip or left in the care of whoever remains behind—the father or an elderly relative. By mid-morning the house is usually empty and the village is all but deserted. In search of company I would sometimes enter a house to find a solitary old man in possession, cradling a child in a palm husk and swaying from side to side across the floor with a rhythmic gait. After midday children come home from school and fetch water or are put to grate coconuts for the meal—sweet potatoes or rice and cassava leaves stewed in coconut milk. The afternoon is spent in pounding and winnowing rice, drying grains or tobacco on mats, or in tending the fields. Women make a final trip to their gardens around 4 or 5 p.m. and come back at dusk, bearing huge loads of tubers and leaves to feed the pigs. They stop on the way to bathe in the Susua, lingering in its cool rapids while they exchange gossip. Their husbands follow them up to the village, empty-handed unless they have been cutting firewood. There is a brief period of gregarious bustle before the privacy of the evening meal. A woman carries a glowing ember from a neighbour's hearth across the square; small boys chase a piglet with stick-spears; a youth sits at a window strumming a ukelele. Then the roof-flaps are lowered, leaving the front public room in darkness, and the family withdraws into the rear apartment. The meal is identical to lunch, though perhaps enlivened with a little salted pork or prawns netted in the flood. The family sits on the floor to eat, by the light of the fire or a tiny oil lamp. It is a moment of quiet and intimacy. Fathers croon to their children or feed them on their laps, while mothers comment on the gossip they have heard, or mildly scold their daughters as they serve the food. After chewing betel, the women return to pounding rice or cassava flour while the men mend nets or chat with neighbours. On moonlit nights they sit outside on the big stones which are still warm from the sun. By about 10 p.m., unless a feast is in preparation or a dispute is being negotiated, the village is silent.

2

Descent and Local Groups

If the village gives the individual a primary orientation in the world, his or her social identity within that world is defined crucially by descent. The present chapter considers how descent operates as a principle of social organization in conjunction with institutional arrangements concerning residence, property, and succession. In Chapter 3 I consider the relation between descent and alliance.

Descent in Nias is reckoned patrilineally. Incomplete payment of bridewealth, bride service, child betrothal, and uxorilocality have no influence in determining the child's recruitment, which is always to the clan of its social father. In this respect Nias differs from certain other Indonesian societies in which patrilineal descent predominates.[1] Fostering of children occurs, but very rarely full adoption or other transfer involving a change of clan. The instances of clan change which I discovered were all in the remote past and involved the sheltering of fugitives. A woman retains her natal clanship on marrying.

This unambiguous patrilineality partly corresponds in Nias thinking to father-to-son succession, male ownership of property, inheritance through males, and patrilocal post-marital residence. It is an idea at the service of a number of purposes. When I presented informants with a counter example—matrilineal descent among the Minangkabau—and asked why Niasans trace descent exclusively through males, I was told, 'Because it's the men who stay and continue the line (*samatohu nga'ötö*); whereas women are taken away for bridewealth.' At another level of indigenous explanation, the tracing of unilineal descent is associated with the regulation of marriage. Clans exist 'so that we don't marry our sisters or mate promiscuously like animals'.

---

[1] Compare the *ambil anak* institution of South Sumatra (Moyer 1984), the Atoni of Timor (Schulte Nordholt 1971), and other eastern Indonesian societies discussed in Barnes (1980*b*).

1   The Clan

The generic term for clan and subclan is *mado*. Each clan bears the name of its apical ancestor (e.g. *mado* Ndruru). Subclans are named 'children of' the eponymous founder (e.g. a Ndruru subclan descended from Tafulu is called Ono Dafulu) or add some qualifier to the clan name (e.g. Great Laia, Gold Laia). The internal structure of clans varies. The Bu'ulölö clan is said to be undivided in the sense that it contains no named subclans and is the largest unit of exogamy. Segments can be traced back to apical ancestors, usually village founders, but these reference groups are not called *mado* and they may not intermarry. Some of them are designated 'sons of X' in the manner of subclans. The Laia clan is divided into a number of subclans (seventeen by one account) deriving from the sons of Laia by successive wives. Some of these subclans are further subdivided into dispersed exogamous groups named 'sons of X', etc. The Ndruru clan is similarly subdivided. Thus what counts as the strict unit of exogamy varies among clans, although there is a general preference for clan exogamy. (See diagrams of lineage structure in Appendix 1.)

According to legend, subdivision of clans came about in two ways: either through the separation of half-siblings, as in the case of the Laia, or by endogamous marriages which were legitimized by clan division. Ultimately these divisions are probably related to clan density and the isolation of particular settlements. It is noticeable that the preference for clan exogamy among the Laia and Ndruru varies locally. In mixed communities, such as the Sifalagö complex, it is much stronger than in relatively homogeneous and isolated settlements such as Böe and Hilizamurugö.

All clans trace their origins back to the legendary first men who descended to earth from the upper world. Their sons and grandsons, founders of the hundred or so clans in Nias, migrated from the four or five sacred points of origin to all parts of the island. The sons of Hia, the first man on earth, settled most of the area south of Gomo. The three largest clan groups in Sifalagö and its neighbouring villages, the Laia, Ndruru, and Bu'ulölö, stem from three brothers who settled in the area about five or six generations after Hia— about twenty-three generations back in contemporary pedigrees. The membership of these clans, which runs into several thousand, is dispersed across a wide belt of central Nias as far as Lölöwa'u in the west. Ordinarily there is no contact between geographically dispersed members. Great chiefs sometimes meet to honour each other and to fill in the gaps in their clan pedigree. Otherwise, common clanship is recognized only in the rule of clan (or subclan) exogamy and, in the days of head-hunting, in the ban on taking the head of a fellow-clansman. Both of these rules were sanctioned by the retribution of ancestral spirits. Between clansmen of neighbouring villages there is a more palpable solidarity, which in the old days took the form of co-operation in feasts and war.

Between members of a clan who belong to different lineages there is a solidarity of both a moral and practical kind over against other clans. Thus, on the one hand, there is a sense of being different, even superior, to other clans, expressed in heroic legends, abusive rhymes, and unfavourable comparisons. On the other, there is an obligation to co-operate in festive ventures of fellow-clansmen, and a tendency to unite in political factions along clan lines. In principle the clan is exogamous, and most dealings between members of different clans are coloured by affinity. To some extent, affinal relations play a part in determining the compass of agnatic groupings, as I shall explain in the next chapter. As a dispersed group the clan holds no property in common.

2   The Lineage

Since the lineage appears as an amorphous and often fragmentary group it is perhaps useful to list here the aspects in which it is, or once was, conceived to be corporate.

1. As a group which worshipped a single set of ancestors.

2. As a residential group, occupying a communal house or line of houses. The simplest type of village/settlement (*banua*) is identical with the lineage.

3. As a landholding group. In principle a lineage holds in common all the land ever cleared by its apical ancestor. Each household has rights of use in lineage land.

4. As an independent political group. The lineage acted in concert under the leadership of its senior men in war and defence. It carried out head-hunting raids and acts of revenge.

5. As a feasting group. It unites behind its leaders who sponsor feasts of merit.

6. As a wife-giving group. The whole lineage (though internally differentiated) receives bridewealth for its women and appears as a guest group at the feasts of merit held by its members' wife-takers. For reasons explained in the next chapter, the lineage is not corporately involved as wife-taker.

The ideological or ritual group which I call the lineage derives from a common ancestor usually four to seven generations back from the generation of young married men. However, there are no rules concerning the size of a lineage, and fission is governed by a number of factors extrinsic to descent. Within this group exact genealogical relations can be traced by most adults. Ideally (i.e. in normative statements), the membership of groups convened or identified for all the purposes listed above is consistent. In practice of course it varies. Not surprisingly, then, the terms by which descent groups are identified are vague and fluid in application. They should be considered as segmentary terms for reference groups rather than as sociocentric terms analogous to *mado* ('clan'). The concept of segmentation is expressed in the term *rahu-rahu*. This term, which derives from *rahu* ('grasp'), denotes both the apex and the compass of a group. (I have also heard it used to denote groupings in the hierarchy of animal classification.) The group itself may be called *sambua motua* ('those of one ancestor/grandfather'). Usually this means the whole ritual group or some segment defined in relation to it. Several other terms exist: *sifamakhelo tua* ('those whose grandfathers called each other brother'); *nafulu*, a southern dialect word meaning here the married men of the lineage; *nafu*, ('clump'), as in a clump of bamboo, signifying strength in numbers; or simply *nga'ötö* ('descent line').

Lower levels of segmentation can be referred to by the term *sambua mo'ama* ('those of one father'), thus brothers (or sometimes FBS) and their descendants.[2] Ordinarily any grouping is referred to by clan name, by the name of its senior men or by its location in the village. In this sense there are no fixed labels of agnatic groups below clan level. Use of segmentary terms like *sambua mo'ama*

---

[2] In south Nias (Maenamölö) *mo'ama* can be used of descent groups at any level from lineage segment up to phratry (the clans descended from Mölö, tribal progenitor) (Marschall 1976: 136).

implies an appeal to agnatic solidarity at that level rather than the identification of a fixed group. Consequently, the process of inclusion/ exclusion in corporate groups is a matter of 'negotiation' rather than principle or precise rule of recruitment. Nevertheless, lineages did indeed have a certain loose corporate coherence which was unlike the purely conceptual framework of a classic segmentary system such as Evans-Pritchard identified among the Nuer.[3] This corporate structure was based on joint participation in the activities listed above, within the overarching framework of groups defined by ancestor worship.

The ancestor cult, at least in its external manifestations, was abolished about sixty years ago, and with it went the ideological unity of the lineage. Since then, there are groupings of inconsistent and sometimes fluctuating composition associated with the concept of the lineage and giving the genealogical abstraction more or less reality. Lineage boundaries are no longer identifiable by any single or dominant criterion. Agnates who own separate plots of land may be identified as a unit in the division of bridewealth or at feasts of merit. Father's brother's sons may dispute ownership of a plot which theoretically cannot belong to either since it is impartible lineage land. In Sifalagö, a segment connected to the chief's line seven generations back and with its own separate land, claims to belong to the 'chiefly line' (*nga'ötö zalawa*). In so far as it supports the chief morally and materially, it is indulged in this pretension by the chief, if not by other lineages.

It is perhaps useful, then, to begin with the lineage as a ritual unit before proceeding to the more complicated arrangements associated with residence and property.

Ancestor Worship and Lineage Fission

Each local lineage worshipped a common set of patrilineal ancestors. Carved wooden figures called (in the central Nias dialect) *azu zatua* represented male agnates and their wives. Pairs of these figures were tied together on staves, row above row, and were fastened to the wall of the front room, where they were consulted and propitiated on every important occasion. It was the immediate ancestors who

---

[3] A close parallel to Nias descent group organization and its terminology is the Toba Batak: *marga = mado* (clan), *saompu* (lineage/'of one grandfather') = *sambua motua* (lineage/'of one grandfather') (Vergouwen 1964: 30–3).

were addressed, and they passed on the request upwards. Each lineage also possessed several other idols used in particular rituals. The most important of these was the *azu horö* ('idol of war/transgression'), a man-size ithyphallic figure associated with warrior heroes, which was sacrificed to before mounting a raid or a headhunting expedition.

Reliable information on the traditional processes of lineage expansion and fission, and how these processes were represented, is difficult to obtain and can only be pieced together from the oral history of the village. In modern times extraneous factors have intervened and disrupted the pattern. It seems that a new lineage made a duplicate set of ancestral figures which required the inaugural blessing of the parent lineage. The notion that the spirits were attached to their images (as their seat or abode) thus did not prevent them from being at the disposal of two sets of descendants. If the lineage division was acrimonious, the original core group would deny their blessing and instead cursed the offshoot. There are unexplained mentions in colonial reports (Korn 476/42) from north-central Nias of a payment for 'splitting the stave of the idols' (*fabali katia nadu*) to legitimize an anomalous union. This suggests a formal division of lines back to an apical ancestor, prompted by a breach of marriage prohibitions.[4] My informants knew of no such customary payment in the Sifalagö area. No examples of anomalous unions, past or present, of which I was told led to lineage fission (in contrast to some explanations of clan fission). Informants thought that those irregularities which escaped the radical solution of execution could only be patched up nominally—there was no fundamental reorganization of the descent group.

The community of ancestors was seen as existing separately, parallel to the world of the living, and with its own special needs and demands; but there was also regular contact between the two realms, and an intimate—sometimes unwelcome—participation of the dead in the activities of the living. The spirits were addressed as 'father' and 'mother', and were respected and feared. But they were easily bribable, greedy for tribute and pork, and capable of such unpaternal acts as strangling their progeny. When a child fell ill, its father sacrificed to the ancestors and said, 'Release your hands,

---

[4] It is not a breach of clan exogamy but of an asymmetric marriage prohibition which is referred to in this payment, as I explain in Ch. 7.

father. Let him live. Here's pork for you!' Nevertheless, without their aid there could be no prosperity or success in any venture.

Lineage Rituals

Propitiation of the ancestors was a matter for each household, rather than a collective ritual. The lineage united in ritual at planting and harvest. An important prelude to any co-operative activity, then as now, was the settling of quarrels, for resentment between members brought ancestral disapproval which would blight the enterprise. Reconciliation was followed by a renunciation of faults beneath the ancestor figures.

At harvest, a priest summoned the rice spirit ('he who fills the rice') and asked it to replenish the ears. The priest would despatch the spirit to neighbouring fields to 'take the *uvu vakhe*', the immanent spirit of the rice. This could only be achieved by reducing the harvest of the neighbouring descent group.

After the harvest there was a period called *famongi* ('placing of taboos'), a time of 'joy' and 'purification' which is now only dimly remembered. During *famongi* the whole lineage remained indoors for four days and refrained from work. People dressed up in their gold ornaments and festive clothes. All day long there was singing, dancing, and the recitation of narratives. Rivals were reconciled; people confessed their acts of spite to each other. Senior men of the lineage reviewed the conduct of juniors and harangued them on customary law. Members of other descent groups could not enter the lineage house or share its consecrated food, which was *salakha* ('cursed/prohibited') to them. Wives and uxorilocal husbands, as resident members, were exempt from this prohibition. Each household killed a pig which it had previously bathed in coconut milk beneath the ancestor figures and dedicated to the ancestors. The pig was cooked and hung up in the front room where it was consumed little by little in the company of other lineage mates, as if the lineage were one big household (normally each household eats privately in its apartment). After four days, everyone in the lineage went down to the river to bathe. A priest beat a drum and invoked the ancestral spirits, then he sprinkled water on the ancestor figures. A small stone bench was placed for the spirits. At the end of ritual aspersions to 'cool' the participants and their property, i.e. to bring them health and prosperity, each person took a handful of sand from the shore (thus something cool) and brought it back up to the house. This concluded the *famongi*.[5]

Very little remains of traditional lineage ritual, centred as it was on the pagan ancestor cult. However, ancestral spirits remain part of the Nias cosmology—albeit in a ritually impoverished world—and are frequently taken into consideration in daily affairs, in the explanation of illness and death, in divination, and in determining auspicious days.

The mortal illness of the chief of Sifalagö, which dominated many weeks of my stay, was assigned differing causes. Villagers whom he had worsted blamed his 'wickedness and corruption'; church elders, for years piqued at his indifference to Christianity, harassed him with biblical citations and blamed his failure to confess his sins to God. It was an opportunity for all to censure the great man with impunity. But a female diviner, Ina Ria, provided the explanation most acceptable to him when she attributed the illness to his 'sin against the ancestors' in deserting the ancestral house. On her advice he moved back up to the *omo sebua*, living out his last weeks in the big front room surrounded day and night by family, villagers, and visitors from afar. During his prolonged and intensely public death agonies, various repairs to the building were undertaken, pleasing to the ancestors, and more important, a farewell feast was organized: the *fangandrö hovu-hovu* ('request for blessing'). On this occasion all the wife-takers and kinsmen assembled to receive his blessing, and six pigs were slaughtered to 'satisfy my filial obligations' (i.e. in tribute to his deceased parents). Each person was sprinkled with water blessed by the chief, and each was given a morsel from the pig's lower jaw which he had consecrated. From his deathbed he made a speech reviewing the history of the village, his own great role in its making (modesty is not expected of a chief), and his hopes for the future. This was followed by a candid airing of grievances by senior kinsmen of a kind I had never before heard in the chief's presence. It was intended to be a 'straightening out' or 'reconciliation' (*fangatulö*) between agnates necessary to a peaceful death. On a smaller scale, a reunion of this kind is expected of any important man, paving the way for a smooth succession and distribution of the inheritance.

---

[5] A variant of this ritual was the cooling of wealth which had been obtained dishonestly (see Ch. 8 on this theme).

The Local Lineage as a Residential Group

A 'compromise kin group' (Murdock 1949: 66) which I call the local lineage is constituted by patrilineal descent, clan exogamy, and patrilocal post-marital residence. It is based on a core of co-resident male agnates, with their unmarried daughters and wives obtained from other clans. In the Nias language there is no term for this group distinct from the terms indicating patrilineal descent (*sambua motua*, *nafulu*, etc.). For the most part there is no need to make such a distinction since incoming wives, although they retain their natal clanship, are identified for practical purposes with their husbands' lineage, just as daughters are lost from the lineage on marrying. A deceased wife joined her husband in the pantheon of lineage ancestor figures. In the following discussion, the terms 'lineage' and 'local lineage' both refer to this descent/residential grouping unless otherwise stated.

Sahlins has noted that 'in major territorial descent groups, there is no particular relation between the descent ideology and group composition' and that 'a descent doctrine does not express group composition but imposes itself upon the composition' (1965: 104). In some societies, cognatic infiltration, as Sahlins calls it, may be ignored or interpreted as unilineal descent. In contrast, the Nias lineage (or its segment) may have one or two sons-in-law living in, but neither they nor their sons are counted as members of the ritual or property-owning community (neither may sister's sons be counted as honorary brother's sons). The rigorous exclusion of cognatic relatives from the agnatic estate ensures that uxorilocality has no permanent consequences for group composition, and the pure agnatic framework is retained. Similarly there is no genealogical revision brought about through widow-inheritance and the consequent matrilateral links generated among half-siblings, such as Kelly describes among the Etoro (1974: ch. 3). Genealogical knowledge within the lineage seems to be objective, as far as it goes, and anomalies are tolerated rather than revised or absorbed into the agnatic structure.

The composition and structure of local lineages is variable. Very large lineages, such as the Bu'ulölö lineages of Sifalagö, have unnamed segments four or five generations deep (traced back from adult members) which are discernible as an intermediate stage in the formation of a lineage. In the traditional context, if they continued to expand there would be a division of the ancestor figures and a geographical separation. If the segments are unequal (e.g. B1 and B2), in that one is larger or contains more illustrious members, patron–client relations may develop among the members. The boundary of the lineage may be drawn differently depending on which segment one belongs to, and who gains (in meat, prestige, etc.) or loses by inclusion. In the B3–B4 lineage the two major segments are of roughly equal strength and status in the village, and there is broad agreement that they are *sambua motua*. In some lineages (e.g. the Ndruru of Hilisibohou) ancestral land is held in common. In others, ancestral land has been divided between segments, or among households either singly or in groups. The same factors are at work in the subdivision of lineage land as in the growth and fission of the lineage itself: expanding numbers, shortage of land, dispersal of holdings, dispersal of lineage members, strained personal relations within the lineage.

Likewise, residential composition of lineages is extremely variable. A number of households of various types may be joined together under a common roof or in adjoining houses which have a common social area in front like a longhouse. This is the local lineage in its most readily identifiable and corporate form. In Sifalagö two such rows of houses face each other across the village square (see Village Plan). The B3–B4 lineage consists of two segments occupying two adjacent communal houses. The B4 segment comprises the descendants of five brothers, *dalima mo'ama* ('five men with one father'). Ideally, each group thus formed would have a separate apartment of the house, with its own kitchen and front door leading into the communal front room, and bedrooms for each nuclear family (*ngambatö*). In fact, the composition of the house is fluctuating, as some families live on a temporary or semi-permanent basis in field huts outside the village and others have set up separate houses in the village.

3   The Household

Sifalagö exhibits a range of household types of varying complexity, from the nuclear family with its own land, up to the joint-family of brothers with their sons and grandchildren farming a section of lineage land. This variety is not only a function of the developmental cycle of the domestic group but relates to the development and fragmentation of the lineage as outlined above.

It is the household, not the lineage, which is the unit of production and consumption. This unit is variously referred to (depending on household type and context of utterance) as *sambua omo* ('one house[hold]'), or *sambua ngambatö* ('one married couple'), or simply *ösi nomo* ('contents of the house'). These alternatives are loosely applied, overlapping labels, not synonyms. One large house may in fact contain several households, which may in turn consist of more than one married couple. A minimal definition of the household, and one which conforms to indigenous thinking, is that its members eat together, from the same pot, food which they have produced in common. In polygynous households each wife feeds her own children separately from the produce of the field she cultivates. But the husband is the nominal owner of everything his wives produce and the household has a certain fractious unity. In some houses, several households share a single kitchen but eat separately. As an economic unit the household may be internally differentiated. Thus even in the most solidary joint-family household, brothers or sons may pursue certain enterprises separately from the pooled household fund.

4 Adoption

In the literature a term frequently given for adopted child is *ono nisou*. In central Nias this term is regarded as a euphemism for household slave. Under certain circumstances a debtor or criminal could redeem himself by handing over a child (as servant) in payment. The child might later be married off by his or her adopter but did not acquire the full rights of true offspring. Not surprisingly, when I began my household survey and asked questions on adoption, no one admitted to having fathered or accommodated an *ono nisou*. As I explain in Chapter 7, there are a number of roles which can be summed up in the phrase 'exploited dependant'—among them, adopted child (especially if orphaned), uxorilocal son-in-law, widow, and household slave/servant. None of these roles is clearly defined and movement between them is common. For example, an adopted fugitive could confirm his subservient position under his protector by becoming his co-resident son-in-law.

Fostering (*fondrorogö*) of an agnate's or sister's child is without these connotations of servility. Nowadays it is common in families where one of a set of brothers has a public service job for him to bring up several of his nephews and nieces. In the traditional context the children of a sister sometimes live for extended periods with their mother's brother if he is well-to-do.

A childless man can adopt his brother's son, but the degree of transfer varies. Full adoption is rare. A minimal commitment on the part of the adoptive father is to pay the core of the boy's bridewealth. Inheritance in this instance is not affected, since B and FBS are co-heirs of their fathers' property. This would not apply if the adopted child were a more remote agnate: he would be passed over in favour of collateral heirs. Adoption or fostering is not a strategy for producing an heir but a form of mutual aid and a token of agnatic solidarity. In Sifalagö one branch of the chief's lineage is unique in having two state employees who live away from the village. The elder of them, who is childless, has adopted fully a nephew; he also fosters several others on a temporary basis. His younger brother, a teacher, has adopted a son and a daughter of different brothers. The unity of the family is thereby said to be assured.

I consider in Chapter 7 how rights in children are affected by widow remarriage.

5 Inheritance

There is no clear division between private property and lineage property, since wealth obtained by personal effort is passed on and in time the number of potential heirs grows. A man has the right to dispose of what he has obtained during his lifetime as he thinks fit, e.g. his pigs, rice, gold which he has purchased or obtained through trade, consumer goods, and his own house if he built it. The primary heirs to a man's disposable wealth are his sons, followed by his brothers and their sons. In poor lineages there is usually nothing left once the dead man's debts have been paid off. In wealthier lineages there may be a few pigs, a little gold, and possibly land obtained by the deceased during his lifetime, either through purchase or as a bridewealth prestation. Gold heirlooms, Chinese plates, gongs, lineage land, coconut trees, and the ancestral house remain the joint property of the lineage or its segment. If lineage gold is divided up, its *lakhömi* ('lustre, inherent power') disappears.

The actual division of the patrimony among sons depends on age and ability, as does succession to authority in the family. The dying man determines his legacy, but other senior men of the lineage and village elders have a say, and may arbitrate if there is competition among heirs. Usually problems do not arise until years later when a particular ornament or plot of land is needed.

If all the sons are married, shares may be equal, the eldest son getting slightly more if he replaces his father as head of the family. If there are unmarried adult sons, they receive extra to help towards their bridewealth. If they are still children and the eldest son acts as their guardian, he receives half of the inheritance. Although the house remains joint property of surviving sons, in the event of overcrowding the son who is nominated as his father's successor remains and his brothers move out, although they remain joint-owners until they build substantial houses of their own. The successor is expected to contribute to the expenses of his brothers' new houses. A daughter inherits at most one or two coconut palms, and perhaps some money, but no land, pigs, or gold. An uxorilocal son-in-law can occupy the land of his deceased wife's father, but as soon as he moves out the land reverts to agnatic heirs.

The question of division of lineage land is more complicated and is considered separately below in Section 7 'Land Tenure'.

6 Succession

Succession to chiefship is treated fully in Chapter 10. There is no formal position of head of the lineage or its subdivision and so no formal succession in the strict sense. Authority is exercised by the men most senior in years and in achievement. A man who has achieved eminence in feasting, who has oratorical skills and other qualities of leadership, may wield influence beyond his years, so long as he pays due regard to his elders. At every level of social organization this double sense of seniority applies—age on the one hand and experience or ability on the other. A younger man can be said to be the elder (*sa'a*) in achievement or notoriety. In a set of brothers seniority in age is always subject to seniority in ability. The one who takes a lead in providing for the others is recognized as the successor, the one who 'follows in his father's footsteps' (*tarai lahe nama*). To him it is said:

Ölö mo mate namau,	Though your father has died,
hulö zilö'ö	it's as if he hasn't
Ölö mo mate namau,	Though your father has died,
hulö ziso,	it's as if he's present
Me ono famatete börö zisi	Since [you are] the son next to the heel
Ono famatete gavono.	The son next to the ankle.

During the father's lifetime, his successor is sometimes confirmed in the role of 'replacement' (*fatanga nama*) by a feast given in his honour. The importance given to succession among surviving sons (and the degree of formality involved) depends on the rank of the father. In a chiefly line it is a matter of great significance to the whole village, and succession accomplished at a feast or funeral is a major public event. But even among the sons of a minor village elder there may be some public acknowlegement of the succession.

In assessing the meaning of succession to seniority in the household, joint family or lineage segment, we have to make a distinction between succession to authority and what might be more accurately called spiritual succession. These do not always coincide. Again, for the most part these matters concern only the sons of a village elder or chief.

Succession to authority brings the right of decision, the right to speak for the others in public meetings, the biggest share of meat, priority in inheriting agnates' widows, and so on. Spiritual succession is accomplished by the deliberate transfer of the father's qualities, which are thought to be concentrated in his dying breath. The nominated son leans over and receives in his mouth the *era-era* ('thought'), *fa'atua-tua* ('wisdom'), and *söfu* ('authority') of his father. In northern Nias, these attributes were thought to be contained in a spiritual element belonging only to high-ranking men which was called *eheha* and was passed on in the dying breath. (The Bible translators chose the word *eheha* for Holy Ghost.) In Sifalagö this word means no more than the father's superior qualities. Reception of the father's breath in itself confers no rights or privileges. Though this ritual is still said to occur, nowadays it is more common to transfer the paternal qualities nominally, in the form of a blessing with a laying on of hands—a compromise between traditional and Christian practices. A form of spiritual succession associated with leadership is described in Section 2 of Chapter 10.

Seniority has its ritual aspect in that the household idols were in the care of the eldest son (Schröder 1917: 424). It was usually he who was instructed by the dying father to obtain human heads for the funeral ceremony. Likewise, in the lineage as a whole, the ancestor figures were kept by the oldest member. For practical reasons as well, the natural successor is the eldest son. Usually he is many years older than his youngest siblings and acts towards them as a father. If he is unsuited to this responsibility, the next oldest son succeeds. However, if there is an outstanding figure among a set of adult brothers, it is always he who succeeds, irrespective of birth order. During his lifetime, a father may nominate an outstanding younger son as successor in the household.

The elder/younger contrast is important in many Indonesian societies and may be used to express a relation of inequality in binary oppositions which have nothing to do with relative age. In Nias, elder/younger expresses the notion of seniority-in-equality, *primus inter pares*. The parent/child opposition expresses a more absolute inequality. In the traditional cosmology the upper world is governed by Lovalangi and the underworld is governed by Nazuva Danö, his younger brother. Nazuva Danö won a trial of strength and Lovalangi conceded to him seniority; as the stronger of the two he went down below to hold up the earth.

In the Nias relationship terminology, eldest and youngest brothers are distinguished from each other and from the middle brothers, who are lumped together. After the eldest son it is the youngest son who is ideologically marked, as it were preserving the simplicity of the opposition. He is thought to have missed out in life. He loses out by his father's death, and his extra portion of the inheritance compensates for 'what he never ate'. But he also misses out on education. The eldest son, groomed as successor, has learned all his father's wisdom. A father can choose to endow his youngest son spiritually if he wishes, in compensation for the benefits and opportunities he has missed. Such is the case with my oldest informant, Ama Huku, whose only surviving sons were born forty-five years apart. If, as is usually the case, it is the eldest son who is spiritually endowed during the father's life, the youngest son can receive a sort of consolation prize at the funeral. A piece of string is tied to his right arm and to the left little toe of the deceased (left and right are reversed in death), who is told to 'pick your son; give him your wisdom and chiefly dignity (*fa'asalawa*)!'

In ritual, then, but not in customary law, middle sons are passed over, and there is a suggestion of optional primo- or ultimogeniture. This may once have corresponded to the developmental cycle of the household. The scenario would run as follows. Eldest and youngest sons are born up to a generation apart and as such are not in competition for control of the paternal house. Succession would run from father to eldest son to youngest son. It is the middle sons who are squeezed out, forced by overcrowding and the heavy hand of the oldest son to move into remote field huts. These middle brothers would be the pioneers and founders of new settlements. A controversial example of ultimogeniture by merit is furnished by the story of the three brothers Laia, Ndruru, and Bu'ulölö, founders of the three clans of Sifalagö (see Sect. 3 of Ch. 1).

In the narrative poem recorded by Lagemann (1906) in north Nias, known in various forms all over Nias, there is a competition among nine sons for succession in the heavenly village, Teteholi Ana'a. Sirao has three 'equal' (*sifagölö-gölö*) wives, each of whom has three 'equal' sons. Eight of the sons dispute the succession and inheritance; only Luo Mewöna is silent. Sirao organizes a contest. Whoever can perch on the point of his spear like a cock will reveal himself as the true successor. One by one they try, but only Luo Mewöna manages the feat. In this contest winner takes all. There is not enough room in the upper world for the rest, so they are lowered down to earth. Luo Mewöna, the successor, is the youngest son of the first wife. The youngest of the second wife is Hia Walangi Adu who is the first man lowered down to earth and the origin of men. Hia also has nine sons, but in this case it is his eldest son who succeeds him.[6]

It is interesting that this myth makes no distinction of rank between the wives or between the sons. In practice, in central Nias, polygyny introduces a certain inequality among half-brothers which derives from a priority among the wives. Unlike south Nias, where a son's rank depends on both parents, in central Nias sons of women of different rank are theoretically equal in customary law and can claim equal shares in the patrimony. Sons of a favourite or senior wife (who need not be the first wife) may be made guardians of the

---

[6] In the interesting version collected by Marschall in south Nias (Maenamölö), the successor, unnamed in the translation, is the youngest of the nine sons (1976: 20 ff.).

father's gold, with the result that their descendants, in the event of a division of lineage property, have the advantage of control and may exclude the others. In recent years in Sifalagö much bitter argument has centred on this very question of differential endowment and its consequences. In the section on land tenure below I give an example of the kind of problems which may ensue in the division of a polygynous man's estate.

7 Land Tenure

Although this topic takes us beyond the bounds of descent, it is convenient to outline here the main features of land tenure, as they are closely connected with the corporate aspect of the descent group.

Niasans practise shifting cultivation, and land is classified according to its stage in the swidden cycle. Virgin forest is called *atua* ('old'); land under cultivation is *benua* (cf. *banua*, 'village'); and land which has been cultivated but stands fallow is *benua savuyu* ('young *benua*').[7] Rights of tenure are created by the clearing of virgin forest, which in the area around Sifalagö was considered to belong to no one. (In some parts of Nias there were village federations and *atua* belonged nominally to the district.) A piece of land which has once been cleared belongs in perpetuity to the pioneer's patrilineal descendants. All of the land surrounding Sifalagö was cleared several generations ago and is collectively owned by local lineages. There is no virgin forest within about five or six miles of the village.

While the lineage is the landholding unit, each constituent household is responsible for cultivating its own fields. The choice of plot is made by arrangement with other households of the lineage. If there is insufficient land for the whole lineage in a particular season, younger households may be expected to open new fields at or beyond the limits of lineage territory, possibly entailing removal to a remote field hut. However, there is no clear rule of priority in allocation, and some older men choose to live in huts away from the constant demands on their resources for bridewealth contributions,

[7] The terms 'young' and 'old' refer to the age of the trees. Land which has been left fallow for over twenty years is called *atua eu* ('old trees').

etc. Currently a number of households are farming land on a semi-permanent basis in Amoroa, four hours' walk from Sifalagö in the wilds between central and south Nias. Much of this land was in fact cleared long ago by villagers of Aramö, but the present tenants have chosen to regard it as *atua* and have defied attempts to repossess it.

Another option in the event of insufficient land is to borrow from affines (especially wife-givers) or from other villagers who are on friendly terms. No subordination is implied in this arrangement unless the borrower actually moves in with his father-in-law. Through marriage alliance one has access to land which may be more fertile or otherwise better than one's lineage land. The loan of land can be a purely friendly arrangement or it can be based on mutual self-interest, with payment of a prestation called *fanö'ö* which is said to be in lieu of rent. The borrower is not allowed to plant perennials or coconut palms, and he gains no permanent rights in the land.

Lineage land cannot in theory be sold. However, a study of land tenure in Sifalagö shows that large areas have in fact been transferred for a variety of reasons. Land can be substituted for gold in payment of bridewealth. Unless the plot is individually owned (i.e. a newly cleared plot) the transfer requires the agreement of the whole lineage. It can also be given in ransom for the life of a lineage member. In the past the high interest on loans and the huge fines for certain crimes meant that a wealthy lineage could profit by bailing out an offender to save his life. In exchange, the individual would pledge a daughter, or his labour, or land. The chiefly line of the Bu'ulölö obtained a great deal of land by these means and there has been a net transfer of land between the Laia and Bu'ulölö clans. Now that land is scarce, the economic advantage of this transfer is beginning to be felt. Inheritance of land transferred in this way is always a matter of dispute in the event of division, as its status as individual or lineage property is unclear.

The question of the division of land is complicated. There is no fixed or ideal point in the development of the local lineage at which land division should occur. It is theoretically independent of lineage fission, though the two processes are connected in practice. Land division is a gradual process, as particular households or lineage segments assert their claims to particular plots. Usually an informal allocation of plots precedes a definitive division by one or two generations. The leading man in the lineage monopolizes the best land closest to the village for his own descendants and assigns parcels of the rest to each segment. As long as no borders are determined the land remains nominally the collective property of the lineage. As demarcation disputes grow more frequent, and individuals try to consolidate their hold over plots by planting coconut palms or converting them to permanent irrigated rice fields, the need for a definitive division becomes apparent. Land disputes have a periodicity as potential heirs reach maturity and as the plots in question reach the end of their eight- to ten-year fallow period. Then the agnates and village elders meet to 'tell [the story of] the land' (*facunö danö*). Usually this means an exhaustive discussion of genealogy, land transfers through bridewealth, fines and tribute, plantation history, and so on. Borders are determined, and hardy fire-resistant *buasi* trees are planted in each corner of the field, while curses are uttered on those who transgress the border.

I referred above to the inequality among half-siblings that results from polygyny. There is rarely a formal division of land among half-brothers during their father's lifetime, but each son has a superior claim on the use of land worked by his mother (her *halösö*). The son of a diligent mother therefore has access to more land. This means that the descendants of a principal wife (the one shown favour, the most diligent) tend to occupy the best land closest to the village. Nevertheless, as legitimate patrilineal descendants, sons or grand-sons of secondary wives claim equal rights of ownership in the lineage estate. Since priority among the wives is not clearly formul-ated (unlike in south Nias), and tends to be denied by later genera-tions, there arise very bitter disputes over the eventual use or division of land. Such disputes are of greater significance than formerly, now that land has become scarce.

Example: Division of land in a lineage segment in Sifalagö
Currently there is a dispute regarding the subdivision of land belonging to a segment of lineage *A* (see Fig. 2.1).[8]

An eminent elder named Dara had four wives, two of whom gave birth to sons. Wife 1 was his *tuho wo'omo* ('the primary/favourite wife'). Wife 2 was captured on a raid and no bridewealth was paid for her. Descendants of sons by wife 1 are now disputing a plot occupied by descendants of sons by wife 2, claiming it is the field worked by their grandmother. Since the branch descended from

[8] Here, as throughout, my policy has been to use pseudonyms in controversial or disreputable cases.

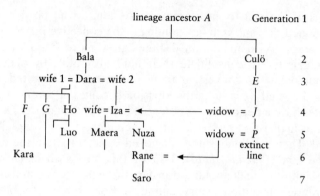

FIG. 2.1. Division of a lineage

wife 2 is firmly entrenched, having converted the plot to an irrigated rice-paddy, and is prone to violence, there is little that can be done. In former times, the rival claims might have been settled by war, and one branch would have been wiped out or expelled. But nowadays, lacking this option, there can only be negotiation. Unfortunately this too is rendered extremely difficult by the sensitive nature of the issue. Whereas in south Nias there is a clear grading of sons by different wives, in central Nias mere mention of a secondary or inferior wife (*erua*) as such is offensive and would immediately provoke violence. Perhaps feeling that the best method of defence is attack, and in disregard of all accepted standards, the occupier of the land in question (Rane) fortified his claim over those of weaker lines (*F* and *G*) descended from the primary wife by denying their paternity, claiming outrageously that they were *ono nisou*, adopted/ ransomed orphans who have no right to any land. He has avoided a direct confrontation with Luo, the senior man of the lineage. In 1988 the dispute, which had been simmering for years, erupted in violence and the usurper murdered Kara, one of his bitterest rivals. Now that Rane is removed from the scene to prison, his close agnates, Maera and Saro, are left to come to some compromise with the rival claimants.

It may be wondered how such disputes were resolved in the past. In the first place, there was much less pressure on land, and each segment could carve out its own territory. With unlimited land surrounding the village, there was less at stake. In the case of limited land some kind of division or exclusion had to be made. The myth of succession in heaven described earlier provides an example of winner takes all, which is one way of preventing the fragmentation of the estate. Samson (1925a), writing of west Nias, notes that, in the event of a division, if the land is insufficient for an equal sharing among sons, the whole territory is given to the eldest son and the younger sons are obliged to move away. A policy broadly along these lines has been followed in recent generations in Sifalagö.

Land disputes unfold over generations. In the same lineage, after the death of Dara, his successor Ho, the leading man of the lineage at the time, made a rough allocation of land among the branches descended from his lineage brothers. Lineage gold remained under his guardianship and the land as a whole remained jointly owned. When Ho died, thirty years ago, his sons denied their agnates access to the gold, maintaining that their father had financed the bride-wealth of Iza and Nuza, and that he had sponsored the funeral feast of their common grandfather Dara. In retaliation, the branch descended from Iza has monopolized a tract of land formerly worked by a now extinct line descended from Culö. They have been able to do this by marrying widows of that line, and taking over the land worked by each widow. In theory, all the descendants of Bala have an equal claim on the land worked by Culö's line in that agnatically they are equally close. But the practical consequences of widow-inheritance make it difficult to dislodge the descendants of Iza. In the last couple of years the dispute has flared up and violence has been in the air as women of the two branches (through Ho and Iza) compete to cultivate the same plot. A formal discussion of tenure history followed by a planting of permanent borders is now in prospect.

As might be expected from this example, the degree of lineage fragmentation and land division is variable and subject to a number of factors. The Ndruru lineage of Hilisibohou hamlet have not divided their land, which was cleared two generations ago. The chiefly lineage of the Bu'ulölö (B1) is currently in the throes of redefining the land of its segments. In the other Bu'ulölö lineage land has been divided in two, corresponding to the two largest segments (B3 and B4). In B4 the sons of five brothers (thus FBS) have divided their land, and in one case, two brothers have formally divided their father's plot. The other major segment B3 has as yet only an informal allocation among households, many of which have voluntarily moved to Amoroa, beyond lineage territory.

In some parts of Nias (in the west and north-east) a classification of villagers according to their settlement history cross-cuts social stratification based on criteria of birth and rank achieved through feasting (Samson 1925a and 1925b). Briefly, in those areas there are three categories comprising descendants of village founders, later settlers granted land, and temporary first-generation settlers without land. They have unequal rights in land and village government. This system derives from the co-existence of large immigrant groups and original settlers within a district federation which is nominal guardian of district forest. In Sifalagö and surrounding villages no such threefold scheme applies. All landholders are in principle of equal status as *ono mbanua* ('members of the village'), and only recent arrivals (e.g. fugitives, or nowadays teachers) lack land and a say in village affairs.

8 Relations among Agnates

Relations within the lineage are the most intense and often the most strained. This is hardly surprising given the constant interaction of agnates and the complexity of rights and obligations among them. The behaviour of agnates tends to be further from the ideal than is the case with affines, who are usually careful to observe the proprieties. A breach between brothers often hardens into a perpetual enmity between their descendants. On the other hand, brothers are often like fathers to each others' children and take a major role in their upbringing. They are expected to moralize and even administer discipline, but at the same time they tend to be more indulgent figures than the real father. One Sunday morning when I was practising the Nias martial art with my teacher, his young nephews came in to watch. Ama Yeri does not like boys to learn *sile* because he gets blamed for their scrapes, so we had to stop. When I suggested we send them away he replied: 'I can't. They're my nephews. They'll be resentful towards me.' The boys were sitting there more or less quietly when their uncle suddenly began to scold them. 'I've been watching you and taking note of your conduct, and it's not good. It's not the behaviour of schoolchildren. By a person's deeds we know if they are educated. You should know better . . .', and so on. The boys' attitude was not that of respectful attention; they hardly seemed to be listening. And the uncle delivered this apparently uncalled-for sermon somewhat half-heartedly and without even looking at them. But it was just what a father's brother is supposed to say—which they fully understood and could therefore take lightly—and it was a good opportunity since they had spoiled our *sile* session.

Brothers share the burden of each other's feasts and bridewealth payments—or at any rate they are among the principal contributors—and they represent each other in disputes and negotiations. On occasion one may be obliged to bail out another if a fine is beyond his means. But the lines are quite clearly drawn, if differently from case to case, between their separate household expenses. And debts between brothers are kept, though one must exercise tact in reclaiming them, as the following example shows.

Ama Zari borrowed a piglet from his younger brother, Ama Budia, to feed the men who were helping to build his house next door. When Ama Budia, a zealous churchman known for his stinginess, demanded the piglet back after only three weeks, the elder brother decided he had overstepped the mark and dismantled his kitchen while he was at church. The wailing of Ina Budia, who was in the kitchen, could be heard all over the village. After some days a settlement was reached and Ama Zari killed a pig in reconciliation, but the younger brother, who was widely blamed for pressing the debt, continued to complain.

Between cousins this sort of petty dispute is less likely as they are not usually involved in each other's immediate household expenses. Their quarrels concern lineage property and land and therefore take on a more serious character. But short of moving out of the village there is little that agnates can do to avoid each other; they are needed in all the most important activities—bridewealth funding, feasting, housebuilding, planting, and harvesting—so there is a positive necessity to maintain a semblance of good will and civility. 'It all comes down to solidarity,' as I was often told, 'especially when you're dealing with the in-laws.' Consequently, agnates are prepared to put up with a great deal more from each other than they would from non-kin. One man will refer, seemingly without rancour, to how he was cuckolded by a cousin; another to how his daughter was molested in the fields by her classificatory uncle. The close proximity of agnates' living quarters and of their fields creates opportunities

for assignations with each other's wives, and these events, if discovered, are followed by fruitful and protracted litigation. But part
of the settlement is always a reconciliation, and the quality of
continuing relations is measured not in what the agnates might once
have done to each other, but in mutual aid and the sharing of food.
Time and again I heard judgements such as 'He's a vicious brute,
but he never forgets to give me a portion of his pork'; or, 'He has
cheated me more than once, but when it comes to helping with
bridewealth you can count on him.' Loyalty, solidarity, and tolerance are the key values of kinship and are nowhere more evident
than within the circle of the lineage.

One who acts against his brother harms himself; but among
agnates who are further removed genealogically—especially those
living apart—there is a tension between their diverging interests
and what custom demands. As the lineage expands and a division of
ancestral property draws near, or as power and advantage begin to
accumulate in one branch to the detriment of another, the solidarity
can crack. Open confrontation is rare, but violent when it happens.
More often there is a steady accretion of resentment and envy
(*afökhö dödö*)—the prime antisocial evil in Nias—which sometimes
leads to covert action. During my stay I saw fishponds filled in, fruit
trees vandalized, clothes smeared with itching powder, and pigs
speared in the sty. There were also illnesses and deaths attributed to
poisoning and sorcery. A vivid memory is of the dead chief's cousin
publicly swearing his innocence over the coffin, while grasping the
hand of the corpse. The giving of poisoned betel is the very image of
perverted solidarity and shows how *afökhö dödö* can infect the most
potent symbols of sociability. To be sure, such malicious acts are
uncommon, but they are part of the experience of many, and they
leave a strong impression.

Predictably, it is equals or rivals who are most sensitive to
emerging differences in status and prosperity and who ascribe envy
to each other (direct accusations seldom occur). Envy and spite
belong to the illicit side of status competition—the positive, public
side being the quest for prestige through feast-giving. Thus one
sabotages the efforts of others where one cannot match them. But
agnates who feel themselves cheated in a bridewealth division or
who have got the worst of a land settlement are also typical suspects
(as are disgruntled neighbours, for *afökhö dödö* is not restricted to
the lineage, even if it tends to appear there in its strongest form).

The many small acts of generosity characteristic of agnates are, among other things, intended to deter suspicion and preserve an atmosphere of mutual good will. Similarly, people take care not to excite envy in others, either by sharing what they have or by concealment. Adjoining apartments in lineage houses have numerous holes and cracks so that one can keep an eye on what is being eaten next door. Occasionally it is necessary to stop up the holes. One night, when I was at the house of an informant, he disappeared for an hour and came back with a sack of rambutans, picked by torchlight, which we ate with the family by the light of the fire. In general, though, privacy within the lineage is next to impossible. Women talk through the walls to each other as they are cooking, and children run freely from one house or apartment to another. In the big front room there is nearly always an agnate or a neighbour who has dropped in to chew betel and pass the time. With a few exceptions, between the members of a lineage there is a trust and relaxed comradeliness that comes of a lifetime spent in each others' company.

9 Conclusion

The definition of lineage boundaries is a matter of context: it depends on which apical ancestor is chosen as the point of reference (*rahu-rahu*), and for what purposes agnation is being reckoned. Theoretically a lineage is identified with a particular undivided tract of land, but as we have seen this is not necessarily the case since variation in the means of segmentation occurs and land division is a gradual process. Neither is co-residence a criterion by which we can identify a lineage: the most far-flung agnates in remote huts may continue to assert their attachment to an ancestral house in the village. Nor can exogamy be taken as a criterion, since it is the (dispersed) clan or subclan which is the unit of exogamy. As I shall show in the next chapter, an asymmetric marriage prohibition, such that one cannot marry a woman whose mother or mother's mother is one's agnate, can apply to the lineage or its segment or to the whole clan. The level of segmentation involved and the boundaries of the segment identified are variable. The very fluidity of reference groups in practical arrangements, if not in ideology, is an essential feature in the working of the alliance system.

Lacking the overarching scheme of ancestor worship, which once imposed a clear ideological framework on agnatic relations, and lacking the corporate function of warring groups, descent today has become an idiom in which a number of different types of relation are formulated, rather than an independent system.

3

Asymmetric Alliance

Central Nias offers a singular example of a society having a system of asymmetric alliance without prescription. Marriages are contracted unilaterally, according to a rigorous system of asymmetric prohibitions, but there is no corresponding positive marriage rule, either terminological or jural, ordering unilateral exchange. It is a 'system' because certain structural implications of the prohibitions are recognized and are elaborated in an ideology of affinal alliance. This ideology is similar in many respects to the well-known prescriptive systems of eastern Indonesia and the Batak region of north Sumatra. But although there are institutional, symbolic, and formal parallels with prescriptive systems, there are also crucial differences, as we shall see.

While there is no obligation to marry a woman from a wife-giving group, such as in an elementary system, there is nevertheless a rule which prohibits the return of a woman to a wife-giver. Accordingly, the patrilateral cross-cousin, among others, is prohibited as wife. Correspondingly, there is a weak preference for a woman from a wife-giving group (including matrilateral cross-cousin). The range of prohibited women is very wide, comprehending a chain of wife-takers' daughters. This prohibition of reciprocal exchange gives a distinct asymmetric slant to affinal relations. Consistent with this pattern, the relationship terminology has a pronounced asymmetric cast, though it entirely lacks prescriptive equations.

There are two simple rules on which the system is founded:

1. A prohibition applies to women of a man's own *mado* (clan or subclan as locally indicated).
2. A man is prohibited from marrying a woman whose M, MM, MMM, MMMM, etc., belonged to his descent group (ideally his clan).

Neither of these rules excludes sister-exchange. But the repetition of sister-exchange is excluded since in the second generation the man would marry a woman whose mother comes from his own clan (his bilateral cross-cousin). In addition to these two rules, which are expressed in Nias speech more or less as I have described them, there are further considerations which do not quite amount to rules but which weigh heavily in favour of asymmetry:

3. The direct reciprocal exchange of bridewealth, which would amount to a return, is poorly regarded.

4. A marriage which leads to mutually contradictory roles, such that the parties are simultaneously direct wife-givers to each other, is strongly disapproved.

Both these considerations exclude sister-exchange.

1   Alliance Groups

The alliance network is seen most clearly from the point of view of the wife-taker. It emerges with particular clarity in the distribution of bridewealth (see Fig. 3.1). A man is indebted first to his wife's agnates—members of her lineage clustered about her father and father's brother, who are called in this context *so'ono* ('those to whom the child belongs'). Next in importance to F and FB are the bride's brothers. They receive prestations at the wedding and a promise of more later, which will go towards financing their own bridewealth payments. This promised exchange has to be solicited by small gifts to the groom which are said to be a token of the brothers' continuing care for their sister. Other agnates are endowed according to genealogical proximity and seniority, but men who have redistributed their own daughters' bridewealth generously get more than misers. Thus there is no simple lump sum payment to the bride's lineage. Roles are differentiated and payments depend partly on reciprocity between agnates and partly on reciprocity of a different kind between the bride's brothers and the groom. Each of the dozen or so prestations is named differently and the conditions and timing of the exchanges differ. Each is negotiated separately, both between the agnates and directly with the groom's party.

Second in order to the bride's agnates are her mother's agnates, represented by the bride's MF, if alive, and her MB (*sibaya*). Their prestation is called *maso-maso*, said to be an archaic ritual term for heart. It consists of pigs and gold, like most of the bridewealth prestations, and is given in a lump sum direct to the MB and MF. They and their company of agnates are called *sanema maso-maso* ('recipients of *maso-maso*'). Only in cases of a high status marriage, entailing a large bridewealth, would the whole lineage attend as *sanema maso-maso*. In most cases only the senior man of each lineage segment (*sibaya si tambai*, 'collateral *sibaya*') receives a portion. Others get a few morsels and are fed at the wedding feast. So again, there is a differentiation within an outwardly solidary group. As with the *so'ono* group (bride's agnates), the size of the *sanema maso-maso* group mobilized on the wedding-day partly depends on its internal relations of patronage. The bride's MB wins glory if he arrives at the head of a large company, who will perform a dance and song flattering the groom and asking for more gold. But if he brings a large company the MB has to kill a pig for them at rehearsals and he is obliged to divide his bridewealth portion among a wider circle. Thus there is a kind of internal agnatic patronage going on separate from the affinal exchanges, and the empirical composition of the group is determined by a combination of both considerations.

The third group to receive bridewealth is called *sanema hië dödö*, represented by the bride's MMB or his patrilineal descendant (successor). Usually only two or three men of this lineage attend, unless they live in the groom's village or unless the groom is anxious for some other reason to establish good relations with them. The fourth group, *sanema tahövu*, receives only one or two pigs, not enough to be subdivided among the lineage, so only one or two men are called. The *sanema tahövu* is the patrilineal descendant of the bride's MMMB. A further one or two ritually named bridewealth groups may be invited (*sanema gölumbola* and *so'aya za'a*), each one reckoned as MB (*sibaya*) of the previous group.[1]

Moving down the rank-order of the bridewealth-receiving groups there is a progressive reduction in the size of prestation and in the extension of the group, from the solidary but internally differentiated bride's lineage down to the individual recipient who represents the fifth- or sixth-order group. In the south of Nias this gradation is evident in the names of the groups: *sibaya si felendrua, sibaya si*

---

[1] The meaning of these bridewealth terms is obscure. Informants gave sociological glosses and rough etymologies. Thus *hië dödö* means 'strings from which the heart hangs' (i.e. on which life is dependent?).

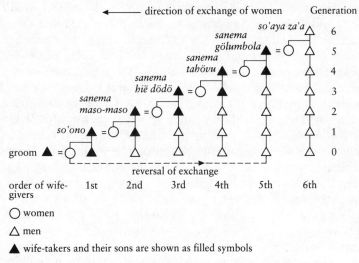

FIG. 3.1. Alliance structure

önö, *sibaya si tölu*, *sibaya* who receive twelve (units), six units, and three units, respectively.

The relation of these bridewealth recipients to each other and to the groom is as a series of patrilineal groups linked together by affinity. The *sanema hië dödö* is wife-giver to the *sanema maso-maso*, who is wife-giver to the *so'ono*, who is wife-giver to the groom. If we imagine the series extended through time, the key partners in each group figure as both wife-givers and wife-takers, but the direction of exchange is always unilateral.

An analytically separate feature, consistent with the asymmetric tracing of past affinal links, is the rule that one may not reverse the flow of women and return a bride to one of these wife-giving groups. For example, a man belonging to the group which received *hië dödö* for a particular woman may not marry her daughter (for whom he can claim *tahövu*). The rule is sometimes relaxed for remoter wife-givers, and a reversal of the original exchange as shown by the dotted line in Fig. 3.1 can occur.

Collectively these wife-giving groups are called *sokhö ya'ita* ('those who own us') or *si tenga bö'ö* ('those who are not other'). Separately, the groups are denoted by their bridewealth names (as above). In the weeks or months before a wedding each group negotiates its own prestation with the groom and the *so'ono*. There are no parallel exchanges among the wife-giving groups in connection with this latest union. They are brought together on the basis of their common relation to the groom as wife-givers, direct or indirect.

In formal terms the relation between wife-givers and wife-takers is transitive, so that if *A* has given a wife to *B*, who has given a wife to *C*, *A* is therefore automatically considered wife-giver to *C*, independently of whether *A* gives a wife to *C* directly on a later occasion. This principle of transitivity, such that direct and indirect wife-givers are classed together, is evident in the collective terms (*sokhö ya'ita*, etc.); but it is more than a matter of names. It appears in the division of bridewealth as described above, in the groom's ritual obligations to each group (such as at feasts of merit), and in other jural and mystical aspects of the relation which I will discuss later. In short, transitivity is a fundamental principle of marriage alliance in Nias.

Unlike a system of prescriptive alliance which simultaneously imposes (in the terminology) a tripartite structure on all past and present marriages, the Nias system identifies a historical series of marriages and leaves present unions indeterminate except that it prohibits a reversal of the prior exchanges. Wife-givers of wife-givers are therefore not WBWB as in asymmetric prescription, but MMB; and bridewealth prestations circulate not among current affines (whose links, in prescriptive alliance, are ideally renewed by repetition of marriage), but follow a path of past marriages.[2]

It is the historical emphasis of the Nias alliance system, the tracing of past unions, that gives it its property of transitivity. In a historical series, if *A* precedes *B* and *B* precedes *C*, by that very fact *A* precedes *C*. A similar instance of transitivity is evident in the tracing of patrilineal descent; and this similarity permits the alliance system to be represented by Niasans in language characteristic of descent institutions, giving at first sight a misleading impression of double descent. For each wife-giver is MB of the next in the series, and the women who link up the affines are M, MM, MMM, MMMM, etc., of the present bride. The series of women is sometimes referred to as a *nga'ötö* ('line') or *nga'ötö ndra alave* ('line of women'). The same word, *nga'ötö*, is more commonly used of what

---

[2] I use the word 'path' here without implying that this is how Niasans necessarily conceive of the series, although occasionally the word *lala* ('path') is used when the transfer of women between villages is traced.

we would call a descent line or a patriline. Thus the chart of a patrilineal pedigree is a *sura nga'ötö*, and a man of a noble line is *nga'ötö zalawa* ('line of a chief'). *Nga'ötö* does not mean 'line' in the graphic or geometrical sense. It is the plural of *götö*, generation, a word which may in turn derive from the verb *ötö*, 'to cut across' (e.g. a river) or 'to slice thinly'.[3] This suggests a horizontal or lateral imagery rather than the vertical line with which we represent descent; a succession of units (generations) rather than a continuous line. Nevertheless, as regards spatial imagery, literate men draw downward-branching pedigrees, and older, unschooled, men would tear up betel leaves and arrange the pieces in vertical lines to represent patrilines for me. In genealogical narrative, descent lines go up (*yawa*) and down (*tou*).

Aside from the question of how a genealogical series is represented, it is striking that the same word can be used of descent and of the series of women exchanged asymmetrically between affines. In discussion of anomalous marriages, informants sometimes speak of clan endogamy (a disregard of the patriline) in the same breath as anomalous 'symmetric' unions (a disregard of the affinal series), suggesting that the two principles of social organization are conceived as being in some respects at the same level and, although different, comparable in the native model. I believe this verbal assimilation of two structural principles, affinity and descent, is largely a matter of idiom and results from the stepwise method of tracing genealogical connections. What is at issue in any discussion of bridewealth entitlement or marriage prohibition is a girl's relation through M or MM to a patrilineage. There is no group or category of persons conceived or constituted, for any purpose, by matrilineal descent, so the existence of double descent—whether 'weak', 'submerged', or 'full'—must be ruled out (Goody 1961).[4] Members of different patrilineages connected through a 'line' of females do not have a common identity as such, since they are mutually distinguished as either wife-givers or wife-takers to each other. Only from the point

---

[3] A euphemism for menstruation is *ötö idanö* ('to cross the river'), suggesting that *ötö* connotes periodicity. *Inötö* means 'time, epoch'.

[4] On similar grounds Watson rules out double descent in South Sumatra (1984: 103). We must be careful to distinguish descent from institutions which may be contingently related to descent such as inheritance and succession. Interestingly, asymmetric prescription and double descent, two systems with which Nias has certain tantalizing resemblances, are the poles of variation in parts of eastern Indonesia (van Wouden 1977; Needham 1980).

of view of an individual Ego do they fall into a single category (*sibaya*).

The tracing of affinal links which precedes any marriage is a historical enquiry similar to the tracing of patrilineal descent, an enquiry which follows what Fox, writing of Roti in eastern Indonesia, has called the 'line of maternal affiliation' (1971: 233). In Roti, as in Nias, recognition of the line of maternal affiliation is the basis of a system of marriage alliance which 'require[s] neither a categorical prescription nor a jural rule of cross-cousin marriage' (Fox 1980c: 132). I shall return to the symbolic aspects of the relation and will explore first what is formally entailed by the system.

The principle of transitivity in the exchange of women combined with the asymmetric prohibition would seem to exclude the possibility of closing the circle of marriages: a possibility allowed in prescriptive systems since the affinal relation is not transitive (or only for a very small number of exchanges). This would mean that if whole lineages were the exchanging units, and no wives could be brought in from outside, the lineage at the beginning of the chain could not obtain wives and the one at the end could not marry off its daughters. There are two features of the system which prevent this predicament from arising. First, it is not whole lineages which are conceived as being the exchange partners; I will return to this point. Secondly, in practice, recognition of remote affines, namely those who are outside the four or five bridewealth-receiving groups, depends on the prior exchange of supplementary gifts (gifts soliciting tribute from wife-takers), and where this exchange lapses or where the genealogical links are forgotten, the erstwhile affines become estranged and are considered as *bö'ö* ('other'). This designation contrasts with the term for wife-givers, *si tenga bö'ö* ('those who are not other'). Estranged affines, as 'others', become once more marriageable against the original direction of exchange.

Where the line is drawn, or rather at what point the line of maternal affiliation is cut off, is an index of status. Among noblemen as many as seven or eight generations of wife-takers to their patrilineal ancestors may be recognized, but there is no rule fixing a number and making a simple correlation with status discernible. In any case, recognition of wife-takers is inconsistent for a given individual: a fifth-order wife-taker in one nearby village may be recognized, while a fourth-order wife-taker in a remote village may be ignored.

Relatively fewer wife-givers are recognized: it is not in one's material interest to extend their number. Unless one receives solicitory gifts from remoter wife-givers, one recognizes—and owes tribute to—only the five or so bridewealth-receiving groups.[5]

The wide range of wife-takers recognized by nobles greatly restricts their choice of spouses and often forces them to marry outside the area. For this reason local exogamy tends to correlate with high status and is therefore itself a practice which enhances prestige. It tends also to be associated with a large bridewealth, another index of status. In Sifalagö, where about half of marriages are within the village, the chief's grandfather's four wives all came from other villages, as did the four wives of the chief's father. The chief himself and his two brothers married noblewomen from other districts and all their sons have followed suit.

For most ordinary villagers, who lack ambition and the means to solicit tribute from remote affines, the range of recognized wife-takers (and givers) is much smaller, and therefore their range of potential spouses wider. Among ordinary men, in reckoning un-marriageability there is said to be a cut-off point above *tahövu*, the fourth-order wife-givers. This means that a man who belongs to one of the four bridewealth-receiving groups (up to *tahövu*) for a particular woman may not marry her, but a man from the fifth group, *gölumbola*, may do so (as shown in Fig. 3.1). His bridewealth prestation would simply be cancelled. In fact only the first four orders of wife-givers are said to receive the *boto mböli*, the 'body' or 'substance of bridewealth'. Remoter affines, usually not more than one or two, receive only token payments. *Gölumbola* is said to mean 'a (mere) mat'.

The asymmetric prohibition is frequently expressed as follows: one may not take as wife a woman for whom one could expect to receive bridewealth, that is *boto mböli*. This rule, which represents entitlement to bridewealth and the marriage prohibition as two sides of the same coin, we might call the native model. In this limited form the rule is practically never violated. Whenever I asked why a particular woman was ineligible the answer would usually be 'we receive bridewealth for her' (*matema mböli niha*). Character-istically, it is a sociological formulation conceived as an exchange model.

---

[5] I have borrowed the useful term 'solicitory gift' from Malinowski (1922: 354) who gives it a slightly different meaning.

Although no more than five or six wife-giving groups are invited to a wedding, noblemen recognize a much wider range of wife-takers than those from whom they receive bridewealth; and all these are prohibited from returning a bride. This would seem to invalidate, or at any rate to qualify, the simple association in the native model between bridewealth entitlement and marriage prohibition. However, the tribute from remote wife-takers is explicitly analogous to bridewealth in native ideology (indeed it may even be called *böli niha*, 'brideprice'), so the model still applies, if not in a literal sense. Moreover, the benefits and blessings conferred on wife-takers in exchange for their tribute are held to be analogous to the prestations given by wife-givers at a wedding and the benefits which accompany the gift of a wife.

When a man rules out a woman as a possible spouse because, as he says, 'we receive her bridewealth', he may be stating a realistic expectation or he may be including himself in the widest group which can, in principle, receive bridewealth, i.e. the whole clan of the girl's M or MM, etc. Although the actual composition of a bridewealth group on the wedding-day is an empirical question, in the calculation of the prohibition the whole clan may be implied as potential bridewealth recipient. In contrast, descent groups—of whatever level—are not conceived as wife-takers. This points to a crucial distinction: a whole clan theoretically gives a wife but only an individual receives. (His sons have a special obligation to their mother's agnates but do not pass it on to *their* sons.)[6] There is no simple tripartite structure of lines linked by affinal exchange as in a system of asymmetric prescription. Instead there is a curious structural imbalance.

Since there is no categorical prescription and no jural rule of marriage to matrilateral cross-cousin, it follows that two brothers can take wives from different clans provided they conform to the asymmetric prohibition.[7] This means that each brother has his own set of wife-givers and each owes nothing to the wife-givers of the other. On the other hand they share the same set of wife-takers (ZS,

---

[6] Among the Karo Batak, who practise a form of asymmetric prescriptive alliance, the *anakberu* ('wife-taker') category includes 'ZH's ascendant and collateral agnates', who are Ego's '*anakberu* by marriage', as well as ZH's descendant agnates, Ego's '*anakberu* by birth' (Singarimbun 1975: 100).

[7] In prescriptive alliance agnates may belong to different alliance cycles, but formally they are in an equivalent position (Barnes 1974: 246; Needham 1957, 1973).

FZS, DH, BDH, etc.) even if own DH and brother's DH are not under the same degree of obligation.

The wife-taker is faced with a number of lineages or part-lineages as his exchange partners, but the wife-giver has only individual wife-takers (and their sons) belonging to a variety of clans and villages. These wife-takers do not include siblings: thus DH, BDH, but *not* DHB, BDHB, who have their own wife-givers to worry about (*umönö* = DH ≠ DHB). This is one reason why the range of recognized wife-takers is so difficult to assess in any given case. For whereas one's wife-givers are a single series, one's wife-takers belong to series which derive from different points in one's descent group (e.g. Z, FZ, FBD, etc.).

The structural imbalance, which opposes individual wife-takers to wife-giving groups, has important implications at the global level. First, it means that no descent group as a whole (at whatever level of segmentation) stands as wife-taker to another, therefore the inequality of affines, according to which wife-givers are always superior, does not affect the overall relative status of descent groups. The inferiority of an individual wife-taker does not even apply to his brother. Only if most members of lineage A married into the same lineage B—which never occurs—would they be collectively inferior to their wife-giver (even then they might have different second- and third-order wife-givers, so affinal statuses would be out of step).

Given this structural imbalance, the transitivity of affinal relations—which I have argued is a feature of the system—cannot lead to a hierarchy of classes. If A is superior to B, and B is superior to C, then A is superior to C in the Nias system. But since, in each case, the inferior partner is only an individual, and there is a multiplicity of affinal chains which may contradict each other, the system cannot form a basis for classes.

Leach (1961: 84–7) has argued that 'matrilateral cross-cousin marriage' in combination with affinal inequality tends to lead to a class system. But this is true only if (1) the inequality is transitive—which has been found generally not to be the case in asymmetric systems, and (2) permanent or fixed groups are involved as exchanging units.[8] If we grant that alliance status can contingently have a political (class) aspect, we must add as a third condition for the fulfilment of Leach's hypothesis: (3) a consistency among alliance

[8] On 'non-transitivity', see Needham (1980: 41). On the variable constitution of alliance groups, see Needham (1957) and Barnes (1980a: 86).

cycles (such that the status differences in one series are harmonious with those in the next).

In Nias, where prescription is lacking but asymmetry, affinal inequality, and transitivity are present, the egocentric basis of the system and the practical recognition of only four or five wife-givers (in series) to an individual works against the establishment of an alliance-based class system. This is not to say that marriage alliances do not have a political content—many do, which is another reason why nobles choose not to marry locally; it is merely to deny that alliance inequalities are consistent enough to form the basis of all political relations.

2 Alliance and Local Exogamy

There is great variation in the compass of alliance groups and in the interpretation of the equivalence of bridewealth entitlement and marriage prohibition. Consequently, the number of local women considered marriageable varies from one individual to another. There are, moreover, two dimensions to the extension of the prohibition:

1. The extension of Ego's own descent group conceived as wife-giver: for example, do the second-order wife-takers of remote agnates count as one's own second-order wife-takers?

2. The extension of the asymmetric series of affines: does one recognize fifth- and sixth-order wife-takers and beyond?

Noble lines tend to prohibit a return of women from any wife-taker (direct or indirect) of the whole clan. This means they are forced to look outside the village and even outside the district for wives. Lineages or lineage segments which include men of high rank likewise tend to adhere strictly to the rules and regard themselves as wife-givers to any man whose wife's line of maternal affiliation can be traced back to their *clan*. The daughters of such men are prohibited as spouses. (Thus, the asymmetric prohibition does not apply to all the women of a certain clan, only to those connected through the line of maternal affiliation to the man's clan.)

Among ordinary lineages there is a tendency to reduce the span of one's group—conceived as wife-giver—in proportion to social distance. Thus, lineage *A1* regards as prohibited any woman whose

M or MM comes from clan *A*, but a girl whose MMM comes from lineage *A2* may be allowed, while a girl whose MMMM belonged to a different segment of lineage *A1* from that of the groom may be allowable as spouse, at a pinch. The reversal of asymmetry is excused by appeal to the formula: 'we don't receive bridewealth for her', applying it in a literal sense. Only a single individual will turn up to claim *gölumbola*, and his agnates may regard the girl in question as effectively unrelated (*aefa khöma*, 'free of us') and therefore marriageable.

Lineages or lineage segments without any pretensions to high rank are usually prepared to limit the extent of the prohibition at an earlier stage and prohibit only women of their own clan and women to whom the clan is first- and second-order wife-giver. For remoter wife-takers it is the actual rather than theoretical alliance groups which are taken into account. The operative question becomes, 'Can we expect to receive a pig for her?', rather than 'Did her maternal great-grandmother belong to our clan?'

Nevertheless, even a liberal interpretation of the rules cuts out a sizeable proportion of local women, with a consequent tendency towards local exogamy. Consider Table 3.1, which shows the origin of wife and wife's mother (thus of wife-giver and wife-giver of wife-giver). A girl whose mother comes from Sifalagö is likely to marry out because men of at least one locally represented clan (apart from her own) regard her as prohibited. If her MM comes from the

TABLE 3.1 Local exogamy in Sifalagö

Man's clan	Bu'ulölö	Laia	Ndruru	Other	Total
Number of marriages	56	49	20	6	131
Origin of wife					
Sifalagö	36%	44%	70%	67%	46%
outside	64%	56%	30%	33%	54%
Origin of wife's mother					
Sifalagö	7%	14%	25%	33%	15%
outside	93%	86%	75%	67%	85%

Note: The table shows a record of all 131 marriages of the inhabitants of all 103 households in the village (except temporary residents), including marriages where only one spouse survives. The figures refer to the central cluster of historically related hamlets, not the administrative unit (*desa*).

village as well, two clans are excluded to her, and so on. Likewise, daughters of women from outside the village are more likely to find husbands within it. The difference between percentages of wives and wives' mothers from outside Sifalagö is a function of the rules and the local exogamy they encourage, not a reflection of a change in the pattern of exogamy in recent generations. In 54 per cent of marriages the wife came from outside Sifalagö. But in no fewer than 85 per cent of marriages the bride's mother came from another village. Second-order wife-givers are therefore mostly outsiders. Third-order wife-givers can of course belong to the 'home' village, but they are more likely to come from further afield, and may even be unknown to the prospective groom. A large proportion of alliance chains therefore radiate outwards from the village up to a point where knowledge of them fades out. A proportion of local marriages are alliance renewals (*sangawuli ba zibaya*), a few are anomalous, and a few open alliances with 'unrelated' lines, though there are very few cases where no relation could ultimately be traced.

As noted above, descent groups vary in their interpretation of the rules and their attitude towards breaches. The Bu'ulölö lineages resident in Sifalagö are very strict and proud of their record in this respect. Bu'ulölö men are obliged by their reputation to comb wide tracts of central Nias and beyond in search of unrelated women.[9] The Ndruru (also the Halawa and Giawa, listed as 'Other' in the table) form an instructive contrast in that 70 per cent of their wives come from within the village. On balance their members are wife-takers to other local descent groups. Moreover they are not strict in applying the asymmetric prohibition at the clan level so long as actual alliance groups are not confused. Correspondingly, they lack prestige and influence within the village. The maintenance of asymmetry in affinal networks pays dividends in prestige. A noble maintains his networks by means of occasional solicitory gifts (*so'i-so'i*) which oblige the wife-takers, on pain of being cursed, to render lavish tribute at his feasts of merit. In this sense the exchange of prestations is constitutive of social structure. Men of rank who cannot afford to solicit tribute widely among their wife-takers avoid a reversal of alliance ties locally to protect their reputations and to

---

[9] The rate of local exogamy for the Bu'ulölö would be even higher were we to exclude the Ono Goyo lineage whose history has obliged it to marry anomalously for protection.

avoid creating too many importunate wife-givers within the village. If they marry locally it is preferably to existing wife-givers, confirming a prior alliance.

Thus the notion of a cycle of affines is certainly not an ideal as it is in some prescriptive systems. It is permissible, if at all, only if the main alliance groups are not implicated in a reversal. The closing of the circle (as we should call it) by giving a wife to a fifth- or sixth-order wife-giver, is far from being a desirable form of marriage. It can be a source of embarrassment (especially from the man's point of view, since he is making a superior of his inferior) and is only contracted for pressing reasons: that the girl is pregnant or that the immediate parties are keen on an alliance of this kind. Sticklers for the rules would oppose it, arguing that as long as the previous affinal relation can be traced the girl cannot be truly a *niha bö'ö* ('other, unrelated'). There is no conception of 'purity' in descent or alliance, but there is a firm belief that clan endogamy and alliance reversal are morally reprehensible and cause supernatural displeasure. Since in many cases remote affinal links are forgotten it is assumed that ordinary men, especially those marrying in the village, often 'sin' in ignorance, marrying related women who are, if they knew it, *salakha* ('the prohibited/unthinkable'). In the absence of accurate knowledge, outsiders can more confidently be assumed to be *niha bö'ö*. The penalty for anomalous liaisons in the past was execution; nowadays the sanction is a heavy fine. Very rarely, remote relatives who were ordinarily prohibited could be reclassified as 'other' by a nominal change of clan enabling a marriage to take place.[10]

There is no official record of alliances comparable to the patrilineal pedigrees which most people know at least in outline. In former times the row of lineage ancestor figures included women who had married in (though they actually retained their natal clanship). These would have been of limited use as an *aide-mémoire*, since each ancestral pair was separated from the other pairs in its alliance chain which were to be found in other houses. There are the bridewealth-group terms, but these are conceived egocentrically and could not have the generality and permanence of a pedigree. It happens, then, that an alliance is either kept alive through the exchange of prestations or, at a practical level, it may be ignored or forgotten. Misfortune and illness are sometimes interpreted as signs

[10] See further Sect. 6 of Ch. 7 on anomalous unions.

of divine (or ancestral) disapproval for men's laxity over affinal regulations. For God, at least, remote affinal links continue to exist. In the past, epidemics would be remedied by expiatory sacrifices and legislation enforcing the marriage prohibitions (including clan exogamy) by imposing a curse on offenders. But lacking a simple means of identification (comparable to, say, a clan name), remote affines who do not figure as bridewealth groups inevitably tend to be forgotten.

3 Tracing the Bride's Line of Maternal Affiliation

The feasibility of a local marriage is initially calculated in terms of the bridewealth groups. Any young man or boy knows that if his lineage received the *maso-maso* prestation for a girl's mother, then his own lineage gets *hië dödö* for the daughter and she is prohibited (*salakha*) to him.

In making a match outside the village, the groom's negotiator first asks, 'How many (patri)lines (*nga'ötö*) are involved in the girl's bridewealth?' There may be no living descendants of the fourth-order wife-giver, for example, and so no claimant for the *tahövu* prestation. This is a bad sign. One looks for longevity, fertility, and good fortune in the bride's background. Assuming the signs are favourable, the negotiator begins his genealogical enquiry, asking where the girl's mother comes from—her clan and village—then he asks about her MM and so on until he has exhausted his informant's knowledge and excluded the possibility of the groom's own descent group being among the wife-givers. This is called investigating the girl's *tanö-tanö* (from *tanö*, 'ground, earth, to plant') or her *ananöma* (a synonym from the same root, with the further meaning of 'the thing planted' in the southern dialect). What seems to be implied in the present context is the soil from which a plant grows, and this is how informants explained it. 'If there is no ground there is no grass. Just so, I am the *tanö-tanö* of my sister's child.' This is strikingly reminiscent of the 'botanic idiom' of Rotinese MB/ZC relations (Fox 1971). However, the terms *tanö-tanö* and *ananöma* can also be used of patrilineal background, and one cannot press the analogy with the Rotinese usage very far. There is no elaboration of a conception of 'sister's child as plant', if such it is.

It is important to note that the investigation is not simply a tracing of any cognatic links which might lead from the potential spouse back to the groom's clan. Only direct, uninterrupted affinal links matter, or as it is sometimes put, the *nga'ötö ndra alave*, the 'line of women'. Thus FFZDD is prohibited, but FFZSD is marriageable since her mother does not derive from Ego's clan via the line of maternal affiliation: she comes from *niha bö'ö*.

The word *nga'ötö* cannot be used of other cognatic links. It is only used of a patriline and a line of maternal affiliation. This poses an interesting question. What is transmitted through females such that the line of maternal affiliation is—in Nias eyes—comparable to patrilineal descent? Or, to put the question in alliance terms: what is the ideological complement or basis of the transitive relation between affines? To begin with a negative answer: there is no transmission of group membership through the maternal line. Maternal affiliation is conceived egocentrically. Secondly, the line does not represent simply the inheritance of one's father's affinal obligations. If this were the case there would be no distinction between MB and brothers of the father's other wives. In fact, the latter category of men have no significant role in one's life. (Neither does a son inherit his father's matrilateral ties: a ZSS has no obligation to FMB.) Therefore a simple reduction of maternal affiliation to affinity is invalid. Neither does recourse to folk biology help in the analysis. There is no generally accepted theory by which each parent contributes some element to the child's make-up.

The tracing of a line of maternal affiliation derives from the idea, common in eastern Indonesia, of the asymmetric exchange of women as a gift of life from wife-givers to wife-takers, which is represented in that area as a cumulative 'flow of life' (Fox 1980*b*: 12). In Nias, if one asks why bridewealth is due to the bride's mother's agnates, the answer is 'because the bride's mother comes from them, and without her there would be no bride'. Similarly, without the bride's mother's mother's agnates the bride's mother would not exist. On the same principle a man is indebted to his own MB, MMB, etc., for his existence.[11] There is no parallel obligation to F and FF: patrilineal ties are differently conceived.

---

[11] This rationale for the special relationship between MB and ZS is the same in Kédang (Barnes 1974: 248) and parallels the 'representation of the mother's brother's group as the source or origin of the sister's sons' in Rindi (Forth 1981: 288) and among the Karo Batak (Singarimbun 1975).

In the historical series of affines, each clan is the *tanö-tanö*, the 'origin' or 'ground', of the next. The *sanema tahövu* is the origin of the *sanema hië dödö*, etc. This relation is felt to be axiomatic and self-evident. To repeat the aphorism: 'Without the ground there is no grass. I am the ground/origin of my sister's child.' Rather than there being a life-principle or substance transmitted through women, as in some eastern Indonesian ideologies, what is passed on in marriage and maternal affiliation is the means to life in two senses: a woman's reproductive capacity and her labour. These two life-giving attributes are separately recognized in prestations given both to direct wife-givers and to mother's agnates. For example, there is a prestation called 'debt for the child' (*ömö nono*) claimed by the wife's parents for her first-born son and daughter. The notion that the incoming wife assures the continuity of the line is a familiar one. But it is not only the living who benefit: Schröder (1917: 258) writes that for Niasans the purpose of marriage was to create descendants to venerate one after death. The association between life and a woman's labour is evident in a host of daily expressions, attitudes, and formal prestations. She is the provider of daily subsistence and of the surplus needed to finance her son's bridewealth and her husband's feasts (rituals aimed partly at promoting life and prosperity).

For both life-giving services—reproduction and labour, or life and livelihood—the immediate beneficiary is the husband, and he offers bridewealth as a counter-prestation. But it is the son who owes his very existence to the exchange, and whose continued well-being depends on his mother's efforts. *His* benefactor is his MB or, more generally, mother's agnates. At a feast of merit the two main guest groups are the wife's agnates and the mother's agnates (called respectively by the terms for WF and MB, *matua* and *sibaya*)— acknowledging simultaneously the feastgiver's debts as a husband and as a son.[12]

By virtue of the exchange of women and all this implies, wife-givers (including own mother's agnates) retain a power over the wife-taker. They are collectively called *sokhö ya'ita*, literally 'those who own us'. Paradoxically, then, in the transfer of a woman it is the wife-givers who come to 'own' the groom, who becomes their *ono* ('child, wife-taker'). They own him in the sense that he is dependent

[12] Cf. the Karo Batak, who make a distinction within the wife-giving category of '*kalimbubu* by birth' (e.g. MB) and '*kalimbubu* by marriage' (WF, WB, etc.) (Singarimbun 1975: 98).

on them for prosperity and fertility, both in the immediate transfer of female labour and reproductive capacity, and in a symbolic and mystical endowment which derives from the affinal relation. They have the power to bless and to curse, and their formal blessing is requested at all life-crisis rituals.[13] The wife-givers, then, and among the mother's agnates especially the MB line, control the 'flow of life' (to borrow the Timorese idiom). The mere payment of bridewealth cannot requite this gift, which is lifelong and depends on their continual regard. Not surprisingly, given this conception of marriage alliance, the brothers of the father's other wives (who are 'not true *sibaya*') are of no account. One derives neither life nor sustenance from them.[14] In polygamous households each wife provides for her own children, who owe nothing to the co-wives' agnates. In both a practical and symbolic sense, then, the system emphasizes not simply affinity but the matrifiliation deriving from affinity, and this matrifiliation is conceived as cumulative and transitive, a descending line of females which links up the affines. Hence Niasans can discuss descent lines and alliance chains in the same terms. The line of females so identified might give an illusion of matrilineality, but as I have argued, what is at issue is obligation to patrilineal groups traced through this line. Depending on which aspect of the alliance relation is being stressed (debt for one's existence, genealogical connection, or transfer of labour), Niasans are 'descent theorists', 'alliance theorists', or something in the middle, to borrow the terms of a well-worn anthropological controversy.[15] Matrifiliation is a function of affinity, but in the Nias form of marriage alliance these concepts are not equivalent to each other unless we ignore the ideology of exchange and the distinction, jural and terminological, between MB and FWB.

The mystical powers vested in wife-givers, their superiority over wife-takers and the obeisance due to them (the wife-taker 'kneels')

[13] There is no term equivalent to the Toba Batak *sahala* (spiritual power) (Vergouwen 1964: 54) or Karo *tuah*. The conception of affinal power is relational rather than substantial.

[14] Similarly, one is under an obligation to the true MB for one's life rather than to the brothers of a stepmother, even though the latter may replace one's real mother as provider.

[15] Fortes (1959: 208–9) reduces alliance to filiation and consigns it to the 'domestic domain', while descent is held to originate in the 'politico-jural domain'. This allocation of descent and alliance to different structural domains is untenable in the Nias context as in other Indonesian societies. See replies of Leach (1960) and Dumont (1961).

puts them in a position analogous to God and the ancestors. The affinal epithet *sokhö ya'ita*—'he (or those) who own us'—is also a common epithet for God, both in the old religion and in contemporary Christian prayer. This analogy is another common feature of asymmetric alliance systems in Indonesia, for example among the Toba Batak (Vergouwen 1964: 54) and the Karo, for whom the wife-givers are a 'visible god' (Singarimbun 1975: 137).

There is a further, less explicit, analogy between wife-givers and patrilineal ancestors, who alike are guardians of one's fortune. Ritual invocations performed at the houses of wife-givers prior to a feast of merit imply that their mystical power derives from their ancestors, a set of spiritual beings parallel to one's own patrilineal spirits. Wife-givers are also able to curse in the name of their ancestral spirits.

4 Categories of Alliance

I have identified the ways in which wife-givers are identified, classified, and their place in ideology. I now consider the meaning of the categories of alliance in more detail. Due to the structural imbalance which pits individuals against groups, wife-takers are an amorphous category of persons of diverse origin. *Ono alave* (lit. 'daughter, female child') is the commonest designation for all types of wife-taker, e.g. DH, ZS, FZDH, FBDDH. It is interesting that the term for WF (*matua*) also means 'male', hinting at an opposition between a 'male' wife-giver and a 'female' wife-taker, as attested in other asymmetric alliance systems such as Rindi (Forth 1981: 284). A male/female opposition is not, however, manifested in other ways in Nias marriage alliance, and there are no complementary masculine and feminine prestations. Another alliance category derived from the relationship terminology, *ono* (lit. 'child'), usually denotes direct wife-takers of one's descent group, e.g. DH, FBDH, ZS, FZS. *Ma'uvu* (lit. 'grandchild') refers to indirect wife-takers, i.e. wife-takers of wife-takers and so on. Any members of the wife-giving group (potentially a whole clan) may employ the terms *ono* and *ma'uvu* to refer to individual wife-takers, irrespective of the relative genealogical levels of Ego and alter. This use of descending relationship terms expresses with economy the juniority of wife-takers, and is another feature common to many societies practising asymmetric prescriptive alliance. The principle of transitivity is once more evident in the use of the term *ma'uvu* ('grandchild') for wife-takers of wife-takers. The corresponding equation of wife-givers of wife-givers with grandparents is lacking, though, as already remarked, there is a symbolic association between patrilineal ancestors and wife-givers. The asymmetric marriage prohibition is frequently expressed in the form: 'I cannot marry her because she's our *ono* (or our *ma'uvu*).' The double meaning of these terms conveys well the prohibited nature of the union, putting it in the same light as marriage with a kinswoman. The Bu'ulölö clan, which is austerely exogamous and equally strict over the asymmetric prohibition, has an abusive rhyme about the Laia clan who, they say, marry endogamously and are lax about asymmetry: 'Laia, red-eyed fornicators, they marry their *ono* (wife-takers).' This usage of the terms for C and CC accords well with the emphasis I have identified on matrifiliation—on the consanguinity that derives from affinity.

When someone refers to a wife-taker as *ono*, he nearly always adds the first-person plural possessive suffix *-ma*, as in *onoma* ('our child/our wife-taker'), as it were speaking on behalf of his descent group. If he wants to specify more precisely his genealogical relation to the wife-taker, he chooses an egocentric relationship term and attaches the singular possessive suffix *-gu*, as in *umönögu*, my DH. In reckoning bridewealth calculations and marriage prohibitions, since the wife-givers are always a group in such calculations, *ono(ma)* and *ma'uvu(ma)* are usually the terms used rather than egocentric relationship terms. Needless to say, given the conception of affinity outlined above, only persons directly connected through the line of maternal affiliation are classed in this way. ZS is *ono*, but ZSS is (strictly speaking) neither *ono* nor *ma'uvu*: his mother 'does not derive from us'; she is *niha bö'ö*, and therefore he belongs to a different alliance chain. The use of these terms is therefore selective. It does not cover the whole range of cognatic kin.

There is a vaguely defined penumbra of relatives who are one or two genealogical steps away from *ono* and *ma'uvu*, belonging to different alliance chains, e.g. ZSS, and these are called *sahatö* ('those who are close'). Their recognition depends on the quality of the personal relation between the parties, whether they engage in mutual aid, etc.

To summarize the range of categories, wife-givers are *sokhö ya'ita* ('those who own us') or *si tenga bö'ö* ('those who are not other'). The category includes all the affinally linked groups culminating in wife's agnates and mother's agnates. Wife-takers are *ono*, if direct, *ma'uvu* if indirect, or *ono alave*. Besides these categories there are fellow-clansmen and -clanswomen (*talifusö*) and the penumbra of cognatic kin, *sahatö*. Beyond these are *niha bö'ö* ('others').

A *niha bö'ö* is someone with whom there are no ascribed relations, no rights or obligations, and no prescribed forms of behaviour. *Niha bö'ö* are quintessentially strangers, outsiders who are therefore potential enemies from whom (formerly) heads may be taken, and also potential spouses. The mothers of several men in the village were obtained on raids. In informants' descriptions of matchmaking it is always assumed that the man roams among remote and hostile villages before picking a wife. At feasts of merit affines confront each other in warlike postures; guests arrive as raiders, re-enacting the hostility which precedes the peace created by alliance.

To marry an 'other' and thus make affines of her family is to transform them into 'those who are not other' (*si tenga bö'ö*). In contrast to the hostility that exists between *niha bö'ö*, *si tenga bö'ö* are traditional protectors of their wife-takers and will defend them to the death. Men who had committed a capital offence in their village would often flee to the village of their WF or MB and live there permanently. (In recent cases, too, murderers have sought refuge with their affines.) The threat of annihilation by one village faction could be averted by marrying into a lineage of the same clan as one's enemy. This type of political marriage was usually uxorilocal and the husband became a subservient dependant of his wife-givers. (The example of the Ono Goyo lineage is related in Sect. 3 of Ch. 1) It also happened that settler-fugitives gave wives to their protectors, thus reversing the normal superiority of wife-givers and making a tribute of their women in exchange for safety. It is only after several generations of judicious matchmaking and political manœuvring—and perhaps only nowadays under the relative security of national law—that the yoke of this kind of protection can finally be cast aside. However, even today the old affinal loyalties of settler lineages are still a force in village politics. Most of the settler lineages in Sifalagö have a history of political alliances behind them. The Halawa lineage has taken wives from the chief's line four generations in succession since arriving in the area. Its land was obtained in bridewealth and as a reward for services in war, giving it an independent position as self-reliant ally to the chief. The Giawa, refugees from a feud in Gomo, have chosen to diversify their alliances in the village.

The incorporation of *niha bö'ö* into the category of affine is thus a transformation fraught with political and symbolic significance. As mentioned earlier, the reverse process of estrangement comes about through geographical dispersal, the lapse of gift-exchange, or through the reclassification of an anomalous union.

Despite a certain flexibility in practice, the location and mainten- ance of the kin boundary (to use a Nias metaphor) is not simply a matter of convenience: there are powerful sanctions involved. To fail in one's obligations to a wife-giver is to 'act as a *niha bö'ö*'. The offender is branded as 'no longer *ono* or *ma'uvu*'. He can be brought into line by afflicting him with a curse, which forces him to beg forgiveness and offer tribute. Unlike the curse of a sorcerer, the curse of a wife-giver cannot be counteracted by magical remedies. The curse is said to be effective because of the power vested in the wife-giver: he can curse because he can bless; he can bring fertility to crops or he can blight them. The wife-giver's curse, particularly that of the MB line, is also said to be powerful because it confirms the customary law (which enjoins the giving of tribute by the ZS or other wife-taker); by virtue of their genealogical position they are figures of mystical authority. Wife-givers are *mosöfu bava* ('author- itative') or *salakha bava* ('curse-mouthed'). The sorcerer's curse, in contrast, transgresses the customary law; he relies on magical means, having no inherent authority. The only person who can undo the wife-giver's curse is the curser himself or his own wife- giver, who has power over him (*mosöfu*). Again the principle of transitivity comes into play. At feasts of merit, where wife-givers receive tribute, one of their tactics for squeezing more out of the feastgiver is to threaten him with a curse. They ask, 'Have you invited us today to obtain our blessing or our curse?' If the feastgiver has fulfilled his obligations and a curse would be unjustified he need not greatly fear their threat. He can always appeal over their heads to remoter wife-givers.

5   Renewing the Alliance

There is no rule enjoining marriage to a female matrilateral cross- cousin (*ono ba zi matua*) corresponding to the ban on patrilateral cross-cousin (*ono ba zi alave*), but there is a slight preference for women of wife-giving lineages. The groom in such marriages is called *sangawuli ba zibaya* ('one who returns to the *sibaya*'). *Sibaya* is a term used loosely of all males connected through the line of maternal affiliation. Primarily it refers to mother's agnates. So, to marry a woman of mother's clan is to return to the original wife-giver, *sibaya*, for another woman.

Why should a man 'return to his *sibaya*'? He is able to marry thanks to the labour of his mother who raised the pigs that form his bridewealth. He is indebted to his MB for this service, since his gain is his MB's loss. Marriage to an outsider, a *niha bö'ö*, is a further alienation of the fruits of the woman's labour, and the groom must acknowledge this fact with a prestation to his MB called the 'sow's toe'. One informant explained the meaning of this prestation as follows: 'My sister's son has given away the "value" (*ösi*, lit. 'content') of my sister to outsiders (*bö'ö*), so he asks my permission.' Hence the proverb: 'When the sister's value departs one brings [gifts] to the *sibaya*' (*me mofanö nösi makhelo alave, ladoro khö zibaya*).[16] Marriage into the clan of M or MM, on the other hand, implies a return of the fruits of the labour of the woman originally given away, in the form of bridewealth for her clan-brother's daughter.

Marriage to the MBD would seem to be the neatest formulation of the preference: a repetition of the original union in the same direction, breaking neither the rule of clan exogamy nor the (patri-lateral) asymmetric prohibition. In fact, in the centre of Nias, marriage to the MBD is not strictly allowed, even if such unions— where they occur—are not regarded as gravely anomalous.

The relation between cross-cousins is multifaceted. Accordingly, there are several ways of classifying MBD. The MB is said to be a kind of second father, who may be addressed as *ama* ('father'), and also a potentially dangerous figure deserving of special respect. The child of MB is likewise a playmate and classificatory 'sibling' but also a member of another clan to whom one is born in debt. The whole constellation of relationships is a ritual and structural focus, located at the crossroads of affinity and consanguinity.

---

[16] In south Nias, where there is a jural rule enjoining marriage to the matrilateral cross-cousin (see Marschall 1976), a similar payment is claimed as a kind of fine if a man marries someone else.

While marriage to MBD is, then, at best a controversial practice, marriage to the daughter of mother's clan brother is desirable, and entirely lacks any connotation of the forbidden. Most marriages which are called 'returning to the *sibaya*' are of this kind. I consider below some of the varieties of alliance renewal.

1. Marriage to MFBSD, the closest possible matrilaterally related spouse, eludes the ban on MBD by a collateral step. In this form the alliance is repeated in consecutive generations but not between the same descent lines, that is, not by the lineal descendant (MBD) of the first wife-giver.

2. Another possibility (see Fig. 3.2) is to elude the ban by missing a generation and repeating not father's marriage but grandfather's (marriage to FMBSD). This is a repetition of the alliance in alternate generations. It remains asymmetric, confirming the direction of the original alliance. In the intervening generation the direction cannot be reversed as this would lead to patrilateral cross-cousin marriage which is explicitly barred.

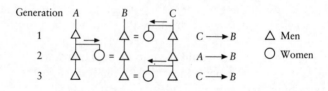

FIG. 3.2. FMBSD marriage

3. A third possibility (Fig. 3.3) is to renew the alliance at one affinal remove. This occurs 'when the children of cross-cousins marry'. In what sense is this a repetition of a union? In the first generation B gives a wife to A; in the second generation B gives a wife to C; in the third, C gives a wife to A. Given the principle of transitivity, if $B \rightarrow C$ and $C \rightarrow A$, therefore $B \rightarrow A$. To convert these formal terms back into institutional arrangements, in the third generation B becomes *sanema maso-maso* as the wife-giver of wife-giver of A. This repeats the $B \rightarrow A$ marriage at one affinal remove. Instead of taking another wife from B, $A3$ takes a wife from the wife-taker of B. In this way the alliance between A and B, which would have lapsed in the third generation, is renewed.

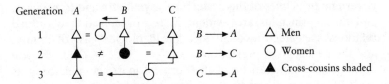

FIG. 3.3. FMBDD marriage

4. In the contrasting possibility (Fig. 3.4), when the sexes of the children of the respective cross-cousins are reversed (union with MFZSD), there is no renewal, rather a new alliance is opened. Although it appears that the $B \to A$ alliance is repeated indirectly, in fact the alliance chain is broken in generation 2. In the third-generation alliance, A owes tribute and bridewealth to C and D who are his wife-giver and wife-giver-of-wife-giver respectively. Line B has no material claim on $A3$ for this marriage.

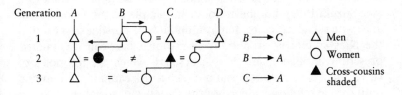

FIG. 3.4. MFZSD marriage

These genealogical considerations are only involved in cases where the closest permissible relatives marry. In most cases of renewing an alliance a man simply marries a woman of his mother's clan or of any clan which is wife-giver (direct or indirect) to his father, the men of which are *sibaya*. In all such cases the groom is a *sangawuli ba zibaya*.

6 Conclusion

The foregoing analysis has demonstrated that we are justified in speaking of a system of asymmetric marriage alliance in Nias. The governing principles of this system are asymmetry and transitivity, and these principles are evident in the organization of affinal relations, the categories of alliance, the ideological basis of affinity, and the exchange of prestations.

A special characteristic of this form of marriage alliance is its explicitly historical construction, its concern with origins, which is bound up with religious conceptions and notions of the person. In marrying, one enters into a long historical series, and one acknowledges past unions in tribute, just as one expects bridewealth at the marriages of one's D and DD. This transitive conception of alliance relations is quite unlike the simple dualism of wife-giver/wife-taker which underlies the tripartite structure of asymmetric prescription (Needham 1962: 96). In Nias the entire series of affines is constantly kept in view. We are in a different world from the discrete triads and the ideal conception of past, present, and future relations embodied in prescriptive systems. And we look in vain for a simple comprehensive scheme of ideas embracing social structure and symbolic classification such as can be found in eastern Indonesia and other parts of Southeast Asia. Nias is not without its binary symbolism (see Suzuki 1959), but this is not in any simple relation of concordance with social structure. It may ultimately be possible to show that the Nias system is structurally transitional between asymmetric prescriptive alliance and double descent, which are the poles of variation in eastern Indonesia; but such a task cannot be attempted until we have fuller evidence of the varieties of social structure in other parts of Nias.

4

Relationship Terminology

In this chapter I discuss relationship terminology, beginning with a presentation of terms of reference, followed by notes on principles of classification. The remainder of the chapter is devoted to a consideration of the line of maternal affiliation and categories of alliance, ending with an attempt to characterize the terminology.

1 Terms of Reference

1. *tua*   FF, FFB, MF, MFB, MMB, FMB; FFF, FMF, MFF, MMF
    and their brothers; EFF, EFFB, EMF, EMFB, EMFB;
    MBWF, MFZH, MZHF
    akhi dua ('grandfather's younger sibling') MFyG, FFyG,
    EMFyG, EFFyG (the masculine specifications, e.g. MFyB,
    can be termed *tua sakhi*, 'younger grandfather')
    tua, ama dua   ('grandfather, father of grandfather') FFF
2. *ave*   FM, MM, FFM, FMM, MMM, MFM, EPM; FFZ, MFZ,
    MZHM, MFBW, MFW (co-wife of MM)
    ave sa'a FF_1W, FFeBW
    ave lave   FMZ, MMZ
3. *ama*   F, FFBS, M_2H, HF, MB (in some contexts)
    ama sa'a   FeB, EFeB, FFeBS,
    ama talu   FmB, EFmB, FFmBS
    ama sakhi   FyB, EFyB, FFyBS
    ono nama sakhi   FyBC, FFyBSC
4. *ina*   M, female agnates of +1 genealogical level, HM
    ina sa'a   FeBW, FFeBSW, mother's senior co-wife
5. *ina lave*   MZ, FZ, HMZ
    ina lave sakhi   MyZ, FyZ
    fo'omo nina lave   MZH, FZH
    ono nina lave   MZC, FZC, HMZC

6. *makhelo nina*   ('mother's sibling') MB, MZ
   ono makhelo nina   MBC
7. *sibaya*   male agnates of M, MM, and MMM
   ono zibaya   D of mother's agnates and MM agnates
   ono nono zibaya   MBDC (or *ono nono makhelo nina*)
   sangai ono zibaya   MBDH, H of mother's agnates' daughter
   sibaya vo'omo   male agnates of spouse's M and MM
   fo'omo zibaya   MBW, MFBSW, wives of *sibaya*
   sibaya nama   FMB
8. *makhelo*   B, Z, FBC, FZC, MBC, MZC
9. *ka'a*   eB, eZ, PGCe, HeG, HFBCe, eBW (ws)
10. *akhi*   yB, yZ, PGCy, HyG, HFBCy, yBW (ws)
11. *talifusö*   B, Z, agnate of same genealogical level
12. *ono*   S, D, CC, SW, SSW, DSW, BC, ZC, FBSC, MZCC, ZSC
    ono nakhi   yBC, yZC, HyBC
    ono makhelo   BC, ZC
    ono makhelo(gu) alave   ZC, HZC
13. *ma'uvu*   CC, BCC, ZDC (all of these are also *ono nono*, 'child of child'), CCC
14. *ono mbini'ö*   ms: ZS, ZD, ZDS, ZDD, FZS, FZD, FFZC, FZDC
    ono nono mbini'ö   ZSC, FZSC
15. *tahö nono*   ms: ZS
16. *fo'omo*   (also *donga*) W, H
    fo'omo ga'a   eBW
    makhelo vo'omo   WZ, HB, HZ
    fo'omo makhelo vo'omo   HBW
    fo'omo nono   SW, BSW, HBSW, CSW
17. *matua*   WF
    matua(gu) ira alave   WM
    matua ga'a   eBWF, HeBWF
18. *mbambatö*   SWP, SWPP, SDHP, SSWP, SWFB, SWFBW, SWMB, DHP, DHFB, DHFBW, DHFP, DDHP, BCEP (ms), HBCEP, BSCEP (ms), HBSCEP
    ono mbambatö   SWB
19. *la'o*   ms: WB, ZH, FBDH, FZDH, ZHZH, WBWB, ZHB, ZSWP, BWG, WZHB, DHMB, DHMF, DDHF (or *mbambatö*), DSWF, SWMF (or *mbambatö*)
    la'o ga'a   eBWB

la'o nono   SSWB, SWB
fo'omo la'o   WBW
makhelo la'o   ms: ZHZ
ono la'o   WBC
20. *sangai makhelo(gu) alave*   ZH (ws), HZH
21. *sovöli makhelo(gu) alave*   ZHF
22. *sovöli ya'o*   HF, HM, HFB
23. *umönö*   DH, SDH, DDH, ZDH (ms), HZDH, BDH (ms),
      HBDH, DH of classificatory B and S (ms)
    makhelo numönö   DHB, DHZ
24. *gabalö*   (or *cuhi*) WZH

The following notes are numbered in accordance with the order of
listed terms.
   2. Female lineal ancestors of Ego and his/her spouse, and wives of
      male lineal ancestors are all *ave*.
   3. Apart from this category, in the remainder of the terminology I
      give only one of the terms indicating relative age in each case,
      for the sake of brevity. See remarks on relative age below.
   4. Sometimes the form *ina sa'a* is used for MeZ or FeZ instead of
      the more long-winded *ina lave sa'a*; however, usually relative
      age is not indicated for MZ and FZ and the term *ina lave* is
      preferred.
   5. *Lave* is a contraction of *alave* ('female'). Little girls are some-
      times addressed '*lave*'. Alternative terms for MZH/FZH are
      sangai ina lave ('he who took [married] MZ/FZ') or *sangai akhi
      nina* ('he who married MyZ').
   6. This term is a compound, but I give it here separately as it is
      commonly used to distinguish MB from mother's classificatory
      brothers.
   7. See below Section 5 'The Line of Maternal Affiliation'.
  11. *Talifusö* means, literally, 'navel string'.
  12. *Ono* can be qualified as male or female by adding *matua* or
      alave respectively. BC and ZC are usually specified as *ono
      makhelo* or *ono ga'a/ono nakhi* rather than simply *ono*.
  13. *Ma'uvu* has the sense of 'descendant', as well as indirect wife-
      taker, and usually the compound term *ono nono* ('child of
      child') is used to specify CC. An obsolete term for CCC is
      madou, again with the sense of 'descendant'. A man who died

childless was said to be *si lö madou* ('without descendants'), therefore worthless.

14. Usually this term appears as a reciprocal of *sibaya*, thus restricted to ms.

16. An alternative to *fo'omo* is *donga* (cf. Batak *dongan*), which is considered less polite. *Donga* has the sense of 'sexual mate', whereas *fo'omo* has the sense of 'house-spouse' (*omo* means 'house').

17. *Matua* can also refer loosely to wife's male agnates of a senior generation, and even, though rarely, to WMB (wife-giver of wife-giver). As an adjective, *matua* means 'male' (boys are sometimes addressed '*matua*'). See Section 4 of Chapter 3 regarding this double sense of the word.

18. *Mbambatö* applies primarily to CEP. Its wider application is imprecise, and for a number of the specifications *la'o* can be used.

19. *La'o* can be used by ws for HZH instead of term 20. Generally, though, it seems to be a term confined to ms.

20. Means 'he who married my sister'.

21. 'He/she who purchased my sister'.

22. 'He/she who purchased me'.

23. *Umönö* denotes an individual wife-taker of a junior genealogical level, but especially DH. Ordinarily in referring to the DH of an agnate one would specify the relation as *umönö ga'a*, etc., unless one was referring to his obligations as wife-taker to the descent group.

As the above list shows, there are several ways of distinguishing between cousins. Context and intention determine which is appropriate. The addition of a proper name or the tracing of the relation by another route ensures that no confusion arises.

There is a pair of terms to designate cross-cousins. These are *ono ba zi matua* (BC, 'child by the male') and its opposite, *ono ba zi alave* (ZC, 'child by the female'). They are not relationship terms, in the sense that a speaker would not say 'my/his *ono ba zi matua*'. Rather they are used to draw attention to the customary aspect of the relation or to define it precisely to someone else. Whereas, according to traditional rules, cross-cousins are not allowed to marry, their children are ideal partners, and the man in such a union is called a *sangawuli ba zibaya* ('one who returns to his *sibaya*'). I have also heard a pair of MZC referred to as *faoma ono ba zi alawe* ('both children through females', i.e. children of sisters). Again, this is not a relationship term as such. In the southern terminology a similar construction is in fact a regular feature of relationship terms for cousins, distinguishing cross- from parallel-cousins, and FBC from MZC.

The relationship terminology does not exhaust all the categories of person with whom some relation is traceable. Categories for which there is no special term (e.g. FZHB) may be denoted by a term of the appropriate generation (e.g. *ama* for a senior man), by compound terms or by proper name. As unnamed categories they are *bö'ö* ('other'), unrelated.

Even where simple terms exist, compound terms are often used for clarification. For example, FFZ is ordinarily called simply *ave*, but she is sometimes distinguished in practice from other *ave* because her son is someone from whom one can expect tribute. Thus she might be referred to in discussion as *makhelo dua alave* ('sister of grandfather').

Sex

In the case of neuter terms the sex may be denoted by adding *matua* (male) or *alave* (female), e.g. *makhelo alave* (Z, FBD). Usually, in forming compounds, possessive suffixes are inserted between the terms, e.g. *makhelonia alave* (his Z). Sex of linking relative and alter can be distinguished as follows: *ma'uvu makhelogu alave* (ZCC) 'grandchild of sibling-female', *ma'uvu makhelogu ira alave* (GCD) 'grandchild-of-sibling woman'. In the second compound term, *ira alave* is a substantive used in apposition to *ma'uvu*. ZDC can also be termed *ma'uvu ba zi alave* ('granddaughter through females').

Relative age

Akhi ('younger sibling') and *ka'a* ('elder sibling') are used adjectivally in many relationship terms, indicating (1) relative age within the sibling set of the referent or the sibling set of linking relatives, (2) relative age within the sibling set of the referent's spouse, (3) seniority (i.e. priority) of wives of an ascending male relative. The adjectives are *sa'a* or *sia'a* ('elder') and *sakhi* or *siakhi* ('younger').

A third modifier *tatalu* or *talu* ('middle') is used to denote the intermediate category, indicated in specifications by the letter 'm'.

The terms *ka'a* and *akhi* are used far more commonly than the term *makhelo*, for two reasons: first, relative age is a crucial factor in behaviour between siblings; secondly, *ka'a* and *akhi* are used both in reference and address. Terms for relatives linked through siblings (especially through B) usually preserve this distinction. Thus eBS is usually termed *ono ga'a* rather than *ono makhelo*, and eBWF is *matua ga'a* rather than *matua makhelo*. It is possible (though rare) to distinguish eldest and youngest siblings from those in between who are older or younger than Ego. Thus *ka'a talu* (mBe), *akhi talu* (mBy). Normally one would simply say *ka'a* or *akhi*, adding the name if necessary.

In the −1 level the distinction is again crucial: *ono sa'a* eldest child, *ono tatalu* middle child(ren), *ono sakhi* youngest child. In the +1 level relative age is always used in terms of reference for FB, and for others linked through him: *ama sa'a* FeB, *ama talu* FmB, *ama sakhi* FyB. One can be more pedantic and specify whether the middle brother is older or younger than F, but this is a hypothetical usage and probably rarely occurs: *ama talu sakhi* father's junior middle brother. The wives of these individuals are as follows: *ina sa'a* FeBW, *ina talu* FmBW, *ina sakhi* FyBW. But the latter terms also refer to Ego's mother's co-wives: *ina sa'a* F_1W, *ina talu* F_2W, F_3W, *ina* M, *ina sakhi* F_4W. In the case of widow-inheritance, the FeBW often becomes the F_2W, but the original term of reference is retained. FBC are distinguished according to the relative age of the linking relatives; thus, *ono nama sa'a* FeBC, etc. But they are addressed according to the relative age of Ego and alter, thus FeBCy is *akhi*.

At the +2 level relative age may be distinguished among FFB with the terms for their wives conforming (consistent with the pattern for FBW and FW). Thus: *tua sakhi* FFyB, *ave sakhi* FFyBW or FFW who is younger than FM.

Apart from these cases, distinctions of relative age are not normally made. It is possible, though uncommon, to distinguish MeB, MmB and MyB, and in theory one could construct compound terms for most positions using relative-age adjectives. But such precision is only needed in abstruse genealogical discussions, not in the normal course of daily life. Relative age is usually distinguished only when referring to members of the local lineage, thus agnates, their wives and unmarried daughters. Female agnates marry out and their importance is as links with affines: as such their age relative to a male Ego becomes of secondary or no importance. Within the lineage such distinctions correspond to nuances of behaviour—respect, indulgence, authority, submission—as well as to customary laws determining precedence in bridewealth portions, other payments due to lineage mates, and inheritance.

Relative age is not necessarily indicated in both terms of a reciprocal set. For example FFyB : eBSS would normally be given as *tuagu sakhi* : *ono nonogu*.

2 Terms of Address

1. *tua*   men of +2 level
2. *ave*   women of +2 level
3. *ama*   men of +1 level
4. *ina*   women of +1 level
5. *sibaya*   man of +1 level belonging to lineage of M, MM, or MMM (also *ama*)
6. *mbambatö*   DHP, SWP
7. *ka'a*   senior of same genealogical level
8. *akhi*   junior of same genealogical level
9. *la'o*   WB, ZH
10. *ono*   persons of −1 and −2 levels

As terms of address, choice between *ka'a* and *akhi* may depend on the relative age of the linking relatives. Thus WeZHy is addressed as *ka'a*. This follows from the fact that the relation is traced through the spouse: for certain categories, a husband adopts the frame of reference of his wife, and vice versa. In contrast, FeBSy is *akhi*, even though his father is *ama sa'a*.

Husband and wife address each other by name—formerly by given name, nowadays by teknonym.

When discussing which relationship term should be used, Niasans verbalize the term of address by prefixing it with '*o-*', for example, *la osibaya ndra'o* (they call me '*sibaya*'); *i'o'ama ndra'o* (he calls me '*ama*'). When self-reciprocal terms are indicated a different verbal form is employed: *si fa-*, meaning 'he/those who habitually do such-and-such'; thus *sifala'o ira* ('they call each other *la'o*', i.e. 'they are

WB/ZH'), *sifagabalö ndra'aga* ('we call each other *gabalö*'). This form is frequently used to indicate levels of segmentation; thus *sifatalifusö ama ira* means 'their fathers called each other "*talifusö*" (B)', i.e. they are FBS to each other. *Sifatöi* means 'those who address each other by name (*töi*)', i.e. who are unrelated.

In addressing by name a person who is one's senior (including eG) one must always prefix the name or teknonym with an appropriate kin term. To omit this is disrespectful. In daily intercourse individuals are often referred to not by the terms of reference listed at the beginning of the chapter, but by this same combination of term of address plus name. For example, a FyB who bore the teknonym Ama Uco would be referred to as '*amagu* Ama Uco', rather than the anonymous *ama sakhi*.

3 Teknonymy

The practice of teknonymy has spread from northern Nias this century and has been generally adopted throughout the centre but to only a limited extent in the south. It was encouraged by missionaries dismayed by the use of grandiose feasting titles and was readily adopted as a neutral means of address, and moreover one which avoids use of proper names (which may imply lack of status). In the south given names are still used alongside teknonyms, but in the centre it is now considered very impolite to use a married person's given name. Some bachelors adopt a teknonym to signify their adulthood, and they keep this name upon marriage. My wife and I were assigned teknonyms some time before we were given clan names and eventually titles. We never acquired given names but were not thereby socially disadvantaged. Given names are used only in genealogies (if no title exists), in drawing up official lists (e.g. for a census or tax survey), and at funerals—a Christian custom intended to strip the deceased of his earthly vanity.

Usually teknonyms incorporate the name of the first child, but the name of an elder brother's son may be adopted 'to show solidarity'. A child's name is usually abbreviated in the teknonym and may thus lose its meaning. Husband and wife are identified by the same teknonym (Ama X and Ina X) but this is not always the case. A person who remarries does not usually adopt his or her spouse's teknonym.

In parts of the north, where the custom originates, teknonymy is more systematic and less idiosyncratic in application. The eldest son adopts the name of his ZS or other relative, becoming known as Sibaya X (MB of X). The second son assumes a teknonym incorporating the name of the first brother's son—Ama Y; the third follows the name of the second brother's son, and so on.

4   The Use of Possessive Suffixes

I have already mentioned the use of possessive suffixes in compound terms—a purely technical point. Possessives are also used in a courteous or manipulatory fashion to include or exclude the interlocutor, to emphasize his juniority, and so on. The expressive potentialities of the we-exclusive/we-inclusive contrast are exploited much more extensively than in the Indonesian *kami/kita*. The our-inclusive suffix *-da* can be used to imply that the speaker is sharing what he has with his guest (*yae rokoda*, 'here are our cigarettes'; *lö afoda*, 'there is no betel [of ours]'), or impudently to include himself (*Hadia göda?* 'What's "our" food? What are you eating?'). The same suffix can be used where one would expect the we-exclusive form to be used. People asked me if it is cold 'where we (inc.) live in Inggris', i.e. 'where you live'. When added to relationship terms *-da* can equally refer to 'your father (not mine)' or 'my father (not yours)'. Both must be rendered *amada* ('our (inc.) father'). It would be extremely impolite to say *amau* ('your father'), putting a distance between the speaker and his audience. (Even worse is *inau*, 'your mother', which is an abbreviation of an obscene taunt.) Likewise, to say 'our father' instead of 'my father' embraces the interlocutor in a fictive triangular relationship. One can only use the 'your' form (1) to a junior, as in 'Where's your mother, child?', or (2) fictively, to someone who is *not* related to alter. Thus a senior man might say to a junior, 'Go and speak to the chief, your father, about the problem.'

If it would be absurd to say 'our father', because speaker and hearer are of widely different generations, there are two options. Supposing A and B are unrelated, and A belongs to a generation junior to B; A would refer to B's father, C, as *tuagu C*, 'my grandfather C', rather than 'our father C', which would be presumptuous. Again, the term implies a triangular relation and is therefore 'close' or 'familiar' but respectful. Alternatively, one can make use of the two ways of indicating possession, using both suffix and possessive pronoun, e.g. *amada khöu*, 'our father yours' (i.e. your father). An elder who intends to assert himself against a younger man may stress the difference of genealogical levels by harping on the fact that 'my father' is 'your grandfather'—that the triangular relation is not equilateral.

The use of possessive suffixes with affinal terms is particularly complicated and usually has some manipulative aspect. Mastery of the status implications of affinal terms and how to use them is an important part of oratory.

Another way of avoiding the bluntness of directly naming someone is to prefix the name with *ira*, the equivalent of the Indonesian *si*. This form is impersonal in that no kinship relation or intimacy is implied. It is particularly useful in referring to young unmarried persons who have not yet acquired a teknonym but who cannot simply be named directly as one does with a child. It is often used when listing people because it is simpler and quicker than saying 'our father Ama *X*', 'our grandfather', etc. Instead one just says, '*ira* Ama *X*, *ira* Ama *Y*, *ira Z*'. This form is also employed to refer to the family, group, or even lineage of the named person. A rough equivalent in English would be the form 'the Joneses, the Smiths'.

5   The Line of Maternal Affiliation

The classificatory range of the term *sibaya* and its derivatives, and the reciprocal *ono mbini'ö*, varies according to context.[1] This contextual variation can best be appreciated by comparison with the more straightforward case of south Nias. In that area *sibaya* is MB, and his daughter, with whom marriage is preferred, is *ono zibaya*, MBD being distinguished from other cousins and siblings. Signi-

---

[1] There are no folk etymologies of *ono mbini'ö* and *sibaya*. *Si* means 'he who', and the verb *baya(gö)* means 'to touch or anoint'; but the participle 'he who anoints' takes the form *samayagö* rather than *sibaya*. According to Sundermann's dictionary *bini'ö* means 'married out daughter' in the north; so *ono mbini'ö* would mean literally 'C of married out D'. (Cf. cognate forms in other Indonesian languages.) In central Nias the word *bini'ö* is not used independently, except with an entirely different, and unconnected, meaning: 'to conceal'.

ficantly, according to Marschall (1976: 131), use of the term *sibaya* implies the intention to marry MBD, and a ZS without this intention prefers to address his MB as *ama* (F).

In central Nias marriage with classificatory MBD is permitted, but genealogical MBD is usually equated with siblings and is prohibited as spouse. In daily intercourse MB is referred to as *ama* (F) or *makhelo nina* ('mother's brother'), the more 'distant' term *sibaya* being reserved for more formal usage. MB is 'equal to' mother, therefore his daughter is 'sister'. It is other agnates of the mother who are ordinarily termed *sibaya* (men whose daughters are marriageable).

There has been a relaxation of the ban on marriage to MBD in recent years—though it is still discouraged—and perhaps because of this, younger men tend to refer more readily to MBD as *ono zibaya*, rather than always to equate her with Z, which implies unmarriageability. The reasons for this relaxation are not easy to discern. Influence from the south due to increased contact, and the abolition of harsh punishments for anomalous unions are possible causes. In the face of elders' objections to the new-fangled MBD marriage, young men point out that it does not upset existing alliances (as would marriage to FZD), nor does it breach clan exogamy. Nobody's material interests are harmed. My records show that it was allowed occasionally in the past as an exception, whereas marriage with other first cousins never occurred. The tendency to distinguish MBD from Z more frequently than was the case in the past is a matter of contextual emphasis rather than a substantive difference between the usages of older and younger generations. On basic principles there is no disagreement, and there is no reason to suppose that the terminology is changing.

Sibaya in its widest application is used of all the agnates of M, MM, and MMM. It is not a cognatic category, which would include all men related through M; it comprises, rather, the men of a series of affinally linked patrilineal groups. As such it denotes a category of alliance and comes into play when affines gather for a wedding, feast of merit, or any other important occasion in which affinity is central. In face-to-face relations with particular individuals finer discriminations are made and it becomes important to distinguish MB from MFBS.

The extension of each set of *sibaya*/affines is something which depends on context as the following examples show.

1. In reckoning the asymmetric marriage prohibition *sibaya* can refer to whole clans. The rule is formulated as follows: one may not marry a woman whose M, MM, MMM came from one's own clan (therefore to whom one is *sibaya*).

2. In division of bridewealth, there is a progressive reduction in the size of the (bride's) *sibaya* groups involved, down to one or two individuals in the case of fourth-order wife-givers.

3. At feasts of merit the host's own *sibaya* (roughly, his mother's lineage) form one of the two major groups, the other being the *matua*, the wife's agnates. Groups linked through MM, MMM, etc., on the side of either the host or his wife, are identified on the occasion with the two main groups. If they are distinguished it is as *sibaya mori furi* ('*sibaya* from behind/in the background').

A close parallel to this fluidity in the determination of the 'mother's brother' category is to be found in Roti (Fox 1971: 226 ff.), where there is a similar tracing of a line of maternal affiliation between contextually defined affinal groups. As in Roti, within the 'mother's brother' category finer discriminations relate to important ritual functions. In Nias it is the agnates closest to the line of maternal affiliation who are said to be the 'ground' (*tanö-tanö*) and 'origin' (*böröta*) of one's existence. They are conceived not merely as affines but consanguines (in contrast, agnates of mother's co-wives are of no ritual importance). The use of the term *ama* (F) for MB is significant in this respect. In native ideology this usage derives from a parallel role with the true father and from an identity of mother's brother with mother. M and MB are 'equal', 'the same' (*sifagölö-gölö*), and 'on a level' (*sifelalawa*). MB is thus a kind of second father, in whose house one can expect to be fed, and who has a share in one's upbringing. Unlike MFBS he has the same ultimate origin as Ego; that is, his MB is the MMB of Ego. Significantly, a mother's half-brother (different mother, same father) is *sibaya*, while full MB is *ama* or *makhelo nina*. The mother's half-brother is simply a man of the mother's clan. But full MB belongs to the same line of maternal affiliation (the same alliance chain) as Ego. The term *sibaya* therefore implies (as I was told) a certain genealogical and metaphorical distance, whereas *ama* is 'close'.

Of all the *sibaya*, those who have most claims on Ego belong to the mother's patriline. Members of this same line possess mystical powers (to a much lesser extent, so do collateral *sibaya*) but they are somewhat differently disposed towards him. Those to whom Ego is closest are usually referred to by consanguineous terms. As well as being, in other contexts, *sibaya*, MF is *tua*, MB is *ama*, and MBS is *makhelo*. MBSS, by contrast, is merely *sibaya*, like the other agnates of M. He belongs to the crucial line, but he tends to be neglected, therefore he is dangerous. MBSS, and sometimes MBS, are said to be *salakha bava*, 'liable to curse' (lit. 'whose face is prohibited').[2] The efficacy of their curse seems to reside in the fact that they share a common ancestor with Ego; that is, their patrilineal ancestor is his 'origin', his ghostly wife-giver (MF). In cursing, it is this person's spirit which is invoked; just as in requesting blessing, the nearest ancestral spirit of the *sibaya* was, in former times, offered sacrifice. The MB, by contrast, is more reluctant to exercise his power to curse, since he regards his ZS as his 'own child'.

In trying to define the category of *ono mbini'ö* (or *ono mbene'ö*) one encounters similar problems. Etymologically the term means 'child of a married-out daughter'. As a rough approximation it is the reciprocal of *sibaya* in its most inclusive sense; thus it includes the child of a 'clan daughter', child of a second-, third-, and fourth-order wife-taker. As such the term coincides with the asymmetric marriage prohibition. The rule is sometimes formulated: you cannot marry your *ono mbini'ö*. How far the category extends is a matter of individual or lineage-segment policy. As a rule, all those women for whom one can expect a portion of bridewealth are termed *ono mbini'ö*. This is usually up to and including fourth-order wife-taker. Beyond this point one speaks of remote wife-takers as *sahatö* ('close') or *ma'uvu* ('descendants'). Chiefly lines, however, solicit bridewealth portions and festive tribute among remoter wife-takers by occasional gifts. As such, their affinal network is much wider, and the category of *ono mbini'ö* more inclusive.

Within the vaguely bounded category of *ono mbini'ö*, distinctions may be made by the same criteria as distinctions among *sibaya*. A MB or MBS who is in regular contact with his ZS/FZS develops a more intimate and informal relation than one who perhaps lives far away and whose contacts are limited to ritual occasions. In the former case the term *ono* or *ono makhelo* is more appropriate to everyday contacts than *ono mbini'ö* or the more precise and formal term *tahö nono*. But the MB/ZS relation is of manifold character,

---

[2] Cf. the Kachin *tsa*: 'mother's brother', 'wife's father', 'to curse' (Leach 1967: 141).

and different contexts call for different terms. To call a ZS *tahö nono* is to draw attention to his status as inferior wife-taker whom one can press for tribute and help. To call him simply *ono* implies a parental and less demanding attitude in the speaker. This does not imply that the former term is the correct one and the latter usage 'fictive'. Likewise, MBS addressed as *ka'a* is brotherly, a playmate; as *sibaya* he is a drain on resources, a possible source of curses and blessings. *Sibaya* is therefore a term more likely to be used in ritual contexts, in which MBS (and his agnates) appear collectively as affines; but in daily contacts MBS is equated with B. Use of the term *sibaya* and its derivatives corresponds to an emphasis on alliance (group relations) while the alternatives correspond to individual relations, complementary filiation.

In sum, variability among speakers, inconsistency in particular speakers, optional terms, and contextual variation all conspire to make a single list of specifications a less than perfect guide to the subject.

6 Categories of Alliance

I have discussed categories of alliance in the context of ideology in the previous chapter. The following remarks concern classificatory principles and also touch on some affinal terms not yet considered. Wife-takers of one's line (contextually defined), singly and collectively, are *ono* or *ono alave* (lit. 'daughters'); wife-takers of wife-takers (and so on) are *ono* or *ma'uvu* ('child' or 'grandchild'), irrespective of genealogical level.[3] As categories of alliance, *ono* (*alave*) and *ma'uvu* are more comprehensive than *ono mbini'ö*, since they include pure affines (FZH) as well as children of wife-takers (FZS).

The structure of alliance, as described in Chapter 3, is reflected in the terminology. Consider the specifications for *umönö*. In each case it is only the individual wife-taker who is listed; his brothers are not included. The reciprocal term *matua* stands primarily for WF, but it can also be used of the lineage or its segment. The indirect wife-givers, e.g. the WM agnates, who may be termed 'wife's *sibaya*', 'woman's *sibaya*', or 'recipients of *maso-maso*', also call

[3] A distinction between wife-givers and wife-takers is of course an essential feature of asymmetric prescriptive systems.

their ZDH *umönö*. Thus groups of wife-givers are opposed to an individual wife-taker. However, members of the groups do not have equal claims on the wife-taker, and discriminations may be used, such as *umönö ga'a* (eBDH).

Despite the superiority of wife-givers over wife-takers, evident in numerous observances, certain affinal relations have a more egalitarian nature, and these are marked by self-reciprocal terms. *La'o* denotes WB and ZH, thus a wife-giver and a wife-taker. The obligations of each side towards the other are unequal, but the tone of their relation is comradely and relaxed, without the deference of the DH–WF relation. Indeed, unrelated people with a friendly intention used to address each other as *la'o*. *Mbambatö* likewise corresponds to a relaxed, friendly, and co-operative relation between the parents of a married couple. Although the balance of obligations falls on the side of the HP, this does not detract from the mutual respect required of *mbambatö*. Like *la'o*, the term can be used to cover a wide range of persons connected through affinity with whom one is not in a wife-giving/wife-taking relation.

The term *gabalö* is a self-reciprocal which denotes the parallel relation of sons-in-law to their WF. It was defined to me as 'those who have the same *matua*' and 'those whose wives are sisters'. Such men frequently meet at their *matua*'s house to pay him tribute or to be pressed for contributions, and form a sort of community of suffering.[4] A term sometimes used as an alternative to *gabalö* is *gasiwa*; others defined *gasiwa* as 'those whose mothers belong to the same clan'. In the latter meaning the term defines the same common relation to a wife-giver *in the next generation*. According to this interpretation, men who are *gasiwa* to each other share a *sibaya* rather than a *matua*; they are sons of *gabalö*. Neither term is much used and a decisive translation cannot be found.

A term which I have not included in the list is *lakha* ('widow'). In central Nias it also means 'agnate's wife whom one may inherit', and reciprocally 'husband's agnate to whom one may be remarried'. Thus a man can refer to his BW as 'my *lakha*', even while his brother

---

[4] Waterson (1986: 106–7) reports similar self-reciprocal terms for WZH and CEP among the cognatic Toraja. But she sees these as a reflection of reciprocal ties and a mutual interest among sons-in-law in inheritance. In Nias the distinguishing of this category is a function of alliance. Schefold's (1986: 77) observations on Mentawai apply to the Nias case: 'the reciprocal term *saulu* for WZH underlies the openness of matrimonial alliances (contrast the asymmetric terminological identification of WZH with B in Barnes 1974: 270).'

lives. This word comes up only in the context of widow-inheritance, and normally other relationship terms would be used. In south Nias it is used, somewhat differently, as a relationship term.

A woman calls her HM, HF, and his brothers *sovöli ya'o* ('he/they who purchased me'). This suggests wife-takers are a group, which apparently contradicts the structure of alliance. In fact this group relation applies only to the wife, and concerns her relation to her husband's lineage as a whole—it is a usage which signifies her practical incorporation into her husband's local descent group. It does not imply a group relation between the lineage of her husband and her own natal lineage.

A woman retains her natal clanship, and marriage does not lead to a confusion of her position in the alliance network with a corresponding distortion of alliance terms. I have heard women who have married into Sifalagö say that (due to repetition of alliance) most of the men of their husbands' clan are *onoma*, 'our wife-takers' (lit. 'our children').

7 Characterizing the Terminology

Unilineal descent is indicated by the following equations and distinctions:

$$B = FBS \qquad\qquad B \neq MBS$$
$$F = FB = FFBS \qquad F \neq MFBS$$
$$Z = FBD = FFBSD \qquad Z \neq MFBSD$$
$$D = BD = FBSD \qquad D \neq MBSD$$

The equation $F = MB$ is anomalous in this respect, but it disappears if we accept *sibaya* in its broadest application, referring to all agnates of M. This same term *sibaya* indicates a patrilineal tracing of descent. With the exception of *tua*, *ono*, and *ma'uvu*, no agnatic categories employ equations across genealogical levels, and many make distinctions within a level between elder and younger. In contrast, affinal categories make extensive equations across levels. *Sibaya* (depending on context) equates all the members of a clan regardless of age.

The terminology has a pronounced asymmetric character based on a tracing of the line of maternal affiliation. This is indicated by the following equations and distinctions:

$$ZC = FZ = FZC \qquad BC \neq ZC$$
$$(MB =) MBS = MMBS \qquad MBC \neq FZC$$
$$ZSC \neq ZDC$$

However, there are no equations indicating asymmetric prescription.

Needham (1970: 257) has listed as features which are 'significantly coherent' in the context of prescriptive alliance: 'arranged marriages, corporate involvement of descent groups in marriage payments, widow-inheritance, sororal polygyny, and the absence of divorce'. With the exception of sororal polygyny, all of these features are found in Nias, in addition to a terminology with an asymmetric cast, asymmetric marriage prohibitions, separate terms for wife-givers and wife-takers, and, in the south, a jural rule of marriage to matrilateral cross-cousin. It will be evident that the listed features are coherent in a system of asymmetric alliance even in the absence of prescription.

The central Nias terminology is not 'constituted by the regularity of a constant relation that articulates lines and categories' as is the case in a prescriptive system (Needham 1971: 32); nor are there any equations suggestive of prescription. It may, however, prove useful on some future occasion to consider further the asymmetric peculiarities of Nias kinship in comparison with asymmetric prescriptive systems and also non-prescriptive systems of asymmetric alliance, such as are found among the Rotinese (Fox 1980c) and the Mapuche (Needham 1967).

5
The Context of Marriage Alliance

1 Women and Alliance

Women's subordination is both expressed in cultural representations and is a feature of the organization of social and economic relations. Women are perceived by men as providers and labourers for the household—a perception they largely endorse. Their work, which is more or less continuous from before sunrise until night, is mostly concerned with producing and preparing food in a monotonous daily round which leaves little time for social activities. They also bear the greater share of the work for bridewealth and festive resources. The rhythm of women's work is so regular that it provides certain time indications. For example, 'return from the fields' means just before sunset, around 6 p.m. Men's work, in contrast, fluctuates in intensity and derives its rhythm from the demands of the swidden cycle, and as specific tasks crop up, such as collecting firewood, repairing the roof, or hunting. Men spend a good deal of time engaged in formal debate over disputes, weddings, and so on, as well as in idle conversation. Making speeches is man's work, and a good speaker, besides gaining influence in the village, provides for his family with pork from the slaughter that accompanies any such debate. Woman's role as labourer in the fields contrasts to man's orientation to the village and thus to questions of customary law (*hada, huku*). This is expressed in the traditional blessing spoken at the wedding ceremony when offspring are wished on the couple:

Otu zi matua ziagö banua	One hundred sons to the village
Felendrua zi alave ziagö tanö/	Twelve daughters to the land/field huts
halama	

A similar distinction between women as producers and men as the guardians of custom is evident in casual remarks. Once when I asked a couple why women possess or inherit nothing in their own right, the husband replied, 'Because they are only workers' (*sohal-*

övö). I heard the same comment from women—though not without irony—on more than one occasion. It is worth noting here that the subordination of women is not founded on a sharp distinction between a 'domestic' female sphere and a 'public' male sphere as reported in some societies; at any rate, such a dichotomy is not prominent in gender stereotypes.[1]

When they are not working alone in the fields, adult women are nearly always in the presence of men. Apart from certain rituals associated with childbirth and now discontinued under pressure from the Church, there are no exclusively female social activities and there is no forum in which a distinctive female point of view could find expression (cf. Ardener 1975). Neither can such a view be discerned in oral tradition. As for specialist knowledge, apart from the skills of the midwife, I am not aware of any body of magic or esoteric lore which is exclusively female.

Women's participation in social events is always in an ancillary capacity. At debates and social gatherings, men are seated along the window benches while women sit on the floor whispering or move about serving betel. They do not make speeches unless their testimony is called for (neither do junior men). There are exceptions: a very few senior women may rise above these restrictions if they possess ability, and some are capable of dominating a gathering of ordinary folk. I once saw the chief's sister, a redoubtable matron of 60, hold an audience in nervous subjection to her bullying humour. A few great ladies are supposed to have organized feasts in the past. Such women would have had slaves and were free of the burden of constant work which oppresses the ordinary woman. However, the point is that they attained this stature by emulating men, not by some distinctively feminine achievement. Other women of ability become notable as diviners or healers and are treated with special respect; they may exert influence privately, though they do not have a public voice. Notwithstanding these examples, women in general are not credited by men with the intelligence or the strength of character needed to make judgements and deliver speeches, and they tend to concur with this stereotype. Nearly all are illiterate, a fact which further devalues them in their own eyes. 'Our lips are hard [from chewing betel]. We cannot learn,' they say. Even today, when an increasing number of girls attend school beyond the

[1] Moore (1988: ch. 2, 3) criticizes the supposed universality of this dichotomy.

primary level, only two (both of the chief's lineage) have ever graduated from high school. But illiteracy is a symbol of women's inequality rather than its cause. After all, very few men have more than the rudiments of literacy, if anything; and the skills of a clerk are useless in the oral culture of the village. More significant is the total submersion of women in back-breaking agricultural work and childbearing.

The regime of drudgery begins early. A girl of 5 works alongside her mother for part of the day. While her brothers play or spend their time fishing, a girl of 10 already knows complete physical exhaustion. As her share of the tasks grows she may become the economic mainstay of the family, especially if her mother is old and worn out. None of the deaths which occurred during our stay was treated as more calamitous than that of the only daughter of a neighbouring widow, a girl of 17. More than the family's subsistence depended on her: the bridewealth of her brothers would come mainly from the efforts of she and her mother. As a result of her death, the brothers will not have any direct wife-takers (sister's husband) from whom they can expect services, so their long-term fortunes are damaged as well. Moreover, they lose the bridewealth that would have been paid for her. This kind of evaluation of a tragedy sounds somewhat cynical, but in the harsh conditions of village life the practical consequences of an untimely death are in the forefront of discussion. Likewise, expressions of mourning and grief tend to focus on the deprivation which follows such a loss, rather than on the sentiments of personal bereavement. The same anxieties arise of course when a man dies, but my impression was that there is more concern with the reason or cause of his death (Was it his time? Had he sinned?) and with other matters of no practical weight, such as whether he was a good man, hospitable and kind, or bad-tempered, and so on.

The subordination of women is of course closely connected to limited control over resources as well as to the division of labour. Women cannot own or inherit land. Native explanation sometimes relates this fact to the separation of a woman from her lineage estate at marriage. She retains no rights in the natal estate unless the marriage is uxorilocal. As with land so with its product: no part of the rice crop is regarded as her own separate from the household fund. Livestock, too, belongs to the household under its titular head, the husband. The central role of women in subsistence is recognized and valued but this does not lead to any degree of economic independence.

The sexual division of labour underlies the economy of festive exchange as well as the symbolism of certain gift exchanges. The economic value of a woman is explicitly recognized in certain bridewealth prestations, which are intended to compensate the loss to her family when she marries and moves out. In negotiating an overall sum for bridewealth, the father of a girl who is known to be hard-working expects a better-than-average figure, as his loss is greater. Ironically, the huge debts incurred by the groom for bridewealth are paid off mainly by his wife's labour. A wife is the provider of daily subsistence, but she also labours to provide the surplus for feasts which will raise her husband's status. In the Nias conception, the fruit of a woman's labour is returned by her husband to his wife-givers as tribute; his feast of merit, and thus his reputation, is partly a product of her effort. Labour, or effort (*ölö*), is a key concept in all types of exchange and is particularly prominent in the exchanges surrounding marriage alliance. The wife of a feastgiver shares in the prestige of her husband, and she receives a title analogous to his; but unlike him she is not addressed henceforth by title, and she does not become a 'village elder'. In so far as she can be said to have a rank, it is as a 'daughter or wife of a chief/ elder'.

On a different level, the division of labour has consequences for the development of personality. The contrast between a middle-aged man and his wife is remarkable. He is generally in his prime, sharp-eyed and self-interested, articulate and knowledgeable, still physically strong and perhaps looking out for a second, younger woman to marry. His wife is typically dull and worn-out after a lifetime of unceasing toil, and having given birth up to a dozen times. I shall comment later on the moral appraisal of a bride, but it is worth making the point here that the denial of full moral responsibility to a young woman, which begins as an idea, gains a kind of proof through a regime of work which allows little room for intellectual or moral development.

Despite their practical subordination and their limited social opportunities, a few women have strong personalities and one or two even dominate their husbands. It is said that decisions of importance to the family require the private consultation of husband and wife. How much the wife actually influences the decision, or merely accedes to it, I cannot say; but it is sometimes a mother who chooses her son's wife—the woman who will be her helpmate. At feasts, spouses are honoured as a pair and carried in state, side by side. Husband and wife are sometimes said to be 'equals' in the marriage bond (*sifagölö-gölö, sifelalawa*), in the sense that they are two halves of a whole. They are 'of one body, one heart, and one speech'. They spend a good part of each day in each other's company working in the fields, they eat together and share confidences; and long into old age they continue to share the same mat at night. Their individual fates are tied together, and this mutual dependence forges a powerful bond. The unity of husband and wife is thus both a dogma and a reality, and this is no doubt part of the reason why women accept their poor situation and fail to recognize and act upon their common interests. Indeed, to pose the problem in terms of sexual antagonism or group interests is quite foreign to the Nias way of thinking.

In outlining the main aspects of gender relations relevant to alliance I have not touched on the incidental ways in which women sometimes exert influence and try to make something of their situation—but that is beyond the scope of this treatment. I should say, though, that if my account has given a strong impression of women's passivity, this is truer to the practical organization of male–female relations than to the tone of everyday life. Women participate freely in informal conversation, and they enjoy banter and innuendo. In private they can contradict and even berate their husbands. If they feel they are being maltreated, or suspect their husbands of infidelity, wives complain loudly. Usually a woman's brothers or father will intervene if the husband is particularly neglectful or violent, and they may beat him or take back the wife.

The relations between men and women are traditionally subject to strict codes. Nias is notable for the fact that the introduction of the austerest Lutheran decrees actually led to a liberalization of sexual mores. Severe punishments for adultery—execution or ransom—were abolished and mere fines could not have the same deterrent effect. Nevertheless, immorality as defined by the Church and custom is still infrequently uncovered, and within the bounds of the village community probably not much escapes notice. (Men sometimes boast of intrigues with women in remote huts or other villages.) This fierce public morality is not accompanied by sexual reticence or prudishness: the Rhinish missionaries did not succeed in instilling a sense of guilt or aversion to the body. Sexual misdemeanours are mostly judged in public terms for their disruptive consequences. The assumption is that custom sets limits to natural appetites in the interests of order.

The advent of Christianity has, perhaps, had a greater effect on the lives of women in indirect ways than in its message, as locally interpreted. The prohibition of work on Sunday and the weekly church service provide some respite from work and the opportunity for joint activity which may eventually have some influence on women's sense of their identity *vis-à-vis* men, and thus on their cultural evaluation.

My purpose in explaining the broad outlines of gender relations is to situate them within the subject of marriage alliance and affinal exchange. We are now in a position better to understand the mixture of motives and considerations which influence the choice of a spouse and we may therefore begin with the first stage in the matrimonial process.

2   Factors in the Choice of a Spouse

Local Exogamy

As noted in Chapter 3, asymmetric marriage prohibitions oblige a large proportion of men to take wives from other villages. Strictness in applying the rules correlates with high rank. Local exogamy is itself therefore a prestigious form of marriage. For political reasons as well, the leading men have traditionally obtained wives from their peers in other villages, and have thereby avoided creating alliance superiors (*famatua*, lit. 'to make a *matua* [WF] of someone') within the village. Ordinary men, who are more likely to marry within the village, prefer to renew existing local alliances, maintaining the political status quo, rather than open new alliances. Otherwise they marry out.

Discussions of the process of looking for a wife almost always assume marriage between unrelated persons or strangers (*niha bö'ö*). This assumption, also evident in songs, fables, and proverbs, no doubt derives from the traditional pattern of clan/local exogamy. It is predicated, moreover, on the notion of a search for one's match. The search is a recurrent theme of biographical or autobiographical accounts, even in cases where the man marries a neighbour.

Men who have married locally say they first of all made an exhaustive tour of the surrounding villages and further afield before arriving at their choice.

Moral Appraisal of the Candidate

Among the criteria involved in choosing a spouse the most important are said to be diligence, moral qualities evident in conduct (*amuata*, 'deeds'), status (which I discuss separately below), and background (*tanö-tanö*). Individuals vary in where they place the emphasis, but all agree that diligence is crucial in choosing a wife. This was stated bluntly: 'if she is lazy there is no food.'

Diligence (*fa'owölö-ölö*) is valued in both sexes, but while a lazy or physically weak man can achieve a measure of respect if he has compensating qualities, a lazy woman is said to be 'useless'. During my stay, two women living in remote field huts were driven to suicide by beatings meted out by their husbands for their alleged laziness. Often the poverty of a particular family is attributed to the wife's laziness. If the husband is blamed, it is his stupidity or dishonesty which is said to be the cause. The stress on diligence in the appraisal of a possible spouse reflects both the facts of domestic production and the ideological devaluation of women. Other moral qualities in the candidate are of less interest. 'Good conduct' in a girl means diligence or a lack of bad characteristics.

In contrast, the girl's family pays great attention to the positive moral qualities and the reputation of the suitor. They have an eye on his virtues as a lifelong (and subordinate) ally. Consequently, they are looking for a respectful and attentive bearing towards seniors, generosity, and constancy in word and deed. The wife-taker is regarded as a source of material fortune (*löfö*), so the young man's economic prospects are of great concern. Initiative, skill in speech, and a basic education are highly valued, both as prestigious personal attributes and as lucrative assets in an ally. These qualities are only appropriate to the individualism of the men's world; they have no place in the roles expected of women. An unmarried man is considered as 'only a boy', with no right to speak in public, and he does not attain full adulthood until he becomes a father. Even so, he has often already made his mark and become a conspicuous individual by the age of about 20: a keen traveller and visitor of relatives, attender of feasts, source of information, and with a sharp eye for enterprise. Unmarried and newly married men are the innovators in agriculture and trading, trying out new crops and market goods, and investing in loans of pigs which they can recoup with interest to pay bridewealth.

A young woman rarely, if ever, acts as an individual. During the years of adolescence any respite from work is spent in peer groups, as a member of dance troupes at feasts or in choral groups at church functions. At marriage she is torn from her friends and returned to the unrelenting labour and relative unsociability of domestic life, in the alien surroundings of a new village. The bride's moral nature is thus as yet unknown. In the early stages of negotiating a union there is considerable emphasis on the use of omens to reveal her future moral nature, as I shall show later. A potential wife is appraised not as a morally autonomous adult, but as a product of her family. Her sexual purity is vouched for by the men of the household and lineage who will lose substantially from a hasty and injudicious marriage brought on by pregnancy (there are no unmarried mothers). Nubile girls are therefore chaperoned and guarded from mischief.

In choosing a wife (or approving a suitor) there is a careful scrutiny, on both sides, of family background (*tanö-tanö*) which is at the same time a moral vetting and a genealogical and biographical investigation. These different aspects of 'background' are inter-woven in the conception of the person. Three elements or aspects of the moral personality can be distinguished. First, there is a certain uniqueness in human character. This God-given individuality is cited proverbially in explanation of conduct, especially where it runs counter to 'background'. A second element is that which is instilled by education or example. It is assumed that children imitate their parents, so parents are liable to be castigated for their children's behaviour with the proverb 'parents teach, children follow'. This proverb is also used to criticize misconduct in the public sphere, and refers to the setting of a bad example or precedent. Thirdly, there is a hereditary aspect of one's moral nature. This may consist of a simple inheritance of parental characteristics or a form of atavism which is linked to concepts of sin and punishment. Sexual transgressions are the paradigm of sin (*horö*), constituting a violation of the social order. A special category of *horö* is sex between prohibited categories of person, *horö salakha* ('sin which is cursed'), an offence against laws protected by ancestral curses. These curses visit the sins of the fathers on the sons in Old Testament fashion, bringing misfortune, illness, and the extinction of the line. In Sifalagö the daughters of a certain respectable man have passed 20 without receiving a proposal because (according to a sympathetic informant) their father was the issue of a union between brother and sister. Despite the exemplary behaviour of father and daughters there is an atavistic expectation that immorality—or the baneful effects of the original sin—will re-emerge.

Immorality and misfortune are mutually confirming: a history of early deaths or infertile marriages in a lineage points to undisclosed *horö*, just as occurrences of rape or adultery presage misfortune. Hereditary or congenital diseases are usually interpreted as punishments by God or the ancestors for some past offence against custom. Since the prospective wife-givers are dispensers of fertility, it is particularly inauspicious if one of the bridewealth-receiving groups (e.g. third-order wife-givers) has died out. Although the wife-taker would therefore have less bridewealth to pay, he would be reluctant to contract such an alliance. In the investigation of background, illicit unions and anomalous marriages come to light and fresh anomalies are avoided. Both sides, but particularly the groom's, are anxious to avoid a symmetric marriage, which is an unnatural reversal of the correct order.

It is not clear whether moral characteristics are transmitted exclusively along the institutionalized channels of patrilineality and the line of maternal affiliation. All that can be said is that enquiries focus on recognized relations, namely wife-givers, wife-takers, and the clan of the marriage candidate. There is no interest in other cognatically related persons.

In moral evaluation the distinction between the influences of education and heredity is often blurred or omitted as superfluous. It is simply asserted that bad character runs in families; thus whole families are branded as bad, lazy, immoral, or thieving. The child of an adulterer is regarded as a risky choice as spouse and is viewed with suspicion: there is no need to specify nature or nurture as the ground of the suspicion. There are 'good' families and lineages as well as 'bad' ones, and it appears that positive qualities are to some degree heritable as well.

Status

Transmission of status is discussed more fully in Chapter 10, but before leaving the subject of inherited characteristics and their consideration in the choice of spouse, it is worth noting here that while chiefly status cannot be transmitted through females, it can, apparently, be foreshadowed. Thus, if any of the wife-giving groups in the bride's line of maternal affiliation have numbered chiefs among them, the bride's descendants (if not her own sons) will, it is thought, include a chief—a definite asset to her party in negotiations. This mystical foreshadowing, which has no institutional correlate, contrasts with the practical determination of chiefly succession, which is always by a combination of patrilineal succession and other factors (wealth, achievement).

What part, then, does status play in the choice of partner? In south Nias, where there are hereditary classes, strict rules govern mixed marriages. In central Nias it is expected that marriage take place between the children of men of roughly equal rank, but there are no hard and fast rules. This flexibility is due to the relative fluidity of ranking and to its complexity. There are three broad divisions: chiefs (*salawa*), that is, the leading man of the village or hamlet; elders (*satua mbanua*), that is, men who have held feasts of merit and who bear a title; and thirdly, ordinary villagers (*ono mbanua*). Within these divisions there are differences of title and informal gradations of status, according to the number and size of feasts given. These gradations are constantly under review and are very much in mind in the negotiation of an alliance. Traditional ranking is further complicated by status in modern systems: office held in the standard Indonesian village staff (headman, ward head, etc.) or in the Nias Protestant Church (evangelist, church elder). Occupational status is a further complicating factor. Government jobs (teacher, paramedic) are more prestigious than traditional crafts, trading in market goods, or farming. Any particular alliance involves a weighing up of status in traditional and modern systems. This can be seen quite clearly in the case of the chief of Sifalagö. He himself combined traditional eminence with a position in the modern system. He was the son of the last district chief and was government headman and traditional chief of Sifalagö for over thirty years until his death in 1988. The marriages of his three daughters differ considerably in respect of status, but what they all demonstrate is a careful balancing of advantages in the separate spheres of Indonesian life.

The first daughter had only a primary education and now works in the fields like most women. She is married to a schoolteacher who is the grandson of the deputy district chief, a man of very high rank.

The bridewealth was large and the wedding was combined with an *ovasa* staged by the groom, pushing the costs up to 127 *batu* (units of wealth), about £3,000—a fortune by local standards. The groom was given a title at this feast validating his noble ancestry. The alliance was thus for both sides highly prestigious in traditional terms, but not wholly without a modern aspect. The groom continued to render tribute and aid as requested after the marriage.

The second daughter, high-school educated and now a teacher, was married to a paramedic, the son of an elder in the next village. The bridewealth was less than half that of her sister. Lacking better candidates, and not entirely happy about the bridewealth, the chief consented to the alliance, knowing that he could count on ready cash when he needed it, since a paramedic makes a good living giving injections. During the last year of his life the chief was nursed with devotion and at great personal cost by his son-in-law.

The third daughter, also a teacher, married a policeman whom she met in town when still a student. He is another source of cash to his father-in-law (he is helping to pay the university education of his wife's brother) and of bureaucratic string-pulling in town. Although he attends all important family events, his own family background is virtually unknown and he is referred to simply as Officer X. In each case, then, the alliance has a different basis, with different benefits and expectations on each side. Traditional rank is weighed—to use a very Niasan concept—against tribute and service, or access to cash, or to other sources of power. Among ordinary villagers and elders there is a similar weighing of pros and cons—title, reputation, and connection to eminent men—besides factors which are closely linked to status, such as wealth and land holdings.

Other Factors

Marriage to a woman of a wife-giving lineage has certain advantages from the point of view of ideology which I have already discussed. The practical advantage, on both sides, is that one already knows what to expect from one's affine. The investigation of (or worry about) the conduct of the other side is therefore unnecessary. One is simply renewing an alliance or making direct an indirect affinal connection. The negotiations in such marriages are generally less protracted and tense than is usually the case. Renewal of an alliance also affects the status quo less than marriage between *niha bö'ö*, and there is not the 'negotiation' of relative status which accompanies the usual bridewealth negotiations.

A suitor takes into account the strength of the lineage which is to be his wife-giver. A lineage with numerous members and a high degree of solidarity will (aside from what status commands) expect a high bridewealth as there are many recipients. The groom can expect to be tapped frequently for contributions to the feasts of its members. There are corresponding advantages to such an alliance. The groom wins more glory than by marrying into a small and fractious lineage, and he expects firm backing in disputes. His allies are a deterrent to troublemakers and cheats.

3 The Concept of a Match

More than simply a suitable candidate, the chosen woman has to be a 'match' (*tambali*, 'match, counterpart, partner'; Indon. *jodoh*) in two senses. She has to be the daughter of a man whose status and background correspond to those of the groom and his family. The status-match is stressed by prominent men and nobles. The woman also has to be a match in the sense of the unique one-and-only (or if the man is a polygamist, two-and-only) woman with whom he is destined to spend his life. A spouse is 'what is granted', one's lot (*sinema zi samö-samösa*), and this 'comes from God'. In the past, divination was used to determine whether the ancestors had approved the union—whether they had joined the couple. Nowadays, omens are thought to be as important in finding a spouse as the practical considerations, advice, and personal impressions which guide one's path. One man related this idea of the unique bond which draws together strangers in a match to the creation of woman from man's rib in Genesis. Husband and wife should be matched as if made from the same substance: Christian and indigenous theory concur in this.

In illustration of these ideas, one informant described what happens when a young man and his companion out prospecting for a wife enter a strange house. They announce to the man of the house, 'We've come to see the fat piglet!' Understanding their intention, the householder calls his daughter to the front room to prepare betel, giving the potential spouses a first chance to look at each other. If the visitor likes her he makes his proposal and expects her to agree, 'because if you are sympathetic (*ombuyu dödö*, lit. 'soft-hearted') to the girl, it's because you are suited therefore she will be sympathetic towards you.' If the visitor does not experience this shock of recognition (however fine the girl, however convenient an alliance), he withdraws politely, having eaten, saying, 'the house is not suitable' (*lö fagöna nomo*). Neither side loses face.

Evidently a match can be conceived (by Niasans) ideally as independent of other circumstances. Indeed, several people insisted that, having made up his mind, a suitor would not be put off by subsequently discovering disadvantages in the union. Nor should he be deterred by a large brideprice if 'no other woman will do'.

In fact betrothals are quite commonly broken by either party as new facts or situations appear. Moreover, in most cases, preliminary enquiries have already been made before the suitor pays his first formal visit to 'view the bride' (*famaigi niha*), as this first official step is called. Usually all the important details of background and character are known before he commits himself, and before the bride's side give their consent.

In cases of child betrothal personal wishes are not of course involved; but the marriage cannot go ahead, when the couple are grown, without their agreement. Often the girl's agreement to a marriage may be a question of her acceding to her father's wishes, but, as far as I could gather, rarely is she forced against her will. Schröder (1917: 263) makes a similar observation, so this cannot be due to the influence of modern urban ways. The girl's wishes are relevant to the success of the alliance, since it is assumed that an unwilling bride will be an unfaithful or rebellious wife and a source of friction between the parties.

4   Access

One has access to other villages via weekly markets, exchange visits between churches, as a member of guest groups at feasts of merit, and through regular contacts with affines. Market dealers make frequent trips to town for supplies and are known in villages along the way. Government employees may be posted away from home or work in town and their jobs usually involve travel within a district. These men and women are a source of information on eligible spouses outside the usual range of contacts, and they can arrange meetings. One prominent extended family in Sifalagö, close to the chief, has obtained four wives from a village in south Nias as a result of the eldest son's posting there as a teacher. The marriages were all prestigious since the women belong to the noble class. Moreover, two of the marriages conform to the southern preference for matrilateral cross-cousin. Prestige is further enhanced by the geographical remoteness of the villages, giving an inter-district aspect to the alliance. The family was an impoverished branch of the chiefly line in Sifalagö and unable to afford the high bridewealth required for a local match. It was the great disparity between bridewealth in the centre and the south that enabled them to contract appropriate alliances.

Ordinarily one's own affines or those of neighbours living in other villages provide the necessary contacts. A young man has regular informal access to perhaps half a dozen villages in the district via existing affinal links with his own village. Between strangers the traditional hostility persists, and a man out prospecting for a wife approaches an unfamiliar village with caution and always in the company of a kinsman or friend. However, it is said that even total strangers, if 'good-hearted', will inform him of any marriageable girls and will warn him off girls of bad character.

Due to pressure on land around Sifalagö there has been a steady migration in recent years to outlying districts. A number of families have settled in Aramö, the former buffer zone between the villages of the centre and the south, which was once depopulated by headhunting raids from both regions. Several marriages between Sifalagö and its traditional enemies in the south have thus come about, made possible by the frequency of contact and the improved safety of modern Nias.

5 Affines and Marriage Parties

In contracting a marriage a man does not act alone. He depends on neighbours, his wife-takers, and above all his agnates for support in raising bridewealth and in financing all subsequent prestations to his wife-givers. His supporters are involved at every stage: in searching for a suitable spouse, making the first approaches, negotiating and handing over bridewealth, attending the wedding feast, and escorting the bride to her new home. Support is drawn from the same sources throughout his life in dealings with wife-givers.

How does the corporate involvement of agnates of the wife-taker square with an essential feature of the working of the alliance system in Nias, namely the opposition of an individual wife-taker to a group or groups of wife-givers? This apparent contradiction disappears when a number of points are taken into consideration. First, it is significant that neighbours and the groom's own wife-takers are among the contributors. This should alert us to the fact that we are not dealing with an alliance group comparable to the wife-giving group. Secondly, the contributions are nearly all in the form of loans (*naekhu-naekhu*) which must be repaid when the lender or his son set about raising their own bridewealth. These loans are a form of mutual aid which is entirely separate from the payment of the bridewealth to wife-givers and is of no interest to them. It is an internal matter for the village or the lineage, played out in the sphere of village politics where material support wins—or neutralizes—advantage or influence.

The bridegroom's supporters, or sponsors (*sanaekhu*), receive no acknowledgement or prestation from the bride's party for their service. It is the groom who kills a pig for them, either when he requests their support, or at the feast following the fetching of the bride. The supporters themselves give nothing directly to the wife-givers. Even the groom's closest agnates (F, FB, FBS, etc.) whose contributions are usually not returned, and who therefore have a personal stake in the exchange, do not appear as bridewealth-givers, except on behalf of the groom. Neither, with the partial exception of the groom's father, do they ever give tribute to his wife-givers, and their tribute cannot be solicited: they each have their own wife-givers to honour.

The groom's negotiators (*si so ba huhuo*) are picked for their skills, reputation, and perhaps because of their contacts with the bride's side. Usually an agnate is entrusted with this job but he need not be a close agnate. It would be demeaning for the groom's father or brother to plead his case. The groom's closest agnates sit through the entire proceedings in silence, occasionally having a quiet word with their representative. The negotiators thus have a sort of professional independence recognized in the fact that they receive a reward for their services from *both* sides. A special honour is attached to the role of speaker (as on other public occasions) and the respect that goes with his prestation would be inappropriate if he were simply identified with the groom as wife-taker. It is precisely because the negotiators are not addressing their own wife-givers that they are given licence to speak freely.

Thus it can be seen that the groom's party is composed of heterogeneous elements, convened for different purposes. It would be a mistake to identify them simply with the groom as 'wife-takers'. The bride's side, for its part, is a more or less solidary group. Members of the bride's side involved in negotiations and in the division of bridewealth are identical with the set of wife-givers. The bride's speakers may include her father's brother as main negotiator, and even her father is expected to make speeches. Thus, despite initial appearances, the structure of affinal relations is consistently that of an opposition of individual : group. There are separate terms (discussed below) for the parties involved in arranging the marriage and for the affines or allies, though of course their membership overlaps.

The groom's party initiates all the moves. Girls make sure that they are seen at social events, but their families wait for proposals. The groom, as suitor and later as wife-taker, is inferior. He courts or 'pursues' (gohi) the girl's father, and figuratively 'kneels' (manalulu) to him. To reverse the inequality and make approaches on behalf of one's daughter or kinswoman invites public derision and gives a decisive advantage to the groom's party in negotiating the bride-wealth. I describe in Section 8 of Chapter 6 the tragi-comedy that ensued in one such case.

The groom's inferiority attaches to his party during all formal and informal contacts with the bride's side. His party is called soroi tou ('those who come from below'). The term relates to the fact that they have entered the house from below—in former times through a trapdoor in the floor—to supplicate to the girl's party, the sovatö. The latter term, which means literally 'those in possession of the floor', refers to the hosts on any festive occasion. The host of an ovasa, who entertains his wife-givers and thus appears in the role of wife-taker, is called sovatö. The pairing of sovatö with soroi tou implies an opposition of high and low, or at any rate a figurative difference in height, which in Nias always denotes a difference in status. But it is important to recognize that the terms referring to the parties are occasional, limited to the context of a wedding and its preliminaries. Similarly, the inferiority of the soroi tou (excepting the groom himself) is occasional or situational. *Soroi tou* and *sovatö* are not synonymous with terms meaning wife-taker (*ono alave*) and wife-giver (*so'ono, si tenga bö'ö*, etc.). They are not categories of alliance, and the members of the *soroi tou* are not conceived to be allies of the *sovatö*. The groom owes lifelong allegiance to his wife-givers, but his kinsmen (and others who together make up the *soroi tou*) have no such obligations. The situationally limited opposition of the two groups, *sovatö* and *soroi tou*, thus contrasts with the permanent structure of the alliance, which is an opposition of a group of wife-givers to an individual wife-taker. The ritual relations evident in the wedding preliminaries, then, do not accord with the persisting reality of social relations. Only the groom's position *vis-à-vis* the bride's party is consistent.

The groom's father occupies a somewhat ambiguous and marginal position in alliance relations. He is the groom's major sponsor and is most closely associated with him. A prime factor in the wife-givers' consent to the union is the status and reputation of the groom's father. But he does not take part in the preliminaries of the marriage, even as a spectator. Instead he keeps a dignified distance and is sent wrapped portions of food, which confer honour on him, from the meals served to the groom's party. Usually he does not even attend the wedding, held in the bride's village, but sends his wife or brother as his representative.[2] His absence makes the position of the other agnates among the *soroi tou* somewhat clearer. They can attend, and act with the required subordination, because there is no danger of their being classed as affines. Their inferiority is temporary.

The groom's father has a few, strictly limited, ritual obligations to his son's wife-givers, and in this sense can be regarded as their affine or ally. But he is anxious not to compromise further his status by attending the negotiations. His obligations are to render tribute (*sumange, ana'iwa*) at the *ovasa* of his SWF and to bring a pig to the latter's funeral. If he fails in these obligations, or is dead, his son must perform them on his behalf in addition to his own much heavier obligations to his WF. Some fathers shirk this duty and say to their sons, 'I've got my own *matua* (WF) to do homage to, so you take care of your own.' In contrast to the marked inequality between a DH and his WP, there is a relation of friendly solidarity

---

[2] As in south Nias (Marschall 1976: 122).

and mutual respect between DHP and SWP (*mbambatö*). Evidently, then, there is some ambiguity in the groom's father's position. His obligations imply the subordination of a wife-taker. His egalitarian bearing towards his SWP and their reciprocal terms of address imply otherwise.

6
Marriage and Bridewealth

In this chapter I describe the sequence of events leading up to a wedding. The major theme, as always in Nias, is the exchange of prestations, and I shall be concerned with the symbolic and sociological import of these exchanges. Analysis is interwoven here with descriptive ethnography as the most convenient method of presentation.

1 Terms for Bridewealth

In the literature on Nias usually two alternative names are given for bridewealth, *bövö* and *böli niha*, with the implication that they are synonyms. Some authors assign these terms to different dialect areas.[1] In fact both terms are encountered throughout Nias. In the centre, *bövö* has the following meanings:

1. The commonest usage is for the solicitory gifts or counter-prestations of wife-givers (*bövö moroi khö zo'ono*), as opposed to bridewealth, *böli niha*.
2. A polite and somewhat euphemistic term for bridewealth, as in *bövö moroi khö zi faöli* (prestations from the groom), equivalent therefore to *böli niha*. This term is not often used by village people when talking about bridewealth.
3. The whole complex of prestations and counter-prestations involved in the marriage alliance. Thus tribute to wife-givers at an *ovasa* (feast of merit) is *bövö ba govasa*.
4. Custom, as exemplified in meaning (3). 'Good *bövö*' means something like 'the correct observance and discharge of mutual obligations between affines'. It is not a simple equivalent of the Indonesian word *adat* ('custom, customary law').

[1] Schröder (1917: 273) assigns *bövö* to north Nias and *böli niha* to the south. But on p. 272 he uses the word *bövö* for a wife-giver's counter-prestation in Savö (north).

Böli niha is more straightforward. *Niha* means 'human being' or 'person', and in the phrase *böli niha* refers to the object of the exchange, the bride. The bride is also *niha* in the phrase *fangai niha* ('the fetching of the bride'). In other contexts she is *ono nihalö* ('the child taken (in marriage)'), or *ni'ovalu* ('the (one) married'). *Böli* is the word for price or market value. *Böli niha* means, literally, 'brideprice'; but how little the conception equates with a price will, I hope, become clear.[2] In discussing bridewealth, *böli niha* is an indivisible phrase. It is not the same thing to ask, 'how much was the bridewealth (*böli niha*) for Yui?' as (a solecism) 'how much did Yui cost (*hauga mböli*)?' The exchange of bridewealth has an undeniable economic importance, but nobody confuses the concept of commercial price with *böli niha* even if the connotations are there (hence recourse to euphemism among the educated townsfolk). While the bride has a 'purchaser' in her HF or HFB, whom she calls *sovöli ya'o* ('he who buys me'), her own family are not considered as sellers. Only if a nakedly commercial motive determined her father's choice of suitor and he forced her to marry against her will, could it be said disparagingly that he had sold (*amawa*) his daughter. This was said privately to me of a few individuals. A linguist might be able to explain why the transitive form of the verb 'to buy' (*öli*) is never used of marriage exchanges, being reserved exclusively for commercial transactions; whereas the participle of the intransitive form (*sovöli*) is enshrined in the relationship terminology.[3]

A number of characteristics clearly distinguish *böli niha* from a true price. First, there is no conception of a sale or seller, and no price-fixing by a market mechanism of competition among buyers and sellers. Secondly, rational economic motives only partly enter into negotiations. More is at stake than wealth or what wealth can buy. A groom may choose to pay a high bridewealth if it enhances his prestige. Thirdly, a sale involves no continuing relation. The

---

[2] Cf. Fischer's criticisms of the notion of bridewealth as a purchase price (1932: 65–6) and Forth (1981: 359 ff.) on the mix of economic and symbolic elements in Rindi bridewealth.

[3] In Sisarahili, in the Middle Susua region of central Nias, I recorded the relationship term *sifa'avö ovöliwa* for HBW. *Ovöliwa* means 'purchase', 'the thing bought' (from *böli*). The whole phrase means, literally, 'she who is a fellow purchase'. In Sifalagö I was told that a widow is the *ovöliwa* of her husband's lineage, and as such can be passed on to his surviving agnates with a reduced payment to her family. If the widow remarries elsewhere, she is 'half-price'. Informants rejected my supposition that the term for suitor/groom, *si faöli*, derives from *öli*, maintaining that there is no connotation of purchase in the term.

verb used by older men for a commercial transaction, *aecu'ö*, derives from *aecu* ('cut-through'), such that payment severs the relation between parties to a deal. Bridewealth, on the contrary, opens a lifelong relation between the parties to a marriage. In a simple purchase there is a transfer of ownership to the purchaser. But in giving bridewealth, paradoxically, the groom becomes the *ono* ('child') of his wife-givers, whom he henceforth calls *sokhö ya'ita* ('those who own us'). The ritual superiority of the wife-givers partly consists in the fact that the gift of a wife creates a debt which can never be paid off. Marriage involves the first set of exchanges in a complex, lifelong relation between the affines, an alliance which entails much more than the exchange of a woman for pigs and gold.

2   The Sequence of Prestations

Despite the fact that gold is believed to have certain inherent mystical, as well as symbolic, properties, and although affinity is a relation with a mystical aspect, there is no evidence that items of bridewealth in central Nias are required to have a 'magical' character, such as Fischer (1932: 67) perceived in the institution elsewhere in Indonesia: 'For brideprice, only that which has "mana", magical power, has worth.' Gold and pigs, the main bridewealth items used in Nias, are exchanged in a variety of transactions, both commercial and non-commercial. Neither is there an equivalent of the Toba Batak *ulos* cloth, given by the bride's family, which is 'permeated with sacred powers' (Vergouwen 1964: 58).

Most of the bridewealth prestations are said to be intended as a reward for some service to the bride or groom which has been performed by the recipient. Some of these services are integral to the particular relationship. For example, the indirect wife-givers are endowed in recognition of the bride's 'origin' and the blessings which flow from this. Other prestations are due for particular ritual acts performed during the sequence of events from the betrothal onwards. For example, there is a pig for the 'escorting of the bride', and gold for her agnates for 'bringing her from the bedroom'. Others still refer to the groom's symbolic progress—his entrance into the bride's house when he grasps the 'end of the staircase', his 'treading of the floor', and so on. The schedule of prestations suggests, then, a prescribed order which we would expect to be tied to a prescribed sequence of actions. However, the two are often out of step. The order and timing of prestations are matters of both contingency and strategy as well as of custom, and are always intensely debated. Moreover, the original meaning of some prestations has changed as the practices they once symbolized have been abandoned. Some stages in the matrimonial process have also changed and are now integrated with the schedule of payments in a different fashion from formerly.

It is a difficult problem to reconstruct past nuptial practices. There are no records of marriage customs in the centre based on direct observation. Father Johannes Hämmerle's valuable account (1982: 27–43) is based largely on the recollections of an expert informant, Cosmas Baene of Hililaora. My own informants' versions of the past diverge more widely from present custom than does the account of Hämmerle. This may be due to the fact that the Upper Susua area (which includes Sifalagö) was Christianized some years later than the eastern-central region where Hämmerle's informant lives. However, that does not mean that the Sifalagö versions of the past are more authentic or pristine. The many social changes of the last sixty to seventy years in the Upper Susua make it impossible to establish an agreed picture of past practices. (And, of course, we may not hypostatize the past as informants are apt to do.) The existence of variant forms of union (uxorilocality, widow-inheritance, etc.) further complicates the picture. When we also take into account the variation in customs between areas only a few miles apart, and the influence of present context on the informant's testimony (depreciation or idealization of the past) it becomes virtually impossible to establish a certain pattern.

In the following description I shall try to show the main shifts of emphasis and changes of meaning in marriage customs but I shall not hazard a full historical reconstruction. The main purpose is to elucidate the present situation, and unless otherwise stated it is to the present that I refer.

3   Initiating an Alliance

Due to the secrecy and delicacy of the first approaches, unfortunately I was not able to observe the process directly and have had to rely on villagers' descriptions of actual and hypothetical cases. Taking a typical example, let us assume that a young man has discovered his match in a neighbouring village. Initial impressions have been formed and discreet enquiries made about the suitability of the partners. The suitor's go-between (usually an agnate or affine) has canvassed the possibility of an alliance without yet declaring officially the suitor's intentions.

The first formal visit is, as mentioned above, referred to as viewing the bride (*famaigi niha*). This term is also used, however, of earlier informal approaches. A tentative proposal (*fame li*) can be made on either of these occasions. The young man sets off to the girl's village with his negotiator, reassured by auspicious dreams he had the night before. He should have dreamed he was given the bride or was handed money. Coconut palms are also auspicious. Floods and fire are not and would lead to a postponement of his visit.

From the moment they depart the men are alert to omens. The names of people they meet on the way are significant. Anything with negative connotations would cause them to turn back. Such names as Lö'ö (No), Ide-ide dödö (Resentful), and Holebali (Vacillating in Speech), which are actually encountered in Sifalagö, would be examples. Sökhiniwa'ö (Well-said), Arozanolo (Constant in Help) would be auspicious. Certain activities are inauspicious, for example, carrying. If they meet someone fetching water in a bamboo tube they will return home. The water in the tube signifies *oboula*, the rotten remains of a corpse: the bride will die. A sick person on a stretcher also portends the bride's death if the wedding goes ahead. A sack of rice symbolizes the maggots that feed on a corpse. These omens probably derive from an analogy between the festive carrying of the bride from her house and the object being carried. In cases of child marriage (*solaya ono*), the groom or his father is told to 'take up his burden', that is, to pick up the infant girl and carry her on his back. Schröder (1917: 266) reports a similar formula phrase spoken to a man about to marry.

Other ominous activities encountered on the way to the girl's house relate to her moral qualities as a wife. If a bather is encountered (causing shame if it happens to be a woman), the groom will be 'shamefaced' and 'pale' later over the waste of bridewealth and the conduct of the bride. As they enter the girl's house the men note what meets the eye. It is inauspicious if a dog runs past them. A dog is 'ignorant of law', promiscuous, and like the bather is naked: the girl will be an adulteress. If the floor is not clean (*ohahau*) they are not happy (*ohahau dödö*, lit. 'clear-hearted') about proceeding. Good signs are a well-swept floor, a woman preparing betel (the token of hospitality and civility), and the girl combing her hair. Thus nudity or uncontrolled sexuality (the surprised bather, the dog), death, dirt, and bad names are contrasted with civility, modest feminine beauty or controlled sexuality (hair grooming), and good names.

The girl's father, who has been forewarned of the visit, welcomes them and his wife or daughter offers them betel. They announce that they have come to see the 'fat piglet' or to 'eat the chicken', that is to arrange an engagement if all goes well. The host questions them on the omens encountered on the way (*tanda zi fazuzu*), which are presumed to be good or else they would have returned home. The guests are fed and stay the night. The next day the host asks the suitor to describe his dreams. It is auspicious if the suitor dreams of coconut palms (which are firm and proverbially fertile) or if he dreams he is given the bride or a child, or if he has no dream. It is inauspicious if he dreams of the dead (marriage is a gift of life). Provided the signs are good, the host now kills a pig and entertains the guests. Even at this stage things can go wrong. I was told of an engagement being called off when miraculously a crack suddenly appeared in the suitor's glass. In summary, the omens have three functions: to reveal the bride's character, to reveal whether the match is destined, and to provide a pretext for withdrawing if other impressions fail to satisfy.

The meal is called *fe'a manu* ('the eating of the chicken'), a term which stands for the contracting of the betrothal. The guests are given the pig's lower jaw (the portion of honour) and take away with them raw and cooked portions for the suitor's father. He is thus associated with the wife-taker but at the same time distanced from him—an ambiguity which is characteristic of his role *vis-à-vis* the bride's parents.

The significance of the *fe'a manu* meal has changed considerably since the advent of Christianity, not merely in the substitution of a pig for the eponymous chicken. Old men in Sifalagö still remember the traditional ritual as it was performed in the 1930s and earlier, when Christianity had not yet become fully established in the village. The parties to a marriage sought the approval of the girl's ancestors and the Creator, Samailo. A forked piece of *kapok* wood (*afasi*) with a carved face, arms, and waist, called a *siraha afasi*, was used to communicate with the wooden ancestor figures. According to my informant, the *siraha* represented the suitor. A feather of the cock to be killed was attached to the waist of the *siraha* and possibly another was attached to the ancestor figures. A ritual specialist or priest (*ere*), who was the suitor's speaker, held up the *siraha* to the ancestor figures and pronounced the names of the young couple. In doing this he would 'bind together' their names with the *siraha*. He would then ask the ancestors and the Creator (who are identified in this task) to give a sign of their approval: 'You, O ancestors, fathers! You, Samailo! If you approve, let the chicken's heart be good. If you refuse, make it rotten.' The chicken was then dispatched and its heart removed and cut open before witnesses. If the heart was spoiled or scarred the marriage could not go ahead: the bride would surely die. A clean heart signified that the ancestors had united the couple. While the chicken was roasting over the fire the specialist would perform a ratification of the union. The couple would stand with him beneath the ancestor figures, all three grasping a sword (*gari*) or a length of iron. The priest intoned:

Hear us, fathers, unite these children! May you [the couple] be as enduring on earth and as firm as iron. May you be as cool as iron. May you have descendants (*ya mocuho ami*, 'may you put forth a trunk'), one hundred sons to the village, twelve daughters to the land.

This done, the couple then ate their first meal together in celebration of their union: hence the term 'eating of the chicken'. A small piglet was slaughtered to accompany the meal, and a portion of this was later wrapped and sent with the groom's speaker to his father who was informed of what had passed.

After the meal the groom would hand over a sum of gold (say 10–30 g.) which the bride's father weighed. This prestation, called the *böbö ziraha* ('the *siraha* tie') signified the uniting of the couple by means of the *siraha* figure. The bride's mother was the official recipient. A prestation called *gari* ('sword') is still given as part of the bridewealth, although the 'sword' rite is no longer performed. The *böbö ziraha* is less commonly given nowadays: possibly only in cases of child betrothal, in which case it is forfeited if the groom's side later withdraws. In former times, as today, after the 'eating of the chicken', the wife-givers determined the size of the *be'elö* prestation ('offering'), brought some days later, which confirmed the alliance. The *böbö ziraha* and the *be'elö* were paid before the formal negotiation of the schedule of bridewealth prestations at the *fangerai ana'a* ('the counting of the gold'). This has not changed.

In the simplified procedure followed today, all the steps leading up to the contracting of the betrothal can be accomplished in a single visit (though there may be informal enquiries made beforehand). My account differs from Hämmerle's in the absence of the groom's father, the significance of the *siraha*, and the order of rituals.[4] The sword ritual, according to Hämmerle (1982: 36), could take place in the house of either party, depending on the availability of a traditional priest, after delivery of bridewealth. In the version I was told, it is explicitly the girl's ancestors who join the couple in matrimony. Therein lies the power of the wife-givers to bless and to curse. I would suggest that the order I present above makes sense, in that the ratification follows directly on the divination of ancestral approval. We can, however, expect to find considerable differences between regions in these customs.

Whatever the order of the rituals, it seems clear that the significance of the 'eating of the chicken' has changed considerably. It once signified the definitive joining of the couple by the ancestors (as Hämmerle writes, 'the wedding has taken place'). With the abolition of the ancestor cult it became downgraded into a mere betrothal. Ratification of the union came to depend on a ceremonial 'joining of hands' by a Christian priest, following the main wedding feast. This, in turn, is nowadays conditional on the delivery of the bulk of the bridewealth.

The shift of emphasis altered the positions of the two sides in respect to bridewealth negotiations. In the traditional procedure the 'wedding has taken place' before negotiations begin, and the girl's agnates, the *so'ono*, are therefore already wife-givers, not merely prospectively, and as such are invested with powers over the groom. Their sanction on failure to deliver bridewealth is not merely the withholding of the bride, as nowadays. They can curse the groom and blight the marriage. This ultimate sanction, acquired later in the modern sequence, makes comprehensible the assertion

---

[4] In terms of my analysis the father's presence would compromise his status. According to Marschall (1976: 122), in south Nias, if the groom's father attends the wedding, 'this would be an extraordinary honour to the bride's parents and he would be derided in his own village.' At a wedding described later in Sect. 7 (case 2) the groom's father did indeed attend the wedding, but the circumstances were extraordinary.

by some older informants (others disagreed), that the marriage was consummated immediately after the 'eating of the chicken'. The couple then remained in the house together for a week. This early consummation would be an inconceivable ceding of the advantage to the wife-taker in the modern sequence, as well as being in Christian terms a sin. Younger men, listening to these elders' accounts, scoffed at the folly of granting sexual rights to the groom before he had paid bridewealth.[5]

The elders say that abuses began to occur, and wife-givers were increasingly cheated out of bridewealth, as paganism began to be discredited, so that in the late 1930s the district chief held a meeting at which customary law was made to conform to Christian practice and the present sequence of events was inaugurated. The increase of cheating and the need for reform would, in my analysis, relate to a decline in the ancestor cult under the impact of Christian influence.

Leaving aside these sometimes conflicting reports, what is clear is that the decisive stage in the contracting of an alliance now occurs much later in the sequence of events. There are nevertheless continuities, even in the cosmological framework of the process, which we might have expected to have undergone the most profound changes of all. Particularly notable is the emphasis on omens. Without the possibility of a direct invocation of the ancestors, the problem facing both parties today is still to discover whether the pair are meant to marry, whether the match is 'approved' (*sinehe*), and this is revealed through omens. This is why the notion of a match, which I explored earlier, is ultimately conceived to be independent of earthly concerns: it depends on a higher approval. As in most other such cases of divination (e.g. the foretelling of a feastgiver's fate in the death of his 'dedicated' pigs), there is, since the abolition of the ancestor cult, a vagueness about the supernatural agency responsible for giving the signs. Just who is approving is never specified. But, in descriptions of invocations and blessings as they were once performed, there is an evident tendency to pass easily from the ancestors to the supreme deity, so it required no great revolution in world-view for pious Christians to begin speaking of God's approval. The present emphasis on omens (and even the pious fatalism of today's Christians) is therefore a feature

---

[5] A letter from Pieper to Kruyt of 15 Mar. 1921 regarding the *adat* of Sa'ua (southeast Nias) says: 'One marries here first and then gives the brideprice. In contrast, in the north the brideprice is given at the wedding' (in Korn 479).

of the contemporary folk religion which has obvious continuities with the past. As one elder put it, 'In the old days we were guided in marriage by the ancestors, now we rely on divination (*fama'ele'ö*).'

Let us return to the safer ground of present-day practices. Up to two weeks after the 'eating of the chicken' the groom brings the *be'elö* ('offering'), a prestation of 3–12 pigs, to confirm the betrothal. He also 'returns the sack' in which his father's portion of food was sent, now with quids of betel inside it. If we discount the obsolescent *böbö ziraha*, the *be'elö* is the first substantial prestation given by the groom's side. It counts towards bridewealth, but how it is allocated is only determined much later when the entire schedule of prestations is discussed at the 'counting of the gold'. Meanwhile the groom obtains an approximate figure for the total bridewealth at a private meeting with the wife-givers. During the engagement period—typically one to three years—he sets about raising this sum.

4   The Calculation of Bridewealth

The quantity and relative proportions of gold and pigs in bridewealth are determined by long negotiations. Although the market integrates the prices of all commodities in commercial exchanges and converts everything to a cash value, in customary transactions other rates of exchange apply. These rates were fixed by ancestral decree and were periodically adjusted to meet changing conditions in the district. The present rate of exchange goes back at least fifty years. A full treatment of this topic is presented in Chapter 8; but a few particulars of the system need to be introduced here.

Gold is weighed against Dutch coins and metal counterweights. The gold unit, which has subdivisions, is the *batu*, 10 grams (8 g. in bridewealth transactions). Pigs are measured by girth in *alisi* units (*alisi* means 'shoulder, girth'). Rice is measured by volume in *tumba* (about 1.5 litres). The customary rate of exchange for the three commodities is 1 *batu* of gold = 5 *alisi* pig (about 50 kg.) = 8 *so'e* (8 × 30 *tumba*) rice. The relative cash value of the commodities has changed considerably since the rate was set. Prices in 1986 were as follows:

1 *batu* gold (16 carat) = 150,000 rupiah (about £60)
5 *alisi* pig = 50,000
8 *so'e* rice = 120–140,000 (depending on season)

1 *batu* of the rarely used 24-carat gold, worth Rp.250,000, counts as 2 *batu*.

Bridewealth is reckoned in *batu*, regardless of the mix of pigs and gold. A typical total figure for a marriage between ordinary villagers is 24 *batu*. This might consist of 4 *batu* gold and 20 *batu* pigs (i.e. 20 × 5 *alisi* or other combination of pigs making up this average). In former times the proportion of pigs to gold was much smaller than now. Pigs were in short supply, whereas gold was comparatively plentiful—a situation which has reversed within living memory. Rice, once harvested in vast quantities, is now scarce as land holdings have diminished. This change is reflected in the present undervaluation of rice in the customary rate of exchange.

Given the wide discrepancy between market and customary values it is not surprising that a hotly debated point is the quantity of gold included in bridewealth. There is a kernel of gold called the *ikhu mböli niha* ('nose/point of the bridewealth'), which is divided among certain prestations, such as *gari* ('sword'). The bride's father's demand is a compromise between what he wants and what he thinks he can reasonably expect. If it is a local marriage, he will have some idea whether the groom can obtain gold within his lineage or whether he will have to buy it on the market—a much heavier burden. In such a case he may make allowances and ask for less. Nevertheless, he has a certain minimum figure, usually 1–3 *batu* (6–12 in a noble marriage), which he sticks to tenaciously in negotiations. In an example I refer to later in Section 7 (case 2), a wedding between children of ordinary villagers, the girl's father insisted on 6 *batu* as the kernel. So far only 1 *batu* of this has been paid, and no one expects him to get more than 3. The rest will be substituted by pigs *at the customary rate*. This makes a considerable difference to the overall cost (a saving worth 300,000 rupiah) while not affecting the nominal total of *batu*. Such figures have to be seen against the stark poverty of the population. The few men who work for wages earn 1,000–2,000 rupiah per day. A primary school teacher earns 50,000 rupiah per month.

As a rule of thumb, the bride's father expects a figure for the total bridewealth equivalent to what he gave for her mother. This following of precedent stabilizes the system and provides an approximate guideline in negotiations. The bride's father is anxious to recoup the effort (*ölö*) which he put into his own bridewealth, especially if part of it was paid off in labour for his own father-in-law. The groom's side have made enquiries and know roughly what was given for the girl's mother, but they have to limit their objections if the *matua* exaggerates. After all, he is not soliciting offers of marriage and he is not to be bargained with as if his daughter were for sale. Instead the groom pleads for moderation and indulgence from the *matua*, who may then insist only that certain prestations, e.g. the 'sword', be equal to those paid for the girl's mother; or he may change tack and demand a bigger kernel while remaining flexible on the total bridewealth figure. But this is to anticipate a discussion of negotiations. My point here is that precedent is a factor in determining the total figure.

A related factor is rank. According to the oldest villagers, ranking may once have been more systematically integrated with bridewealth figures than at present. One man spoke of seven *bosi* ('steps') of bridewealth, corresponding to ranks. This unprompted (if uncertain) information suggests similarities with districts of north Nias where a man's rank was determined partly by the sum of bridewealth he had paid, in a single system of *bosi* (Korn 475/51). The details of the old system in Sifalagö are, unfortunately, beyond recovery. Nowadays the word *bosi* is applied to the schedule of prestations, the *bosi mböli niha*. The size of bridewealth nevertheless continues to reflect broad divisions in rank which existed also in the past. These can be summarized as follows:

For the daughter of an important chief   100 *batu*
an ordinary chief   50 *batu*
a titled elder   30–40 *batu*
an ordinary villager   24 *batu*

These are, on the whole, only differences of quantity. The basic schedule of prestations is the same in all cases. The figures above are no more than a rough guide, a description by informants of typical payments. In practice, as everyone recognizes, the status of both parties affects the size of bridewealth. The son of a great chief or a high-ranking elder of a chiefly line would expect to pay more for the same woman than would the son of an ordinary chief. A high bridewealth is a validation of status and usually involves a feast of merit which further pushes up the overall cost. Thus sisters may be married off for different sums, as the example of the chief of Sifalagö shows, depending on the status of the groom's father.

One of the elders of Sifalagö, Ama Huku, married off his first three daughters for 30 *batu* each to men of approximately equal background to their own. The bridewealth for his fourth daughter was put at 40 *batu* because the groom was the DS of the chief's grandfather and is therefore an *ono zalawa*, of 'noble birth' (lit. 'son of a chief'). The importance of maternal affiliation (the groom's 'background') is striking in this case. Even if the groom had lacked this distinction he would still in all probability have had to pay more than the others since his wife is the youngest daughter, the 'last of the children', and her marriage left her father without labour except for his ageing wife.

The village secretary (presently candidate for headman) stressed the factor of status in the modern system as the main determinant of bridewealth, while acknowledging that it tends to overlap with traditional status. Thus, in order, the daughters of headman, deputy, secretary, and ward head command the biggest bridewealth. If we are to judge from typical bridewealth figures, a priest and evangelist correspond roughly in status with, respectively, a headman and deputy. There is a predilection among the local bureaucracy (and men on the lowest rungs such as the secretary) for stressing the complementarity of the three systems: custom, government, and the Church; or to use the mixture of Indonesian and Niasan used in this formula: *adat, famareta, agama*. We might construct a table of rough correspondances with appropriate bridewealth figures (see Table 6.1).

TABLE 6.1 Status and bridewealth

Custom	Government	Church	Bridewealth
chief	headman	priest	50 *batu*
elder	deputy	evangelist	30–40 *batu*

Given all the possible combinations of status and all the other factors involved in the making of an alliance, clearly any young man about to marry is faced with a variety of options in terms of how much bridewealth he can expect to pay. Why then pay more rather than less? This question has already been answered in part, but it is worth listing the reasons again and adding a few further considerations.

1. A big bridewealth wins prestige and enhances status, especially if the wedding is combined with an *ovasa*.

2. One pays as much as is necessary to make one's match, in the sense of marrying an equal.

3. One pays more than the girl's background merits if she is a match in the other sense: 'No other woman will do.'

4. A large bridewealth (40–50 *batu*) requires custom to be performed in full: the bride's party gives counter-prestations (*bövö*) which add up to between 6 and 12 *batu*, consisting of pigs, gold ornaments, household goods, etc.

5. 'One gives as much as one is able and willing.'

This last reason is only puzzling if we persist in regarding bride-wealth as a simple price, which it is not, despite its economic importance and the partly commercial aspect of negotiations. More is being negotiated than price: reputation, status, goodwill, and the terms of the alliance. The bride's party therefore accept less if their favoured suitor is unable to pay the appropriate sum. The *soroi tou*, for their part, want the prestige of a high bridewealth but want large counter-prestations and flexible terms of payment, which may involve a reduction of the officially declared figure. Once the parameters are agreed there is a lot of room for hard negotiation within them.

It is at the first, private meetings between the two sides that an approximate overall figure is agreed upon. The first matter to decide is whether to 'reckon step by step or by the total' (*hadia latörö mbosi ma amarahuta*), that is, to reckon up the prestations (naming recipients) one by one and arrive at a final figure or to begin with the total and leave it to the wife-givers to subdivide it. The lump-sum method generally works out at less, but it depends partly on the number of potential claimants. So an initial question is how many lines of wife-givers there are. The groom has an idea of the numerical strength of the lineage and may be anxious to avoid a reunion of far-flung agnates of the bride at his expense. The bride's father takes into account his own position in the lineage—his desire for influence and patronage, whether he has received large portions of the bridewealth for his agnates' daughters and therefore is expected to return the compliment, or whether he wants to punish their meanness.

If the lump-sum method is agreed on, the next point to be

clarified is whether certain 'extras' are included in the figure. Besides the basic schedule of prestations, the *töla mböli niha* ('bones/trunk of bridewealth') or *boto mböli* ('substance/body of bridewealth') there are a number of minor prestations which are due to participants who do not necessarily belong to either party, such as the chief and the Christian priest. Some of these extras can be quite substantial and the object of fiercer negotiations than the bridewealth itself.

5   The Schedule of Bridewealth Prestations

It is a fairly simple matter to collect lists of marriage payments. Any young man can provide such information, and older men or experts can offer interpretations of archaic terms and symbolism. This type of data lends itself readily to tables and diagrams of the kind common in ethnographies. Such a presentation loses something of the meaning of prestations, leaving out of account the crucial matter of timing, and the particular considerations of personal relations which are involved in the negotiation of every payment. After a long and perhaps exhausting description of bridewealth in this section (my excuse being that such matters are long and exhausting), I therefore end the chapter with two case-studies, which reveal in more vivid form the concerns of participants.

Case 1: The wedding of Fau Ndruru to Ateria Bu'ulölö of Sifalagö
To introduce the subject, however, let us take as an example the marriage of Fau Ndruru to Ateria Bu'ulölö, both natives of Sifalagö, who were married in 1984. The background to this union illustrates points made above concerning the calculation of bridewealth as well as earlier points relating to the choice of spouse and leads into the schedule of exchanges.

Fau is the son of an ordinary villager with a minor title, whose wife was a cousin of the chief. Ateria comes from a separate lineage of the chief's clan (B4). The union is therefore a repetition of an alliance and Fau is a *sangawuli ba zibaya*, but since Ateria and the chief are connected eight generations back, the alliance-renewal aspect of the marriage is unimportant. What is more important is that the marriage does not alter the status quo or reverse the previous union. The girl's father, Sorombövö, a respected and prominent village elder, had received a proposal from a man in a village twelve miles upstream. The suitor was willing to pay a high bridewealth, partly because he wanted to renew an alliance with Ateria's MB. However, the union would have been polygamous and Sorombövö risked expulsion from the Church if he consented to it. In opting for the local man (his next-door neighbour) he sacrificed financial gain and prestige for a more convenient and practical alliance which suited his daughter as well.

Some twenty-five years ago Sorombövö paid a bridewealth of 50 *batu* for his own wife, and in addition held a feast which cost 20 *batu*. His father-in-law demanded a 'kernel' of 6 *batu* gold. He gave 4 *batu* at the wedding and worked for his father-in-law to pay off the remaining debt. In successive seasons he gave 7, 6, and 9 *so'e* of rice—a very large quantity by today's standards—which was reckoned as 2 *batu*. It was with this tremendous effort in mind that he asked Fau for 6 *batu*, to recover what he had given for the girl's mother. He eventually accepted a figure of 3 *batu*, since Fau is a readily available source of free labour (Fau is currently helping him to build a new house), and the agreed kernel was delivered before the wedding. Sorombövö demanded from Fau 50 *batu* total, excluding extras, but settled for a comprehensive total of 40.

The following is a description of prestations with values asserted to be standard by informants and examples taken from Fau's case (recorded in Sept. 1986).

1. *fanarai mbatö* ('the treading of the floorboards'). 3 *batu* to the *so'ono* (bride's father *et al.*). This is the first of several prestations which refer to parts of the bride's house, or rather the groom's entrance into the house. The relative status of the parties is symbolized in their names which denote position relative to the house. The bride's party, as mentioned earlier, are *sovatö*, the hosts (lit. 'those who have the floor'); the groom's party are *soroi tou* ('those who come from below'). As the former term indicates, the floor is representative of the house as a whole and its occupants.[6] Unlike many Indonesian societies, however, social groups are never referred to as 'houses' (*omo*).

---

[6] A number of other terms associated with kinship and domestic roles incorporate the word for floor (*batö*). One of the words for wife or married couple/nuclear family is *ngambatö* (south Nias: *gagambatö*). SWP/DHP are reciprocally *mbambatö*. (*Nga-* and *mba-* are particles which do not have any independent meaning.)

In the traditional residence pattern the entire local lineage lives under one roof. At a wedding or feast, the host—'he who holds the floor'—therefore, in an obvious way, represents the whole lineage. In the traditional wedding ceremony the couple were joined under the lineage idols kept together in one house. The groom's entrance is therefore a licensed intrusion into lineage territory and is accompanied by formality and a certain trepidation on his part. Guests in Nias were traditionally honoured but were also vulnerable. Stories of feuds are full of tales of treachery towards the guest.

As these first prestations indicate, then, the scene and symbolic focus of the betrothal and the wedding is the bride's house, and the groom's entrance is therefore 'sacred' or 'marked with taboos' (*ni'amoni'ö*). Each stage of his progress is represented by prestations. The first of these, *fanarai mbatö*, is large: at least 3 *batu*, 6 or 12 for the daughter of a chief. A point stressed by informants is that, unlike some of the other prestations, this one is not sued for or solicited with counter-prestations. Nothing is conceded actually or metaphorically to the wife-takers and the very first payment is thus emblematic of their power over the wife-taker, setting the official tone for the exchange of bridewealth as a whole and demonstrating their advantage in negotiating positions.

Fau's bridewealth: 3 *batu* (i.e. 3 pigs of 5 *alisi* girth).

2. (*fanufa*) *balö nora* ('[holding] the end of the staircase'). 3 *batu* to the *so'ono*. Logically one would perhaps put this first, but informants usually place it second. Perhaps the 'treading of the boards' once referred to the first visit as husband-to-be and the *balö nora* referred to the second. The staircase is the point of entry into the house. Formerly, entrance was via a trapdoor in the floor. Nowadays staircases are usually at the side of the house. *Ora* has a sense of 'in-betweenness' (go-betweens are sometimes referred to as *ora*).

According to Hämmerle (1982: 40) the *balö nora* prestation signifies the groom's sexual rights in the bride; his grasping of the rounded end of the staircase signifying possession of the bride. In the Upper Susua the *balö nora* seems never to have had this connotation. What, then, does it signify? I was told that the groom's entry was barred by a string of coconut leaves stretched across the doorway. The wife-givers cut the string to allow him in. The 'payment' for this is the *balö nora*. I would interpret the first two prestations, therefore, as signifying the groom's ritualized access to the house. We might go further and say they (and the actions they represent) symbolize his incorporation into an alliance with the wife-givers, which was completed formerly by the wedding rites under the household/lineage idols. Henceforth he is their *ono* ('child').

It is worth referring at this point to another prestation (now obsolete) which relates to this theme. This marked a further stage in the groom's incorporation when he 'crossed the threshold' (*fanötö vosiavu*) which divides the front and rear halves of the house. The rear section of the house is private and associated with domestic activities (cooking, sleeping, sex). The threshold is a symbolic boundary with the front, public section. Until the time comes for the bride to be taken to the groom's house, she remains most of the time sequestered in the bedroom. The groom's crossing of this boundary is therefore indirect evidence that the marriage was formerly consummated in the girl's house as some informants reported.

Both the *fanarai mbatö* and the *balö nora* are paid at an early stage, long before the wedding feast. The *be'elö*, which confirms the betrothal, is frequently allocated to these retrospectively. Only in cases where the engagement is very short would they be paid all at once with the other prestations.

Fau's bridewealth: 3 *batu*.

3. *gari* ('sword'). 3–6 *batu* to the *so'ono*. See description of former wedding ceremony above in Section 3.

Fau's bridewealth: 3 *batu*.

4. *ono sebua*. 3 *batu* (often including 1 *batu* gold). The term means literally 'child who is big/grown up'. It is given to the eldest son (*ono sia'a*) of the bride's father and is so-called 'because the recipient is the first to be grown up'. He claims it at the wedding, or if he is still unmarried, he claims it later as a contribution towards his own bridewealth. This is the only prestation which is explicitly intended to be re-directed in this way. As with African cattle-linking it symbolizes also the bond between brother and sister.

Fau's bridewealth: the recipient, age 12, was given 2½ *alisi* as an instalment.

5. *ono tatalu* ('middle child'). 2 *batu*. The middle sons may get 2 each or a larger sum is divided among them.

Fau's bridewealth: not yet paid.

6. *ono siakhi* ('youngest child'). 3 *batu*. The eldest and youngest sons are supposed to receive more than the middle sons 'because

they are the most trouble to their parents'; whereas the middle sons have elder siblings to help look after them. The size of payments to the bride's brothers, however, partly depends on the quality of the ongoing alliance relation they individually establish with their sister's husband. This is an important point of difference with the earlier bridewealth prestations given to the bride's father. The latter are given in a spirit of indebtedness and formal tribute, whereas payments to the bride's brothers are, in part, solicited.

The nature of the relation between brothers-in-law is further revealed in a payment called *fo'ekhe* (lit. 'endow with a knife'), which is not part of the formal bridewealth schedule. When the eldest son claims his *ono sebua* to put towards his own bridewealth, he claims a 'supplement' or 'extra' (*hude*) which is the *fo'ekhe*, usually equal in size to the *ono sebua*. He gives a chicken and demands a pig in return. The chicken is said to be 'what extracts the pig'. When my wife and I were given clan names I was immediately deluged with offers of chickens by my wife's 'agnates', who now addressed me eagerly as *la'o* (brother-in-law). Fortunately one of my own 'agnates', from whom I could expect material support, warned me strenuously not to accept anything or I would be indebted for a pig.

This unequal exchange illustrates an important class of gifts in Nias: the solicitory or obliging gift—*so'i-so'i*. To *so'i* is to endow someone in expectation of a later and greater reward. Any prestation from wife-givers to wife-takers can be classed as *so'i-so'i*. The size of the return is proportional to the solicitory gift, and (apart from bridewealth) if you aren't 'solicited' you don't give. Certain gifts are said to 'draw out' or 'extract' return gifts. For a *fo'ekhe* prestation of 3 *batu* a mere chicken from the bride's brother would be inadequate. He would be expected to entertain his sister's husband formally, killing a medium-sized pig (3½ *alisi*), serving him the portion of honour, and would send him off with a live pig of 2½ *alisi* and a hen. The total value of the solicitory gifts would therefore be more than 1 *batu*. These formal prestations to a wife-taker, added to intermittent small presents of food when a married sister is ill or pregnant, are tokens of 'caring'.

Interestingly, only the first and last sons can claim a *fo'ekhe* supplement. Their equivalence and their superiority over the middle sons is evident also in their larger portions of bridewealth. This superiority is not a question of formal priority. Rather, it recognizes the likelihood of either the first or last sons' succeeding their father. The first son is the one who deputizes for his father and receives any portions due to him when he has died. The youngest son tends to be the one who looks after the ageing patriarch and who remains in the house when his older brothers have set up field houses elsewhere. So there is a kind of optional *de facto* primo- or ultimogeniture, which is recognized in these affinal payments.

One informant interpreted for me the purpose of the *fo'ekhe* supplement as follows. It is intended to compensate the bride's brother for the fact that the bulk of the bridewealth went to his father. He will say to his sister's husband, 'I received only 1 *batu* for the *ono sebua*, where's my extra?' By this supplement he is made 'equal' with his father. He is therefore his father's successor in the special sense that he inherits the affinal relation. But, importantly, he has to consolidate and keep alive this relation by solicitory gifts. Thus the alliance relation is inherited but it changes in the process, both in terms of obligation and characteristic behaviour. Brothers-in-law are on friendly and relaxed terms as well as being firm allies. (I know of several cases of brothers-in-law setting up adjacent homes in the wilderness.)

Payments to the bride's brothers may be staggered over many years, and, of course, the youngest son receives his portion much later. If the bride has no brothers the payments are simply made to her father: a general principle of bridewealth is that no steps (*bosi*) can be omitted.

Fau's bridewealth: not yet paid.

7. *talu'i gerua* ('co-wife's girdle'). 1–3 *batu*. This is given to the bride's mother's co-wife or, if there is none, to the bride's father. A second wife is called (*g*)*erua* a term which derives from *dua* ('two'). A woman carries a child on her back in a girdle or sling called a *talu'i* (Steinhart 1937: 32 n. 65). The prestation thus refers to the co-wife's minor share in the bringing up of the bride. Relations between co-wives are usually strained. It is important therefore that no one is taken for granted. As one man said, 'The co-wife is resentful if she receives none of the bridewealth, and she won't look after the bride or her mother any more.'

All payments to women are in name only: the recipient's husband or son (if the woman is a widow) is the actual beneficiary. The pacificying of co-wives therefore might mean in practice the endowing of one half-brother over another.

Fau's bridewealth: 3 *batu* promised to the bride's father (not yet paid).

8. *uvu dödö*. 3 *batu*. A literal translation is meaningless, and informants regard the term as obscure. In the Upper Susua *uvu* has several, mostly archaic, senses, including mother's or MM agnates and, in some contexts, wife-givers and their ancestors. Here the latter sense is possibly implied since the *uvu dödö* prestation goes to the girl's FF or, if he is dead, to her FeB.

Fau's bridewealth: 3 *batu* to the bride's FeB. Half of this has been paid.

9. *aya gave satua* ('ornament of the old grandmother'). 3 *batu*.

10. *aya gave savuyu* ('ornament of the young grandmother'). 2 *batu*. These payments are made to *talifusö* (agnates, lineage mates) of the bride's father. In all the examples I collected, the first payment is made to the one or two most senior men of the lineage, with small supplements of cash to their sons. The second payment is made to other adult men of the lineage. The meaning of the terms derives from the fact that the prestations are not simply lineage payments; rather they acknowledge the role of incoming wives (in time 'grandmothers') as wealth-producers. As one man explained: the *aya gave satua* is given to the bride's father's agnates in commemoration of their common ancestress (their FM), who was the *sovöli* ('purchaser') of (i.e. provider of bridewealth for) the mother of each agnate. The bride's father gives it to his agnate with the words, 'take the food of (on behalf of) our mother, the food of our grandmother'.

The *aya gave savuyu* is supposed to be given to the bride's father's half-brothers, who receive it on behalf of their mother, who was co-wife to the bride's FM. Like the *talu'i gerua* payment which pacifies the resentful co-wife, the *aya gave savuyu* smoothes over a potentially difficult relation between the children of co-wives. Nowadays, when polygyny is rare, this prestation simply goes to lineage mates. If the lineage is large, the prestation may be much larger than 2 *batu*. The size also depends very much on the relations of patronage and reciprocity within the lineage. The bride's father is obliged to be generous to his agnates if they have done likewise with the bridewealth they have received. He may wish to over-reciprocate to win their allegiance, or he may requite their meanness.

Fau's bridewealth: for the *aya gave satua*, pigs of 3 and 4 *alisi* to the senior man of the lineage, and 2 *alisi* to his younger brother. Cash for their sons. For the *aya gave savuyu*: pigs worth 3 *batu* divided among the heads of five families.

11. *maso-maso*. 3–6 *batu* to the bride's mother's agnates (see Sect. 1 of Ch. 3 for the definition of bridewealth-receiving groups). *Maso-maso* is a ritual term for heart. Two other archaic senses suggest an analogy between wife-givers and other figures of authority: 'tribute for a chief', and, according to Steinhart (1934: 353), 'food offered to the ancestor figures'. The size of the prestation is ultimately at the discretion of the bride's father, the *so'ono*, but if the recipients demand more, he can hardly oppose them and risk their displeasure or curse. They are sometimes asserted to be 'equal to the *so'ono*', and their portion is second in size only to that of the bride's father. Usually the *maso-maso* includes gold from the 'kernel of the bridewealth', signifying its great importance.

Fau's bridewealth: 6 *batu* (including ½ *batu* of gold) divided among six brothers. Not all of this sum has been paid. The recipients are an influential family, hence the large prestation.

12. *hië dödö*. 2½ *alisi*–3 *batu* to the bride's MM agnates.

Fau's bridewealth: 3½ *alisi* + 18 *saga* to two brothers in Hililevu'ö, 5 miles downstream, plus 5,000 rupiah divided among their retinue.

13. *tahövu*. 8 *saga* to the wife-giver of the *sanema hië dödö*.

Fau's bridewealth: not invited, even though the genealogical links were traceable, since the family in question have never shown any 'care' for the bride's father. They could safely be ignored. More remote affinal links were not investigated.

14. *gölumbola*. A token gift of pork, or traditionally a mat, is given to the wife-giver of the *tahövu*.

15. *so'aya za'a*. Only the oldest villagers remembered this prestation, which was given to the wife-giver of the *gölumbola*.

Of these higher-order affinal groups only the recipients of *maso-maso* and *hië dödö* are of any real importance in the life of the married couple, and their portions are correspondingly large. They are minor guests at any future feast of merit held by the groom when they receive tribute in exchange for their solicitory gifts.

16. *fanuyu mbö'ötö* ('the taking by the wrist'). 1 *batu* gold. At the wedding the girl is handed over in the bedroom. The groom's mother grasps her wrist and places gold in the palm of the girl's mother (or the co-wife). The latter says something like, 'My child is now yours, for good or ill', to which the groom's mother replies, 'She's mine, I'll take her!' Note that this critical moment takes place

unseen, in the privacy of the rear section. It would be an intrusion if a man were to enter this area. Moreover, the girl is passed from one woman to another—she ceases to be the domestic helper of her mother and becomes that of her husband's family. There are other instances of women as it were standing between men at critical encounters between affines, such as at the highly charged arrival of guests at a feast of merit, when women on both sides link arms to form a cordon.

Fau's bridewealth: this prestation was omitted. The bride's father told me he would have insisted on it if the groom had come from another village.

17. *labusö*. A pig of 8 *alisi*. To the bride's mother, to 'replace the girl in the home' and 'gladden the heart of her mother' who loses a valuable worker. A recurrent theme of exchange is the concept of labour or effort. Here the concept appears in two senses. First, the loss of labour to the family; secondly, the labour that went into bringing up the girl. The *labusö* is therefore often glossed as 'the cost of the upbringing' (*böli veroro*). Although the entire bride-wealth is sometimes conceived as 'what replaces' the bride, this prestation in particular makes this concept explicit. Payment of *labusö* is regarded as concluding the bulk of the bridewealth schedule. It may be paid on the couple's return visit to the *so'ono*, or months or even years later. The literal meaning of the term is lost.

Fau's bridewealth: 8 *alisi* promised, not yet paid.

18. *tambali labusö* ('counterpart of the *labusö*'). A pig of *sazilo* (6 *alisi*). Paid to the bride's mother's co-wife, or if there is none (as is usually the case) to the bride's FBW as a sign of 'brotherly love'.

Fau's bridewealth: 4 *alisi* to the bride's FeBW. Sorombövö's own bridewealth was arranged, but not paid for, by his brother. He intended this payment to be understood as a reward, but not a generous one because the brother has since shown himself to be mean.

19. *famokai lövö-lövö* ('the opening of the parcel'). 1–2½ *batu* (including 1 *batu* of gold) to the bride's father. On the return visit of the couple when the *labusö* is usually paid, the groom brings a cooked piglet, wrapped in a parcel with rice. He gives it to the bride's father, who says 'give me something to open the parcel with'. The groom responds with the prestation of this name.

Fau's bridewealth: 2½ *batu*; not yet paid.

20. *taroma vakhe* ('prestation of rice'). 3 *batu* to the bride's

father. The prestation represents the possibility of substituting rice for gold. The value of 3 *batu* in rice is 30 *so'e*—a vast quantity by the standards of today's small harvests, so in most cases *taroma vakhe* is paid in pigs.
Fau's bridewealth: up to 3 *batu*; not yet paid.
   21. *balaki mböli niha* ('[fine quality] gold of the bridewealth'). 3 *batu* to the bride's father. This and the prestation above are paid years after the wedding and they are regarded as the conclusion of the schedule of payments. Among other things they show that 'bridewealth isn't over and done with in a day.' They are also symbols of the ongoing alliance, and therefore as one might expect they are solicited with *so'i-so'i* gifts.
Fau's bridewealth: up to 3 *batu*; not yet paid.[7]

Certain other expenses are sometimes included in the 'grand total' of bridewealth-plus-extras, as follows:

taroma zalawa: 3 *alisi* for the bride's village chief.
aya mbanua ('ornament of the village'): nowadays this consists of 50,000 rupiah cash (i.e. 1 *batu*) divided unequally among the bride's villagers according to rank.
agama (Indon. 'religion'): 10,000 rupiah for the priest or church evangelist who performs the Christian wedding ceremony.
böli nukha ('cost of clothes'): 200,000 rupiah to pay for wedding clothes and jewellery. Often the bride's father simply keeps half of the money himself. This sum, which is fiercely contested, and tends to be seen as exploitation of the groom, is paid after the 'counting of the gold', before the wedding. This is not a traditional payment. In former times the bride was decked out in gold and clothes belonging to her lineage, which were returned after the wedding on a visit called 'the returning of the ornaments' (*famuli gama-gama*).

6 Summary Remarks on Bridewealth Prestations

It is evident that the schedule of prestations is heterogeneous. Some acknowledge a particular service or ritual action, some are given in

---

[7] The above schedule, if paid in full with extras, would exceed the agreed total of 40 *batu* (some 24 *batu* having been paid so far); but remaining debts are ideal 'official' sums, and will be reduced or commuted by further negotiation.

virtue of a relation and repay whatever benefit flows from that relation. Only one prestation is explicitly intended to 'replace' the bride, and then only in her capacity as labourer. It is not at all clear whether the bride's sexual services are symbolized in any payment, and recognition of her reproductive services awaits the actual birth of her children, when a 'debt for the child' is claimed by her father. Certain prestations are particularly associated with the continuing alliance, and these are staggered over some years and typically are solicited. The tribute given to higher-order wife-givers is sometimes referred to as a *fangombakha*, a 'proclamation' or 'announcement' (of the marriage), given in return for their blessing (*hovu-hovu*). As such it is analogous to the tribute formerly given to the ancestor figures (cf. the archaic sense of *maso-maso*) and underlines the analogous roles of wife-givers and patrilineal ancestors.

In negotiating prestations and in explaining their meaning to me, speakers commonly referred to the emotional and ethical aspects or purport of the particular exchange: to avoid resentment, express gratitude or recognition of a service, to encourage or show 'caring' (i.e. material support), to 'cheer up', or to pacify. These emotions tend to be attributed to or linked in speeches with exchanges which involve a degree of optionality (in size) or reciprocity. They are mentioned in discussion in order to apply pressure on the wife-taker to fulfil his obligations. Prestations given to the *so'ono*, the direct wife-giver, are, in contrast, conceived more in a spirit of straight-forward obligation, or as Niasans put it, 'debt' (*ömö*).

Another aspect of many of the prestations is the reinforcing of bonds between the bride's father and the other recipients, such as his wives, agnates and their wives, etc. Bridewealth is the occasion of a redistribution of wealth and his generosity is under intense scrutiny. He is subject to a variety of pressures and obligations as well as conflicting desires: for personal enrichment, prestige, and influence. He is usually brooding and irritable, and his speeches are often testy challenges. The groom's position, in contrast, is fairly clear. He is crushed under the weight of obligation and is expected to act with appropriate humility.

Redistribution is also a sharing of the glory (*lakhömi*) which a gift confers. The head of each guest group (e.g. the recipient of *maso-maso*) asks for more so that his members will share in his glory. In the bride's lineage, all the married men expect a pig. In a lineage with a depth of seven generations there could be as many as fifteen claimants.[8] When every claim has been satisfied and the total has been further reduced by counter-prestations and the costs of feasting, the bride's father is said to be left with about a quarter of the original figure.

This long description of prestations glosses over the perhaps obvious point that the objects of exchange are in nearly every case the same: pigs. Only the names of the prestations are different. As for the pigs, they are differentiated only by size. Although the language does not lack terms for varieties of pigs, these discriminations are not involved in the exchanges. There are no masculine and feminine affinal prestations, such as are found in other Indonesian societies with marriage alliance. Objects of the same kind—if of different value—are made to symbolize a variety of relations merely by a change of name, so a great deal depends on the designation of a particular pig as x or y prestation. Much of the negotiations is taken up with just such quibbles, as speakers try to establish the interpretation which is most to their own advantage in terms of size. Just as recipients can be reshuffled (giving one man the pig earmarked for another, perhaps to his loss), so can prestations: the x pig can simply be called y, and in this way the whole sequence of events can be reordered by a change of name, perhaps shifting the negotiating advantage from one party to the other.

The fact that pigs are easily substituted or transferred invests them with something of the abstractness of currency, a quality which is further enhanced by their convertibility into gold. All this means that bridewealth negotiations can be pitched at a fairly abstract level of figures and quantities. There is no reference to particular objects with unique characteristics. This tends to be true even of gold ornaments and jewellery, which are simply referred to by their weight and quality, rather than as, say, 'the necklace made for the chief's wife at her husband's feast'. While the talk is all of weights and measures, the gross objects of negotiation remain out of sight, corralled beneath the house and are not even examined during negotiations.

It is a point of difference from other transactions that bridewealth pigs are not measured publicly or in front of the groom's party. Although the girth of pigs can be roughly estimated by sight to ½ *alisi* there is a tendency to exaggerate, so that a pig of 4½ *alisi* is

---

[8] According to a villager who married a woman from Onohondrö (south), in south Nias only the actual brothers of the bride's father can claim a pig.

given as 5, equivalent to 1 *batu* gold. In marriage payments this is acceptable. The recipient loses a little materially, but he gains in prestige by the higher figure. There is no question of either side cheating in the size of the prestations. However, nothing is conceded, in debate at least, without a struggle. A claimant's honour is satisfied if his portion is promised, but he cannot obtain it forcibly and the actual size depends partly on circumstances.

Thus the bridewealth negotiations give a slightly misleading impression of exactness to outsiders. In south Nias there is a wide discrepancy between the official total and the sum actually handed over. In central Nias this difference is not systematic, and in any case, it is much smaller. Since payments are spread over many years, it is not possible to check this difference independently, but I was told that it only becomes significant in the case of a very big bridewealth. For example, an official figure of 100 *batu* for the daughter of a great chief might represent a real payment of 70 *batu*. In an average bridewealth of 24 *batu*, there would not be enough pigs to go round if substantial reductions or omissions were made.

7   Bridewealth Negotiations

When the groom has assembled a large proportion of the bridewealth, his party pays a formal visit to the wife-givers to 'count the gold' (*fangerai ana'a*) or 'reckon up the debt' (*fangerai gömö*) and 'set the date' of the wedding (*labe ginötö*). This particular stage of the matrimonial process may be referred to by any of these terms, though the first is commonest. Usually the two parties have met a few days earlier to confirm the rough guidelines established at the outset and to make arrangements for the formal visit when all the main recipients will be present.

Since the 'counting of the gold' is the occasion when bridewealth is formally negotiated, it will be helpful here to consider a particular case with brief excerpts from speeches.

Case 2: The wedding of Rata Laia of Botohili to Bene Ndruru of Sifalagö (October–November 1987)
The groom, Rata, is the son of an ordinary villager, but he is well connected as an agnate of the ex-chief of 'Botohili'.[9] He is high-

---

[9] In cases 2 and 3, fictitious names are given to the protagonists and the grooms' villages.

school educated and has a stall at the weekly market in Sifalagö. The couple were betrothed in 1984, and by October 1987 the wedding had been considered imminent for some time. The groom's father, Ama Rata, held out and delayed the wedding because he dislikes the bride's father, Ama Bene, an unpleasant and querulous man with a reputation as a poisoner (which is shared by his elder brother, the bride's main spokesman). The bride's lineage as a whole is without any particular merit. A further disadvantage to the match is the fact that the bride's father is a remote wife-taker of the Laia of Botohili. This means that the recipient of the *tahövu* prestation (fourth-order wife-giver) for Bene is actually an agnate of the groom, though the connection is remote, going back seven generations. This kind of reversal, while not very serious at this level of the alliance structure, is nevertheless a drawback and lowers the prestige of the marriage.

There were two inducements to proceed. First, the groom, as a schoolboy, was known to have exchanged letters with the bride, which in the puritanical ethos of Nias is tantamount to 'womanizing'. Since then both of them have been unwilling to consider marrying anyone else. Secondly, very recently the groom's mother was discovered to be having a liaison with one of his friends, an unmarried man. This brought shame on the family and led to her excommunication from the local church. I was told that this event scared the groom's father into action: he thought that misfortune had befallen him because he had made obstacles to the marriage, breaking the promises of the betrothal. The fine imposed on the adulterer added 6 *batu* to the family resources, which may have been a further reason for choosing to go ahead now. The scandal did not put off the bride's father, who was worried she might become the centre of a similar scandal if the couple were not soon married. Moreover, being a greedy man (in everyone's estimation) he was more worried about pigs than prestige and could press home the advantage gained by the wife-taker's present troubles. So for very different reasons all parties were keen to see the wedding go ahead; though, of course, it would have been a serious error in negotiating tactics to say so.

With these inducements, the groom's party, about fifteen of them, arrived in Sifalagö one day to 'count the gold'. Among them was Ama Rata, the groom's father. His visit, an honour to the bride's side, showed the seriousness of his intent and required some material response (tribute) from the hosts which was not forth-coming. A few days previously the groom's speakers, including the ex-chief of Botohili, had come privately to arrange the official meeting. These private discussions were referred to frequently in the speeches. As is customary, the groom's party brought with them a large instalment of the bridewealth pigs (12 in this case), which were tethered beneath the house. They entered and were greeted formally by women proclaiming the purpose of their visit: '*Ya'ahovu zangerai ana'a!*' ('Greetings/Bless you, Counters of gold'). All the claimants of bridewealth had already gathered: the bride's lineage, and the second-, third-, and fourth-order wife-givers, as well as several village elders from Sifalagö. Altogether there were about eighty people assembled in the large common area of the lineage house. Betel was passed around but not everyone partook. The 'recipient of *hië dödö*' from Gomo, despite having the blackened teeth of an inveterate betel chewer, declined, perhaps nervous of his host's reputation as a poisoner, and felt obliged to smoke cigarettes throughout to justify his abstention. After speeches of welcome the negotiations began. Throughout the speeches the groom and his father remained in silence and impassive. The bride's father, Ama Bene, spoke in brief, ill-tempered outbursts, and he frequently disappeared into the back part of the house as if not wishing to hear the speeches of the groom's party.

In formal debates each side listens in silence to the other and there are no interruptions. A speaker addresses a respondent belonging to his own group, who punctuates the speech with rhythmic interjections and prolonged piercing cries of 'true' or 'yes' which raise the emotional pitch and add emphasis, sometimes drowning the speaker's voice. A show of anger from the bride's party is customary, and an impassioned speaker will stride into the centre of the floor, with out-thrust finger jabbing the air, and stamp on the spot in a fit of rage. If they are well armed with a reply, the groom's men smile at these tricks, and may even cluck appreciatively. More often they maintain a dignified silence; rarely are they dis-composed. In reply they are conciliatory, but keen to probe for weaknesses in the other side's position, drawing attention to omis-sions in the correct procedure and easily taking offence. In this way they can take some of the pressure off themselves and wrest tactical advantage from the wife-givers. This is evident in the speeches cited below.

Much of the debate focused on the bride's trousseau, the *böli nukha*, which is usually around 200,000 rupiah in cash (always difficult to obtain in the village). Ama Bene was demanding an excessive 500,000 rupiah and wanted to make this a precondition of the wedding.

Bride's side:

Add the trousseau to the marriage licence money and there's nothing more to be said. We will be satisfied. Nothing stands in the way of solemnizing the marriage.

Groom's side:

Let us not waste breath over the trousseau. Haven't you got clothes and ornaments of your own, you who are men of substance? [in the old days the bride's family lent her wedding gear] . . . We are not saying we'll refuse it: we've already made good what our grandfather, the ex-chief here, promised [at the previous meeting]. We'll face your anger; we can provide no more . . . In any case, whether the marriage is solemnized or not, it would be like ratifying half a marriage [since half the bridewealth has already been paid; i.e. it's a *fait accompli*: it's no good stalling now]. People will say: 'it must go ahead, even if the debts are not settled all in one day'.

So when you greeted us this morning as 'Counters of Gold', I asked myself, Why so? Have we not already reckoned up the debt [at the private meeting]? But 'nine times' we were hailed thus.

If your speeches are going to carry on like that, and if they are devious, we'll go home. We'll leave it up to Ama Rata, your *mbambatö* [DHF], to decide; or rather your *la'o* ['brother-in-law']—let's not say *mbambatö* yet, that's for the future [i.e. let us revert to the more casual and classificatory term for affine. Who knows, the wedding might not go ahead!].

This kind of quibbling over relationship terms (which may have implications of relative status, seniority, or familiarity) is a typical feature of formal speeches. The use of affinal terms in negotiations is always manipulative since the status of the parties has not yet been decided. To use the term *mbambatö* would imply a positive result, anticipating the alliance. Moreover, as a self-reciprocal term it implies an equality which contrasts with the strict inequality of the parties in negotiations. It may be generous of the *sovatö* or presumptuous of the *soroi tou* to use it. The groom's speaker, then, disconcerted by the excessive demand for the trousseau (which is strictly outside the main bridewealth debt) is accusing the wife-givers of shifting ground. Hence he objects to his party being welcomed as 'Counters of Gold'. He prefers to stick to the more moderate demands of the previous meeting which he wishes to be recognized as 'the counting of the gold'. He parries their demands by implying that the wife-givers are not corresponding with counter-prestations: why was there no welcoming tribute for Ama Rata who has graced them with his presence? Do they really expect Ama Rata to agree to have slaughtered and shared out the only pig he has received?

Groom's side:

If your *la'o* [Ama Rata] had not come today, you would be anxiously enquiring about him and your other 'brothers-in-law' [his agnates]: 'Why has only the son come? Do they not have the same body?' [is there disunity among them? Are they opposed to the marriage?]. He has come, but there is no incentive for him.

You must be wondering at his meanness. He won't let you kill an extra pig for us all—a pig from which of course you'd claim the 'toe' [leg] and guts. He'd rather have the whole pig himself than see it dispersed. So let him have it and take it away in his pocket! [laughter] And why not? Was there any tribute for him when he arrived? Was there anything 'sweet' over and above our meal here? Why do you bring yourselves to the point of refusing us a quid of betel [i.e. a counter-prestation of gold, since you are demanding so much of us]?

Bride's side:

If Ama Rata wishes to take away the pig rather than slaughter it now and share it, so be it. Let him demonstrate his meanness. The pig cannot be put back in the sty.

You ask me, elder brother (you called me 'father', but we won't quarrel over that) why we greeted you as 'Counters of Gold'. When our grandfather here, the ex-chief, came the other day, did we put down the tokens to reckon up the debt? [no, we didn't]. Certainly that meeting had a purpose, or else Ama Rata would not have come today bringing twelve pigs. But it was not the reckoning of the debt. So let's put a name to your visit. Behold, I salute you as Counters of Gold! That's my word!

With this emphatic pronouncement the bride's spokesman spread a mat on the floor and placed on it rows of tokens—uniform pieces cut from coconut leaves, referred to in the speeches as *era-era* (which also means 'thought'). White coconut leaves are used, 'so that our hearts are white' (pure, clear): there should be no concealed feelings in the reckoning; both sides must be content. But immediately there was disagreement over what the tokens signified. Should they represent the named prestations (the *bosi*) or quantities (*batu*)? The bride's speaker, an experienced elder, broke with this procedure and declared that each piece represented a pig due to a particular claimant, effectively obscuring the question of quantities and enabling him to monopolize what had already been delivered. It also put off the reckoning of sums for another day. There followed a heated debate on the propriety of such methods.

Eventually, as both sides were becoming weary, a provisional agreement was reached, leaving the final details to be worked out after the wedding. The tokens were tied up in a bundle by the bride's speaker and put away, the tally to be reduced one by one as the debts were paid off.

Once the debt has been agreed, the date of the wedding is fixed. The timing is a matter of negotiation. The wife-givers use delaying tactics, hoping that the groom's impatience will lead him to promise more. Once he has taken away the bride they have lost the advantage and depend on his integrity and his fear of their curse.

The session was concluded with a meal. The host slaughtered a pig and served the guests and a few of the village elders from Sifalagö. The young couple ate together off a large antique plate, their portion being the prestigious lower jaw, which they shared with the rest of the groom's party. Other customary portions were taken away raw to be divided among the groom's financial supporters in Botohili.

Four weeks later the groom and his brothers brought another 13 pigs. Again, all the main recipients were present, but this was not a formal confrontation between the two parties. The speeches were all between the bride's immediate agnates (the *so'ono*) and the other claimants, and concerned the redistribution of the pigs.

As I have pointed out previously, redistribution is not simply a matter of following customary rules: it is a function of relations of patronage and reciprocity both within the lineage and between affines. The insistence of the *so'ono* on a pig for every agnate repays similar generosity or obliges it from the recipients on future occasions. The second-order wife-givers live opposite, so their prestation was an indication of the state of relations between the neighbours. They happen to be wife-givers not only to the bride's father, but also to his BS, so the family is doubly indebted to them. The bride's FB told me that he was repaying their 'meanness' (they had neglected his son's sick wife) with generosity to teach them a lesson.

Three days after this meeting the wedding festivities took place.

8   The Wedding Feast

Rituals which have any explicit reference to the ancestors or deities have disappeared from wedding ceremonies. This has led to an even greater focus on the exchange of prestations than was formerly the case, and the ethnography must reflect this concern if it is to have any claim to authenticity. Some of the prestations have become 'secularized' as the rituals to which they referred have become obsolete. But the ideology of affinal relations—and thus of bride-wealth—is still taken seriously, at least in central Nias. The wife-givers' blessing (or curse) is a crucial element in the thinking which underlies exchange. If it ceased to be valid, as incentive or sanction, it is unlikely that the cycle of prestations could continue in its present form. It would become simply a fulfilment of stipulations or a purchase.

One could argue that the institution of bridewealth and the values of affinity are mutually supporting and this is a clue to their survival in the hostile climate of secular and Christian influence, where other traditional institutions have perished. The missionaries have found, to their dismay, that bridewealth appears to be ineradicable, and as long as it persists—which, as one man put it, will be as long as there is marriage—the values and mystical sanctions of affinity will survive in some form.[10] In contrast, the religious aspect of descent ideology has been more thoroughly suppressed. Its corporate values survive largely in a secular form.

The abolition of the ancestor cult, as I have shown above, shifted the emphasis from the 'eating of the chicken' (now downgraded to a betrothal ceremony) on to the feast which precedes the bride's departure, which we can nowadays call with accuracy the wedding feast.[11] This is conditional on the delivery of bridewealth. The Christian ratification of the marriage, which replaced the ancestor's

[10] The Catholic Mission in recent times has argued for moderation rather than abolition.

[11] In the north, where the betrothal was followed by strict avoidance between the partners, the wedding feast was the occasion of the ritual joining of the couple (see Lagemann 1893).

approval, has been fitted into the sequence of events without in any way altering the meaning of the exchanges, and without itself undergoing any modification or elaboration. It is considered indispensable as a legitimation of the union, but it is brief and peripheral to the celebrations. Mostly it is performed after the festivities are over (sometimes days later, delaying the consummation or rendering it 'sinful') and few or no guests may be present. However, it can be done at the wedding feast. At the wedding of the daughter of the chief of Sifalagö in May 1986, there was a neat dovetailing of old and new ways when the *sanema maso-maso*, a priest from Gomo, having argued energetically for a bigger portion in return for his blessing, donned his frock and married the couple, passing from one position of spiritual authority to another.

There are several reports of weddings in other parts of the island which differ markedly from my own account and that of Hämmerle concerning central Nias.[12] Although these reports are superficially quite detailed, the symbolism of the rituals is obscure and does not, I think, shed any light on practices in central Nias. Only one account (Ködding 1868a), which happens to be the earliest, refers to a ritual in which the couple joined hands over a sword, such as was once the case in central Nias. Ködding's account appears to derive from the east of Nias.

The form of the wedding celebrations (*fangovalu*) depends on whether they incorporate a feast of merit. In the literature it is usually noble weddings which are described, sometimes leading to a confusion between the standard elements which are present in any wedding (differing only in scale) and elements of the *ovasa*, such as the exchange of tribute, title-giving, war dances, etc. In a simple wedding the main feast is held at the bride's house. The groom's party, twenty or thirty in number, sets out in the morning, driving before them half a dozen pigs. They carry with them two small gongs and a drum and their progress over the hills can be heard from a distance. As they approach the bride's village, their gongs are answered by the low booming of two huge gongs and a drum from the bride's house. Once inside, the groom's party are seated and given betel. Then they are ceremoniously greeted by women proclaiming the salutations and formulas of self-deprecation with which guest groups are always honoured, whether they are wife-givers or

---

[12] See Lagemann 1893, Rappard 1909, and Schröder 1917. The basis for all subsequent accounts of marriage in north Nias seems to be Lagemann.

wife-takers: '*Ya'ahovu zangovalu-le!*' ('Greetings, bridegroom'), 'Greetings to the Laia clan!', 'We have no betel!', or 'No food!' The bride's main speaker gives a speech of welcome, inviting the guests to 'shake the dust and burrs off their feet' (i.e. to dance). The guests excuse themselves and say, 'Although we don't dance, let it be as if we have done.' Then the formal speeches (*gego*) begin in earnest on the usual topics: the fulfilment of bridewealth obligations, the correct performance of custom on both sides, and other circumstances and obstacles surrounding the wedding.

Assuming all parties are present, the speeches follow a prescribed order, and to speak out of turn invites interruptions and even mockery. It implies that the speaker 'does not know his place'. First to speak is the bride's main representative, who asks the groom's side if all the promised prestations have been delivered. The groom's speaker excuses omissions and says that more will be brought at the visit one week after the wedding. Speeches go back and forth between the two men until the bride's side is satisfied. Then particular claimants have a chance to speak: first, the bride's father, who comments on the agreement just reached by his representative, and may add a quibble or a further demand. The groom's speaker again pleads patience, adopting a humble, conciliatory tone, explaining the groom's straitened circumstances. The father replies, and so it goes on until he is satisfied. Next come the bride's father's brothers, who may already have formed an agreement with the father, or they may demand more and block progress until they are satisfied. In turn, the second-, third-, and fourth-order wife-givers speak.

The marked inequality between the groom's party and the wife-givers is evident in the tone of the speeches. The groom's speaker responds to the vehement and sometimes threatening, or merely dismissive, shafts of the host with tact and eloquence, employing proverbs and citing fables to clinch a point. He 'takes on his back the burden of their speeches'. In return for this onerous but honourable task he expects the esteem of the groom and he receives a pig and a sum of gold. His role gives him the power to bless the couple and invoke good fortune on them (as in the traditional 'sword' ritual). Less than his due earns his ill will, which spells bad luck for the bride.

When everyone is more or less content, which may take some hours, each of the parties (*soroi tou, sovatö,* and *sanema maso-*

maso) performs in turn a square dance, *maena*, accompanied by singing. Mostly adolescents and young married people take part. The *maena* provide a light-hearted commentary on the themes of marriage alliance, enlivened with local references. The groom's side praises the greatness and magnanimity of the host, the beauty of the bride, and pleads for moderation of the claims. The bride's side flatters the groom (his hair is like a cock's comb, his nose is a beak) and chides him for concealing his fabulous wealth. A typical chorus goes:

Faya wa'alumana	It's a lie that you're poor
Faya wa'alö'ö	It's a lie that there's nothing.
Tölu ngaocu zugilö	You have 300 pigs in credit
Baero ziso barö mbatö	Besides those [tethered] below the floor.

Between each chorus the leader improvises witty lines on the characteristics or reputations of members of the other side. The *maena* was introduced from the Soliga area north of Gomo some twenty to thirty years ago. But similar rhymes have formed a traditional part of weddings as far back as memory goes. The group addressed in each *maena* is expected to show generosity, giving cash, betel, and cigarettes, which are waved about ostentatiously by the dancers. Each troupe has already been entertained at rehearsals to a meal by its convenor. The *maena* are sometimes followed by choral singing, again group by group. The same alliance themes are set to the stolid rhythm of European hymns, complete with part-singing and a conductor.

Once these distractions are over the serious business of the feast can be attended to. Two pigs are killed. As could be expected, the division provides a commentary on the relations between the various parties, and a description is therefore unavoidable.

The *bawi huku* ('law pig') or *bawi vangovalu* ('wedding pig') is provided by the groom for the wife-givers. Usually it is at least 5 *alisi* in size as there are many recipients. It is slaughtered and butchered by one of the bride's speakers or an elder and by the *sanema maso-maso* (usually her MB). The most prestigious portion, the lower jaw, is divided in four.

sanema maso-maso	*salawa* (bride's chief)
sanema hië dödö	*sovatö* (host)

Other portions are as follows: the *satua mbanua* (elders of bride's village) receive a portion running the whole length of the pig, called 'one back, one leg'. The *so'ono* (bride's father and close agnates) receive a similar portion. A small quantity is cooked and served to the bride's agnates. The rest is divided raw among the other wife-givers and the chief. The butchers receive one front leg each.

The *bawi daravatö* is the counter-prestation from the host to the groom's party. It is usually bigger than the wedding pig. It is split lengthwise and half is divided up raw among the guests. The groom's speaker(s) gets one back section. As with an *ovasa* pig the donor—in this case the host—claims a leg and receives back the lower jawbone as a trophy. The 'one leg, one back' portion, about one-quarter of the entire animal, goes to the groom, to be divided at home among his supporters (including his wife-takers, e.g. ZH, FZS). The rest is cooked for all the guests, including the other wife-givers. The lower jaw, heart, and viscera are served on a mountain of rice to the groom and his family. He eats off the same plate as his bride. Since the kind and size of portion denotes status, great care is taken in the division and only elders are trusted with the task. Each group sees to the division of its own portion.

The 'law pig' is so called because it is consumed by representatives of customary law in the village: the chief and elders (as well as by the wife-givers, who are not regarded as law-givers). As with the sacrifice of the 'origin' pigs at an *ovasa*, which I describe later, ritual superiority (of wife-givers) and social superiority (of the elders) are combined in the law pig. Wife-givers, direct and indirect, are symbolically united in the prestation.

The meaning of the term *bawi daravatö* is obscure. Etymologically it probably derives from *tara(i) mbatö*, meaning 'treading the floor-boards', and is therefore comparable to the prestation of that name (*fanarai mbatö*) which marks the groom's advent. Informants interpret it simply as 'pig for the guests'.

The meal is eaten without solemnity. The bride and groom, however, always appear embarrassed and reluctant to eat. For most of the day the bride remains out of sight in the rear part of the house. The groom sits through the dances and speeches shame-faced (*aila*) and disconsolate and does not appear to take any interest in the proceedings. When the meal is over, the bride (who has retired again) is prepared for her departure, and is handed over by her mother to the groom's mother in the bedroom. At this moment the *fanuyu mbö'ötö* gift of gold is given. The bride has to be dragged wailing from the room and her shrieks and lamentations cause a general commotion among the village women and girls. There is usually some last-minute stalling, and the groom's party, impatient to be off, may encourage the host with a song:

Alio-lio'ö, sovatö	Hurry up, hurry up, host
Akhömi nono nihalö	For night descends on the bride
Oya idanö ma'ötö	We have many rivers to cross
Oya mbanua ma'erogö	Many villages to leave behind.

At a big wedding the bride is carried aloft on a wooden throne around the village square and is then borne arduously and still weeping to the groom's village. Lagemann (1893) describes a custom in the north called 'lamenting the bride' (*lafe'e niovalu*). Some weeks before the wedding she visits the houses of various relatives and sings a dirge to each of them, bemoaning her fate and reproaching them for not saving her. Her bitterest words are reserved for her mother (ibid. 316):

> Oh, Mother! You are all unanimous in burying me, mother!
> You will not linger after burying me, mother.
> You love gold more than you love me, mother.
> You are mad that you don't retain me as a slave, mother.
> All your effort in raising me was in vain, mother.
> How, if you are ill, mother?
> Who will look after you, mother? . . .
> I'm like a chick without its mother
> When I go to strangers. Oh, mother! . . .
> I'm once more to you a much-abused child, mother.
> Without a thread of clothing that sticks to my body.
> When I own not a single piece of clothing, mother . . .
> You make me a slave of a slave-owner. . . .
> Therefore I grieve. Oh, mother!

Inarticulate suffering seems at last to find voice. Lagemann calls this a time of mourning, implying—we might say—that the bride is symbolically dead to her lineage. She attains a new status when she joins her husband's household. Suzuki (1959: 93) finds other evidence in the sources for an interpretation of the wedding rituals in the bride's village as a symbolic death of both the husband and the wife. There may be some truth in this—it is an aspect of all rites of passage in Nias, including feasts of merit.

The bride's escort (*samesao niha*) consists of female relatives, junior agnates, and others who did not receive pork at the feast. Her younger sister goes along and receives a pig for 'drawing out the bride' (*fondröni niha*). The bride reclaims a similar prestation later when the sister herself marries. Younger brothers may claim on arrival a 'roast sweet potato', a pig which counts as an instalment of their bridewealth portion. There is a formal reception (*famolaya*) by the groom's father who remained behind during the earlier feast. A pig is killed to 'entertain the bride' (*famolaya nono nihalö*) and the married couple are again faced with a huge antique plate loaded with rice and surmounted by the pig's lower jaw, heart, and belly. From the raw half, the bride's speakers get 'one back, one leg' and her father gets a similar portion, which is carried back to him later. A pig for the groom's bridewealth contributors is often killed at the same time. After the meal there are speeches concerning the prestations for the escort, then the latter group departs.

Schröder (1917: 271) records that in the far north of Nias, on arrival in the groom's house, the bride clasped the 'male spar' of the house and then the feet of the lineage ancestor figures, as a sign of her incorporation into the household (she in fact kept her natal clanship). The ancestors were shown the 'prize' or 'what the gold had purchased' and were told the bride's name. A boy was put on her lap and blessings were said so that she would have many descendants. Possibly some such rite of incorporation was practised in central Nias as well, but I do not have any evidence for this.

The last step in the sequence of events, and one which is common to all parts of Nias, is the 'return of the clothes' (*famuli nukha*), i.e. the gold regalia and clothes belonging to the girl's lineage which, in former times, she borrowed for the wedding. The visit, which takes place about a week after the wedding, is the occasion for bringing another instalment of bridewealth and for a final reckoning up of the debt. The bride's father slaughters a pig for the couple and may provide them with one or two pigs.

The wife-givers' counter-prestations are known collectively as *bövö*, or *fobövö moroi khö zatua* ('endowment from the [bride's] parents') in the case of her father's gifts. Some are solicitory gifts; others are a response to a gift from the groom and their size depends on the size of the preceding gift. For example, if the *sanema maso-maso* receives 3 *batu* or more, normally he would kill a pig of 2½ *alisi* for his *umönö* and would give him a pig of the same size to take away: a total value of 1 *batu*. There are also gifts from the bride's side to the speakers and the witnesses to the promises extracted from the groom. In general it can be said that the actual delivery of counter-prestations tends to vary from case to case in a way that bridewealth prestations do not. There are omissions and substitutions and the names of the some of the gifts are no longer stable. This is partly due to the nature of the affinal relation: wife-givers endow the couple in a spirit of generosity rather than indebtedness; their gifts cannot be demanded and there is no public reckoning such as for bridewealth.

Exchange remains a prominent, lifelong aspect of the alliance, but the last exchange which is considered to be an integral part of bridewealth takes place after the birth of the first son and first daughter. The couple visit the wife's father to inform him of the birth, bringing pigs worth 3 *batu* for a boy, and 2 *batu* for a girl. These prestations are called the 'debt for the child' (*ömö nono*). They obviously acknowledge the transfer of rights *in genetricem* in the bride—something which is otherwise lacking from the earlier gifts. It is interesting to note that if the woman is barren she cannot be returned and no bridewealth can be reclaimed. The separation in time which makes the payment of the 'debt for the child' dependent on the actual birth of children accords with this separate evaluation of the various roles of a wife. The wife's father reciprocates with a 'sow for the child', and an assortment of pots and pans: the 'pot for the child'. If he is a village elder he is expected to kill a pig for his guests.

I have tried in this chapter to show exactly how marriage payments are conceived and how they are both constrained and constraining. This has necessitated going into detail over the meaning of particular prestations and setting them in their precise sociological context— something which tends to be omitted from many accounts of exchange, giving the impression of a 'custom-bound' adherence to ancestral decrees or an entirely symbolic world where people never make decisions or worry about the implications of their actions.

Instead of supporting my analysis with hypothetical examples where everything goes like clockwork (which probably never happens anyway), it is perhaps more instructive and revealing of the operative principles and values to consider an extreme case where custom was flouted and everything was done wrong. Here we see as it were the reverse weave of the tapestry, with the joins and mistakes visible, the false starts and patchings up. This 'negative case' sums up better than a mere repetition of the argument many of the points made in the foregoing chapters.

Case 3: The wedding of Yani Bu'ulölö of Sifalagö and Uco Laia of Hiligewo (Dec. 1987)

Yani is the only daughter of a man belonging to the chief's clan but ambiguously placed within it. Ama Yani is connected five generations back to the chief's line and so has no claim to noble birth. Since there is no longer any lineage ritual the bounds of the lineage are not clearly defined and association with the chief or other prominent members depends, for marginal figures, on active participation in their ventures. Ama Yani has no part in anyone else's business as a contributor, and his whole family has a reputation for laziness and thieving. (Despite its bad name it was one of the few houses from which I could regularly hear laughter in the evenings.) His agnates suspect him of damaging their crops, cutting down banana stems out of spite, and petty theft. Nevertheless, his house is a crucial dropping-in place in the village, a sort of neutral ground where members of different factions call to chew betel (their own) in his taciturn, cussed company. Perhaps this is due to his marginality and his detachment from the web of debt-relations in which everyone else is enveloped. He neither gives anything to callers nor expects anything from them.

Yani was betrothed two years ago to an agnate of the chief of Hiligewo, a village one hour upstream from Sifalagö. Her betrothed was an acknowledged good-for-nothing, his father a ruthless and aggressive man with a reputation for sorcery. Neither side could therefore regard the other as a good prospect. But a flirtation had been discovered and Yani's mother arranged a betrothal. She was afraid that her daughter would be ruined and this led her to take the extremely unusual step of making the first approach. A bridewealth of 30 batu was provisionally agreed. When the flirtation was again becoming talked about, and Yani was thought likely to run away with the man, her mother pressed for the wedding to go ahead. There was no 'counting of the gold'—the formalities were simply omitted and one evening the groom came with nine pigs and took her away 'in the dark', as it was related later. 'It was a quick sale,' as one village elder put it. People in Sifalagö understood the mother's concern, but she should have been kept under control by her husband and not allowed to disgrace him by 'running after the groom'. As for the girl, her chastity was supposed to be under the protection of the whole lineage, or at least those agnates who would lose most by a hasty wedding. It was believed that the groom had put a love charm (*fokasi*) on Yani and had worked magic to win her mother's sympathy (literally 'softened her heart'). This is a common explanation of unsolicited approaches by a woman, but it was given particular credence because of the reputation of the groom and his father.

Ama Yani appointed two experienced elders of his own clan but a different lineage to be his representatives. My understanding of the events I witnessed is largely derived from conversations with them. They went to the groom's village with the difficult task of salvaging a bridewealth and managed to obtain a promise to deliver a further 20 *batu*, including 2 *batu* gold. Encouraged by the groom's compliance, Ama Yani subsequently increased his demand to 40 *batu*, including 6 *batu* gold, thereby undermining the credibility of his speakers and provoking the groom's side to challenge him. At this point the speakers resigned. Ama Yani then appointed an agnate from his own lineage, a respected headmaster of the school in Hiligewo, and therefore ideal as an intermediary. Unfortunately Ama Rosa lacked the oratorical skills and authority of the previous negotiators and this was crucial in the failure to achieve a settlement. He extracted a promise to bring 23 pigs for the wedding feast which was fixed for one month after the bride had been taken. But the promise could not be relied upon. Ama Yani had opened himself to exploitation by reversing the usual roles of courter and courted and by allowing the bride to be taken away without waiting for the bulk of the bridewealth to be delivered. In dealing with an untrustworthy or intransigent *soroi tou*, the wife-givers' withholding of the bride is their ultimate negotiating tactic. It nearly always works because the *soroi tou* are deeply ashamed to return home empty-handed, so they commit themselves to give extra pigs. Elders are ready to step in and loan them pigs at interest before witnesses. In the event, nobody knew how much the groom's party would bring. When they finally arrived they brought ten smallish pigs: an insult. To rub in their advantage (or as some said, more sympathetically, to hide the bridewealth pigs), they arrived late—so late that it was already dark and some of the bride's agnates had wandered off home. Their demeanour was wary and tight-lipped. When negotiations falter and offence has been given, violence easily breaks out. The groom's father had come along but clearly this was not out of respect. They had not come 'to kneel', as bride-takers are supposed to do. Most of the speeches came from the bride's agnates, especially two men who are themselves powerful and ruthless figures in Sifalagö. Ama Yani was caught between the anger and scorn of these men and the intransigence of the affines. When he was challenged to say where his agnates' portions were going to come from he retreated to the back of the house, calling out gruffly that it was the responsibility of Ama Rosa to ensure the fulfilment of the promised pigs. Ama Rosa merely shrugged and remained silent. He was also restricted by his position as a 'settler' in the groom's village and his fear of incurring their resentment. Both he and Ama Yani were afraid to confront the groom's father, fearing his sorcery. After a conciliatory speech by the groom's speaker, it was decided to beat the gong in official welcome—an hour after their arrival. The senior agnates protested at this. 'It is a token of gladness, and who here is glad?' After the gongs were beaten the bride's mother and FBW proclaimed the greetings, the latter with unconscious irony which raised a few smiles: 'Welcome, you who are versed in custom!' The speeches continued, with Ama Yani's agnates pushing him to a confrontation. 'Look at what's down there below the floor. Is that your tribute? Is that your glory? If you're satisfied with that then why are you delaying the slaughter of the wedding pig?' The form of oratory, where the speaker addresses a respondent from his own group, allows the expression of anger without directing it at the intended audience. The groom's party were thus able to sit quietly like spectators at a contest between members of the other side, as speakers put forward personal claims and challenged Ama Yani to action. When these appeared to have no effect, one speaker challenged the *soroi tou* directly: 'Am I nothing that I get nothing? Have you come here to earn our blessing or our curse? [outraged mutterings] You who are of noble birth, how can you come here in shame like poor people with ten small pigs to offer.' In reply, the groom's speaker told the fable of the great feaster and titled elder Nine Spans who was travelling far from home. One night he came to a village and asked to be put up. 'Who is it?', they asked. 'Nine Spans', he replied. 'We are poor people with a small house and cannot accommodate you,' they said. He tried another house and was again refused. When he knocked at a third house he told them his childhood name—As big as a rat—and was immediately welcomed in. The meaning of the fable, which he did not bother to elaborate as all understood it, was that although the groom was of noble descent and his father bore a title, they had come humbly in accordance with their reduced circumstances and thus hoped that their meagre offering would be accepted.

Next, debate turned on the interpretation of the promised sums— whether the figure of 23 referred to *batu* or pigs, and whether individual claims, or named prestations were to be added together or a grand total subdivided. The groom's party claimed that the latter method had already been agreed, so they could not be held responsible if Ama Yani left out his agnates.

It was interesting that the closest agnates did not speak. One of them explained to me that it was inappropriate and shaming for them to argue for more since Ama Yani had already shown his disregard of them by giving them a tiny proportion of the pigs already delivered. To press a demand implies the ability and likelihood of being satisfied, and secondly it depends on a certain mutual respect, which Ama Yani had forfeited. The sanction for his neglect was that when his teenage sons come to marry, they cannot count on contributions from these disgruntled agnates. Remoter agnates, who can expect less of the bridewealth automatically, need to assert their claims. One of them even made the absurd claim (unchallenged) that he had paid the bridewealth of Ama Yani, a man ten years his senior.

Speeches continued in this way with the agnates' anger met by intransigence from the affines, until Ama Yani emerged dramatically from the back and shouted a curse: 'May you be struck down by filth!' The groom's party, stunned and suddenly vulnerable, dared not reply. Other guests tittered nervously. Such curses had not been uttered for many years and no one knew quite what should happen next. Ama Rosa, the bride's negotiator, thinking the curse was directed at him, sprang up and renounced his portion, pointing to heaven and inviting God to strike him down if he kept it. It now seemed impossible that the wedding pig should be eaten. It was 'a mockery of custom' and the correct procedure. However, the senior men who had been most outspoken and were half-delighted with this outrage forced Ama Yani to go ahead, threatening that the curse would otherwise rebound on him and 'what we don't eat tonight will be eaten by the Devil.' The groom's party at this point made a speech of conciliation and promised to fulfil a reasonable figure. Ama Yani killed a guest pig of 4 *alisi* and a wedding pig of 1 *alisi*, a huge disparity which further inflamed the company. As a gesture of conciliation, the groom's father offered to combine opposite halves of the two pigs. Ama Rosa refused to perform the negotiator's duty of butchering the wedding pig, since it was contaminated with a curse. To assuage the tempers of the agnates, short-measured in the pork division, the wedding pig was subsequently reclassified as a 'witness pig': a prestation to the agnates as witnesses and guarantors of the groom's latest promise.

Several lessons can be drawn from this case. The negotiating positions of the two sides depend on a number of premises: the inequality of affines, which is disrupted if the wife-givers make any solicitory approaches; the chastity of the bride, which leaves open the option of withdrawing; the delaying of her removal until the bridewealth is in; the independence of the bride's speaker from obligations or ties to the groom's party; the relations among members of the bride's lineage—of solidarity, patronage, and reciprocity (any perceived weaknesses will be exploited by the groom's party). The case shows as well that a man's success in customary dealings cannot be placed in the hands of others. Ultimately it depends on his own judgement, his abilities, and strength of character. The negotiators and agnates can only give him advice, but their views are not disinterested. Ama Yani failed to capitalize on his side's advantages: the groom's bad character, which meant that he would not easily find an acceptable wife; both sides' attachment to chiefly lineages, which forces up the bridewealth; the large number of claimants in Sifalagö. Among his lineage mates are several of the strongest and most unyielding speakers in the district who would have been more than a match for the groom's men. Instead he chose a mild and 'good' man. As a result he became the victim not only of the affines, but of his own wolfish agnates. He is blamed for lack of authority in his own family (dominated by his wife), greediness and inconstancy (raising the bridewealth total), disregard of formal procedure, inability to play the host and give speeches, disloyalty to his lineage, and blighting his sons' bridewealth prospects.

7
Other Types of Union

This chapter deals with variants of the standard marriage alliance, and other types of union, both approved and illicit.

1 Widow Remarriage

When a wife dies it is usual for a man to remarry as soon as he can afford it. Without a wife he is socially at a loss: unable to serve guests, and totally dependent on relatives for his food and welfare. In the main cluster of hamlets in Sifalagö I knew of no widowers who had been without a wife for more than a couple of years. Even elderly men remarry, taking a wife who may be a generation or more younger.

In contrast, there are a number of widows in the village who, for various reasons, have not remarried. These are referred to as *lakha mbanua* ('village widows')—so called because they 'belong to the village'. Anyone in the village can call on them informally and request betel. A good deal of gossip is circulated in this way. Living next door to an old widow, and with an interconnecting door, I was often present at these cosy chats and was able to obtain much 'off-the-record' information.

Widows are objects of sympathy, though not of charity, and are nominally under the care of the village. In reality they receive little or no help from anyone, and several live alone or with a grandchild for company, in remote huts, barely surviving in great poverty. Others live with their sons, but they are not much better off. They are denied all but the necessities and continue working virtually until they die.

It is usual for a widow who is not yet past childbearing age to remarry, either within her husband's lineage or outside it. If she has not yet borne sons she may be obliged to remarry. But a woman of strong character may prefer to remain as the guardian of her children and to replace her husband as head of the family. In such a case she is 'made an [honorary] male' (*labali'ö ira matua ia*). This does not involve changing her natal clan—indeed rights in a kins-woman are never entirely ceded to her husband's lineage. Her position is confirmed at a small feast to which the village chief and elders are invited as representatives of customary law. Her father is given a pig by her deceased husband's agnates, partly in compensa-tion for the pigs he would have received had she remarried, partly to signify his 'accepting responsibility' in an ensuing dispute if she is found to be unchaste. She is henceforth the *uvu matua* of her husband's lineage. This is an archaism which defies literal translation and could not readily be explained by informants. *Uvu* means here something like 'senior relative'; *matua* means 'male'. I suggest the term means something like 'figurehead' of the lineage. This inter-pretation is supported by the fact that a widow of an important man who had been confirmed in this role could be referred to as the *azu nuvu* of her dead husband's lineage. *Azu nuvu* were the wooden ancestor figures of the lineage (*azu* means 'idol'; *nuvu*, from *uvu*, means 'senior relative'). A widow can thus become a respected senior person in the lineage house. Once confirmed in this role she can receive prestige payments due to her husband, and she can have pigs raised for her by others, like any enterprising man. Within living memory, two widows who had married into the chief's line actually staged feasts of merit in their own names. Such great ladies earned the title of *ina mbanua* ('mother of the village').

This exalted status, now rarely if ever achieved, is remote from the lot of the average woman. In most cases, a woman below middle age is quickly remarried to an agnate of her deceased husband—usually his brother or a son by another woman. Such a man is called a *sangai lakha* ('one who takes [marries] a widow'), and the institu-tion of widow-inheritance is called by this same term or *folakha* (roughly: to 'endow with a widow'). *Lakha* means, besides 'widow', 'agnate's wife' or, reciprocally, 'husband's agnate' of the same genealogical level, and it can be used in a situation in which the husband in question is still alive; the implication being that one of his agnates will marry his widow when he dies. In the literature on south Nias (Marschall 1976: 134; La'iya 1980: 64) *lakha* appears as a relationship term. In central Nias I heard the word used in this way only in connection with widow-inheritance. Other terms such as *donga ga'a* ('elder brother's wife') would ordinarily be used to refer to the relationship. I was told that if a woman is widowed before she has had children she may still be referred to as an *ono alave* ('girl') rather than as *lakha*, which has the flavour of 'matron', and she can be remarried with full bridewealth.

The word *lakha* appears to be connected etymologically to words referring to what is prohibited or cursed: *salakha, lakha-lakha*, which is consistent with the ban on widow-inheritance reported in parts of south Nias (at least in the location Marschall studied).[1] My informants denied categorically that it had these connotations for them. In the local interpretation of the word, *lakha* is synonymous with *ovöliwa*, 'purchase' (from *böli*). The widow belongs to her husband's lineage because bridewealth (*böli niha*) has been paid for her. She is remarried to his agnate by payment of a supplement of 2–6 *batu* to the original wife-givers. This prestation is called *tohu davere*, literally 'extension of the clothes-line'. The widow is, as my informant put it, analogous to used clothes hung out on the line, in comparison with a virgin bride. The 'extension' refers to the continuation of the original bridewealth. One of the reasons why widows are passed on in this way instead of being married out is precisely because the major sum has been paid and that 'it would be a pity to waste it'. The woman is married out if there is no one in the lineage who wants to marry her. Nowadays, when polygyny is outlawed by the Church, a widow is more likely to marry out than formerly was the case.

A widow is said to be 'half-price', in other words about 12 *batu*. (It is noticeable how the language of buying and selling is more blatant in the marriage of a widow than of a girl, consistent with the lack of formality.) A round total is agreed for the bridewealth, rather than a stipulation of prestations. Half of the total goes to the lineage of her deceased husband; the other half goes to her agnates. It is up to the latter how much they give to the indirect wife-givers (i.e. her MB, etc.). The woman's sons remain in their lineage home, as do any daughters who are marriageable. They are looked after by their aunts and uncles. Young daughters may be divided between

---

[1] Sources differ on practices in south Nias. Marschall (1976: 133–4) says that in Maenamölö district a wife is counted as one of her husband's clan, even though she retains her own clan name. Consequently it is impossible for a widow to marry her deceased husband's brother. She should remarry into a different clan and village. La'iya (1980: 53), a native of Botohili, writes that marriage with HB is possible but not obligatory. Tohene'asi district appears similar to the central Nias pattern, according to my enquiries.

the lineage home and the mother's new home. Rights in the daughters remain, in any case, with their natal lineage, which expects to garner most of the bridewealth. A woman 'cannot give her daughter in marriage', and she can only claim the portion due to her for the 'cost of bringing up' the girl, i.e. the *labusö*. However, there is some flexibility in arrangements. Where a daughter is brought up in the home of an unrelated stepfather, it may be difficult for her agnates to assert their bridewealth claims. Such a case was that of Ina Duho, who was born in Orahili. When her father died and there was no one ready to step into his place, her mother remarried in Tuhegewo, a village seven miles away. Rights in the daughter effectively were lost, and when Ina Duho was given in marriage by her stepfather, he received the lion's share of her bridewealth, refusing to endow her true agnates since they had 'neglected' her.

It is said that a wise young man whose father has died will oppose the remarriage of his mother to one of his agnates. It would be a source of shame for him, implying he is unable to take over from his father as head of the family, and involving an economic loss in favour of the usurper. He might even threaten to kill the agnate who intends marriage, even if the man is his senior and his classificatory father. Probably behind such cases (I knew of none directly) lies a fear that the son's inheritance will pass to his FB. A threat is enough to deter the candidate.

It was quite common for a son to inherit a wife of his father, a woman whom he addressed as *ina*, 'mother' (the term of reference, *ina sia'a/sakhi*, means 'elder/younger mother'). Since the Bible does not apparently distinguish between classificatory and actual mother, the prohibition of mother–son marriage is held by dogmatic Christians to apply to all women addressed as *ina*. Most people do not take this extension of the prohibition very seriously, though it is sometimes used by young men, who may be indifferent Christians, as an excuse for not marrying an *ina*.

It is also possible to marry the widow of a son. In lineages where several instances of widow-inheritance have taken place within the lifetime of an individual the structure of relations within the localized lineage can become quite complicated with alternative means of tracing cognatic relations among the members. This contrasts with the relatively unambiguous tracing of relations among agnates, as the following example shows.

Example 1

Let us consider the career of Barasi, a woman who had three husbands from the same lineage. She comes from the Little Laia subclan in Hilimböe, as do the other women mentioned below who have married into the lineage (see Fig. 7.1).

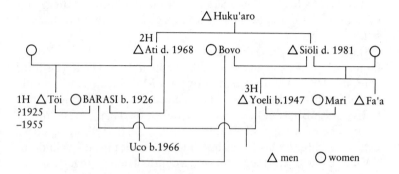

FIG. 7.1. Widow-inheritance within a lineage segment

1. Her first husband was Töi, of the Great Laia subclan in Sifalagö. The bridewealth was 45 *batu*. He died in 1955 having fathered two children by her.

2. She was remarried to her husband's father, Ati, in 1959, when Ati's wife died. Ati had paid most of Barasi's original bridewealth, which gave him priority over the claims of other agnates to her. He now paid a supplement of 3 *batu* to the wife-givers. She bore him two children before he died in 1968.

3. She was immediately passed on to Ati's yBS, Yoeli, then a youth of 19, over 40 years younger than her last husband. He was the closest unmarried man. A supplement of 6 *batu* was paid. Yoeli did not like the arrangement since she was 'like his mother'. At this time she was already over forty and had given birth many times. Nevertheless he had two children by her. Before marrying he called her 'elder brother's wife', tracing the relation through his cousin, Töi, her first husband. This implied that they were of the same generation.

In 1977 Yoeli decided to take a second wife. The reasons he gave were that Barasi could no longer bear children and that he could no longer sleep with an old woman. He married a girl from Hilimböe, an agnate of Barasi, and paid full bridewealth. About three years later he was semi-officially separated from his first wife, Barasi. There could be no divorce, since there were no grounds for one. But as a respectable church-goer he could not be a practising polygamist. So at a meeting with church elders (ratified with a meal) Barasi was reclassified as his 'mother'. She remains in the house as the senior woman. His children by the two women call each other brother and sister.

Barasi was not the only widow to remarry in the lineage. Yoeli's father, when already an old man, had married a girl of 15 (his third wife) in 1979 and had a daughter by her. When he died in 1981 only half of the 30 *batu* bridewealth had been paid. The girl was remarried to Uco, his eBS, (i.e. the son of Ati and Barasi) age 18. The rest of the bridewealth was paid off at their wedding. Uco is bringing up his wife's daughter by his FB as his child along with his own children.

Thus in one lineage segment with a depth of only four generations there are three instances of widow-inheritance. The unions are with FyBW, FeBW, and SW. Widow remarriage may involve a discrepancy of one or more genealogical levels between the partners and one or more generations. This obviously leads to complications in the definition of roles in the household and an ambiguity in the determination of kin terms (see Needham 1974). It is worth looking briefly at how the problem is solved in this instance since all the relevant facts have been presented.

Yoeli called Bovo (his father's third wife) *ina sakhi* ('younger mother') even though she was 15 years his junior. When she remarried Uco, Yoeli's FeBSy (whom he calls *akhi*, 'younger brother'), he henceforth called her *donga nakhi* ('younger brother's wife'), or simply *akhi* ('younger sister'). Thus, in this instance, the change of category following a remarriage happened to conform to age group (age-wise Bovo is much more like a sister than a mother to Yoeli). By the same remarriage, Uco was able to reclassify his WD (= FyBD) as *ono* ('child'), instead of *akhi*, again consistent with relative age. But these corrections are purely accidental. Inconsistencies between age and category are just as likely to be found, as are inconsistencies of usage between siblings. Take the case of Fa'a, Yoeli's younger brother. He calls Barasi *donga ga'a* ('elder brother's wife'), tracing the relation through her first husband, his classificatory eB. She happens to be his actual eBW, but since this marriage is no longer active, his eB vacillates between calling her 'mother' and 'elder sister'.

As a general rule category predominates over age: that is to say, a wide discrepancy between age and category is allowed to subsist. Inconsistencies between categories are tolerated. But remarriage tends to readjust categories, narrowing the discrepancy with age. An exception in which category yields place to age is when a father inherits his son's wife. The other sons would not begin calling her *ina sakhi* ('younger mother') if she belonged to their generation. They would simply continue to call her 'elder' or 'younger sister', tracing the relation through her first marriage. A further exception is when the roles of the persons are clearly at odds with their classification, e.g. when someone acts *in loco parentis* he will be addressed as 'father', 'younger father', or at the very least 'elder brother'. Even if genealogically he is BS, for example, it would be inappropriate to call him so. Precise genealogical links are not disguised or forgotten because of such terminological revisions.

Kelly (1974: 72–4, 106 ff.) describes a system among the Etoro of New Guinea in which agnatic links are revised to conform with closer consanguineous links deriving from leviratic marriage. The internal structure of the lineage or patriline is thus dependent on matrilateral kinship. Clearly, in the Nias case no such revision is involved: the strict patrilineal framework is maintained in all circumstances, in conformity with the rigid patriliny of descent group recruitment, succession, and inheritance.

The classic instances of widow-inheritance described by Radcliffe-Brown and his collaborators, in which a widow is passed on to a younger brother, are held to exemplify 'the unity of the sibling group' (1950: 64). In the examples described above it would seem to be the principle of the 'unity of the lineage group' which is involved. But does this not contradict my earlier argument that the structure of alliance opposes an individual wife-taker to a group of wife-givers? It appears that the whole lineage is a wife-taker, and it is only a matter of secondary importance who is the actual husband. Such an interpretation would be incorrect for the following reasons. First, there is a supplementary prestation paid to the wife-givers, and a meal at which a 'law pig' is killed. It is a wedding, albeit on a reduced scale, implying a real transfer and therefore leading to a reclassification of the parties, not merely a shift of emphasis within an unchanging alliance. WF and DH are henceforth *matua* and *umönö* to each other (where previously they were 'brother's *matua*'/ 'brother of *umönö*'). The groom takes on a new set of obligations towards his WF which none of his brothers share. Agnates of a bridegroom have a stake in his marriage as sponsors (actually, for the most part, lenders); but then so do neighbours and wife-takers of the lineage. They cannot thereby be considered as joint holders of rights in the bride, or as collective wife-takers. Their part in sponsoring the original marriage is a matter of internal lineage politics; it does not concern the wife-givers. But the choice of who shall marry the widow is both a matter of internal politics (as with inheritance of property) and also of alliance relations. It is not necessary therefore to invoke an abstract principle of lineage solidarity. Alliance solidarity is just as much involved. In fact the arrangement suits everyone: often it is not easy to marry off a widow outside the lineage; the alliance is disturbed as little as possible; the man's lineage saves on bridewealth; the children by the first marriage remain in the lineage household.

If we look carefully at cases of widow-inheritance, it usually appears that the widow is passed to the nearest, most senior, unmarried agnate of the deceased man. In the absence of such a candidate (or passing over him) the widow may be married polygamously to another agnate. The choice between these two options may perhaps depend on the degree of fragmentation of the lineage. An independent lineage segment may prefer to keep its women at all costs rather than endow a related segment. But I doubt if a general pattern can be established here. The gift of a widow with four children to look after is not perceived as an unequivocal blessing. It is as much a transfer of responsibility.

Widow-inheritance needs to be seen, then, in terms of two aspects: alliance on the one hand, and inheritance or succession within the lineage on the other. The obvious complicating factor is that the direct heirs of a man are his adult sons, who are debarred from inheriting their mother.

Example 2

Ruti had a son and a daughter by her first husband. She was about 35 when he died. There were no surviving brothers to marry her or to support her as a 'confirmed widow'. Her husband's lineage segment (B4) had already divided its land. This meant that the widow would pass to an agnate who was not an heir or a co-parcener of her husband's property. There were no unmarried men among his FBS, so she was given to the oldest unmarried man among his FBSS, Ama Yuliati, a man who called her 'mother' (as wife of a +1 agnate). In this way one minor segment of a lineage (represented only by her infant son) became the benefactor of another. In a sense there was no alternative. No outsiders wanted her; neither did the lineage want her son to be done out of his land in a struggle with an alien adoptive father. The boy lived with his mother and her young husband until he was old enough to marry. The husband helped to pay his bridewealth, thus reciprocating the transfer of the boy's mother.

Marriage to a widow does not win prestige. It saves on bridewealth, and saving never won anybody prestige in Nias. Even so it is and was practised among leading lineages, which could afford virgin brides for all their members, as well as among ordinary men.

2 Polygyny

The custom of widow-inheritance in central Nias is complementary to, if not actually conducive to, polygyny in two respects.

1. Old widows are difficult to marry off; young widows are an asset which the lineage does not want to lose. It follows that if there are no unmarried men in the lineage (or if married brothers claim priority over unmarried remoter agnates), polygyny results.

2. The disregard of an age discrepancy between partners makes it likely that a youth who inherits an older widow will want to take a second wife—in order to bear him more children, because of personal preference for youth over age, and to win the prestige that goes with paying a full bridewealth.

Most of the cases of polygyny in the village have been, as a matter of fact, a result of widow-inheritance.

However, polygyny in the sense of successive marriages is virtually the norm, since no independent man can survive materially or socially without a wife. The premature death or barrenness of a wife is just bad luck. Nothing can be reclaimed by the bereaved or childless husband from his wife-giver. The payment of bridewealth for a wife does not entitle one to rights in her sister.

If a man marries the sister of his deceased wife he has to pay full bridewealth. This type of union has the advantages of an alliance renewal. The Church now forbids such unions since a man calls his WZ 'sister' and 'the Bible says one cannot marry one's sister'. Sororal polygyny is occasionally found but it is poorly regarded and attracts mockery. It is assumed the man seduced or raped his wife's sister. For this reason adolescent girls are not allowed to reside with their married sisters.

In most cases of simultaneous polygyny the wives come from different backgrounds and are acquired over a wide span of years. Priority among wives theoretically goes to the first, who is the 'one who shares her husband's secrets', the mother of his successor, his consort at feasts of merit, and so on. She is the 'trunk wife' (*tuho wo'omo*) in contrast to secondary wives, (*k*)*erua*. The latter word probably derives from *dua* ('two').[2] It is somewhat pejorative in tone; and to call someone the 'son by a second(ary) wife' (*ono ba gerua*) is a definite slur, likely to lead to violence, since it may imply in practice an inferior claim to the inheritance. (No disadvantage or inferiority attaches to second wives or their children in serial polygyny, and they are not referred to as *erua*.) Despite the general cultural emphasis given to seniority, there is a countervailing recognition of merit, which in many cases predominates. This applies equally to male successors as to co-wives. Matanihela, the chief's father, had five wives and it was the fourth who always took precedence.

Given this flexibility or ambiguity in arrangements, there is considerable scope for rivalry between the wives, and a polygamous household is often said to be a domestic hell. Each wife competes for the favours of her husband. The respective wife-givers are alert to any slight or neglect of their daughters. The husband is expected to sleep with each wife on successive nights, even if he does nothing with his oldest wife.

The domestic arrangements were traditionally as follows (nowadays polygyny is less common and more variable in form). Each wife had her own small bedroom and would take it in turns to use the kitchen. She would cook for and look after her own children, providing for them with sweet potatoes and cassava grown in her

---

[2] Snouck Hurgronje, in *Het Gajoland*, p. 277, gives the following cognate Gayo words: *roa* = two, *keroa* = second, *bekeroa* = to be polygynous (cited in Schröder 1917: 260). The Nias word for two, *dua*, becomes *rua* in 22, 32, etc.

own gardens. She cultivated rice and raised pigs for her husband. Since pork and rice are festive food, they were usually eaten communally by the whole household. However, the wife responsible for a particular pig could expect a bigger share of it when it was slaughtered. And her sons might benefit from the prestations due to her (e.g. in bridewealth) to the exclusion of their half-brothers.

The land worked by each wife was carefully demarcated. If the wives got on well they might combine in weeding. But since each wife farmed her own plot the husband knew exactly how much each produced. He would redistribute the total harvest among his wives. He would show favouritism towards his most diligent and productive wife, perhaps giving her precedence over the co-wives. If a wife was lazy and unproductive he would beat her. To some extent, then, the wives were (and still are) like labourers managed by their husband and competing for advantage.

Merit in a wife therefore means above all diligence. The favoured, usually most productive, wife would get a bigger share of her husband's prestige payments (*urakha*) from feasts of merit. The priority of wives could have important consequences for the children, especially regarding land tenure (see Sect. 7 of Ch. 2).

When a man took a second wife, there was a ritual in which the wives were sworn to co-operation and domestic harmony beneath a roughly carved figurine called an *azu wama'erua* ('idol/figurine of polygyny'). If they broke their promise, the *azu* would make them mad.

3 Uxorilocal Marriage

In the standard form of marriage—entailing payment of full bride-wealth and patrilocal residence—alliance status and social status are in principle separate. Alliance partners are usually roughly equal in rank. A wife-taker's inferiority is largely confined to formal interactions marked by reciprocal exchanges in which some honour accrues to each side. In uxorilocal marriage this inequality has a different basis. Not only does the groom become a dependent member of his father-in-law's household, and subservient in a practical way, but in so doing he loses (or fails to acquire) a voice in village affairs which is the privilege of the independent married man.[3] In other words his affinal position involves a demotion in society as a whole.

One must distinguish between this arrangement and bride service, in which a proportion of the bridewealth (e.g. 6 *batu*) is paid off by labour in the fields of the father-in-law. In bride service the groom may continue to live at home and there is no loss of status.[4] A son-in-law who has paid a low bridewealth is expected occasionally to help his in-laws in particular tasks, such as building, repairs, some agricultural work. This is a simple substitution of labour for bride-wealth. The son-in-law nevertheless has full rights in his wife's labour. In the case of uxorilocal marriage the wife-giver not only withholds these rights, he acquires rights in the groom's labour. It is this reversal which is particularly demeaning in Nias eyes. It contra-dicts the ideology of affinal exchange, in which part of bridewealth is explicitly a compensation to wife-givers for the loss of the bride's labour. The corresponding reduction in bridewealth for uxorilocal marriage cannot make up for the groom's loss of prestige. Moreover, his labour pays off the bridewealth debt at an exploitative rate of one or two *batu* annually—much less than he produces.

The groom is referred to as his father-in-law's 'fetcher of wood' or his *enoni* (one who does work or errands for others). These epithets have undignified connotations. A household slave would formerly be referred to in this way, as would an adopted poor relation who is a kind of servant. Without being the same in essence, there are nevertheless similar characteristics in these roles which we might define as 'exploited dependant in a pseudo-kinship relation'.[5] The uxorilocal son-in-law is termed *ono yomo*, a 'child in the house' and he is sometimes said to be 'like a son' to his WF. In fact, although he is expected to show filial piety he does not have a son's rights. His

[3] Patrilocally married sons are not considered as dependants of their father. They are under no obligation to remain and can set up a new house or move temporarily to a field hut if they wish. Each married couple in the lineage house is considered as an independent unit or family (*ngambatö*) even if resources are pooled.

[4] Marschall (1976: 121) reports that in south Nias it is usual for a betrothed youth to work in the fields of his prospective father-in-law. Schröder (1917: 261, 265) writes that the suitor may live in the girl's house after the engagement, giving him a chance to observe her and make sure of his choice. Schröder contrasts this arrangement with the northern practice of strict avoidance between the engaged partners.

[5] Leach (1954: 160) has remarked (of a strikingly similar society) that the position of a Kachin slave or permanent debtor to a chief 'resembled that of an adopted son or bastard of the chief, or even more perhaps that of a poor son-in-law working to earn his bride'.

position is somewhat ambiguous (as in some cases of adoption), varying according to circumstances. If the bride has no brothers he may indeed be treated more like a son and he can acquire a limited amount of property if it belongs solely to the WF. Otherwise everything goes to the WFB. Other factors affecting the quality of the relation and its public evaluation are whether the groom is an orphan or has the backing of agnates, how much bridewealth has been paid and how much promised (in labour or in kind), and whether the term of residence is indefinite. My example below shows that the similar circumstances attending adoption and uxori-local marriage make for an easy transition between the two, and in most of the cases I know this is what has happened.

Since uxorilocal marriage is devalued, there is no neutral term available to refer to it. It is impolite to draw attention to a son-in-law's dependent status. One can simply say 'he's gone to his father-in-law's' (*mo iagö matuania*), but this can refer equally to a case of a properly married man moving to the village or house of his WF. This sometimes happens after an irreconcilable dispute with agnates. More commonly, a man moves to, or near to, his in-laws in order to use their land. (I do not know of a case of moving to one's wife-takers'.) This type of temporary move is quite common, especially in the early years of marriage. It does not imply losing rights in the natal village. A definite move (e.g. following a dispute) makes one a political dependant of one's wife-giver. Assuming bridewealth had been paid the son-in-law would not be in the subservient position of an *ono yomo*, but as a stranger he would not have the right to own land, and lacking agnates he would depend on his affines for backing in disputes. Thus he is socially disadvantaged for different reasons.[6]

We therefore have to distinguish between bride service, uxori-locality following standard marriage, and uxorilocality involving remission of bridewealth and incorporation into the wife-giver's household. In none of these is there a change in the principle of patrilineal descent. The child belongs from birth to its father's clan with full rights in lineage property.

The situation of the married-in son-in-law is unfavourable but not hopeless. In most cases after several years the debt is paid off or is arbitrarily cancelled. Anything he contributes to his *matua*'s feasts

---

[6] See comments on the political alliances of settlers in Ch. 3.

of merit or other enterprises is deducted from the tally. In cases where the WF dies, the son-in-law stays and provides for his WM until his debts are paid. If there are no sons to take charge of the land worked by the WF, the son-in-law may possess it for as long as he remains in the village. If he moves, it reverts to the agnatic heirs. This same rule applies in the case of a settler. A schoolmaster came twenty-five years ago to Sifalagö and married an only child, agnate of the chief. If he is transferred by the government to another school, his children, who have grown up in Sifalagö, lose all rights in the land.

The social devaluation of the uxorilocal husband ceases when he sets up on his own. Some men who begin humbly in this way are 'emancipated' and go on to attain high rank. An initially small-scale, almost private and informal arrangement between the parties can later be put on an alliance footing, with the usual lifelong reciprocal exchange of prestations and honour all round.

Example
Tali Laia, an orphan, was brought up by his MM in Böe, his native village. When she died, he came, at the age of 12, to live in Sifalagö with his MZ who had married into the chief's lineage. She was a widow and lived in the house of her daughter's husband, the schoolteacher mentioned above. The schoolteacher took on the responsibility of marrying him and arranged a loan-raising meal to fund the bridewealth. Many of the lenders were men of Sifalagö. The bride, Wati, is the only daughter of a branch of the chief's line. The father had died and the eldest son was at school in town. The family was therefore somewhat impoverished and needed extra labour. Moreover the boy and girl were particularly keen on marrying and the match was accepted as 'what God had approved'. As the daughter of a noble, Wati could have fetched 40 *batu*, but a figure of 25 was agreed with the provision that Tali would live with his in-laws and work for them. This he did for ten years, by which time he had paid off his debts and had tired of the embarrassment of his position. He built a hut on a remote part of the chief's land and was so successful in his enterprises that he recently moved back to the village and set up a store, with a stall in the market. His income, which exceeds that of most native villagers, derives from this source, and from subsistence farming practised on land belonging to his wife's lineage.

This case is characteristic in that an informal adoption or fostering led to an uxorilocal marriage. The fosterers, Tali's MZ and MZDH, are both affines of the chief's lineage and it was natural that they should find a wife for him from this lineage, thus consolidating the link.

4 Child Betrothal and Child Marriage

We have to distinguish here between the betrothal of children or of an infant girl to an older male, and actual marriage of children where the transfer is definitive. Child betrothal is quite common. It is reconciled with the increasing emphasis on personal choice of a mate by giving the grown-up fiancés (or at least the man) an option on withdrawing from the engagement, with loss of the sums so far paid. Likewise the girl's side can withdraw on return of these prestations. A typical sum in token of engagement (*famohu*) is 6 *batu*, or more for the daughter of a man of rank. When the girl is grown the rest of the bridewealth is paid and the wedding takes place.

Lagemann (1893: 304) reports that in the north (and probably elsewhere) child betrothal was common as a means of settling debts. I was told that in the Susua area betrothal 'in the womb' was arranged for political reasons (see also Hämmerle 1982: 27). The usual reasons for child betrothal now are a desire to make an alliance with a particular man and to spread the burden of payments over a span of years. There is no implication of low status in this economical arrangement. In Sifalagö the grandson of a high-ranking noble was betrothed at the age of 8 to the daughter of a neighbouring chief for 13 *batu*. Ten years later the couple were married and the wedding was combined with a feast of merit at which both partners received titles.

Child marriage is now rare. The groom in such cases is called *solaya ono* ('one who entertains/feasts the child/bride'). A girl of about 10 is taken home by the groom (who may be adult) or his father, following payment of a substantial portion of bridewealth. In the local idiom, she is 'carried home on his back' like a daughter. She is already referred to as a wife (though, formerly, to satisfy Dutch government and missionary objections, she might be called a helper). She lives as a member of the groom's household until she becomes sexually mature. Then the remainder of the bridewealth is paid, the wedding feast can go ahead and the marriage is consummated. The total sum in a *solaya ono* marriage is less than in the standard form, since the groom's side has borne part of the cost of bringing up the girl.

5   Divorce

Divorce (*fabali*) is very rare. In former times adultery led to execution. Nowadays it is usually settled by compensation. In childless marriages, it seems to be the woman who is initially assumed to be barren. The husband can take a second wife if the first wife consents, but there is no divorce. Some people denied that the husband could remarry; he would simply have to accept his 'fate'. If the husband is thought to be sterile, again, he must accept his lot. His brother cannot father a child by the woman on his behalf.[7] It is common in such cases to adopt a brother's child. I learned of only two cases of divorce in the whole village. In one (originally a child marriage) the wife was ostensibly rejected because 'she was lazy'; in the other, she was suspected of having committed adultery. The divorces were easy to arrange, since there were no children.

6   Illicit Relations and Anomalous Unions

Sexual relationships outside marriage are strictly forbidden. Customary law decreed the death penalty for illicit relations, or a very large fine which was given in ransom for the life of the miscreants. In most cases the couple were tied together and drowned in the Susua river. Nowadays a fine of 6–12 *batu* is paid in compensation to the woman's agnates (and husband, if she is married).

All sexual misdemeanours are termed *horö* ('sin'). Settlement of cases of *horö* are concerned only with the judicial, not the moral, aspects of the case. Hence the important facts are the genealogical relation between the partners, whether they are marriageable, and

[7] Schröder (1917: 419) reports that in the north a barren wife could be sent back to her parents and replaced by a sister. Correspondingly the woman's parents could take her back if the husband could not fulfil his (unspecified) duties.

who will look after the child. The question of whether the woman was willing or forced is considered irrelevant. In the past a victim of rape would be executed along with her assailant. It is interesting that a woman's complicity in a liaison is sometimes attributed to the man's love magic; and if she makes the first approach, or pursues the man, this is attributed to sorcery by a third party aimed at shaming her. But these interpretations of illicit female sexuality do not affect the legal position of the parties. In every case it is the woman's lineage which is considered to be the injured party. They have been insulted, and the bridewealth prospects of their kinswoman (if unmarried) have been damaged. The type of settlement depends on the prior relation between the parties. If the couple are not in categories prohibited to each other the simplest solution is to marry them, even if the husband already has a wife. Failing this a fine is imposed.

A few examples will illustrate the varieties of settlement. Ama X married his agnate's widow after their liaison was discovered. His first wife wanted to go back to her family but was persuaded to accept the new wife. A fine was added to the widow's bridewealth. This settlement involved the minimum of disturbance in alliance relations. Ama Y raped his son's fiancée and later took her as his second wife (the son having withdrawn). Another man raped his son's wife and nothing further was done. The woman's agnates were all afraid to sue for compensation, and the son could not act against his father. The same man was involved in a legal wrangle over several years in a case of adultery and abduction. He had 'put a spell' on the wife of a fellow-villager and took her into the forest for a month. He was tried in his absence and his agnates paid a fine of 12 *batu* which was divided among the first- and second-order wife-givers and the husband's lineage. The fine is referred to as 'what shuts our eyes' (to the offence). In the settlement of such cases much depends on the political backing of the parties and individual strength of character.

I knew of no unmarried mothers and illegitimate children. In the past, in cases of adultery where the death penalty was commuted the woman might be kept on as a labourer by her husband, who would then take a second wife. A child by the adultery would be killed or else would be adopted by the husband as his own. In a recent instance during my stay, a new bride from Böe was abducted by her FB (who had 'put a spell on her') and kept in hiding in the forest for some months before being recaptured by a posse from Sifalagö. Her child by this relation was adopted by her husband without formality. In other cases the couple are forcibly married, or a heavy fine is imposed on the lover if another man agrees to marry the girl. Traditional law, which allows the chief to seize the assets of an offender or his agnates, is now backed up by local government officers who are sometimes appealed to if the man refuses to co-operate.

The most serious offence is *horö salakha* ('sin which is prohibited/cursed'). This involves a relation between persons who are in prohibited categories to each other, either as members of the same clan (or especially the same lineage) or where the man belongs to the woman's wife-giving group (i.e. he would be among major claimants for her bridewealth). Offences of this kind are perceived as a threat to society and there is no possibility of marrying the couple. There are fears that a precedent would be set and the prestige of the man's lineage would be harmed. There are also fears of supernatural sanctions since such a union would be affected by ancestral curses. Clans differ in where they draw the line.

What happens in cases where the couple may not marry and no husband can be found for the pregnant woman? Lacking the traditional recourse to execution, my informants were unclear as to the best solution. Only one case could be cited in which close agnates were married (no bridewealth was paid). The man is something of an outlaw and the shame attaching to the union has not therefore had any serious social consequences for him. In less flagrant violations of marriage rules there is an improvised, and not necessarily satisfactory, settlement.

However, some elders spoke of an expedient by which the parties could be reclassified, allowing an anomalous union to be legitimized. This would be regarded as an exception, not a precedent. There are no current examples in Sifalagö, so I can only relate what is supposed to happen in such cases. The man is nominally assigned to another clan. His children take their father's true clanship. The agnates will not contribute to the bridewealth and will try to distance themselves from the marriage. They disown the man and henceforth regard him as *bö'ö*, unrelated. If the marriage is to go ahead a prestation called *fondröni nola* ('pulling up the border/limit') is paid.

Two interpretations of this term were suggested. It 'pulls up a

PLATE 1. *Chief's house in Mazinö*

PLATE 2. *Chief's house in Sifalagö*

PLATE 3. *The senior elder of the village, Ama Huku*

PLATE 4. *Building a dam on the Susua river*

PLATE 5. *Villagers*

PLATE 6. *A village elder*

PLATE 7. *A village woman*

PLATE 8. *The chief's deathbed oration*

PLATE 9. *Wedding of the chief's daughter*

PLATE 10. *Watching the village square*

PLATE 11. *Elders ponder the division of portions*

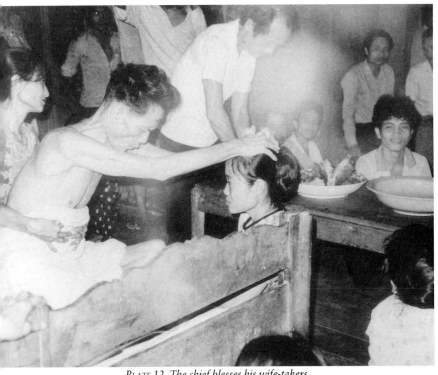

PLATE 12. *The chief blesses his wife-takers*

PLATE 13. *A view of the square in Sifalagö*

PLATE 14. *Lölömoyo hamlet*

PLATE 15. *Women pounding rice*

boundary' between prohibited persons. Or it is a kind of fine compensating for the violation of a boundary. The language probably derives from an analogy with territorial boundaries. In transfers of ownership or land disputes, the participants ritually traverse the boundary, marking it with a *buasi* tree. Then they utter a curse on 'he who uproots the border'. In similar fashion the integrity of the clan was protected by a curse on offenders of the marriage rules. Each clan performed its own cursing ceremony.

The curse is resorted to in cases of personal affront or neglect. Then it is private, sometimes secret, informal or even spontaneous, and is a response to some past offence. In contrast, the formal ceremonial curse is performed in public by a specialist. It is legislative and proscriptive, and concerns the well-being of a group or the whole of society. It is used to protect boundaries of several kinds— land, categories of relationship (thus marriage rules as we see here), and standard measurements used in exchange. The 'uprooting of the border' in anomalous marriages thus entails the lifting of a curse. Nevertheless misfortune and illness suffered by the couple and their descendants (or later recurrences of immorality) tend to be attributed to this original sin.

PART II

The Politics of Exchange

8
Measurement and the Regulation of Exchange

> When a Kachin talks about the 'debts' which he owes and
> which are due to himself, he is talking about what an anthropo-
> logist means by 'social structure'.
>
> (Leach 1954: 141)

The first half of this book has been concerned with exchange in the
realm of kinship and marriage. In the second half I will show how
political integration (and sometimes disintegration) within the village and over a wider field is achieved through exchange. The
present chapter is a consideration of the technicalities of exchange,
intended to draw out their governing principles and to relate these
to fundamental social values and the dominant concerns of Nias life.
Such matters are rarely considered in detail in studies of exchange,
and it is tempting to pass quickly over the particularities. But it is
frequently in the thick of debate over quantities, techniques, and
principles that the significance of a transaction is to be found. And it
is impossible to make sense of a feast of merit (the subject of the
next chapter) without first grasping the systems of measurement. In
giving them such importance I am reflecting a prime Nias concern.

Niasans, like Leach's Kachin, tend to characterize social relations in
terms of debt. Even those relationships which are basic to human
life, such as that of an infant and its mother, are conceived in some
contexts as incurring debt. Indeed, one owes a debt to one's
mother's brother for one's very existence; and—to cite another
example—a wife's father collects a 'debt for the child' from his son-
in-law for the first-born of each sex. *Ömö*, debt, covers many types
of relationship including at one end of the scale commercial debts
and at the other what we would call a moral debt. But there is no
radical discontinuity between the extremes, and just as a commercial
relationship has moral elements, so may a moral debt be given a

numerical value which is symbolic but at the same time has an economic significance. The web of debts traces out a moral order, and violation of this order may have ethical, and sometimes religious, significance. Perhaps this much can be said of many societies in which economic relations are embedded in social organization. But there is a peculiar development of this theme in Nias—it is elaborated in ethical judgements and in eschatology, in a hundred proverbs, and in a passion for measurement.

Virtually all social relations in Nias involve exchange, and most exchanges involve quantification, even those which seem to deal in intangible or purely symbolic elements such as 'life' or prestige. (This is not to say that the relation itself is quantifiable.) Perhaps the most striking instance of this conception of measure in all things is the belief reported in some sources that the Creator asks the unborn child how long it will live (Schröder 1917: 246). Depending on its answer he then measures out on scales a quantity of life-breath (*noso*). In general, it is meaningless to talk of an exchange without specifying quantities, even if these are obviously exaggerations or inventions. In telling myths or stories from the remote past, a narrator usually specifies the exact girth measurement of a particular pig which is given away or sacrificed. Anything less precise than the size to the nearest *alisi* leaves the listener dissatisfied and with an impression of the narrator's ignorance. After being in Sifalagö for some months I was not surprised, when I enquired how the site of the village came to be chosen, to be told that the founder had first of all measured the length of the Susua river from source to mouth and had founded Sifalagö at the exact half-way mark.

In the Nias language, concepts of measurement and reckoning are closely associated with words for thinking and in some instances are identical. Thus from the root [*era*] the following words are derived: *era-era* ('thought, figure'), *erai* ('count, reckon up'), *angeragö* ('reflect on, think about'), *angeraigö* ('count upon, take into consideration'). The verb *mangera-ngera* ('to think') means 'to have thoughts'; *mo'era-era* means 'to have thoughts' in the sense of 'to be wise'. To 'have a lot of thoughts' means to have a lot of debts or financial worries, to be pondering figures. As in many languages, terms for measuring are associated with moral evaluation and judgement. A difficult moral problem is the 'measure' (*su'a-su'a*) of a man. To debate or consider is to 'weigh one thing against another' (*fatimba-timba*; cf. Indon. *timbang*).

The Nias obsession with measurement provides us with an interesting addition to the literature on traditional exchange, and one which has, as it were, an element of built-in precision, which makes it a useful case on which to test hypotheses developed from often imprecise and speculative reports (e.g. concerning the potlatch).

1   The Origin of Exchange Items and Measures

Schröder (1917: 460 ff.) compiled sixteen different creation myths collected in various parts of the island, including Sifalagö Susua. These are told in paraphrase with occasional brief quotations. Even the earliest sources give an impression of incoherence, inconsistency, and disagreement among informants. Multiple versions seem always to have existed.[1] But let us look first at the creation myths which had a wide circulation and acceptance, concentrating on those aspects relevant to the subject of exchange.

Most of Schröder's examples, excepting those from the south, have in common a fabulous tree called Tora'a, which was engendered by the amorous play of the winds, or else grew from the heart of Sihai, a primeval being who was born of the winds and who died without descendants. The fruit of this tree, or its buds, are given as some or all of the following: sun and moon, gold, rice, pigs, measures for these, customary law, and certain deities and progenitors of men. In Thomsen's version (1979: 231) from central Nias, the tree produced 'nine kinds' of things: 'Padang gold/Dutch gold', a 'wise pig', rice, coconut trees, a chicken, sweet potato (as pig-food), areca nut, betel leaf, and finally tobacco.

A related set of myths, which seems in rough outline to be common to the whole island, tells of how the first men came to earth. There is a contest for succession in the upper world, Golden Teteholi, among the nine sons of Sirao. Since there is only room for the successor, the others are lowered down to earth. The first to arrive is Hia, equipped with all the necessary elements of culture (including, in Thomsen's version, the tree).[2] In Lagemann's version

---

[1]   The creation myth collected by Thomsen (1979) in 1933 in Sifalagö Gomo is the most complete version available. There is no coherent body of myths equal to Steinhart's huge collection deriving from the Batu Islands (1934; 1937; 1954).

[2]   Possibly the name Hia derives from the proto-Austronesian *hi[y]ang, which Dempwolff (1938) translates: *Gottheit, Göttlichsein*. Nias loan words automatically drop their closing consonants, so *hiyang* would become *hia*.

(1906: 394) from north Nias, Hia descends in the south. Under his weight the land tilts; so Sirao lowers down 'Gözö, the counterbalance of the earth' somewhere in the north. The land dips again. One by one all the sons are lowered down until equilibrium is restored. These men are the tribal progenitors from whom all Nias clans are supposed to derive.[3]

In most of the myths collected in central Nias, Hia descends at Sifalagö Gomo, an actual village sixteen miles from Sifalagö Susua. The weights and measures accompany Hia but are not products of the tree. In Sifalagö Susua, as in south Nias, the area which it borders, the fabulous tree is unknown, although experts can still recite the creation myth in detail. In the version I collected the emphasis is on human invention and political association. The measures are inaugurated at a meeting of chiefs, thus providing a paradigm or 'charter' for inter-village exchange. Here is the relevant passage, as related to me by Ama Gamböta.

Me ladada Hia Walangi Azu	When Hia Walangi Azu descended
Me ladada Hia Walangi Luo	When Hia Walangi Luo descended
Ladada ia raovi-raovi si'öli	He was lowered down on an iron chain
Ladada ia raovi-raovi fatao	He was lowered down on a bronze chain
Ladada ia fabaya osali	He descended with a temple
Ladada ia fabaya omo	He descended with a house
Tou ba guli danö ölia	Down to the fortified earth
Ba guli dao daya-daya	Down to the earth-base
Sa ba Gomo sidele i'a	At Gomo, where the fish squeal
Ba Gomo sahuva uro	At Gomo, of the grey-haired [= wise] prawns.
Meno mutaro Hia Walangi Azu	When Hia Walangi Azu settled
Meno mutaro Hia Walangi Luo	When Hia Walangi Luo settled
Solohe bövö oroisa	Bringer of customary law,
Zumange nitehe niha.	Of the tribute approved by men.
Owulo damönö niha	The seeds of men gathered
Faonda damönö zalawa	The seeds of chiefs convened
Ba Zifalagö angorahua zihönö	At Sifalagö the meeting-place of thousands

[3] The metaphor of the earth as scales is explicit in Schröder's version from the south. The notion of cosmic balance occurs in other myths, for example one I collected in Sifalagö, in which Nazuva Danö, god of the underworld is sent down as a 'counterbalance' to his brother, Samailo/Lovalangi, god of the upper world.

Ba Zifalagö angorahua zato.	At Sifalagö the meeting-place of the many.
Andrö lataba yawa mbulu faliera	There they determined the gold scales
Andrö lataba mbulu fanulo	There they determined the weighing scales
Fanulo yawa gana'a barasi	To weigh the fine-grade gold
Fanulo gana'a bovo	To weigh the 'bloom' gold.
Labe gafore mbawi dele-dele	They used the *afore* for squealing pigs
Labe gafore mbawi sihogo	The measuring stick for grunting pigs
Lataba lauru su'a-su'a	They determined the *lauru* rice-measure
Lataba zumba famoto.	They fixed the *tumba*, its subdivision.

Ama Gamböta added an apocryphal couplet (incorporating loan words) to the effect that Hia and the chiefs ratified or fixed the levels of bridewealth and the rates of exchange for trade (*faniaga*). The story goes on to relate how the worship of wooden ancestor figures (*azu*) is introduced by Hia.

The recognized foreign derivation of gold, gongs, etc., is disguised in the 'orthodox', ethnocentric myths by the assimilation of earth (*tanö*) to Nias (*tanö niha*), and of men (*niha*) to Niasans (*ono niha*). These myths simply state that all things needed by men were lowered to earth with the tribal ancestors from the upper world. Yet a regular supply of gold could only be assured by well-established trade links with slavers from Aceh and with Chinese and Muslim merchants from the west coast of Sumatra. The naturalization of these imported goods, the representation of the foreign as indigenous, is a mark not only of the fundamental importance of these goods to Nias culture, but also of its inward-looking ethos. Nias has always relied on external sources to feed its internal prestige economy, but it has denied these external contacts an important place in its world-view.[4] The goods which Niasans traded for foreign gold—slaves—were likewise partially excluded from the social and cultural realm. To represent the exchange schematically: a foreign product, gold, could only be fully incorporated by denying its

---

[4] Compare an eastern Indonesian society, Tanebar-Evav, where foreign-derived wealth objects are similarly conceived as inherent to society (*haratut*) (Barraud 1979: 211); but where the putative foreign origin of law is fully represented in a contrasting conception of society in its relation to the exterior (*lor*). Barraud offers an indigenous etymology of *haratut*, but the word has a striking resemblance to Indon. *harta* ('wealth, property') and Nias *harato*. The myth of the tree of wealth is a further point of comparison with Nias.

origin, while a home-grown product, slaves, could only be exported or alienated by destroying the connection with society (the origin of captive-slaves was suppressed, as was their clan identity; they were expendable). In this respect, the exchange of slaves for gold is the opposite of marriage by payment of bridewealth (*böli niha*, lit. 'purchase of a person'), a permanent relation in which the links between givers and gift (the bride) are never dissolved. This contrast in fact is never made by Niasans, but is worth making here for the light it sheds on the different concepts of exchange involved.

In a myth still told today in various forms, and very widely known, the contradiction between the indigenous creation and external origin of wealth objects is resolved in the story of the heart of Hia, the tribal progenitor. After Hia's death, his heart is washed away in a flood with his gold to distant lands. In a variant of this myth, collected by Schröder in Sifalagö Susua, Hia's daughter goes overseas and becomes the ancestress of foreigners and of the 'nine kinds of seed' from which the following trade goods derive: gold, iron, silk, ceremonial plates, gongs, cannons, and a fine variety of rice. There are also stories, still told, of Hia's golden sow (*sigelo ana'a*) which eats men and excretes gold. The golden sow accompanied Hia into exile, which is why foreigners are rich. Foreigners are rather like the golden sow, in fact, since they too consume slaves and produce gold. As far as I know, Niasans do not draw this analogy; however, the point is that these valuables—men and gold—are conceived as prototypically exchangeable, and that the exchange is international.

Less well known, but also complementing the ethnocentric creation theory, is a myth in which certain wealth objects (cloth, gongs, and manufactured goods) come from the abode of *bekhua*, underworld beings on the eastern horizon 'across the sea'. Dealers who brought the goods to Nias were thought to have made contact with the *bekhua*. According to elderly villagers, foreign goods were brought to central Nias via Ono Limbu, the sparsely populated eastern cape—a fact which must have been perceived as consistent with this myth (if not as its foundation). In a different myth which I recorded in Hiliorahua (rejected by the acknowledged experts as 'wrong') Hia obtained gold scales from these underworld beings in exchange for slaves. These variants show the admission of the foreign to the Nias cosmology, albeit at the margins: an admission made necessary by dependence on the outside world for certain 'essential' goods. All the same, the foreign origin is not itself the source of value.

Certain other myths differ more radically from the standard creation myth and offer what might be called an immigration theory as opposed to a Genesis theory, with corresponding differences in the derivation of goods. In one of these, also told to me by Ama Gamböta, it was Sirao Walangi Azu—not Hia—who was the 'seed of men', the first man on earth. He raises pigs and introduces the feast of merit. Generations later, after several tribal divisions have occurred, Hia descends to earth, crossing seas and coming ashore at the mouth of the Susua. He follows the river up to its confluence with the river Gomo and settles in Sifalagö (Gomo). He gathers the chiefs together and fixes or inaugurates the standard measures. Thomsen (1979: 272) mentions a variant collected in Idanö Mola, just north of Gomo, in which Niasans explicitly derive from fugitive immigrants washed ashore at the mouth of the Susua. Common to all versions is the role of Hia as lawgiver and bringer of weights and measures.

The significance of the creation myths for a study of exchange and social organization is that gold, pigs, and rice make their first appearance as objects of exchange, not merely objects of consumption; they are therefore accompanied by measuring instruments and are linked from the start to political association. In many parts of Nias the ancestral decrees on measurement and exchange formed an important part of the constitution of village federations called *öri*. In the Gomo–Susua area no such *öri* federations existed until the Dutch imposed them, but as the myth I have quoted shows, similar local agreements on exchange seem 'always' to have existed.

The inception of customary law is indicated in the following couplet:

Solohe bövö oroisa   Who brought the commandments of custom
Zumange nitehe niha   The homage approved by men.

Here the word for affinal prestations, *bövö*, stands for customary law as a whole. Customary law is conceived on the model of the mutual obligations of affines, symbolized in exchange. *Sumange* denotes the cluster of sentiments and attitudes we call honour, homage, and respect (Indon. *hormat*), as well as the gift of tribute (Indon. *penghormatan*).

Something on which all the sources agree is that the measuring instruments are themselves symbols of customary law. More than that, they are symbols of permanence and justice. Steinhart (1934: 426) quotes a song from the Batu Islands used to console orphans:

Ma laröi gafore	They have left you the *afore*
Ma laröi mbövö,	They have left you customary law.
Hadödöi zigawa ndaugö	Why then should you be at a loss
Ba zi sagötö tanö?	Anywhere in the wide world?

At a wedding I attended, the bridegroom's party flattered their hosts in their opening speech with the words:

Atage ma'uroi	We have gone to the very source
Atage ma'ele	We have gone to the estuary
Ha tö banua andre	But there remains only this village
Zilö tebulö afore.	In which the *afore* is unchanged.

Titles awarded to great feastgivers—guardians of customary law—frequently incorporate the names of measures, as in Lauruz-omboi (Rice-measure of the creator), Aforezihönö (Pig-measure of the masses), Maeralovalangi (Touchstone of God): all members of the last, glorious, departed generation in Sifalagö. In a different area, Chatelin (1881: 131) reports that the instruments had their own spirits (*bekhu*) which could afflict those who attempted to cheat, while users of false weights were punished by Lovalangi. As both the instruments and symbols of law, the measures are ubiquitous. One often sees house façades with carved representations; indeed some concrete houses in Gunung Sitoli have similar decorations.

So much for the origin and significance of measures. How are they used?

2   Measurement of Rice

In all transactions involving rice, it is always rice in the husk (*fakhe* = Indon. *padi*) which is implied in the exchange rate. Rice which has had the husk removed (*böra* = Indon. *beras*) by pounding is worth double. The standard measure is the *tumba*, a wooden cylinder with a capacity of about 1.5 litres. Formerly the smallest unit was the *nali*, a quarter-*tumba*. But since early this century condensed milk cans (*teko*) became available in town and these eventually found their way to the interior, since when they have been used in the home and for small market purchases. Eight of

these *teko* = 1 *tumba* (in other parts of Nias the *tumba* = 6 *teko*). One *teko* provides enough rice for one adult's meal.[5]
Multiples of the *tumba* are as follows:

$$
\begin{aligned}
\text{\textit{matonga} ('one-half') } \textit{gurö} &= 3\,\textit{tumba}\\
\text{\textit{samba} ('one') } \textit{lauru} &= 5\,\textit{tumba}\\
\textit{sagurö} &= 6\,\textit{tumba}\\
\text{\textit{dua} ('two') } \textit{lauru} &= 10\,\textit{tumba}\\
\textit{matonga zo'e} &= 15\,\textit{tumba}\\
\text{\textit{sambua su'a-su'a} ('one measure')} &= 20\,\textit{tumba}\\
\text{\textit{samba a lima} ('one and five')} &= 25\,\textit{tumba}\\
\text{\textit{sazo'e} (1 \textit{so'e})} &= 30\,\textit{tumba}
\end{aligned}
$$

Of these larger units there exists a measure only for the *lauru*, though this is rarely found nowadays.

The rice harvest is reckoned in *so'e*. Rice seeds are measured in *tumba* before planting. All land except irrigated paddyfields is measured not by surface area but by the amount of rice which could be planted on it (with average density), irrespective of whether the land is used for rice, cassava, etc., or whether it is fallow. Thus a field of about 1 hectare is said to be '2 *tumba* of seeds'. Since the terrain is hilly and irregular this is the most convenient method of measuring. Until recently land was not in short supply, and the precise area of a holding was of no particular interest. In terms of production planning and potential wealth, it is the amount of rice under cultivation which is significant. Moreover, the ratio of seeds planted to rice harvested provides a rough index of soil fertility.

Irrigated rice fields (*laza*) are an innovation in the Susua area, dating back to the 1930s. Since there is very little flat land, and there is neither the organizational capacity nor the techniques for constructing large-scale terraces (and no ploughs or draught animals), *laza* occupy a very small proportion of the land. Interestingly, *laza* are measured by area. The unit is the *boronga*, which has no other application and must therefore have been introduced with *laza* (1 *boronga* = 10 × 10 *döfa* (hand-to-hand armspans)). I was told that this method was chosen because *laza* are often worked by hired labour, and it is easier to pay someone by so much per *boronga* (and to check his progress) than by seed quantity.[6] Planting of hill rice is

---

[5] All measurements and standards in this chapter refer to those of the Upper Susua area unless otherwise stated.

[6] The context suggests that *boronga* derives from Malay *borong*, 'piecework' (Wilkinson 1932: s.v. *borong*).

done by co-operative exchange of labour, but there is no question of checking or cheating: the consequence of planting less than one declares is that one's own harvest will diminish due to supernatural sanction.

Total land holdings are estimated in *so'e*.

3   Measurement of Gold

The word for gold, *ana'a*, is said to derive from the Sanskrit *kanaka* (Schröder 1917: 59). Gold is obtained as dust or leaf from traders and is blended with silver and copper by native smiths to form alloys. The process of blending and beating gold is reckoned by scholars to be an indigenous technique, and is known in all parts of the island. Gold working has an important place in Nias mythology and symbolism. In Thomsen's myth from Gomo (1979: 221), the creation of the earth is depicted as the creation of an ornament. A female deity combs the dirt out of her hair, puts it on scales and weighs it against gold weights. Then she summons 'hammer-faced Mazai' to beat it into the form of the earth (at first he forms it to the size of a *tandrina* head ornament). When the earth is populated, a goldsmith is lowered down with Hia.

The techniques of smithing offer a rich source of symbolism. In Lahömi (west Nias), the titles of officers of the *öri* village federation were derived from terms used in the working of gold (see Schröder 1917: 332; Korn 475/10).

1st officer   *sondrani*, '[gold] blender'.
2nd officer   *samobözi*, '[gold] beater'.
3rd officer   *solewa*, 'cutter' (who cuts up the pieces of gold?).
4th officer   *sananö*, 'he who applies the touchstone'.
5th officer   *samahovu'ö*, 'blesser' (Schröder: 'he who speaks about the gold').

The meeting at which the constitution is laid down is called, according to Schröder, *mondrani* ('to blend together'), a term deriving from the blending of gold with other metals to form alloys. As Schröder observes, this is an apt metaphor for both the fusing of distinct groups into a unity, and for the hierarchy within it. In *öri* O'o'u (also west Nias), at the swearing of the pact, pieces of gold of different quality were placed in a ring. Each clan leader was given one piece corresponding to his rank order in the *öri*. The *öri* chief kept the touchstone and standards of each alloy (Korn 475/6).

Although there are certain ritual observances connected with smithing, there is no record of goldsmiths having an exalted status or ritual position in the village. Marschall (1976: 83) notes, however, that they are respected figures, and their titles may incorporate the word *ere* ('priest, specialist').

Any man who has commissioned a gold ornament, and inaugurated it at a feast, is said to have 'beaten gold'. In central Nias it was said that only those who had beaten gold could enter Golden Paradise. Ordinary men 'became food for the worms'. In most cases the construction of an ornament involves melting down or hammering into a different form an existing ornament. Schröder (1917: 218) makes the significant point that ornaments are again and again reworked and heirlooms are hardly to be found, since 'only a piece made by oneself and inaugurated at a feast has any meaning.'

Gold is weighed on fine scales (*fanulo gana'a, bulu fali'era*) against counterweights, *saga*, which are lumps of bronze or old bullets of various sizes. Metric scales are not used, except in town, though it is known that one unit of gold as presently determined is equivalent to 10 grams. In counting units of gold one simply uses the cardinal numbers—*sara, dua, tölu*—without further qualification. Thus, 'he gave me three' means 'he gave me three units of gold'. Sometimes the unit is referred to as the *batu* ('stone'), a word which does not belong to the central dialect. (For convenience I follow this usage throughout the book.) The unit of value applies both to gold and pigs, but the size of pig which counts as 1 *batu* fluctuates with exchange rates.[7]

It must be emphasized that the gold unit is not a fixed weight but varies regionally and is subject to periodical revision. In most types of exchange the unit is set at 10 *huakete*, that is the weight of 10 colonial 10-cent coins, each weighing about 1 gram. When a deal is transacted, different counterweights are first checked against these tiny coins. For bridewealth prestations in Sifalagö and surrounding villages the unit is set at 8 *huakete*. In Gomo the bridewealth unit is 10 *huakete*.[8]

---

[7] Compare methods of counting: *tölu* = '3 *batu* of gold'; *tölu bawi* = '3 *batu* worth of pigs' (which might consist of five pigs); *tölu nga'eu mbawi* = 'three pigs'. The last phrase uses the numerical co-efficient *eu*.

[8] The actual metal counterweight which corresponds to one gold unit (*sara*) of

Several grades of gold are recognized, from the purest (said to be 24-carat), called *balaki*, down to an alloy of 9-carat. Most gold used in customary and commercial transactions is '16-carat', called 'village gold', and this is the variety usually implied in rates of exchange. Often it comes in the form of ornaments or broken pieces of jewellery. Quality is determined by the mark (*lahe*) produced by rubbing the gold on a touchstone (*maera*). This is compared with the mark produced by a standard piece of gold of predetermined quality.

4   Measurement of Pigs

To measure a pig's girth (*alogo*, 'armpit') you take a string (*su'a*, 'measure'), pass it underneath the body, close behind its front legs, and join the ends of the string together over the shoulder hump (*alisi*); then hold the string against a measuring stick (*afore*) and read off the figure. The *afore* is a length of cane or *hoya* palm (picked because it is very straight) sometimes fashioned into a walking-stick with a curly handle. On lonely paths between villages one often meets a man out debt-claiming, equipped with his *afore*. The stick is about a yard long. Near the handle is a notch called the *tuhe gafore* ('stump' of the *afore*). This is the point from which to measure. The next notch is at an interval of about 48 cm., representing a girth of 1 *alisi*. Thereafter the scale changes, and a notch every 8 cm. represents an increment of 1 *alisi*. The *afore* scale goes up to 7 *alisi* (sometimes less)—enough for all but the biggest pigs. If the string runs off the scale at 7 *alisi*, the corresponding point of the string is simply put back at the 1 *alisi* notch (which then serves as the origin) and the remaining length is read off. (The figure 7 here is arbitrary, it does not represent a base.) The largest pig I saw was raised for an *ovasa*, and measured 15 *alisi*.

One *alisi* is divided into 12 *saga*. Accordingly, some *afore* have 12 intervals between the *tuhe* (the origin) and the 1 *alisi* mark. Up to the 1 *alisi* mark, the point where the scale changes, each *saga* is

the designated size is called *samba saga* (one *saga*). There are lesser weights in a ratio to the *saga*. Some derive their names from pigs' girth measurements, corresponding to a customary rate of exchange. The word *saga* also applies generally to gold counterweights. The smallest unit of girth measurement for pigs is called the *saga*, possibly deriving from an obsolete exchange rate between pigs and gold.

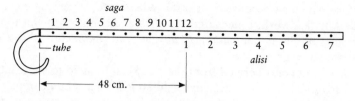

FIG. 8.1. A measuring stick (*afore*)

4 cm. Above 1 *alisi*, the same interval of 4 cm. represents 6 *saga*, that is ½ *alisi*. This change of scale appears puzzling only if we ignore the fact that the system measures a three-dimensional object in only two dimensions, and that therefore its scale must change if the increase in circumference is faithfully to represent the greater increase in volume. If the pig's body were perfectly cylindrical, each regular interval of circumference would correspond to a quadratic (as opposed to linear) increase in volume. Ideally, the value of each interval would grow, or the intervals themselves would progressively diminish. The *afore* scale is a compromise between conservation of volume (by adjustment of a linear scale) and what can be practically achieved and legislated upon under the conditions. The point at which the scale diminishes, 1 *alisi*, is the point at which the discrepancy between the girth and volume progression begins to be significant, and also the point at which hand measurement becomes impractical. Most Niasans are untrained in mathematics; nevertheless, they recognize that the measurement of girth can never be more than a rough guide to 'content' (*ösi*), not only for the reasons given above, but because pigs are an irregular shape, and the *afore* takes no account of length, boniness, etc. In certain circumstances, e.g. when a pig is to be slaughtered, the distinction between girth and 'content' (volume, weight) becomes more important. The relation between girth and content can be estimated on the basis of experience, as I shall show later.

Many measurements are derived from the human body, but the body itself is not measured. A man who has a house built uses his own body measurements (e.g. armspan) as the standards for the house dimensions, which is not to say that he is measured: he is the measure. In certain ritual contexts (e.g. hunting) the size of the human frame is directly compared to that of a pig (the quarry), but there is no question of accurately measuring it, even less of using an

afore, which has a convenient scale. When once, somewhat emaci-
ated by fieldwork, I measured my girth and compared it with my
smaller but fitter companions (7 *alisi* to 5, for the record) this was
treated as a great joke.

Measurements derived from the body can be used to substitute
for an *afore* or to construct a makeshift one from a palm rib or piece
of string. Thus if a real *afore* is not available one can approximate
the 1 *alisi* mark by the distance from elbow to the tip of the index
finger, added to the width of two fingers. Thereafter, increments of
½ *alisi* are reckoned by two-finger widths. Alternatively, and more
commonly, one measures the pig directly by hand, e.g. 2 *alisi* = 3
handspans around the girth. A series of standardized hand measures
are correlated with *alisi* figures as found in Appendix 2.

It must be emphasized that the *afore* scale is not derived from
these hand measurements, which are regarded as variable and
inaccurate—rough equivalents of the linear scale. Hand sizes vary,
hence the need for an independent standard. Moreover hand
measuring is a technically difficult feat and likely to lead to disagreement. It is said that 'the span is more generous than the measuring
string' because a string can be pulled tight, diminishing the girth,
while it is extremely difficult to get your hands round a struggling
pig. However, small pigs are more conveniently measured by hand
(*nitangai*), and most *afore* do not have the *saga* increments on the
scale suitable for measuring piglets. Buyer and seller are well aware
how hand size affects the figure and accordingly they negotiate a
compromise. My informant accurately estimated that my (average
European) hands would give a figure of 4½ *alisi* for a particular pig
where his (average Nias) hands gave 6. This kind of compensation is
a result of years of practice.

There is no explanation of how the *afore* scale is derived. It is
possible that in each area within which an *afore* is standard, its scale
once corresponded to some body measure of the village or district
chief: it is no less standard or invariant for that (see e.g. Korn 475/
6). In the Upper Susua district, a federation of nine villages, the
standard *afore* was held by the district head, who also happened to
be the chief of Sifalagö. At a meeting of the district held in 1933 he
'inscribed the *afore*' and issued each village chief with a copy.
Usually a chief would also inscribe the *afore* scale on the *fulanö*
beam in the front room of his house, where it could be consulted by
anyone. This particular beam was a focus of ritual interest, since it

bore the ancestor figures. Thus the standard measure was an integral part of the house and closely associated with political authority. It was, and still is, a serious offence to try to use a different measure in order to cheat, punishable with a fine of up to 5 *alisi*.

There are various techniques of measuring with a string, and the choice of one rather than another is largely a matter of preference. One method, to *su'a*, is to cross hands with the string over the pig's back, pulling hard so that the string tightens, and cutting the string at the cross-over point. Another method, to *fohu*, means to pull lightly on the string and fold back the ends so that they simply touch. When the string is measured against the *afore*, one digit (i.e. ½ *alisi*) is deducted if the *fohu* method is used, to 'allow for the pig's hair', which is cut through using the *su'a* method. Obviously the measurement depends on how hard you pull and whether you want to exaggerate or diminish the size. Some men heave between the pig's exhalations, almost strangling it to reduce its girth. There are also magical means of increasing your pulling power. A *ladari* twine dropped from a tree by an ape is soaked in coconut oil, which if later applied secretly to the measuring string (not enough to make it slippery) enables you to reduce a pig of 6 *alisi* to only 4. The *ladari* twine is thought to be used by mother apes as a sling to hold their young, as a human mother carries her infant. Apes are proverbially strong in the arm; a mother's sling must not break.

Some years ago a schoolteacher from Oyo who settled in Sifalagö introduced new methods which are regarded as fairer. Palm leaf ribs are now used instead of the almost unbreakable twine once favoured in the Susua area. Another more objective method which he introduced was the use of bottles filled with water. These are attached to the ends of the string and are crossed over the pig's back, hanging down on either side. A pig which measures, say, 4½ *alisi* by the *su'a* method will measure 5 *alisi* using empty bottles, but only 4½ using full ones. The price therefore is adjusted according to which method is used. Generally the *fohu* method is reserved for small pigs, since their flesh is soft and the '*su'a* cuts deep', distorting the figure. The golden rule is: the same method must be used at the loan and at the return of an equivalent pig. Moreover, the same *afore* must be used, ruling out the possibility of variation or cheating. Only the recipient measures the pig at each transaction. Thus a fairly objective method is used which can be clearly watched by the other partner but cannot be contested by him. In this way the exchange does not degenerate into a quarrel. Some types of exchange in which the *afore* is used are described in Appendix 3.

Bridewealth payments and other prestations between affines are not measured by the recipients, although the size is estimated visually (this is something Niasans do habitually when looking at a pig). An exact exchange rate here is neither possible nor desirable, so cheating is not in question. One tries to escape as lightly as possible within the agreed terms, but if the bride-givers feel short-measured they will claim they have been 'mocked' and given 'mist (*sau*) to eat'. Their ultimate sanction is to detain the bride.

The use of the *afore*, with its connotations of exactness and equivalence of return makes it unsuitable for certain categories of prestation. It would be wrong to say that these connotations are identified with economic, as opposed to ritual exchanges, since they apply also to prestige payments made at *ovasa* feasts. However, the *afore* is used in transactions which are largely utilitarian, even if the context of the transaction (to help a neighbour, show solidarity, etc.) and its sanctions (loss of goodwill and influence) lend meaning to the exchange beyond what is economic.

5   Measurement of Prestige Payments

A category of prestations given at feasts of merit has its own measuring system. The meaning of these prestige payments, as I shall call them, is considered in the next chapter. I am concerned here only with certain aspects of measurement.

There are two kinds of prestige payment: *sulö*, live pigs brought to the feast by certain guests, and *urakha*, the portions of raw meat derived from *sulö*, which are redistributed among all the guests. The guest's *sulö* indebts the host; the host's *urakha* indebts the guest. Prestige payments, unlike gifts to affines, must be repaid, and with exact equivalence if the status quo is to be maintained. These debts can only be reclaimed at another *ovasa* feast.

1. *Urakha*. In former times *urakha* were specified parts of the pig which had to be repaid with a similar portion on a future occasion. With the return an extra portion might be added, reversing the debt. Small portions were not measured. The rest were measured

by volume in rice measures—either a *tumba* or, for very big portions, a *lauru*. With the latter, the pig's head would be placed on top as a gratuity. The recipient was said to be indebted for 1 *lauru*. The fact that pork portions were tallied in terms of rice-measures has nothing to do with exchange rates between rice and pork; it is simply a consequence of the technique.

About two generations ago a new method, the weighing of portions, was introduced by the district chief of the Upper Susua. The idea is said to have derived from Gomo via Mazö, a valley a few miles north of Sifalagö. It is remarkable that rice-measures continued to be used as the instruments and as the means of tallying debts, though weight replaced volume as the quantity measured. Portions are weighed on a crude pivot against a stone known to be equivalent to the weight of a standard quantity of hulled rice—usually 1 *tumba*.[9] The word *hië* ('hang, suspend') refers to the unit of weight, the stone or counterweight, and to the action of weighing. There are different sizes of *hië*, that is, different units, which are matched to the category of guest.

The weighing method was introduced to widen the distribution of payments. As the population grew and communication between villages improved due to increased security, the number of guests at feasts grew to the point where the host's resources were stretched beyond limits. The *hië* system was more economical than the generous traditional measures; it was also more accurate and simpler, making the allocation of 100 pigs among 500 guests and the tallying of debts much easier. For the same reason there is a recent trend towards the general use of the smallest unit.

Measuring by weight instead of volume is said to give 'more content' since more units (about twice as many) can be obtained from a pig of the same size. Content is therefore conventionally represented in this context in a relative sense. It means simply number of units. Probably this conception has arisen due to the continued use of the rice-measures, so that whereas a pig of 5 *alisi* (about 50 kg.) formerly yielded 15 *tumba* by volume, it now yields around 30 *tumba* by weight (against rice), an apparent increase in content.

---

[9] Often only one *urakha* is weighed against a stone. It is trimmed down until it balances; thereafter this *urakha* is used as the counterweight for all the others. The same weighing operation is carried out independently on each pig by its group of recipients.

In planning an *ovasa*, a man adds up all his festive debts in a grand total, irrespective of where they originate, and when the debt reaches a certain sum, e.g. 6 *so'e* (6 × 30 units), he may decide to hold a feast and repay the debts. The appropriate threshold depends on the scale and purpose of the feast. This system therefore gives one a precise knowledge of how one's debts stand *vis-à-vis* individuals and one's 'balance of payments' as a whole.

2. *Sulö*. The donor of a *sulö* pig can state whether he wants it to be measured by girth or 'content', in other words measured alive or by the total portions it yields. Whichever method is chosen must be used for the return payment. The variable relation between girth and weight introduces an element of chance and speculation into the exchange. The donor's choice of method depends on what he estimates to be the 'content' (*ösi*) of the pig. Two pigs can have exactly the same girth but vary considerably in content. Supposing in an exchange between *A* and *B*, *A*'s pig is bony so he opts to have it measured by girth. If the return pig of *B* has stout hindquarters (but the same girth), it may yield more *hië*, in which case the original donor, *A*, gains without incurring debt, since he specified girth at the outset. *B* does not want to endow *A* in this way without gaining credit but he may not have a leaner pig available of the same girth; or he may estimate incorrectly. *B* then makes a definite loss, but the unwritten record shows an equal exchange.[10] Loss and gain are not simply neutral economic concepts here, as I shall show.

There is scope for judgement and planning in these calculations, but the content of a *sulö* pig is said, ultimately, to depend on or to exhibit one's luck (*harazaki*; cf. Indon. *rezeki*), a concept which is associated with the notion of gaining something-for-nothing without 'sin', *horö* (cheating is gaining by means of deceit and counts as *horö*). This represents an important, though peripheral, principle of gift-exchange in the *ovasa* and in exchange generally in Nias: gaining as much and losing as little as possible without affecting the official quantities involved and thus without affecting the symbolism of the gift or the social position of the participants. Needless to say, such calculations are not the essence of the *ovasa*, which is intended

[10] In the reverse situation, *A* opts to have a stout pig of 5 *alisi* weighed. It yields 34 *hië*. In order to repay his debt of 34, *B* may have to return a pig of 6 *alisi* unless he can obtain one comparably massive. He loses the equivalent of Rp.10,000: a week's pay for a hired labourer. (Market pigs are priced by girth, with some adjustment for solidity.)

to raise status; they are a side-issue, but one which is important in the motivation of individual participants, in the efficiency of domestic production, and in the practical working out of the exchange. Precision is everything, but even the most precise measurements are imperfect and leave a margin of error, which is where skill and luck enter.

6   Summary Remarks on Measurement in Nias

Measurement in Nias employs bodily units and independent invariable standards. Standard scales are graduated, that is, there is a calculable and consistent relation between units and subunits (unlike in bodily measurements). In general, the individual characteristics of the objects of exchange are ignored (colour, history), and only basic criteria enter into consideration (e.g. for pigs, size and sex; for gold, weight and purity). The relation between girth (circumference) and weight or volume can be estimated by experience, but cannot be calculated. In these estimations, Niasans display a highly developed 'grasp of compensations' (Hallpike 1979: 253) and of the relation between dimensions. However, these relations cannot be formulated with accuracy since the measuring systems are incommensurable. There are no universal systems and there is no need for them. The tendency to specialization leads to different systems for different objects. In linear measure the *afore* is used for pigs, the body for timber; in weight, rice counterweights are used for pork, coins for gold. There are cumbersome ways of establishing equivalence between systems, such as between hand-measures and the *afore*; but there is no common scale. The borrowing of instruments (rice-measures for pork) does not generalize a system, but introduces a new one; likewise the borrowing of terms between systems is not a simplification, but a complication deriving from exchange rates.

The need for precision and objectivity is tied to the exigencies of exchange—payments may be dispersed among hundreds of recipients; gift and return may be separated by many years, necessitating some form of abstraction; in barter or the substitution of prescribed prestations, goods must be quantifiable. But these exigencies are themselves a reflection of the cultural emphasis given to 'full measure' and to exact reciprocity: over- or underpayment on return is always significant (morally, politically, etc.). Likewise, restrictions on measurement (e.g. of bridewealth pigs) or the disdain of measurement (in a vast and profligate *ovasa*) are again highly significant.

There is a sense in which some exchanges, typically between affines, involve gifts beyond measure. Nevertheless, for practical purposes, a figure must be agreed. In such cases the counter-prestation is given a conventional value; it is not meant to express a rate of exchange with the original gift. Who can put a price on a bride or a blessing? But the very idea of a 'priceless' gift can be used to exert pressure to increase the size of the counter-prestation. At the Request for Blessing ceremony held for the dying chief of Sifalagö in 1988, one of the chief's agnates made this appeal for more tribute from the wife-takers, prefacing his demand with a thinly veiled threat to exclude some people from the blessing:

Evidently, this blessing which you request cannot be measured in a *lauru*, cannot be measured in a *tumba*, what lasts as long as a lifetime. We are all here in expectation of blessing. And there are indeed those who say, 'Why haven't I been mentioned yet [in the list of beneficiaries]?' It's as if they are competing for the blessing. Of course we haven't come here today for the food. The blessing goes beyond mere food. . . . It all comes down to our [your] ability and desire [to offer tribute]. It's not obligatory—just whatever one feels like giving. But in requesting blessing, as in all things, one reaps as one sows.

7 Rates of Exchange

The earliest reliable source on Nias, Nieuwenhuisen and Rosenberg (1863: 48), reports that trade in the interior was carried out by barter. Chickens, pigs, and rice could be used as a medium of exchange. Gold was used as a medium of exchange, standard of value, store of wealth, and means of payment, thus having the characteristics of a currency. Schröder, administrator on Nias from 1904 to 1909, introduced Dutch money to the sum of fl.125,000, in order to facilitate trade and to make up for the diminishing amount of gold in circulation. But the purely symbolic value of Dutch money was not immediately fully appreciated, and he observed how, when small coins were not available, large ones might be chopped up into pieces (1917: 202).

The Nias economy has never been uniform. The economy of the coastal settlements, based on fishing and coconut plantations, and the area around Gunung Sitoli, were integrated with the colonial economy and traditional trading networks with Sumatra. In the interior, trade was in pigs, rice, gold, and gongs (ibid.). Alongside these items there must have been a trade in imported cloth, tobacco, salt, and other metals, such as iron and copper. But until very recently the economy of the interior remained for the most part isolated from that of the area around Gunung Sitoli and other ports. Until the 1970s the nearest market to Sifalagö was a day's return journey away at Helezalulu. Today, money is needed for non-traditional purchases such as imported clothing, government taxes, school fees, and church collections. It is also used for a small proportion of essential items, both traditional (rice and pork) and non-traditional (sugar, noodles, kerosene). Households which have turned over part of their land to cash crops, such as coffee and patchouli oil, need to supplement their rice harvest in this way. However, it remains true that most needs can be met from domestic production, and little money is in circulation. In most households at most a few thousand rupiah are available, more often nothing. If money is needed for a specific purpose, something has to be sold in the market to outsiders. Money has intruded as standard of value; its other functions can all be fulfilled by other means.

A customary rate of exchange is maintained alongside market prices. The precise relation between these two systems is difficult to understand given a lack of reliable historical data on the fluctuation of rates and factors of supply and demand. Nieuwenhuisen and Rosenberg (1863: 50) report that in 1848 there were three standards for the *batu*. The lowest was used in settling debts (thus for customary exchange); the middle standard was used for trade with foreigners; and the highest was for bridewealth.[11] Rice units were also different: the commercial *lauru* was 5 *tumba*; the customary *lauru* was 4 *tumba*. It is not clear how exchange rates related to economic conditions. The customary value of rice against other goods did not change with the season, even though there is always a

---

[11] As mentioned, in the Upper Susua district there are two standards of *batu*, one for bridewealth, and one for other purposes (market deals, loans, barter). In Gomo the bridewealth *batu* is 10 *huakete* (10 g.). One Sifalagö man whose daughter married in Gomo insisted that the bridewealth be reckoned in the larger Gomo units. Differences between regional standards make exchange more difficult but not impossible.

shortage before the harvest. This remains true, despite the fact that the cash price fluctuates seasonally.

Evidently rice has increased considerably in value relative to the other items (see Appendix 4). Harvests are much smaller than formerly due to (1) rice being displaced by new crops, and (2) population increase, which has led to smaller land-holdings and shorter fallow periods, causing low yield. Villagers say that pigs were relatively more expensive in the past because stocks were frequently depleted by epidemic and by the constant round of feasts and other ritual requirements. Several people told me that the amount of gold in circulation in the villages has steadily decreased since pre-colonial times—an estimation supported by the literary sources. The slave trade with Aceh provided a steady source of gold which dried up with the establishing of Dutch control after the turn of the century. Since then gold has leaked out of the system. Much is said to have been buried as 'tainted' wealth and is now lost. Much was sold off to merchants in town to obtain imported goods, and this trend continues today. Nowadays, it is said, 'gold is expensive', both in relation to pigs and cash. The current value of gold, as an imported item, is obviously more closely tied to external market prices than are the other commodities.

Customary rates cover barter within the district and substitutions of customary prestations. For certain bridewealth prestations (but not all), gold or pigs can be substituted by rice in the appropriate quantities. Gold and pigs are, to a much greater extent than rice, mutually substitutable, despite the fact that the customary gold/pigs ratio is much less rational than the gold/rice ratio. This says much about the cultural devaluation of rice as a subsistence item, as opposed to gold and pigs as prestige goods.

While customary rates fixed long ago still apply in bridewealth and certain other transactions which qualify as *adat* debts (as opposed to impersonal market deals), the relative value of the goods in the market has changed considerably. In 1986 the price of a pig of 5 *alisi* was, on average, Rp.50,000 (about £20). One *batu* of gold cost Rp.125–150,000. Eight *so'e* of paddy cost about Rp.120,000. In customary rates they are all equal. Clearly, then, the matter of substitution when negotiating and delivering bridewealth is one of great importance. Rice has become so expensive that no one nowadays would consider substituting it for pigs at the customary rate.[12] However, rice is still payable, on these unfair terms, as a counter-prestation (called *fanö'ö*) for interest-free loans. For the loan of a pig of 5 *alisi*, a *fanö'ö* of 1 *so'e* is levied (market value 15,000 rupiah) or a piglet/growth increment of 6 *saga* (value 10,000 rupiah) is added to the return. The lender may specify rice as *fanö'ö*, forcing the borrower to agree or go elsewhere.

Although there are no rigidly defined 'spheres of exchange', such as are found in some societies, certain goods are more associated with prestige than others (gold > pigs > rice); therefore a conversion from one to the other may have a symbolic aspect. This depends on the purpose of the transaction. To sell gold to buy rice in the market would be like 'selling off the family silver'. But to accept rice in substitution for gold as part of bridewealth does not imply a devaluation of either partner in the exchange. The difference is that in the latter case the transaction is not commercial, but remains in the realm of gift-exchange. In the former, rice is reduced from being a gift to a commodity.

Many goods and services which have nothing to do with customary exchange, such as payment for thatch roofing, hired labour on the land, or church duties, can be paid for in kind at fixed rates. One hundred pieces of sago-leaf roofing cost a piglet of 6 *saga* (market value Rp.10,000) or Rp.6,000 cash. The difference between these figures shows that money is a limited good with an inflated value relative to other goods. The cost of a modern concrete house is reckoned in *batu*, rather than rupiah, even though all the pigs sold to buy the materials have first to be converted into cash. In the *ovasa*, money appears solely as a prestige good, becoming *sumange* ('tribute') and losing its primarily utilitarian value.

8 The Regulation of Exchange

Concepts of exchange are central in Nias culture because of their capacity to unite disparate aspects of experience. We have seen how the interrelation of exchange and social organization is given striking expression in the forms and symbolism of measurement. Another manifestation of this interrelation is in the explanation of misfortune.

---

[12] I was told that a ratio of 5 *alisi* = 2 *so'e* is now commonly accepted for certain *adat* payments, excepting bridewealth.

Every society must confront the problem of how to justify or explain suffering, and in Nias illness is often explained as a result of sin (*horö*).[13] While many kinds of offence are punished in this way, both by God and the ancestors, offences against exchange norms, such as profiteering, cheating, and short measuring, are among the most prominent in this kind of explanation. Such reasoning has important implications for thinking about morality. Indeed, what is special about the Nias case is the extent to which ethical discourse focuses on exchange and is in turn expressed in exchange concepts. The full scope of this topic will emerge in the following chapters as cosmological notions are presented. Here I am more narrowly concerned with the regulation of exchange and its ethical functions.

There were practical means to alleviate the effects of sin, on a personal and community level, notably rites of expiation, and the regulation of rates of exchange among different goods, the standardization of weights and measures, and the regulation of interest. The enforcement of such rules was one of the main tasks of the village federations (*öri*) until their abolition in 1967. Such rules are still regarded as the pillars of customary law.

Contrary to what is sometimes asserted, the *öri* was not found all over Nias. In south Nias the same functions were carried out by the *orurusa*—a major village and its satellites.[14] In the Susua valley, where the *öri* system was introduced by the Dutch around 1906 (with effect in Sifalagö from about 1918), similar arrangements regarding exchange seem to have existed traditionally between villages linked by marriage alliance and treaties, without there being a formal constitution of ranked clans or villages.

The standards and exchange rates were revised or confirmed in each area of Nias in much the same way. At the founding of an *öri*, the chiefs of the member villages would gather to appoint a council and determine the measures and rates as part of the *öri* constitution. Some of them even determined the bridewealth appropriate to particular ranks. The constitution was ratified by the swearing of an oath (*fondrakö*) which put a curse on its offenders.[15]

[13] The word *horö* has other meanings, such as 'a state of war' or 'feud'; all are covered by Hertz's definition of sin as a violation of a divinely sanctioned moral order (Hertz 1922: 45–6).
[14] See Marschall (1976: 161) on the standardization of measures at 'law feasts' in south Nias.
[15] Oral histories of various *öri* were recorded by colonial officers in the 1930s (Korn Archive, KITLV, Leiden).

According to an oral history recorded in 1938, *öri* O'o'u (west Nias) derives its regulations from the first *fondrakö* convened by the legendary Hia in Gomo (Korn 475/6). The regulations were renewed and extended at successive *fondrakö* each time there was a migration. The 'present' (1938) *öri* O'o'u traces its regulations back through three such *fondrakö*, performed at the villages of Ambukha, Bavöd-esolo, and Hililovalangi. At the first of these the *öri* was founded as a political federation. This account agrees, in its stress on collective legislation concerning exchange rather than Mosaic lawgiving, with the 'charter' myth which I recorded in Sifalagö Susua.

The *fondrakö* ritual in externals seems to have been the same in west Nias as it was in Sifalagö. A pig was slaughtered, having been dedicated to the deity by means of a makeshift idol (*azu vondrakö*). The oath was sworn over a large stone which had been erected inside a temporary sacred shelter called an *osali*. The priest would utter a curse while cutting a chicken's neck on the stone: 'If any offend against these regulations and diminish the *tumba* or the *afore* may his neck be cut through thus!'

But the *fondrakö* was not restricted to legislation on exchange. In the Upper Susua (and probably in other areas too) public cursing ceremonies, also called *fondrakö*, were performed for a number of reasons: to outlaw sexual relations within the clan or between prohibited categories of affine; to curse an undiscovered thief; to revise the terms of credit. In each case the curse invoked supernatural sanctions on offenders. As it was explained to me, what these different crimes have in common is the idea of 'eating of the forbidden', taking what you do not deserve. To have sexual relations with a prohibited category of person is to 'eat what has been forbidden/cursed (*salakha*)'; to extort, accept a bribe, or obtain by deceit is to 'eat what is not given freely/permitted' (*i'a zi lö aoha gölö*). These examples show how, in discussing exchange, one passes easily from economic to ethical questions, not simply because exchange norms are backed by mystical sanctions, but because commercial debts and moral debts are not radically different in the Nias conception.

An emphasis on full measure and equal return is central, and any deviation from this principle is morally significant. There are licensed exceptions, such as the complementary exchange between affines. A wife-giver is said to be someone who may 'eat of the forbidden fruit of your labour' (*tola i'a zalakha gölöu*); he can take without incurring debt what is forbidden to others, namely, the product of his wife-taker's 'effort'. And there are, of course, numerous occasions in daily life when no direct return for a service is expected, though mutuality and parity are the virtues of good neighbourly relations, and there are very few occasions in which a prestation is explicitly unilateral.

Thanking, in Nias as elsewhere, may imply receiving without the obligation of return. Since this is contrary to the usual expectation, Niasans do not normally express thanks for a gift or service. In fact, the formula for thanking, *saoha gölö* (lit. 'that which is light of effort'), makes the denial of reciprocity particularly clear. It means something like: 'may it be given freely on your part; I do not owe you anything for it'. The recipient's 'thanks' classifies the service as gratuitous, a free gift. (The opposite formula, cited above, is *si lö aoha gölö*: that which is not freely given, the extorted gift.) In ordinary exchange thanks is necessarily excluded, even as a token of politeness. Naturally, I did not realize this at first, and if I thanked my neighbours effusively for some good deed it implied I would not return the favour ('taking for granted', as we should say); if I expressed thanks for some minor courtesy it made them wonder what boon I thought I had received, and therefore what they could extract in return. If ever I gave something (e.g. medicine) without expectation of return I generally received blessing (*hovu-hovu*) rather than thanks—in Nias terms a genuine exchange; or the recipient would transfer the burden of the favour, with the words: 'only God can repay you' (*ha Lovalangi zangulöni*).

Thanking tends to imply, then, nothing-for-something. Significantly, the commonest expression of thanks is in prayer to the Christian God—a being who expects no sacrifice but who takes and gives life at will. When counting one's blessings in prayer to God, one usually adds the phrase *lö sulö moroi khöma* ('there is no recompense (*sulö*) from us'). These words have a peculiar aptness and resonance since *sulö* is the paradigm of symmetrical gift-exchange in the *ovasa*; and failure to recompense implies eventual submission to the creditor. The liturgical phrase takes the form of a refusal of exchange, or at any rate an acknowlegement that one cannot engage in a quid pro quo with the Almighty. While the ancestors and the affines accept tribute, God accepts nothing.

This is a new and sometimes frustrating or puzzling development in religious life, a radical break with the past. No doubt this is part of the reason why Nias Christians are happier dealing with the God of the Old Testament than the Jesus of the Sermon on the Mount: Jehovah is vengeful and capricious, but ultimately amenable to offers. Indeed, the Nias translation of the Old Testament presents relations with God in a wholly familiar idiom. For example, Exodus 34: 29: *La ohe ame'ela saoha gölö khö Jehowa* ('they brought a *willing offering* to the Lord').[16] It is hardly surprising, then, that competitive auctions in church, and donations to absolve sin have become a prominent feature of vernacular Christianity in Nias.

Mauss (1954: 12–15) has shown the contractual nature of 'gifts to gods' exemplified in sacrifice. In Nias, until the advent of Christianity, the terms of the 'contract' with the gods characteristically involved stipulations of quantity and thus measurement. Men may not take freely from the world's wealth, which is in the keeping of supernatural beings. Such notions survive today only in hunting rituals. In former times harvesting involved exacting rites of measuring. Each lineage employed a 'rice priest' to measure the crop in the field. First, the field was encircled by the singing harvesters, and a temporary border was constructed, demarcating a sacred (*ni'amoni'ö*) zone. Then the priest measured one length of a *tugala* leaf (about 1½ armspans) in front of the row of harvesters. At this mark, he would stake in a branch as an *azu* ('idol, temporary abode of the spirit'), while invoking 'he who fills/replenishes the rice', and sprinkling coconut milk on the rice. If he had performed the ritual correctly, and there had been no breaches of the harvest taboos to drive away the rice spirit, the sacks should be full by the time the harvesters reached the mark. If they were not full, he interrogated the harvesters one by one to determine who was at fault. Then he would repeat the operation for the next section of the field. Evidently in dealings with the gods one is careful not to take more than is due, but one expects full measure nevertheless.

These examples have taken us away from the narrow definition of exchange and led to a consideration of wider values and the relations between men and the supernatural. In the last analysis these two realms of activity cannot be separated; rather there is gradation between commercial transactions and religious acts at the two extremes.

---

[16] The Rhinish missionaries and subsequently the Nias Protestant Church have tended to stress the proscriptive and punitive ethics of the Old Testament rather than the positive virtues of the New Testament.

The ethical and religious ideas associated with exchange are not merely of interpretative significance for Niasans; they play a part in the economic and political organization of the community. Concepts of sin (getting something for nothing) operate as a tax on wealth accumulated in profitable activities, encouraging its redistribution. I describe below some of the consequences of 'tax' evasion and the legitimate forms of 'deduction' which allow the rich man to keep most of his wealth.

Power inevitably involves moral compromises. In general, it is assumed that one cannot become rich without being ruthless. A chief or a great man is said to 'crush his fellow men'. Some of his wealth is commonly attributed to 'cheating at the mouth of the *tumba*', i.e. short-measuring, and to simple extortion. Usually he is a ruthless creditor. Loans of gold, rice, and pigs incur interest (*hare*, 'profit') at the rate of 100 per cent per annum. This doubling (*fabali*, lit. 'division') of the principal is recorded by the earliest visitors to Nias, and was customary in all parts of Nias. It can lead to huge profits for the creditor and ruin (formerly bondage) for the debtor. Usually lending at high interest is practised only with unrelated persons, though not with strangers, who are beyond jurisdiction. It is contrary to norms of mutual aid and may lead to a breach between the partners. A chief's rise is achieved at the expense of others, and he expects to make enemies. But he is open to a more serious danger incurred in the pursuit of wealth. For what escapes the sanction of society is punished by God. Acts of deceit and taking more than one's due provoke divine wrath and punishment in the form of illness and death.

There are several forms of insurance against the risks entailed by wealth. One gives it away at an *ovasa*, purchasing the goodwill and indebtedness of guests and the blessing of wife-givers. Nowadays, the Christian repents of his sins through prayer and reformed conduct. In the past there were rituals of expiation, performed on behalf of individuals, local descent groups, the village, or the whole *öri*. There are no descriptions of such rituals in the literature, and villagers' accounts do not always make clear for whom they are being performed. Nevertheless the same set of ideas is common to all types, as will become evident.

In the case of an individual rich man, if his household had been struck by illness or his pigs had died, or to guarantee his prosperity, he would stage a feast at which a slave or captive was rolled off the roof (*nigulu halu*, 'rolled [like a] rice pestle') then beheaded.[17] This sacrifice was called *fanöla zimbo gana'a* ('piercing/letting out [from the roof] the smoke of the gold'). The victim was explicitly a scapegoat, killed to protect the life of the sacrificer. When Matanihela, the late chief's father, 'let off the vapour' (*sau*) accumulated by his wealth, he substituted a piglet for a human sacrifice. The roof was pierced to 'let the heat and steam escape', and the piglet was passed through the hole, then rolled off the top inside a *lauru* rice-measure.

If a big *ovasa* was to be held and new gold ornaments inaugurated, a slave might be made to dress up in all the gold regalia of his master. He was then prodded and tormented, forcing him to declare that he would 'take on my shoulders the smoke and vapour of the gold', i.e. the curses and supernatural wrath which had been defied in obtaining it. Another way of 'cooling' wealth without losing it was to kill a 'ransom pig' (*höli*), which was matched to the characteristics of the sacrificer: a white pig for a pale man.[18]

Part of the rituals ending the harvest, which were performed separately by each descent group, involved a similar expiation of illicit profit. A stone box was constructed beside the river. Into this the priest put a handful of sand taken from the riverbed (therefore 'cool'), with the words: 'Here is the substitute for the excess we have taken (*ya'e zalahi zitöra*); the substitute for the smoke and for the surplus (*ösi töra*, 'extra content'); may it be cool.'

But the most important corrective measure in the regulation of exchange was the *fombuvu*, a ceremony of 'decrease' in which interest rates were lowered or abolished and exchange rates were revised. A *fombuvu* was held in response to an epidemic, either of men or livestock, and the whole population was assembled for the ceremony. A live scape-pig (*bawi salahi*), was tied to a banana stem and carried aloft by six men in offering to Lovalangi, the deity. The priest would then call out:

> *Lali mbanua möi sihönö, lali mbanua möi sato*
> *Yavö a bawi dele-dele, yavö a bawi sihogo.*

---

[17] The same ritual inaugurated a new chief's house and had a similar purpose of protecting the prosperity of the owner. The last such sacrifice was made for the new *omo sebua* in Sifalagö around 1928.

[18] This conception of the danger inherent in wealth (which derives from a denial of reciprocity) invites comparison with the Maori *hau* (Mauss 1954) or Kruyt's analysis of Toraja *measa* (1923). But the steam or heat generated by wealth is a symbol of human and divine sanctions rather than an intrinsic property of gold, etc.

> In place of the village, of the thousands, of the many
> Here is the pig that squeals, here is the pig that grunts.

The pig was then killed and eaten. A pig can substitute for men because men are the pigs of Lovalangi. One of several divine epithets was Sobawiniha: 'He whose pigs are men' or 'He who makes of men his pigs'. The chief would then proclaim the new regulations, sanctioned by a curse.

The ceremonial prohibition of interest could also be prompted by an earth tremor or a period of prolonged rain and floods. The same chain of causes was assumed. It was said that Lovalangi had 'opened the door' and let rain fall in disgust at the sins of men. He had seen people short-measuring and copulating in the fields (taking what belonged to others). Villagers would rush out into the square and compete to confess the collective sins of the community: 'There have been adulterers and sinners; secret profits have been taken; Sobawi (the Pig Owner) is disgusted. Open the door of dry weather! Close the door of rain! Relent, Pig Owner!' On this occasion, a priest would tie a white chicken and a white pig to a makeshift idol and throw them into the river, where they were washed down to the god of the underworld, Nazuva Danö, saying: 'Here is the payment of our profit, our excess, for the infringement of the *afore* and the *lauru*.' The practical aim of such expiation was to deflect retribution, and to 'launder' the wealth, not to get rid of it. People were aware that such laundering involved a different kind of deception, but one which was acceptable.

The last *fombuvu* was held about forty-five years ago and involved an amalgam of Christian and pagan practices. Matanihela's youngest son had died in an epidemic of smallpox, and as head of the *öri* he called together the nine village chiefs and reduced interest from 100 per cent to a small increment of 6 *saga* on a pig of 5 *alisi*, and 1 *lauru* on 1 *so'e* of rice. These payments still stand as the customary counter-prestation on friendly loans, though in other deals high interest is once again charged. It was common for the stipulations to be ignored once the epidemic had passed, and little by little to raise interest rates. It seems that on the same occasion as the last *fombuvu*, the standard measures were reaffirmed and present exchange rates were set. There was no cursing or sacrifice, though six pigs were killed to feed the chiefs. Instead, Matanihela's daughter and another child, who both remember the occasion, prayed in the square for the epidemic to end. The ceremony was incorporated into the confession movement which was active in central Nias at the time. The Great Repentance (*fangesa sebua*), as this movement was called, found a traditional prototype for expiation and public confession in the *fombuvu*.

It would be interesting to know if these ceremonies traditionally operated to maintain the system of exchange by adjusting customary rates to reflect supply and demand, or, in later times when prices began to be determined by the market, by adjusting the relation between customary and market values. It seems that rates would remain stable for many years until they became totally unrealistic. At such a point the system would allow for profiteering, and epidemics were thought to be the result. It is easy to see how the timing of a *fombuvu* could be linked to such economic phenomena. Unfortunately there is not enough evidence to support such a hypothesis.

Not all wealth can be laundered. Gold obtained in fines, such as adultery compensation retains traces of its ignominious origins, possibly through a curse, and may be harmful. It was thought that the Dutch allowed Nias chiefs to try adultery cases to avoid having to 'eat' the fine themselves. It is especially bad to use tainted gold as bridewealth, though it is rumoured to happen.

Profit continues to be seen as a cause of misfortune both to individuals and the community as a whole. The dramatic lowering of agricultural yield in recent years is seen by some people as connected (in this sense) with the introduction of a weekly market in Sifalagö in the 1970s. Goods which could once be asked for in small quantities, such as betel, fruit, and local tobacco are now sold for petty cash, removing one avenue of good neighbourly relations. The market, where pigs and gold can be readily bought and sold for speculation, has disrupted the old means of controlling prices and profits and introduced a different code of practice based on the simple pursuit of profit. Nevertheless, despite market penetration of the economy, customary techniques, rules, and rates of exchange continue to exist as the dominant mode.

9   Conclusion

We have seen how exchange is imbued with ethical values and is intimately related to the conception of sin and suffering; and how the regulation of exchange is not merely supported by religious sanctions, but is in turn a means of controlling those sanctions. In this pattern of ideas, measurement becomes much more than a technical activity; it belongs to a set of exchange concepts which serve as a framework for ethics and for thinking about the relations between man and the supernatural. What has become of this cluster of ideas under Christianity? The explanation of suffering continues to be couched in traditional terms. 'There is no suffering without sin,' as Christians are fond of asserting, and offences against exchange norms loom large among the cardinal sins of vernacular Christianity. At a different level, the language of exchange—indebtedness, credit, quittance—continues to supply Nias ethics with a convenient and apt idiom. We might go further, and say that it has directed the flow of Christian ideas into the old channels and helped to preserve the essential nature of the traditional ethos. Thus the notion of guilt, the interiorization of the disturbance resulting from sin, is construed in the idiom of debt. The word *sugi* is used of both the action of reclaiming a debt and the inner tug of conscience experienced by the Christian. God is said to *sugi* the heart of the sinner, provoking his repentance. Are sins, then, like (bad) debts to God? Though I never heard sins actually described as debts, there are remarkable parallels between the two concepts. During the Japanese occupation of Nias, a Christian repentance movement reached Sifalagö. Church elders heard public confessions and encouraged penitents to 'reckon up' their sins. In similar fashion to the ceremonial 'counting of the bridewealth debt', a sinner would place counters of palm leaf in a row, each piece representing a sin. A church elder kept the tally in a bundle, reducing it one by one as the sins were expiated, much as a bride-giver deducts bridewealth debts as they are paid off. The list of parallels could be extended—church donations as deliverance from sin, the crucifixion as a 'ransom' (*höli*) for men's sins—but the analogy is by now clear enough. Niasans find ample support for their attachment to the exchange-ethics analogy in the Bible, so in one respect at least, they can be both good Christians and good Niasans. Render unto Caesar that which is Caesar's; as you sow, so shall you reap. These sayings are the common currency of ethical discourse in Nias. Since exchange had and continues to have a religious dimension, they have an added and quite unexpected power.

9

Ovasa: Feasts of Merit

Once celebrated all over Nias but now vanished from most of the island, the feast of merit is still performed regularly in the isolated central districts. In this region ceremonial exchange persists as the basis of rank and prestige. There is no detailed empirical account of the sociology of the *ovasa*, and most of what follows has not been described before.[1]

In Chapter 10 I consider the politics of feasting and the relation of the *ovasa* to social stratification. But a few introductory remarks on the latter topic are necessary here in order to make sense of the following description. In central Nias there are three broad social divisions: chiefs, elders, and ordinary villagers (an underclass of slaves was abolished under Dutch rule). Rank and title are attained by feasting, and anyone able to assemble the resources may hold a feast. Sponsors of small-scale feasts (up to 30 pigs) are known as *samahö urakha* ('slaughterers of prestige payments') and bear a junior title. It is within the ambitions of any man of ability to hold such a feast and pay off debts acquired at the feasts of others. Many men do not attain this rank, but only the poorest are practically excluded. Sponsors of major feasts (*ovasa*) are called *satua mbanua* ('village elder'), and bear a 'great name' (*töi sebua*). They speak with authority in customary matters and rule the village with the chief (*salawa*) and the consent of the ordinary villagers (*ono mbanua*). The chief traditionally combines seniority in feasting achievements with other political and economic advantages.

I shall refer to the status won in feasting as 'rank', denoting a publicly recognized position. Thus chief, elder, and 'slaughterer' are ranks; but it is recognized that there are finer discriminations

[1] Early, somewhat superficial descriptions of the *ovasa* are found in Modigliani 1890 and Schröder 1917. For recent worthwhile accounts, see Marschall 1976, which deals with south Nias, and Hämmerle's (1982; 1984) reconstructions of the so-called 'megalithic' culture of central Nias. Suzuki's (1959) Leiden structuralist reconstruction, though it contains many insights, is based on uneven source material and I have not followed his interpretation.

within these categories. The word 'status' is used in a more general sense. According to this usage, affinal superiority and rank are two different types of status, referring to different aspects of social organization.

There is a common structure to *ovasa* and a common set of themes, though emphasis varies with the occasion. This makes it possible to present in outline a 'standard' *ovasa* containing all the essential elements. My description is based on attendance at seven *ovasa* from 1986 to 1988, supplemented by informants' accounts of their own and others' feasts. Historical material derives almost entirely from the recollection of informants. Mostly this was corroborated on separate occasions by different individuals and I believe is reliable item by item: the danger of reconstruction lies in putting these items together. Oral history tends to oppose the present to a homogeneous past. Nevertheless a cautious use of historical material is worthwhile for several reasons. First, I wish to show how the *ovasa* has changed and adapted to the radical transformation of Nias society this century. Secondly, the *ovasa* means different things to different generations and it would be a serious distortion to present a purely synchronic analysis based on what is directly accessible, especially when most such feasts are organized by middle-aged and old men whose ideas of what the feast is supposed to represent were formed many years ago. A further reason is that a number of elements in the ritual are meaningless without reference to practices which are ostensibly discredited or obsolete, such as ancestor worship and sacrifice, but which persist in an inconspicuous form.

I. THE ORGANIZATION OF AN *OVASA*

1   The Purpose of an *Ovasa*

A graded series of named feasts has been reported from many parts of Nias. There is only sparse evidence to suggest that such a series was customary in the Upper Susua valley. It seems that most feasts were—as they still are—clearly linked to a particular occasion, typically a rite of passage, such as a wedding or funeral (of father), or the completion of a house, the successful prosecution of a raid, etc. But *ovasa* can also be events in themselves, without relation to any marked change in the individual's life and without reference to a projected series. They are landmarks in the history of a community against which other events are dated.

The host of an *ovasa* has two declared aims: to win prestige or 'name' and to obtain blessing. Both aims are achieved by gift-giving. The conversion of prestige into influence may provide additional motivation, but it does not form the explicit goal. To make it explicit would destroy the appearance of the gift. Influence in Nias works by applying pressure on those indebted, but never coercion which may rebound on the creditor and lead to the withdrawal of the willing respect from which prestige partly derives. For the most part, *ovasa* are not wars of generosity or fighting with property. The type of feast (now obsolete) in which the host crushed his rivals—the challenge feast—was an exception, having the character of an ordeal. As a rule, the link between rank and influence (not to speak of power) is more subtle and shows itself over time. This is directly related to the fact that the rise in rank is associated with gift-exchange, which works itself out over time and in accordance with a code of morality far removed from simple coercive power relations. However, the individual's political position in the village—his desire to bolster or increase his rank and, ultimately, his influence—is a decisive factor in the scale and timing of the feast.

The initial motivation for undertaking an *ovasa* is often the negative one of not being able to defer it any longer. Participation in feasts as a guest enmeshes one in a web of obligations and debts. When the debts mount up to a certain point one feels vulnerable to criticism, even public rebuke. A man's prosperity is held to be linked to his balance of payments. If he has received without the intention or prospect of return he is vulnerable to supernatural displeasure. His plans may crystallize in response to a growing sense of the insecurity of his prosperity and his reputation. A sudden illness or other inexplicable misfortune is taken as a danger sign, a warning of the risk of putting off the *ovasa*. In several of the cases I recorded some such misfortune was the precipitating cause of action.

2   The Invocation of Fortune

Fortune can be invoked to restore prosperity or as a prelude to a feast. The procedure in former times was as follows. The householder calls together his lineage mates and a priest to summon the ancestors. He adorns the ancestor figures with coconut leaves, and sacrifices a piglet, tucking a tuft of its hairs in the waistband or under the arm of one of the figures. He also offers the ancestors gold as their tribute (*sumange*). The priest tells them that they are being honoured (*nifosumange*) so that they will restore fortune (*harazaki*) to the householder. They may have been angered by broken promises of sacrifices: pigs which the householder should have killed in feasting (dedicated to the ancestors) have been used elsewhere—to settle a debt or pay off a service, or were simply eaten.

The priest sits in the roof flap beating a drum and chanting invocations until the ancestral spirits come.

Faöndru khönia harazaki	Summon to him fortune
Ombuyui löfö lalu'a tönua	Soften the hand of destiny
Löfö laharö gana'a	Fortune weighed in grains of gold
Löfö laharö simo.	Fortune in blended gold.[2]

The sign of the spirits' arrival is when the hairs on the back of the neck stand up, and a shiver passes through the participants. It might take up to three nights of continual drumming (the priest being well fed meanwhile) before the priest can announce: 'They've come!' One of the spirits is said to place a hand on the shoulder of the householder in blessing.

The fortune the spirits bring is not a direct endowment. It is rather the goodwill and co-operation of the deceased patriline (*nga'ötö*). The householder asks them to accompany him on his visits to the wife-takers to claim tribute: 'Propitiate fortune; bring us wealth so that we may eat, O ancestor figures! Soften the hearts of the wife-takers, *X*, *Y*, and *Z*, O fathers!' The householder then announces that he has felt the ghostly hand of blessing upon him and

[2] *Lalu'a tönua* is fate drawn on the palm of the hand; *simo* is tin, but here refers to a gold alloy; *laharö* is a small gold weight. Though sometimes used as synonyms, *löfö* refers specifically to wealth or a 'windfall' brought by fortune, whereas *harazaki* means fortune in a general sense (cf. Indon. *rezeki*).

he will shortly visit the wife-takers to 'see if they are in accord with my plan' (that is, to demand tribute). The gold offering is returned to its bag, and the lineage agrees on a rough date for the *ovasa*, one or two years hence.

The prospective feastgiver then calls on his wife-takers and informs them he has adorned the ancestor figures, asking them to 'endow him with fortune' (*folöfö ndra'o*) and render him tribute (*sumange*). A wife-taker cannot give an outright refusal; to do so would incur his affine's curse. On return home the feastgiver offers up the gold to the ancestors, asking them to 'add to it' on his next trip. The wife-takers' compliance is seen as a result of persuasion and the ancestors' intervention. A close wife-taker will give ½–1 *batu* of gold, and on several trips a haul of as much as 12–20 *batu* may be obtained. Depending on the total amount, the feastgiver decides what sort of ornament he will commission. Since the gold has been given with the *ovasa* in mind, and it has been presented to the ancestors (in some sense it is theirs; the descendant merely holds it), it may not be used for any other purpose. To 'shift' gold away from its true end is a cardinal sin.

Nowadays there is a simple meal for agnates at which the prospective host explains his plans and requests help. The purpose of the gathering is still understood to be an invocation of fortune (*faöndru harazaki*) but there is no request for the aid of the ancestors, as if the collective meal itself is efficacious. The emphasis instead is on agnatic solidarity *vis-à-vis* the wife-takers. The ideology of affinity and its sanctions is unchanged: wife-takers' tribute cannot be allocated to any purpose other than that for which it is solicited, or else the host will fall ill, afflicted by his ancestors.

At any meeting of the kind where, formerly, ancestral blessing on a project was required, a Christian prayer may now be spoken. This substitution shows a certain continuity with the past. Formerly, requests for blessing would move easily from addressing the ancestors to the names of the pagan God (Lovalangi, Samailo, Salöfö). An ancestor figure was the *lovalangi zamösana* ('personal god/idol'). In a sense, the ancestors and God shared the role of guardians of Fortune. Ancestors influenced one's daily life; God, in his various forms, controlled one's ultimate destiny. (The name Salöfö probably derives from *löfö*, 'material fortune'.) The modern practice of requesting the blessing of the Christian God instead of the ancestors' blessing does not essentially disturb the traditional relation between men and the supernatural. Even the name has not changed: Lovalangi is God in the Nias Bible.

The ideology of affinity has not suffered the same direct interference as patrilineal ideology and has survived intact. While the ancestor cult is discredited, and its rituals are derided as the worship of wooden idols, the importance of the affines remains unquestioned. This is surprising since the one may be seen to depend on the other; affines' mystical powers are derived from their agnatic ancestors. The god-like function vested in wife-givers remains explicit in the epithet they share with Lovalangi: *Sokhö ya'ita* ('He who owns us'), as well as in the exercise of their mystical powers of blessing and cursing. Perhaps this paradox shows that the abolition of ancestor worship has merely suppressed one expression of patrilineal ideology, and that the ancestors continue to exert a shadowy influence in other, less obvious, ways.

3   Dedication of the Origin Pigs

At the earliest stage, when the plan to hold an *ovasa* is being formulated, the host picks out from the latest farrow the best pair of piglets, usually males. These are to be the 'origin pigs' (*börö mbawi*) or the 'chosen ones' (*sinuturu*) whose slaughter—when grown into bristling monsters—is a ritual focus of the *ovasa*. They are nurtured with special care and fattened on a rich diet, and their tusks are cultivated to give them a ferocious appearance. Formerly the piglets were bathed in coconut milk beneath the ancestor figures (coconut palms grow proverbially quickly; coconut milk is nourishing and 'cool'). They were then sprinkled with water (a cool and purifying element opposed to what is hot, dangerous, and destructive), while blessings were spoken: 'May they be cool; may they grow like *tugala* shoots, like banana shoots; cool like the earth.' The ancestors were held to have *fohu* ('marked, chosen') the pigs which were dedicated to them. This term *fohu* was also used when a sick or favoured child was dedicated to the ancestors, and when an infant was betrothed. Nowadays, the pigs are still blessed and bathed in the same way, but there is no explicit invocation of the ancestors. Christian prayers may sometimes be substituted.

Once dedicated, the origin pigs may not be used for any other purpose. Only the feastgiver himself (or his wife) can raise them, as they represent, among other things, the labour of his wife which is returned to the wife-givers at the *ovasa* in their portions of the carcass. The symbolism of the 'chosen ones' is explored below.

4 The Organization of Resources

Disposable wealth exists mainly in the form of investments. There are several reasons for this. First, a single household can manage only a few pigs at a time. Secondly, accumulated wealth is dangerous, exciting envy and sorcery: invested it is less visible. Thirdly, wealth is concealed by dispersal from creditors and needy kinsmen or anyone else with a claim which can be put off until an advantageous moment. What one owns is essentially what one has already given away or loaned. These transfers are reversible or reclaimable. What one has in hand, on the contrary, will be consumed or taken by others. Everyone is busy raising pigs not for himself, but for the *ovasa*, funeral, or bridewealth of others. (The 'origin pigs' are an important exception.) As soon as a household has more than three or four pigs, it disposes of them in donations or loans. Like any good system of banking, this is both an investment for the future, and a way of safeguarding wealth until it is needed.

Wealth is thus dispersed and is only reunited for the purpose of a feast, when it is immediately redistributed and consumed. Thus, while differences in rank derived from feasting may be emphasized in daily life, the corresponding material differences are much less evident. Chiefs alone maintain a conspicuously higher standard of living.[3]

It is only field-hut dwellers (about one-third of the village population) who have all their pigs with them. They do not have to worry about envious neighbours or constant requests for loans; moreover, they have the means to feed up to 20–30 pigs, which are simply fenced into a compound. The self-sufficiency and barbarism of the field-hut dweller is often contrasted to the genteel poverty and sociability of the villager. 'Hut men don't know how to count or divide up meat. But what can you expect when their only companions are the monkeys.' It is expected that when the 'hut man' moves back

[3] Cf. Kirsch (1973: 18): 'while economic inequalities are being evened out, these feasts serve to increase status differences within these societies [of highland SE Asia].'

to the village he will hold an *ovasa* to redistribute his wealth and pay off his debts.

The host of an *ovasa* may provide less than one-third of the total resources needed. His third includes pigs which others have raised for him, and loans which he has reclaimed. For the rest—as many as a hundred pigs—he has to draw on a multitude of relationships. Much of this sum, but not all, will become his debt.

The main sources are as follows (in no particular order):

1. The host's own pigs, rice, and gold.
2. Friendly loans (*nira'u*) (see Appendix 3).
3. Reciprocal loans from close agnates (*naekhu-naekhu*).
4. Tribute from wife-takers (*ana'iwa*).
5. Ceremonial donations and repayments made on the day of the *ovasa* (*sulö*).

Differences in the principles and sanctions associated with each type of exchange have a moral and symbolic import. Friendly loans (*nira'u*; from *ra'u*, 'grasp'), which account for a small proportion of the host's resources, are morally neutral since the partners come out even. A counter-prestation called *fanö'ö*, given at the moment of the loan, is proportional to, or less than, the expected growth of the pig. Interest charged on commercial loans, by contrast, is conceived as being explicitly analogous to growth but *disproportional*, therefore profitable and invidious. Of the words for interest, one (*amanöita*) also means growth; the other (*hare*) also means profit.[4]

As the main source of bridewealth, *naekhu-naekhu*, 'support' loans, are canvassed widely among affines, agnates, and neighbours. Some *ovasa* pigs are also obtained in this way, though usually only from agnates, who are obliged to contribute in proportion to the closeness of relation. In principle, support loans are free of interest or *fanö'ö*, though if the loan is inconvenient or pressed for urgently, or if the parties are not closely related, a *fanö'ö* may be charged.

To lend without gain is, in Nias eyes, to suffer a temporary loss, and is thus honourable. Conversely, over-eagerness in reclaiming

---

[4] It is sometimes said that prestige payments (*urakha*) made at an *ovasa* incur no interest because they consist of meat not live pigs and therefore cannot grow. (The same applies to live *sulö* pigs, since they are all slaughtered for *urakha*.) But this is a rationalization: the profit motive is contrary to the spirit of an *ovasa*; prestige payments and loans at interest are at opposite poles, both in their governing principles and in moral terms, and this contrast is implicit in the *ovasa* exchanges.

the loan and the pursuit of gain are a critical test of character, material for gossip and moral evaluation in daily conversation. There is a great reluctance to reclaim a support loan to finance some private project or to lay off another debt. The loan may be outstanding for up to a generation, when the creditor reclaims it to finance another feast or the bridewealth of his son. This approaches the principle of the *ovasa* donation (*sulö*), according to which one can only reclaim for a ceremony of the same type, thus increasing the symbolic value of *naekhu-naekhu* and placing it in the orbit of ceremonial exchanges.

Among close agnates, debts of this kind are often waived. Father's brothers are a common source of such soft loans for bridewealth, acting as patrons of the juniors in return for their allegiance. Solidarity of a more egalitarian kind is created by the typical support loan between junior agnates and between neighbours for bridewealth or *ovasa*. Usually no *fanö'ö* is demanded and the loan is reclaimed in only one or two years. These loans cut across kinship and tie together the village with goodwill and solidarity when in other ways it is often divided and faction-ridden.[5] The solidarity of feastgiver and contributors is further enhanced by a meal held in their honour as part of the *ovasa* (or wedding) celebrations.

The proportion of the total resources which derives from wife-takers' tribute (*ana'iwa*) depends on the host's status. Members of chiefly lines recognize a wider range of wife-takers and can rely on these for one-third to two-thirds of *ovasa* resources. Among ordinary men the proportion might be as little as one-tenth. At a recent feast of merit in Sifalagö, the chief's nephew was able to demand tribute in gold, pigs, and cash from over seventy wife-takers coming from a dozen villages. (This was no empty boast: I have the list they drew up.) In the event, not all of them were contacted, but those who were felt honoured to attend and pleased to maintain the connection; and those who had received substantial solicitory gifts—however long ago—would have been afraid not to come. Most ordinary men can call on not many more than half a dozen wife-takers. The ideological aspect of affinal exchange, however, is the same in every case. Just as the *ovasa* host invites his wife-givers to pay them tribute and obtain their blessing, so, in a parallel set of exchanges

[5] Recently a young man obtained contributions for his bridewealth amounting to 40 pigs from over 30 households in the hamlet.

prior to the feast, he demands tributary contributions from his wife-takers.

Sulö (described below) account for up to one-third of the total resources.

5   Preparations for the Feast

About two months before the *ovasa* is due to take place the host again calls together his agnates and announces that he is going 'to beat gold'. On this occasion the practical plans are formulated. The host gives instructions to a goldsmith regarding the ornaments he wants constructed for himself and his wife; the agnates are told to make a wooden throne or litter (*osa-osa*) on which he will be carried in state round the village. In former times plans would be laid for the installation of a stone monument. Work is divided among the households of the lineage, or if a very big *ovasa* is in prospect, other lineages may be involved. Each receives a measured amount of rice to pound (e.g. *sazo'e*). In calculating quantities, each guest is reckoned to need 1 *nali*. Matanihela, the late chief's father, had a giant rice-pounder for feasts. The pestle consisted of the trunk of a coconut palm, which was raised by a lever operated by the foot-power of six men. The rice-block contained half a sack of paddy.

The day of the *ovasa* is set for some time during the waxing phase of the moon (*tesa'a*), an auspicious period when pigs are said to have more 'content'.

6   Squeezing the Wife-Takers

When the host has amassed about a quarter of the total sum needed, either at home or in the hands of others, he can turn his attention to other sources. He dispatches his agnates to the wife-takers with solicitory gifts (*so'i-so'i*). These are the latest in a series of gifts dating back to, and analogous to, the original gift of a woman. They consist of chickens, piglets, household articles, or pork. The size of the wife-taker's expected contribution is roughly in proportion to the amount of *so'i-so'i* he has received over the years, which is a function of genealogical and geographical proximity. The flow of gifts is increased in the months leading up to any feast or project for which one needs help. One widower with whom I attended an *ovasa* redistributed his entire *urakha* among five wife-takers in expectation of their help for his bridewealth on remarrying.

If the prospective host has not 'looked after' his affine in this way and shown him continuing 'care', the latter is justified in resisting the pressure now applied. The claiming of debts (*fanugi*) is an elaborate procedure, resting entirely on persuasion backed by hints of supernatural sanctions. Customary debts (those which stem from a relation or create one) cannot be claimed by force, unlike commercial debts or fines. The host's representatives are chosen for their skill in speech and their powers of persuasion. The voluntary aspect of affinal exchange and the rejection of the usual precision and exact reciprocity leaves a lot of room for personal abilities in making the most (in all senses) of a relation. A leading man is necessarily one who is skilled in managing his affinal relations, both with wife-givers and wife-takers.

Because affinal relations are based ideally on an exchange of 'care', 'love', and protection by the wife-givers for respect and tribute from wife-takers, it is important to be able to dress up the demands (or to resist them) in appropriate language without giving offence and producing the opposite result. To this end there are many aphorisms and polite formulae which touch on axiomatic values of the society and which are deployed at the right moment when one wants to turn the screws or wriggle out of an oppressive confrontation. A wife-taker who feels unjustifiably 'crushed' or 'squeezed' by demands which have not been adequately solicited may counter:

Manara-nara namada Kalulu Hao	Our father Kalulu only complains.
Lö baluse lö toho	No shield or spear in hand
Aoha me lö fanaro.	He's light without backing.

A wife-giver's weapons are his solicitory gifts. Without these he is disarmed, a lightweight who can be brushed off. The rhyme is typical in its suggestion of contest or antagonism between the affines. In most cases a suitable reply is found, and the banter goes on until agreement is reached; but this particular rhyme is sufficiently shaming to send the wife-giver or his proxy packing.

A wife-taker who is dismayed by the sudden arrival of his affine bearing gifts may say: 'I'll eat it if you're fishing in the sea; but if you're fishing in a coconut shell, I won't (I'll return the gift).' To fish in the sea is to fish without expectation of immediate success: the wife-giver is willing to wait for his tribute. A wife-taker may attempt to forestall a demand or plead patience with the words:

Sahole gambala	If the blanket has slipped aside
Sahole zië	If the mat has moved
Ifagamöi curu ahe.	The toe can shift it back into place.

In other words, what cannot be provided today can be arranged later. This rhyme is said to be wasted on an intransigent adversary. A creditor may fend off a promise with the related saying:

Böi cuani gambala	Don't open the blanket
Böi cuani zië	Don't lift the mat
Oroma zafusi gahe.	The whiteness of the leg shows.

This means: 'We know what's under the blanket; we know you of old and don't trust your promises.' It might equally be said to disarm a creditor: 'Don't show us up; you know us only too well'—a fitting humility in a debtor, which might lead to a compromise.

As the *ovasa* draws near, the wife-takers are invited to a meal at which their 'debts are scored' (*famakhoi gömö*). The same term can be used of the bridewealth reckoning preceding a wedding, and the occasion is analogous. Generally it is only close affines, or those with whom close links have been maintained, who attend such a meeting. Others bring a smaller amount of tribute on the day of the feast. At the session half a dozen pigs are killed as *so'i-so'i*, and firm promises of contributions are extracted. At this stage the host will not brook pleas of poverty or vague intentions. He may simply point imperiously at the hapless affine and say, 'Your debt is three [*batu*]!' If the affine claims that he does not have such wealth at his disposal, one of the host's men steps in immediately and offers to lend a large pig at interest. The affine is obliged to accept this unfavourable solution or face the shame of public rebuke and the threat of the host's highly effective curse. The wife-takers can only be 'squeezed' or 'trapped' (*tolazi*) in this way if they have been duly entertained. Likewise, the elders, who have been invited by the host to represent his case, have been well fed and are therefore obliged to him to do their utmost to milk the wife-takers and offer their own goods as instant loans. To eat and not to respond with this aid is a form of duplicity, 'eating what has not been given lightly'.

The elders are also entrusted with the task of reclaiming friendly loans given by the host and canvassing support loans. Some of these contributions are obtained from wife-takers in addition to their tribute. At a further meeting with the elders, the host informs them of the extent of his *ovasa* debts to various of the guests. Over the years he has received so many *urakha* (weighed portions) of such and such a size from persons X, Y, and Z. He has also donated *sulö* (live pigs for conversion into *urakha*) at others' feasts. The balance of payments is calculated and the total debt is reckoned up. Next a rough estimate is made of the available resources so that any shortfall can be made up. However, in most cases the intention is not simply to settle up, but to overpay, reversing the debts, so the resources assembled greatly outweigh the total debt. Ama Duho'aro of Sifalagö, who held a large *ovasa* in 1985, calculated his debts beforehand at 20 *so'e* (= 20 × 30 *hië*, or roughly 20 large pigs). His total expenditure on the feast was 125 pigs. This outlay put him in credit with most of his guests, but incurred many new debts of his own, both inside and outside the *ovasa* system (for *sulö*, support loans, etc.), in the process of financing the *ovasa*. Having achieved eminence through this feast he now intends to pay off any future *ovasa* debts which he may incur as a guest with a small feast each time the debts reach 5 *so'e* in total.

7 Informing the Wife-Givers

A few days before the *ovasa* the host calls on his *matua* (wife's father) and *sibaya* (mother's brothers) to supplicate and issue a formal invitation. The terms *matua* and *sibaya* refer in the first instance to these men, who are the principal guests, and secondarily to the group which accompanies each. While *matua*, used as a relationship term, refers only to WF, *sibaya* refers generally to men related to Ego through M, MM, MMM, and so on. At the *ovasa* the *matua* and *sibaya* are treated as equivalent and opposed. A third category of wife-givers is the *sibaya ndra alave*, the *sibaya* of the host's wife. This category comprises the series of wife-givers who receive bridewealth at a wedding. At an *ovasa* they play a secondary role and are assimilated to the *matua*. This is logical since they are related to the host through his wife, whereas the *sibaya* group are related to him matrilaterally—an affinal relation by birth.

Collectively all these groups are known as *si tenga bö'ö* ('those who are not other').

The visit to the wife-givers is called 'grasping the feet of the ancestor figures' (*fondra'u ahe nazu nuvu*).[6] This term is still used despite the abolition of the ancestor cult. Formerly the host would make an offering to his affines' ancestors (*uvu*), requesting their blessing on their descendant (his wife). At the *ovasa* this blessing is conferred, now as formerly, by their living representative, the *matua* or his proxy. In a parallel ceremony the host asks for the blessing of his matrilateral ancestors on himself, to be conferred by his *sibaya* (MB or MBS).

The division of roles is expressed as follows in oral tradition:

Andrö wa so zibaya	Therefore comes the *sibaya*
Andrö wa so nuvu	Therefore comes the *uvu*
Si möi mame hovu-hovu	To give blessing
Khö nono azulo manu.	To the child, the chicken's egg.

The wife-taker, and indeed his wife, are cherished and protected like an egg.

The visit to inform the wife-givers can also be performed on the host's behalf by his wife in company with one or two of his agnates. More distant wife-givers may be contacted by a trusted elder. In the affine's village, the host's party are given an official welcome (*lafolaya*, lit. 'danced to'), which means that a gong is beaten to herald their arrival and a pig is killed for them and served ceremoniously. This meal is called, with mock modesty, *öda manu* ('our [the guests'] meal of chicken'). Like all wife-givers' prestations it obliges a much larger return gift, so the hospitality is given with even more than the usual alacrity. The prospective host is free to refuse a large pig and take only the 'blood of the ear', i.e. a piglet, which obliges him to return only 'as much as he can afford'. The return gift is additional to the tribute rendered by the host at the *ovasa*.

In this ceremony, as generally in dealings between affines, there is a secular emphasis on the here-and-now which gives the observer the misleading impression that wife-givers are credited with inherent powers to transmit fertility and confer blessing. The influence of

[6] Although in central Nias the terms *azu nuvu* and *azu ndra ama* are used synonymously for ancestor figures, a literal translation distinguishes them as 'idols of the *uvu*' (affinal ancestors) and 'idols of the fathers', respectively. In reference to the visit described here this distinction is preserved, and the term *azu nuvu* is always used.

ancestors is nowadays made explicit only in the invocation which accompanies a curse. However, although Niasans do not theorize about the origin of affines' powers, the basic premises of the system are clear and unquestioned. If there is no attempt to reconcile these ideas with Christianity, it is because they are not perceived to be in conflict with it.

Could the system exist without some notion of the ancestors' participation? It is possible to imagine it continuing simply because it is a satisfactory and workable form of social organization. A man would accept the heavy obligations towards his wife-givers for the simple reason that he expects as much from his own wife-takers, and he cannot conceive of a society without them. How else would he obtain a wife, seek protection from his enemies, or finance the building of his house? But such a justification would neglect the religious aspect of affinal exchange, which is very much to the fore, not merely as an empty convention or as an idiom for economic relations, but as a powerful and effective sanction.

8 The Installation of a Megalith

A megalith (*behu*) was installed some days before the feast for which it was needed, in a separate ceremony. Monuments, like chiefly houses (*omo sebua*), were permanent symbols of greatness. Most were erected in the lifetime of the individual rather than as memorials. Men of high rank were termed 'stone-draggers' as well as 'gold beaters' or 'slaughterers'.

The practice of stone-raising in the Upper Susua died out some years before other pagan customs, such as head-hunting, were suppressed by missionaries and administrators. Consequently, detailed and reliable information on this subject is not obtainable. In the paved square of Sifalagö there are monuments in front of every house, but nearly all of them derive from the generation prior to the oldest living men, or earlier. It is possible to reconstruct the village layout and the spatial arrangement of lineages as they were at the turn of the century on the basis of these megaliths, which provide informants with a convenient *aide-mémoire*. At most *ovasa* held within living memory stones were merely moved or re-erected. The exception was Matanihela (d. 1968), the *öri* head, who had several large stones brought up from the river Soi to cover his father's grave and for his own personal glory. A number of the most recent (therefore most highly regarded) monuments were destroyed in the iconoclastic frenzy of the conversion movements which swept through the area in the 1930s and after.

In the Gomo and Middle Susua area there was a great variety of carved limestone megaliths, some in the form of mythical serpents and hornbills, others in the form of fluted toadstools or spinning tops, as well as vertical monuments.[7] In the Upper Susua there was no limestone or other soft stone capable of being carved, so the uncut stone had to be brought from downstream, many miles away. At an *ovasa*, the host's wife would dance on a fluted table (*gove nilare*). Only men who had been carried aloft at an *ovasa* were permitted to sit on such tables. None of these remain in Sifalagö. Extant megaliths consist simply of vertical unhewn stones (*behu*) up to 1.5 m. high, and thick slabs placed in front of them as seats (*daodao*). The vertical stone was a backrest (*tendro-tendro*) for the man who raised it and for his ancestral spirits, who were considered to be present during his *ovasa*.

A suitable resting-place for the skull of a great man was under the base of a *behu,* which is itself planted several feet into the ground. Informants differed on whether stone-raising was associated with head-hunting. Some thought there was only an indirect connection. For example, a head might be taken for a funeral *ovasa* at which a stone was erected by the deceased man's successor.

Stones were obtained from the river and were dragged up to the village on sledges by teams of men. These would include members of the *sibaya* and *matua* contingents, as well as men from the host's village. Such an operation entailed the slaughter of a number of pigs. Probably the great expense as well as the dwindling number of suitable stones nearby led to the early decline of this custom.

[7] A collection of these was made by the Dutch at the abandoned site of Tundrumbaho. In the last decade most of them have been plundered by dealers and foreign collectors. Father Hämmerle, who has done much to preserve the old material culture, has written extensively on megaliths (1984). See also Schnitger 1939 and Thomsen 1976.

II. THE *OVASA*

9 The Arrival of Guests

The day of the *ovasa* arrives: it is the first quarter of the moon, an auspicious time for exchange, when the pigs are said to be particularly 'full'. Most *ovasa* take place in the months after the August harvest. In December and January the local calendar is crowded with such events.[8]

Guest groups—usually 30 or 40 in each—converge from the surrounding villages, carrying banners (*laoyo*) and driving *sulö* pigs before them. Usually they halt at a friendly house to prepare themselves before approaching the village. Women change out of muddy clothes into the Javanese-style sarong and kebaya which have, since the abolition of traditional dress (considered indecent by foreign masters), been customary at festive gatherings.

In the host village large gongs and drums are beaten continuously in the lineage house, and these can be heard from miles away. The arrival of each group is a moment of great excitement and tension. As they approach the village, the men form a phalanx, stamping and lunging forward to the rhythm of a warriors' chant. Formerly, they would sometimes come in full battle array carrying shields and spears.

A leader sings out the lines and the warriors sing a raucous refrain between each line:

All: *Hoi ya he!*
Leader: *Ono matua*   Young men!
All: *Hu he! Hoi ya he!*
Leader: *Matua sabölö töla.*   Men of strong limbs.

Ono matua   Young men
Matua salio boto.   Men of swift body.
Sabölö wamahö-mahösi   Strong spear-thrusters
Sabölö sagaro-garo.   Strong shoulder-shakers.
Ya'ita solaya siöligö   We form a fence of dancers

---

[8] In a text collected by Steinhart (1934: 359) *ovasa* is coupled with 'harvest' as a time indication, meaning 'one year'. He speculates whether the *ovasa* was originally a harvest festival, but there is no evidence to support this.Ködding (1868*a*: 278) writes that *ovasa* mainly took place in Jan.

Ya'ita solaya sisindro.	We dance upright
Sifakhai bö'ötö	Joined hand in hand
Sifakhai ta'io	Arm linked in arm.
Ya'ita sovulo	We who have assembled
Sovulo oi faondra.	We who have come together
Tou ba evali ora-	Down on the square, where gathers
Orahua zihönö	The council of the thousands.
Tou ba evali ora-	Down on the square, where meets
Orahua zato.	The council of the many
Tou ba evali site-	Down on the square
Sitegulu halu.	Where rolls the rice-pestle[9]
Tou ba evali site-	Down on the square
Sitegulu hao.	Rolls the bamboo stave.
Ya'ita banua	We are the village
Banua so'evali	The village which boasts a square
Ya'ita banua	We are the village
Banua sitohöna.	The village which is ready.
Fakhöyö tou zonoro	Down where play the bearers
Zonoro bulusa.	Bearers of the spears
Fakhöyö tou zaro	Down where play the strong
Zonoro hulayo.	Bearers of war-spears.
Hadia khöda dödö	How are our hearts?
Khöda dödö somuso	Our hearts are glad
Khö nono zalawa	For the nobleman
Zalawa helanö	The renowned chief
Khö nono zuha	For the son of a lord
Duha terongo	The lord who is acclaimed.
Ilau khönia gondrani	He stages a gathering
Ondrani ovasa.	A gathering for an *ovasa.*
Andrö ikaoni nahö-	And so he summons thousands
Nahönö niha.	Thousands of men.
Iduvagö gölö	He squanders his labours
Gölönia balakhö	His labours as bait.
Aduva mböra ziumene	His finest rice is squandered
Aduva mböra zievo	His finest rice is poured out.
Ife'a manu zihönö	He feeds the chickens of thousands[10]
Ife'a manu zato	He feeds the chickens of the masses.
Ifolau tanömö höva	He scatters [gifts as] spinach seed.
Ifolau löna ndaso	As if he's sowing seed.
Ilabu zilö ölö-ölö	He does it effortlessly

[9] The paved square is so smooth that one can roll a pestle along it.
[10] His guests are mere chickens beside him.

Ilabu zilö naroro	He does what is [for him] superfluous.
Lakhömi wa ono zuha	The prestige that proves he is a lord's son
Bövö wa ono zalawa	The custom that proves his nobility.[11]

Men of the host village respond by swaying and stamping; their chants boast of the ruthlessness and invulnerability of their leader (the host).

Azulo zi'öli, azulo defaö	Iron egg, iron egg
Lacucu ia ba lösu	Pounded in the rice-block
Tegilo-gilo manö.	Merely spins round.

The host is 'hard' in speech and action, like the iron egg which is used in magic. His wealth is not diminished by the *ovasa*, just as nothing comes off the egg under the blows of the pestle.

As the mob surges up the village steps and appears at the end of the square, widows and matrons (guardians of the village) link hands and form a barrier between the groups, like policemen between supporters of rival football teams. The air rings with taunts and aggressive boasts such as: 'We are the origin of war!' (*ya'aga mbörö horö*). The guests then charge forward punching the air and hooting in unison. If they break through the cordon a brawl ensues. Usually, though, the war cries are intended merely to create a *frisson* of excitement which is dispelled in a general loud hoot followed by laughter. The matrons then dance forward one by one with fluttering arms imitating hawks, and proclaim greetings (*la'angona'ö*), naming the descent group or its founder: 'You, sons of Siba'a; you of the Bu'ulölö!'; or they invite the guests to accept betel as the sign of their welcome. Often they humble themselves to the guests by proclaiming, 'You of the nine lineages, there is no betel!', to which a female guest replies, 'We are full!'

The guest group now merges with the villagers in preparation for a similar confrontation with the next guest group who can be heard chanting from below. This can go on for some time. If the *ovasa* is intended to inaugurate a new house, each guest group storms the house and stamps energetically on the floor to test its solidity. Finding it firm—except for a slight trembling of the eaves—they praise the owner for his unshakeable might. On the guests' arrival, the host tethers the pigs due to be slaughtered in their honour as their *famolaya* (official reception).

[11] This and the following chants were provided by Ama Gamböta (the leading exponent), Ama Huku, and others; some were recorded at feasts.

10   The Composition of Groups

Whereas among the Northwest Coast Indians it was a group which potlatched under the nominal leadership of its chief, and the potlatch 'also validated the social rank of the guest group' (Drucker 1967: 485), in Nias the accent is definitely on individual achievement. The descent group shares only indirectly in the prestige of its leading men. This is due partly to the internal organization of the descent group and partly to the structure of marriage alliance. Again we have to distinguish the individuality of the host as wife-taker from the group identity of his wife-givers. Likewise, any of his clan's wife-takers who attend the feast do so as individuals. If the *ovasa* is a big one, the whole hamlet forms the host's group (including of course his own lineage at the core). They are collectively 'hosts' (*sovatö*) or 'home village' (*banua*) to the guest groups (*sibaya* and *matua*, or *tome*, 'guests'), and usually outnumber them. (Note that this reverses the situation of the groups at a wedding, where wife-givers are the *sovatö*.) But all those members of the home village who are not among the closest agnates are themselves also guests who are honoured by the host.

This double role assigned to the villagers reflects the dual aim of the *ovasa*: as a rendering of tribute to wife-givers and as a bid for higher rank in society as a whole. In the first aim, the villagers unite behind the host to honour his affines, much as they did on a smaller scale on the occasion of his wedding, *as a service to him*. In the second aim the villagers are on a par with each of the guest affines, as one-to-one partners with the host in a vast and complex set of exchanges.

As members of the host side, the villagers and lineage mates co-operate in donations of resources and labour in response to the host's patronage—not out of the mere fact of being agnates or neighbours. Their co-operation has been won by careful ground-work; it cannot be demanded on the basis of genealogical or other ascribed relation. Only the closest agnates have a duty to provide backing, but they have a corresponding right to dissuade the host from giving a feast. Part of the reward for this co-operation of the lineage/hamlet is undoubtedly a share in the glory of the host. But it is only he whose rank is raised. Only when feasting achievements have been repeated through several generations, and rank is matched by power and wealth, does a patriline become known as a *nga'ötö zalawa*, a chiefly line, and members who have not personally sponsored feasts are then regarded as above ordinary status. Otherwise, the glory of the host group lasts only as long as the *ovasa*. Feasting does not establish a rank order among groups.

Thus, the degree of identification of agnates in a senior man's feasts depends on genealogical proximity and the strength of their obligations towards him created by his patronage. Likewise, the guest groups at an *ovasa*, who are announced simply as lineage *X* or *Y* (suggesting homogeneity), are internally differentiated *in relation to the feastgiver* according to the same criteria. Although the mother's brother's group (*sibaya*) theoretically comprises the whole clan, only the mother's lineage receives tribute, and within this group MF, MB, and MBS take precedence over their classificatory brothers. Only if the latter have periodically given food or help (*so'i-so'i*) to the feastgiver can they expect tribute: they have to earn the right. Among themselves, the members of a guest group are bound to their representative (the MB, WF, or whoever has received the invitation) as his retinue; he is their patron for the occasion. Of course, merely because he is the host's MB it does not mean that he is himself a man of rank; some of his group may be his seniors. However, as the one invited, he has to kill pigs for them beforehand to ensure their participation and their willingness to perform dances at the *ovasa*. To arrive at the head of a large company brings him glory. He has to pay for it.

Bearing in mind these qualifications, we can nevertheless assert that, due to the structure of alliance, each set of wife-givers receives honour *as a group*, even if their tribute is divided unevenly. The arrival of wife-takers is not formally acknowledged. They come one by one and blend into the crowd. To some extent they are united with the village as co-helpers.

It may be that in the past the lineage did appear more solidary in the *ovasa* and its prestige was more clearly identified with the host. There would have been a basis for this solidarity in the ancestor cult and in the corporate activities of the lineage, e.g. in defence, raiding, clan ceremonies, and harvest co-operation. Descent groups were political units, and in multi-clan villages such as Sifalagö they were in competition. One can suppose that this rivalry was manifested in the *ovasa* in some way, even if not in a systematic ranking of groups as found in the potlatch.

The combative aspect of the *ovasa* preserves something of this corporate ideology in which groups, rather than individuals, wage war and make peace at their leaders' feasts. In mock combat the identity of the groups as affines is disguised—or perhaps, in the play-acting of the arrival, not yet established. They are simply warring lineages or villages, and as such are equal and opposite. Only when peace has been made and the groups formally welcomed are the prescribed forms of affinal behaviour observed. The symmetry of political relations between equivalent villages gives way to the complementarity of affinal relations.

11 Speeches

Once all the guests have arrived the multitude settles down in the square to hear formal speeches from the host's side and each guest group. Some of them are typically concerned with the correct performance of *adat*. The guests analyse the host's omissions and any minor offences given in their welcome, but they stress their forbearance: there is nothing that cannot be put right by his generosity later. The host may admit his offence and even elaborate on it. There is a special emphasis in Nias on explaining how one has maltreated or neglected the other party. I was frequently made to listen to such explanations of offences against myself (by the offender) which I had innocently overlooked. There is in this an element of challenge and testing the mettle of the opposition. The intention is partly to discomfit the guest by calling his bluff. At the same time one pronounces the formulas of self-effacement and pleas for tolerance.

The style of *ovasa* speeches is antagonistic, as at weddings which involve the same participants in a similar exchange. Usually the speaker picks a respondent on the far side of the gathering, which gives him the whole arena in between as his stage. He commands this stage until he finishes with a rhetorical flourish—'that's my word!'—and no one may interrupt him. The manner of the speech is often more important than its content. The themes are familiar to all; there are no surprises or fresh arguments. I was dismayed in the early months of fieldwork when, having listened to an elaborate and dramatic monologue lasting up to half an hour, if I asked a neighbour for a paraphrase, I would always be told: 'He's demanding more for himself.' Certainly, there is an assumption by the audience of self-interest in speakers. But probably this predictability of content was due partly to the fact that most of the *ovasa* I attended did not have a prominent political aspect. With a struggle for succession in Sifalagö currently in progress, and feasts planned as part of the struggle, no doubt the content of speeches will assume greater importance. (Wedding speeches are usually more varied since there are always novel aspects to a union.)

In the 'standard' *ovasa* most of the debate concerns prestations. The host informs his guests of their tribute, how much of gold and pigs, and to whom. This inevitably fails to satisfy. The wife-givers protest that their generous solicitory gifts deserve a much larger response. The host is hardly living up to his reputation or to the standards set by his father. The host, amused but not submissive, pleads for 'patience' and explains that he has many other commitments. The debate swings back and forth, rarely explicit, often couched in rhymes, proverbs or parables (*amaedola*) which clinch a particular point. A skilled speaker can, it is said, 'pay back' and defeat a challenge, capping it with a fitting proverb or riposte. The audience delights in these figures of speech and often chimes in with the end of the rhyme. They are well known; the skill is in their deployment.

At a large *ovasa* it is customary for the guests to flatter the host in conventional terms (which may contradict the tenor of the speeches). This is part of the satisfaction of giving a feast. If the same attitude is adopted by guests at a minor feast, as sometimes happens, the effect can be comic or even satirical. But a great man is expected to 'astonish'; his deeds are supposed to be extraordinary. All is excess, wonder and hyperbole.[12] In former times he would swagger and strut like a king and his achievement would entitle him to act henceforth with arrogance (*fayawasa*) towards lesser men. Now that Christianity enjoins humility on leaders, the host more often listens with false modesty and amusement. The guests for their part, by overpraising him and exaggerating his wealth, intend to disarm him from prevaricating speeches and embarrass him into increasing his gifts. These *manö-manö* ('sayings') which interrupt the flow of

[12] Weber argues that one of the characteristics of charisma (for which a partial equivalent is *lakhömi*) is the extraordinary nature of one who possesses it and recognition of this by his followers (see Schnepel 1987).

speeches are introduced to apply pressure or to acknowledge a concession.

An elder springs forward and with expansive gestures and prancing steps begins his praise:

Samö-samösa ndraugö ba niha	You are unique among men.
Ihalö ndraugö isöndra.	He gets you, he strikes you.
Isasa-ai dödöu bögi	The bat scratches at your heart
Idou höröu tovi-tovi.	The tovi bird pecks out your eyes.
Aitö ndraugö moroi ba ndra'i	You are blacker than grime,
Alu moroi ba zakhömi	Gloomier than the night.
Tumbu khöu lato bakha ba mba'i	Stinging nettles sprout from your penis.
Tumbu nadröu ba mbazili	Wild grass grows on your testicles.
Balazi wa atua-tua	Proof of your wisdom (age)
Balazi wa oköli-köli	Proof that you're dried out.
Zimate ndraugö ihalö emali!	May the head-hunters get you!

This does not sound much like flattery to us, but the host is being praised for his 'hardness' and hoary resilience. It is flattery in the spirit of the enduring iron egg or the boast that 'we are the origin of war', belonging to a warriors' ethic. The birds that peck are the guests, hungry for tribute. The last line is added to all *manö-manö* as a 'shocker' and is followed by a shout from the crowd.

The mark of a rich man versed in custom is that he shares his wealth, as the following *manö-manö* reminds him:

Oi ono zatua sito'ölö	You (the hosts) are all elders versed in custom.
Khömi wa so manu nifalala'ö	All is provided by you: chickens,
Asio wanazökhi dödö	Salt to sweeten the heart.
Adeha mbu movoi davö	A feather pulled out drips with fat
Ahele matona urö	So half a rice-measure overflows.
Alabu ndraono ba zönö-zönö	Children slip over in the grease
Tedou zatua ba zinduhu davö	Elders wax with your real fat.
Oi aero dana ndraono	A handful for every child
Oi aero sakhö-khö	Chopped up to feed everyone.
Oi aero zatua famöfölö	All the elders share in butchering.
Manö me ono zatua sito'ölö	So it is with the experienced sons of elders.
Zimate ndraugö ihalö!	May you be done to death, captured!

Praise of the host's wealth and generosity provokes a quick denial:

Hana öhöni ndraga, özukha-zukha?	Why do you flatter us so,
Hana öhae ndraga mobulu zugala?	As wind raises the drooping
	tugala leaves?
No onösi ndraga momova-mova	We are dry like tree fibre
No afuo ndraga mosalari hoya.	Thin like sheaths of a palm
Zimate ndraugö isöndra!	May you die, get captured!

The guests may then protest that their speeches have no effect on the host: his words are not direct like the flight of the dove, but weave and dodge like the *fule* bird. The banter of flattery and false modesty, cajolery and evasion, is likened to 'fighting with words'. It is said that if one side cannot reply or 'pay back', they are ashamed and provoke a fight, but at the *ovasa* I witnessed these contests of wits were mostly good-humoured. In a method of oratory in which the manner is nearly all, these verses serve not simply as distillations of conventional wisdom in the manner of our proverbs, but as symbols of where the debate has got to, markers of relative position which sum up the feeling (speeches are full of psychological verbs referring to the heart) or which clinch a concession. As such they contrast with the rambling and discursive style of making speeches (*faego*). Transcripts of speeches show that there is very little in the way of direct argument at an *ovasa*; one speaker does not answer points made by another so much as convey the attitude of his side, which may shift in response to the opponents' speeches. Proverbs and sayings are apt ways of summing up or provoking such shifts.

Speeches continue until a compromise is reached, which may be after two hours or more. The host clearly has a limit to what he can promise over and above the resources assembled for the feast. His willingness to concede more may be interpreted as weakness, as may the moderation of the wife-givers. Intransigence and flexibility are both regarded as leadership qualities; but one must know when to show one or the other. A wife-giver who presses too hard for more tribute risks the humiliation of going home empty-handed, which loses him face with his group to whom he is a patron. His sanction is a curse; but this is too dangerous a weapon to be used lightly. At the *ovasa* of the hamlet chief of Hilidanaya'ö in 1988, the *sibaya* group from Hiliwaga pronounced a curse and left in disgust when their *sulö* pigs were returned to them unwanted by the host. He had already accepted and slaughtered the *sulö* brought by the *matua* but he was not willing to incur any further debt: this *ovasa* was his last major feast, after which he would retire in glory almost free of debt. The *sibaya*, in their speeches asked the host if he had invited them to obtain their blessing or their curse. In reply, the host said he had given them enough tribute to merit their blessing (which was true) and he would not add an ounce more. He had won the respect of the other matrilateral groups and was therefore to some extent protected from the unjustified curse of the Hiliwaga *sibaya*. The effectiveness of the wife-givers' curse relies on the fact that it sanctions customary obligations; if these have been met, the victim can appeal over their heads to their own wife-givers to undo the curse.

12 Entertainments

Following the speeches each group performs a square dance accompanied by a song. The principal guests do not take part, since they are the subject of the songs. The *maena*, a custom introduced from the north, is now a regular part of any *ovasa*, gradually replacing the more traditional and demanding entertainments such as the recitation of narrative poems (*hoho*) and war dances. As at a wedding, each *maena* consists of an improvised humorous verse followed by a chorus. The themes are the familiar ones of the host's greatness and generosity, the request for tribute, etc. One such chorus goes: 'The heavens sway and the wide earth trembles, at your earth-slippery [with blood] *ovasa*.' The dancers are rewarded with a shower of coins and cigarettes. Sometimes there is a choir (the only Christian element in the *ovasa*) which elaborates on the same themes at a more stately tempo. There is often a display of *sile* (Indon. *silat*), a martial art developed from the Padang style, introduced into the area after the war and now combined with traditional magical practices. Rarely nowadays a *hoho* is performed. This may consist of a long parable of a great chief (*famaedo zalawa*), interwoven with a dynastic genealogy or a collective sung recitation (*gema*) in which each side 'pays back' the other with a stanza. The merits of the leader extolled in *hoho* are those already expressed in the *manö-manö* quoted above: generosity, ferocity and ruthlessness, and the ability to astound and confound his followers.

13 The Festive Meal and Giving of Tribute

Towards evening food is served. The meal is announced with mock modesty as 'hot water' or 'sweet potato'. Mostly the pork has been cooked the night before. The rice, boiled in huge pots, is unpleasantly undercooked and gritty (there is a word for the consistency of *ovasa* rice). The guest groups are served in squads. Each occupies a large mat spread out over the paving stones. Baskets of rice are brought down from the house and emptied in double handfuls on to banana leaves on the square. Grey coils of pork are passed about by the elders of each group who are responsible for the division among their own men according to rank. The cooked portion counts as an *urakha*, though one which is not measured or included in the debt tallies.[13] Bitter disagreement sometimes arises over the size of portions and I have seen knives drawn in anger. The food consumed at the feast is only a fraction of the total expenditure—as little as one-tenth—but no less important for that.

The most honoured guests, that is the heads of each group— WF, WB, MB, WMB, etc.—as well as chiefs and eminent elders among the groups, are served on old Chinese ceramic plates which are among the few heirlooms kept in central Nias. These guests sit at a table above the masses. They receive the portions of honour, the pigs' lower jaws and viscera.

Iza zimbi tane'a lela	Behold the lower jaw, base for the tongue
Iza dödö nifaigi niha	Behold the heart which is seen by men
Iza mbo soga'a-ga'a	Behold the branching lungs
Iza davö so'arö mova	Behold the fat, soft as under the glands
Ibe yawa ba wiga kumandra	Placed high on the commander's plate
Iza böra ziwaefalihöva	Behold the aromatic rice
Iza nasio samagaolo lela	The salt that makes the tongue curl
Sumange nono ze'ulu	Tribute for the sons of nobles
Sumange nono zalawa.	Tribute for the sons of chiefs.

Added to these tributary portions is gold and money (also classed as *sumange*). The host places the pieces of gold, each wrapped in a twist of red cloth, on the rim of the plate. To each group he gives a sum of money which they divide among themselves according to rank.

[13] Although women do not receive the raw, weighed *urakha* their cooked pork likewise counts as an *urakha*.

After the meal the host invites the guests one by one to offer him tribute. He sits behind a table with his wives and a spokesman calls upon each guest to 'take betel'. The guest comes forward and ostentatiously waves money above his head, proclaiming it as '*sumange* for the great son of *X* of the nine lineages' or his wife. So saying he takes betel from a plate and puts down his gift. Close wife-takers are expected to give gold. Wife-givers, who have just received their tribute, also make a sizeable contribution. Remote wife-takers may give only a few coins. Only the members of the host's own lineage are excepted. At the small wedding *ovasa* held by the chief's nephew in May 1988 a total of over Rp.150,000 was collected in this way—a very large sum in Nias terms.

14   The Conferring of a Title

Titles (*töi sebua*, 'great name') are chosen by the wife-givers after some debate about the characteristics of the host. Ama Duho'aro, who had planned an *ovasa* for many years, was entitled Fadru Sama'anö, Lamp which Plans, or Lamp for short. The late chief's title was Lamp of Fame. A wife's title is a modification of her husband's, usually incorporating the name for fine gold (e.g. Balaki Sama'anö) or a female honorific such as Buruci. Titles in the past testified to the 'arrogance' (*fayawasa*) of leaders: Guest at the Sun's *Ovasa*, God's rice-measure, Heard and Feared. It is customary to address an elder at all times by his title, usually in abbreviated form, rather than by his teknonym. Old men chewing betel together can be heard casually referring to each other as The Sun, Terror, etc. A much-feasted man retains the title given at his greatest *ovasa*. There is no clear rank order of titles, though some are more suitable for bigger or smaller feasts. Tuha (Lord) was reserved for only the very greatest. The chief's father was entitled 'Lord who covers the earth' after killing 336 pigs at a nine-day *ovasa* which is still remembered. A title is one of the few remaining personal emblems of rank. Formerly there were different hairstyles for chiefs and elders, and special insignia worn on important occasions: crowns and moustaches of gold, ceremonial swords, and gold-covered jackets.

Nowadays the titles are conferred in the following manner. The host's *sibaya* (MB) or an elder of his group draws a sword, dashes about flourishing it as if in combat, and proclaims at the top of his voice the new title. The whole multitude then hoots. Next the *matua* (the host's WF) proclaims the wife's title in the same way. The wife's *sibaya* sometimes performs this function. The conferring of the title (*famatörö töi*) is accompanied by the wife-givers' blessing. The newly ennobled couple remain seated and listen in silence. At one *ovasa* I attended in Tuhegewo, the host sat between his two wives and his mother, all wearing gold headdresses, enthroned on specially made chairs. All four received titles. They were then carried aloft around the village square by the guest groups while their praises were sung. This type of ostentation is discouraged by the Church.

The procedure in former times was as follows. The lineage ancestor figures were passed through the roof flap and lowered down on to the square. The roof flap was the channel of communication with the ancestor spirits in an invocation and the route to Teteholi Ana'a, the abode of chiefly spirits. A chief's corpse was passed through the roof flap rather than through the door (which was traditionally a trapdoor in the floor). Since a man secures his passage to paradise by giving feasts, it is appropriate that the ancestor figures should as it were trace out his route for him at his *ovasa*. The entire deceased lineage, including the figures of all the women who married into the house, was figuratively assembled on a mat on top of a newly constructed litter (*osa-osa*) which was placed behind the megalith erected a few days earlier. The litter, of wood or limestone, had a figurehead in the shape of a hornbill—a figure whose significance is now lost but which is vaguely understood to be a symbol of nobility.[14] The *sibaya* then took his nephew by the wrist and blessed him with the words: 'Mount the litter; let the people cheer you, let the thousands acclaim you. May you be like the call of the hornbill, like the crowing of the cockerel.' The crowd responded by imitating the call of the hornbill. The host's *matua* then led his daughter in the same way to her litter, put his hand on her shoulder and pronounced a blessing. As they conferred the titles, the wife-givers handed over to the host and his wife gold as *sumange*. The *sibaya* group then carried the host, while the *matua* group carried his wife on their shoulders, chanting the hornbill's call: 'Haleleleha! Haleleleha!' From his perch the host would fling down pieces of meat for the guests.

[14] According to Schröder (1917: 604), the soul of a deceased noble could take the form of a hornbill. Suzuki (1959: 19, 69) regards it as an upper-world motif.

Thus now, as formerly, the high-point in the host's career is dramatically emphasized by his physical elevation and the reversal of his usual position *vis-à-vis* the wife-givers. First, he is the host (*sovatö*, 'the one who holds the floor') while his affines are the guests. At a wedding they are the *sovatö* and he is the *soroi tou* ('who comes from below'). They have come to his *ovasa* from below, climbing up the hill on which a central Nias village is built. On several occasions I heard the arriving guests referred to as *soroi tou*. While this is not a fixed term for the guest group, it nevertheless has connotations of subordinates rendering tribute. A man is normally expected metaphorically to 'kneel' before his wife-givers, and he must never stand while they are seated, if necessary stooping low to pass them. In elevating the host, the guests cede their usual affinal prerogative. A further reversal is in the giving of tribute (*sumange*) by the wife-givers. Thus, in the ritual elevation, promotion of individual rank in society as a whole is symbolized by a ritual reversal of affinal inferiority. A great man transcends, temporarily, even the universal limitations of (egocentrically conceived) kinship. For a few moments he makes subjects of his wife-givers. What one might have expected is that the host's wife-takers and his own clansmen do him homage. But the wife-takers blend into the crowd: they have virtually no part to play in the ceremony. The implication is that a promotion can only be conferred by those who are of higher status, rather than simply through popular acclaim, and in Nias it is the wife-givers who are intrinsically and uncontroversially superior. How much greater, then, the satisfaction and glory to see them rendering tribute.

A further emblem of reversal is in the naming of the affinal prestations. Whereas at a wedding the wife-givers' counter-prestations are called *bövö*, at an *ovasa* it is the host's gifts which are called *bövö ba govasa* (*bövö* at the *ovasa*). This is despite the fact that the host's gifts are conceived to be analogous to, and even an extension of, bridewealth and are given in a spirit of tribute.[15] The symbolic reversal plays on the two notions of status: the sociocentric (rank) and the egocentric (affinal inequality). The inversion of the latter

---

[15] Since all wife-givers' prestations can be classed as *bövö* (or *so'i-so'i*, a term which has a different emphasis), it appears that *ovasa* prestations from both sides are denoted by the same word, in which case *bövö* could simply be translated as 'affinal prestation'. In my view this translation would be imprecise: it is significant that informants regard the usage *bövö ba govasa* as paradoxical and as limited to this context.

symbolizes promotion in the former. These two kinds of status are again brought into conjunction—but this time harmoniously rather than to effect a symbolic reversal—in the division of the 'origin pigs' which I now describe.

15 The Slaughter of the Origin Pigs

Amid cries of astonishment the origin pigs or 'chosen ones' are now revealed.

Iza mbörö mbawi nama Razi	Behold the origin pig of Ama Razi[16]
Tofali gi'o ba hogu nohi	Its tail coiled round the top of a coconut palm
Tokai nifö ba hogu gavöni	Its tusks hooked round the tops of *gavöni* trees
Hiza me ihöfuni nevali	See when it exhales on the square
Oi toföfö manu safusi	Scattering all the white chickens
Oi tonia manu soladari	Separating the multicoloured hens.
Zimate ndraugö ihalö emali!	May the head-hunters get you!

The slaughter of the origin pigs is a moment of great symbolic import. Whereas ordinary pigs are stabbed in the side with a knife, origin pigs are speared. First, they are held fast in a frame made of four rice-pestles lashed diagonally together, each end of the trestle forming a figure X. It is the *sibaya* or *matua* who spears the pig after pronouncing the words:

Iza khöu zinuturu govasa	Behold your handpicked *ovasa* pig
Iza bawi nifondri ba ndru'a	Behold the pig bathed in coconut milk.
Bawi satabö so'era	The fat pig which is wise
Bawi saho sohalasa	The pig as big as a granary
Zimate ndraugö isöndra.	May you die, be struck.

The dying movements of the pig signify the host's destiny:

Simaöga bagi ndra ama	The ancestors nod [of approval]
To'ele ba zinuturu me ifaöga ia.	Is revealed in the nod of the chosen one.

The origin pig is conceived to represent or be a substitute (*salahi*) for the host. If it drops its head in death, the patrilineal ancestors are

---

[16] This *manö-manö* was recorded at the *ovasa* of Ama Razi in Hoya in 1987.

ashamed of their descendant; he has reached his social zenith with this feast and misfortune will follow. If the pig lifts its head, the ancestors are nodding in approval, and good fortune will follow. These omens are taken seriously, despite the influence of Christianity. A bad omen is talked about privately in the aftermath and is confirmed by subsequent events. The pig represents also the feast-giver's effort (*ölö*) which is an aspect of any prestation but particularly those associated with affinity. A man's efforts can take him only so far; something in his career depends also on fortune (*harazaki*) which is supernaturally endowed. At his *ovasa* he 'pours out the product of his labour' and he hopes thereby to secure fortune. The successful feastgiver squanders, but, as the saying goes, he and his wealth are not diminished.

An intriguing aspect of this sacrifice is the collaboration of the patrilineal ancestral spirits with the wife-givers. The pig is consecrated initially beneath the ancestor figures; it is promised or dedicated to the wife-givers. It is the latter who slaughter and consume the pig, while the ancestors signify their approval through the dying movements. In the *ovasa* as a whole, the wife-givers fulfil a similar function to the ancestors: they confer blessing (i.e. fortune) and they dramatize the promotion of rank. If we take into account the fact that the wife-givers' powers to bless and curse derive from their own ancestors the remaining gap in the picture is complete: a man owes his life and his continuing sustenance to his agnatic ancestors and those of his affines. The wife-takers and lineage mates are temporarily out of consideration. But they too are in analogous positions. They are the primary resources for the *ovasa*, and they are the subordinates of the host (who is their wife-giver and patron or lineage godfather).

This set of equations becomes clearer in the division of the origin pigs. One is split lengthways, half going to the *sibaya*, half to the *matua*; the head goes to the village chief. Thus the wife-giving groups are represented as equal and opposite; moreover, social superiority (the chief) and ritual superiority (affines) are conflated. A conjunction of sociocentric and egocentric statuses was involved in the elevation of the host by his affines earlier in order to effect a symbolic reversal. In the division of the pig the two kinds of status are concordant. The other pig is divided among lineage mates and wife-takers. The agnates are referred to as *makhelo* ('brothers') and the wife-takers are *ono* ('child'). Three levels are thus compressed into two: all types of seniors are equated on the one hand; equals and juniors are equated on the other. Where does the host figure among these groups? Since the origin pigs explicitly represent the host (who retains the lower jaws as his trophies), we might sum up the symbolism of the division as follows. It represents not only the place of the host in the system of exchange relations: the origin pig symbolizes his person as the intersection of these relations. A repeated recognition of his and his wife's origins (personified in his *sibaya* and *matua*) in the form of tribute is necessary to secure his continued well-being; and a recognition of wife-takers in solicitory gifts is necessary to secure his material prosperity in the form of their tribute. What guarantees the integrity of the person and his estate, or as we should say (overstressing the dualism) what keeps body and soul together, is the maintenance of affinal bonds, bringing fertility and life on the one hand, and material fortune (*löfö*) on the other.

The *sibaya* and *matua* appear as equal and opposite. But the *sibaya* do have a certain priority, since the matrilateral relation necessarily precedes the purely affinal relation 'as the ground comes before the grass'. Hence, at the butchering of the origin pig, the *sibaya* takes care of the head end, while the *matua* sees to the tail end. And whenever the wife-givers are called upon to perform some function (give speeches, pronounce a title, perform a dance), it is always the *sibaya* who is called first.

An explanation of these ideas in their traditional setting would have to take account of the well-developed concepts of ransom and substitution, the purchase of blessing by sacrifice, and the analogy between the wife-givers and God—all of which persist in some form—as well as obsolete practices and ideas such as head-hunting and the notion of men being the pigs of God. In today's setting, when the ancestors are feared but no longer worshipped, and when the traditional cosmology has been partially suppressed, partially adapted to Christianity (transforming it in turn), many of the explicit connections between these ideas have been broken. In a surprising way, however, the form and purpose of the exchanges and their supposed efficacy have survived. In banning the pagan practices which corresponded to the usual Protestant targets—excessive ritual, wastefulness, priestly mystification, idolatry, and overt symbolism—the Protestant missionaries inadvertently brought about a sort of Reformation of the *ovasa*, reducing it to its bare essentials, leaving what is (by comparison with former times) a sober and modest festival which nevertheless has little to do with Christianity, the official cult.

The pruning of ritual from the *ovasa* has left a greater emphasis on the actual exchanges than was hitherto the case, and it is to these that we must look in trying to understand what the *ovasa* means to participants today. Basically, there are two separate systems of exchange, corresponding to the two aims of the feastgiver: to pay tribute to wife-givers and obtain their blessing; and to win prestige by the distribution of *urakha*. Affinal prestations account for only a fraction of the total expenditure, the rest being given over mainly to prestige payments. This does not reflect the relative importance of the two kinds of exchange; both are indispensable features of the *ovasa*. In the remainder of this chapter I consider each system in turn before situating them both in a common cosmological framework.

16 Affinal Prestations

The exchange of matrimonial gifts serves explicitly as a model for all future affinal exchanges. Since there is some overlap and use of near synonyms in the naming of prestations as well as certain context-specific usages, a brief list of definitions is necessary here.

böli niha: bridewealth.

ana'iwa: tribute given by wife-takers on any occasion. Bridewealth is regarded in some respects as *ana'iwa*, as are wife-takers' donations for an *ovasa* and the host's gifts to his wife-givers.

sumange: any tribute (affinal or otherwise) or gift which denotes 'respect' (*sumange*) from any quarter. It does not necessarily connote subordination—this has to be judged from context— although it includes wife-takers' tribute (*ana'iwa*).

bövö: wife-givers' counter-prestations, especially those given in a ceremonial context. The term also means, roughly, *adat*.

so'i-so'i: solicitory or obliging gifts from wife-givers in any context, ceremonial or informal (includes *bövö*). The term does not have the symbolic resonance of *bövö*.

bövö ba govasa: the *ovasa* host's gifts to his wife-givers. The same set of prestations may be termed *ana'iwa* or *sumange*, with different connotations. The paradoxical usage of the word *bövö* in *bövö ba govasa* has been explained above.

In native thinking *bövö* is opposed to *ana'iwa*, and they are defined by informants in relation to each other: 'what we call *bövö* is what elicits *ana'iwa*' (*nifotöi bövö fangai ana'iwa*). This definition brings out the complementarity of the gifts and the underlying mechanism of obligation which links them.

Affinal prestations at an *ovasa* are as follows. Each wife-giving group brings for the host a small cooked pig with rice (*öda bövö/so'i-so'i*) with an equal amount of raw meat. One-half or 1 *batu* of gold is given to the host at the 'request for *sumange*'. The affines receive portions of the origin pigs, 3–12 *batu* of live pigs, plus the gold *sumange* placed on their dinner plates. Recipients are the main representatives of each affinal group (thus MF/MB, MMB/MMBS, WF/WFB/WB, WMB/WMBS, WMMB/WMMBS). Other members of the groups get a little cash plus a share of the pork.

The continuity between the exchanges surrounding a marriage and those of an *ovasa* is clear in the naming of prestations, the spirit in which they are given and the ideological aspect. The entire schedule of prestations is conceived as part of marriage alliance. The participants are identical, except that added to the host's own wife-givers (the lineages of WF, WMB, etc.) are those of his father and mother's father (his *sibaya*). These are assigned only a residual role in wedding exchanges. At an *ovasa* the two sets of wife-givers perform complementary functions: the *sibaya* bless the host; the *matua* bless his wife. Each side represents a line of maternal affiliation as well as a series of wife-givers, since the affinal series is projected back in time. The complementarity of the two sets of wife-givers in relation to the host and his wife is not perfectly symmetrical for the simple reason that whereas the host is indebted to both sides, his wife is as it were part of the exchange, herself a prestation. However, in many respects she is conceived as united with her husband, as the choice of titles and every stage of the ritual suggest. This identification of husband and wife is a feature of the *ovasa* but not of the wedding.

Table 9.1 is to be read as a summary of the material gifts. It does not show the intangible endowments made by the wife-givers: namely, life, fertility, prosperity, and labour (in the gift of a bride), and protection in time of war. Some of these endowments

TABLE 9.1 Affinal prestations

Wife-takers	Groom/host	Wife-givers
	MARRIAGE PAYMENTS	
	böli niha ('bridewealth') ⟶	
		⟵ the bride
		⟵ *bövö*
	PRESTATIONS BEFORE THE *OVASA*	
	⟵ *so'i-so'i* ('solicitory gifts')	
ana'iwa ('tribute') ⟶		
		⟵ *so'i-so'i*
	OVASA PRESTATIONS	
		⟵ *bövö/so'i-so'i*
	bövö ba govasa/ana'iwa ⟶	
sumange ⟶		⟵ *sumange*

are symbolized in the named prestations which make up bride-wealth.

Symbolism aside, it is an interesting question whether a wife-taker's gifts are conceived to have any spiritual or mystical *element* which might compensate the wife-givers' mystical endowment. I have already rejected this supposition regarding bridewealth gifts; but what of affinal gifts at an *ovasa*? The etymology of *ana'iwa* is obscure. *Sumange*, 'tribute' or '(token of) respect' (Indon. *penghormatan*), has cognates in many Austronesian languages, e.g. Malay *sumangat* (see Endicott 1970). It is puzzling that these cognates refer to spirit, whereas in Nias *sumange* is a material payment devoid of inherent spiritual quality. Is it possible that the word has become secularized? In a lament collected by Sundermann (1892: 358), *sumange* is coupled with *noso* ('breath, life'); both are 'cut off' when someone dies. In a healing ritual *sumange* is requested from the god Lature in exchange for a sacrificial pig (Sundermann 1905*b*: 84–6). The word means here, according to the author, 'welfare' or 'remedy' and appears as the *object* of tribute. If we accept this interpretation, a greater mystery is how such a semantic change has come about. Fries (1908: 85) defines *sumange* as 'embracing everything which raises one's rank (*Ehrenstellung*)', which is much closer to the present conception and the meaning evident in the oral traditions of central Nias. An explanation in terms of disenchantment or secularization is further weakened by the fact that certain other types of exchange, notably 'prestige payments', have indeed retained a mystical aspect in the concept of *lakhömi* (glory, prestige, spiritual 'virtue'), which I discuss in the next chapter.

17   The Distribution of Prestige Payments

It is principally the host who wins prestige (*lakhömi*) at his feast by the distribution of *urakha*, weighed portions of meat. But the few guests who bring ceremonial contributions called *sulö* also win a certain temporary glory. These donations of live pigs either indebt the host or requite a similar donation which he has previously made at *their* feasts. All *sulö* pigs are slaughtered and converted into *urakha* portions. Incoming *sulö* indebt the host; outgoing *urakha* indebt the guests. In either case no interest is levied on the return. Since pigs grow and increase in value, the return of an equal sum represents a loss. This is part of the reason why such 'prestige payments', as I shall call them, are meritorious.[17]

Sulö may be brought by guests of any category, including the host's fellow-villagers. Those brought by wife-givers are called *sekhe-sekhe* ('prop'). They count as debt in the same way as *sulö*. Unlike the true affinal prestations they can be refused by the host.

The word *sulö* is the nearest equivalent in the Nias language to the anthropologist's concept of 'exchange'. As a verb it means to give back, replace, retaliate, or revenge (*sulöni*). *Sulö* is an exchange of honour or glory which unites potential enemies and consolidates existing relations. Unlike any other type of prestation it can only be reclaimed at another *ovasa*. In this sense, *sulö* (and *urakha*, the portions which derive from them) belong to a self-contained system of exchange. If the donor of *sulö* at someone else's feast never gives an *ovasa* of his own later on, he can never reclaim an equivalent pig. This element of risk, added to the disdain of interest, the ceremonial

---

[17] The details of exchange at *ovasa*, and thus its systematic nature, have hitherto escaped notice. Nieuwenhuisen and Rosenberg (1863: 88) refer to the host's gift of *live* pigs (40–100 in all), which were measured so that an exact equivalent could later be returned. Is this a confusion between *sulö* and the host's gift of live pigs to his wife-givers, a rare local custom, or has the content of prestige payments changed? Schröder (1917: 276), writing of meat exchanges, mentions the addition of an increment to reverse the debt.

'sphere of exchange' restriction, and the nature of the feast as a celebration of rank, all combine to make *sulö/urakha* supremely the prestations which earn the donor prestige. The recipient is also, to a lesser degree, honoured by his prestation.

What insulates *sulö* as a system from other exchanges is that all *sulö* pigs are slaughtered. The donor keeps a leg and the rest is divided up as *urakha* among up to twenty or so men. As it was explained to me, in a practical sense a pig could not be reclaimed for, say, bridewealth, as 'it would come minus a leg'. In contrast, affinal prestations include gold and live pigs, which can be used later as the recipient thinks fit. *Urakha* derive not only from *sulö*, but also from loans, the host's own pigs, wife-takers' tribute, etc. However, once converted into *urakha* they must be paid back as *urakha*. A further restriction on exchange is that *ovasa* debts are not transferable in life (with rare exceptions), though they are heritable.

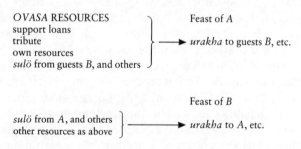

FIG. 9.1. Prestige payments in relation to resources

Once the affinal prestations have been handed over the 'slaughter of prestige payments' (*famahö urakha*) can begin. The distribution is wholly without ceremony. The host and his helpers allocate pigs to several groups at once, usually by lineage or hamlet, and butchering and weighing begin immediately. The composition of the groups is of no special concern to the host since the debts are reckoned individually. The size of *urakha* is specified in a brief consultation between the host's delegate and the elder of the group to which the pig has been allocated (he knows the debts of his own men and their rank). The leading men of the group are given portions which include part of the head. Sometimes there is jostling and grabbing of these portions which do not affect the debt to the host but are relevant to the internal politics of the group. In essence—and in contrast to alliance exchange—prestige payments depend on a principle of symmetry: like-for-like, an expectation of reciprocity. But other factors are also involved in determining the size of a payment as we shall see.

Factors Determining the Size of Prestige Payments

There are two variables in the size of prestation awarded to a particular guest: (1) size of unit, (2) number of units. It is (2) which is indicative of status and is the figure which is remembered and discussed. The number of units given to a guest depends principally on his status and his credit with the host, as I shall explain. In contrast, in any given case the size of unit is matched to the rough category of guest.

1. There are three units (*hië*). The largest has the weight of 1 *tumba* of rice and is called 6 *saga*. The smaller *hië* are stones whose weight has been checked against subdivisions of the *tumba*. A *hië* of:

$$6 \, saga = 1 \, tumba \text{ rice (by weight)} = 1.6 \text{ kg. approx.}$$
$$4 \, saga = 3 \, nali \, (= \text{¾} \, tumba) = 1.2 \text{ kg.}$$
$$3 \, saga = 2 \, nali \, (= \text{½} \, tumba) = 0.8 \text{ kg.}[18]$$

The largest unit is used for those who are closest genealogically and geographically, namely agnates and hamlet neighbours; the 4 *saga hië* is used for other members of the village, and the 3 *saga hië* is used for guests from other villages (which usually includes wife-givers, who are the most important guests). The explanation for this discrimination is that only one's nearest and dearest are likely (that is, feel most obliged) to repay using the same size units: they have to face you every day. Others can more easily get away with repaying the minimum, so long as the number of units is the same. In such a case one has no redress, and one would feel ashamed to protest (it is another matter if the number of units has been reduced). Wife-

[18] The 6-*saga* unit is so called because, when the method was introduced, pork weighing 1 *tumba* of rice was worth a live piglet of 6 *saga* girth in non-festive transactions. A term used in girth measurement thus became applied to a weight. The *saga* numbers are not quite in the same ratio as the weights. This does not affect the tallies, which refer only to the rice-weights. Sometimes a bottle filled with water is used as the 4 *saga hië* since this is exactly the right weight. A few men—market traders—know rough metric equivalents given above.

givers are expected to exploit their superiority whenever possible to win legitimate advantage in an exchange, so they are not given the chance to repay 10 large units with 10 small units. To repeat, the official, socially significant figure is the number of units, not the size of unit used.

2. The number of units is determined by a combination of the following factors:

(a) Whether the host has received *urakha* at his guest's *ovasa* previously. If the host has a debt of 5 *hië* to his guest and he now returns only 3 as an instalment, he remains indebted for 2. To return 5 is called 'paying back' (*famu'a*). To exceed the debt and thus to indebt the guest is called 'planting' (*tanö*), a curious metaphor, since the sum planted cannot grow. Similarly, to give a portion to someone with whom there is no existing debt is also a case of planting. The donor of *sulö* receives back, in addition to the leg, an *urakha* which is deducted from the value of the pig. Thus, if the pig yields 30 *hië* and the donor receives an *urakha* of 8 *hië*, the host's debt to him is 22 *hië*. It is usual for a donor of *sulö* to be given an *urakha* larger than he would otherwise merit.

(b) There are rough guidelines correlating rank with size. The host's own chief receives two or three times as much as anyone else, though this depends on his own feasting record. Elders (men who have given an *ovasa*) are given the same as each other, even though one may be regarded as more influential and higher in rank than another. Men who have given small feasts may receive the same as elders or less, depending on resources. Thus, finer discriminations of status, which may be informal or controversial, are not involved. The payments do not recognize or establish a rank order among individuals. Rather, they recognize the broad divisions of rank (chief, elder, junior feastgiver, the rest).

(c) The social geography of the event and the prior relation between the participants have a bearing on the number of units awarded. Those members of the host's lineage who are involved in the organization and funding of the feast and are identified closely with him as *sovatö* ('hosts') generally receive little. Other members of the host's hamlet (especially fellow-clansmen and affines) are expected to contribute *sulö*, and therefore merit a large *urakha*, irrespective of their rank. Guests from other hamlets do not usually bring contributions of *sulö* unless they are affines because of difficulty in reclaiming the debt. The size of wife-takers' *urakha* depends partly on the size of their tributary contributions and the quality of their relation to the host.

(*d*) Obviously, the size of portions must take account of the ratio of guests to total resources. If more guests come than were expected the portions have to be reduced or some people miss out. Either way, there is no flexibility in assessing the state of credit or debit towards the guest: what cannot be paid now must be paid at a future feast.

The interrelation of these factors in the determination of *urakha* size can be seen in the following example.

Example 1
At the *ovasa* of Ama Duho'aro in 1985, well over 100 pigs were slaughtered. The size of *urakha* was roughly as follows (points are numbered for convenience; they do not correspond to the factors listed above or to fixed groups or categories):

1. In the host's hamlet, most of the men who were elders or expected soon to give a feast brought one *sulö* pig and received an *urakha* of 10 *hië*, using the large units. These included men from all three main clans. Wife-takers living in the hamlet who donated pigs as *ana'iwa* for slaughter received the same.

2. Close agnates were given a token *urakha* of 2 *hië*, which does not count as a debt.

3. The Laia clansmen of Balöhili, the adjacent hamlet which has several affinal ties with Ama Duho'aro's agnates, received *urakha* of 3–4 *hië*, using the medium-size (4 *saga*) unit. There were no elders among them.

4. The Laia of Lölömoyo, a nearby hamlet with no affinal links, received *urakha* of 2–3 *hië*, except for an elder who brought *sulö* and received 9 *hië*.

5. Elders of the host's clan in Hilidanaya'ö hamlet were given 4 or 5 *hië*.

6. The leaders of the wife-giving groups from Orahili village all brought pigs and received 5 *hië* each.

7. Remote wife-takers from other hamlets of the village and other villages received a small *urakha* (1–3 *hië*) or what they could grab, as a gratuity.

Every portion is carefully weighed and remembered. It is a visible sign of worth, a public recognition of rank. Any man remembers all the *urakha* he has received over the years, and guests are sensitive to the slightest reduction in their due. Disputes over the size of a debt quickly turn violent; to overlook someone is a serious public affront. Since the *urakha* confers honour on the recipient and acknowledges his rank and his prior gift (if any), not to award it when due causes shame (*aila*) and anger. At a big feast where scores of pigs may be slaughtered it is inevitable that some people get short-measured or left out. Amid the carnage and clamour of squealing pigs and the incessant din of gongs and drums during the slaughter, tempers flare and the exchange of honour can turn into a brawl. Nowadays some people keep a private written record of their prestige payments, but this cannot be used as evidence in a claim. In a dispute the offended party can challenge a cheat to 'eat the pig's measuring string', a deeply shaming taunt; or he can swear an oath (*möi ba hölu*). Witnesses can always be called concerning the original prestation and it is not difficult to establish a likely figure for the original *urakha*.

Entering the System of Prestige Payments

Prestige payments have no intrinsic relation to other kinds of obligation, such as those derived from kinship and affinity.[19] There are no restrictions on who may be awarded *urakha*: any married man is eligible. Neither is there a formal way of entering the system. It is at the discretion of the host and his helpers who receives what, but in practice virtually every member of the affinal guest groups is a recipient, and a great number of the host's own villagers receive too. Distant relatives and others in credit often send a boy to claim their *urakha* without attending in person. While there are no formal restrictions, a member of another hamlet belonging to the same village would not attend unless he were an elder or in credit, as he might suffer the indignity of being passed over. It is possible to refuse an *urakha* or to choose not to attend an *ovasa*; but attendance by close affines is obligatory. Eventually virtually everyone receives at some time an *urakha* and contracts debts. Moreover, aside from

[19] The exception is the obligation to hold a feast at a father's funeral at which his outstanding debts are paid off. One may hold an *ovasa* in honour of someone else (e.g. father, son, or guardian) but this is unrelated to the question of *ovasa* debts.

the universal desire for respect, the immediate need for meat usually overcomes any misgivings about the ability to return the gift later. A verse sometimes spoken at feasts goes:

Andrö u'ohelua	Therefore I am like a bat
Andrö u'obögi	Therefore I am a flying fox
Ahilu wa'ami mbawi.	Suffering for the savour of pork.

This was paraphrased: 'At an *ovasa* we suffer in the heat, the stench and the filth, like bats hanging in the trees, driven by our pork-cravings.' Until recent years when the weekly market opened, pork was only available at feasts. Even today, for most families feasts (of every kind) remain by far the main source of meat. It is therefore difficult to pass up the opportunity of attending an *ovasa*. For any man of character and ability, even those with a 'modern' cast of mind inclined to disdain extravagance, it is impossible to stay outside the system.

The organizer of a feast can apply considerable pressure on agnates to donate *sulö*. Poor and weak men who have no hope of ever reclaiming feel obliged to contribute. They might need the support of the senior man in a dispute or wedding negotiation later on. Wife-givers (who expect to receive large sums of tribute) are under an even stronger obligation to donate. In this way one can become embroiled, even if reluctantly, as a creditor rather than a debtor. After some years of making such donations, and with debts to others to offset them, aside from the desire for prestige, it becomes a matter of expediency to hold a feast of one's own and settle up all round.

It is common, especially among younger men (30–40) to pay off their *ovasa* debts in a small-scale feast called a *fatome(sa)* ('to have guests') or *famahö urakha* ('slaughter of prestige payments'). The latter term, which applies to only one part of a full-blown *ovasa*, thus stands here for the entire event, illustrating the narrower focus of a *famahö*. It is really an *ovasa* shorn of spectacle and more modest in aim, with only a minimal honouring of affines. It can serve as a stopgap, postponing a major feast, or it can be a first feast.

Example 2
As an example let us examine the *famahö* of Ama Uzia of Sifalagö, a feast held to inaugurate his new house in 1984, when he was 34. He is connected to the chief's descent line six generations back, and he

has no close senior agnates. These unexceptional circumstances of birth mean that profitable links with remote wife-takers have lapsed for lack of solicitory gifts. His contributors were all close wife-takers who automatically owe him tribute (he is their *sanema maso-maso*: recipient of the second largest bridewealth prestation). He has no qualities that would fit him for the role of leading elder, but what gives him an edge over other men is diligence and a taste for independence evident in his reluctance to become indebted.

Altogether 24 pigs were killed. Only one-quarter came from wife-takers, for the reasons mentioned. Unusually there were no *sulö* or loans of other kinds, so the provision for the feast incurred no new debts. Ama Uzia and his brother supplied three-quarters of the resources. The only pure loss in material terms consisted of affinal tribute to the MB and WF groups. Remoter wife-givers were not invited. All the other guests were co-villagers. It was a feast played on a small political stage and the main intention was clearly to pay off *ovasa* debts. In no case did the repayment exceed the original debt: there was no investment in *urakha*. In contrast, Ama Uzia has donated no fewer than eight large *sulö* pigs at others' *ovasa*, which shows publicly that he has the clear intention of mounting a large feast later on. His method of investment represents a choice between two strategies. To invest in *urakha* (that is, to overpay your debts) means that you win glory as a lavish host, but your glory as a guest later is dispersed: you get the *urakha* back one by one. The return is uncertain and depends on your partner's sense of honour and *his* timing. Moreover, the return may put you in debt if he overpays. Investment in *urakha* is hardly appropriate to a modest feast. In contrast, by investing in *sulö* (a generous guest rather than a generous host), you retain control of your fortunes—where possible you can avoid other people's feasts and thus keep out of debt. In practical terms of reckoning and reclaiming, it is easier to keep track of a whole pig than of fifty pieces dispersed among half a dozen villages; moreover, the return of *sulö*—at one's own feast—is certain and the timing no longer depends on the whim of others. To invest in *sulö* means, in this context, putting off the day of glory. Ama Uzia decided to give a modest feast to clear his debts and win respectability; his *sulö* investments are for the big feast to come. At that feast he will kill many pigs and distribute *urakha* widely, guaranteeing his position as a much-honoured guest at the feasts of others. These two strategies correspond to different stages in a man's life, and the policy of Ama Uzia is fairly typical of a first or interim feast held by a youngish man.[20]

18 The Closing Ceremony

After guests have received their *urakha* they depart a few at a time without formal leave-taking. At a large feast the butchering can go on for two days or more. On arrival home, recipients are expected to send small portions to neighbours and others who were not invited as a 'free gift', a distribution called *fegero* (*ero* means 'each, every') which does not transfer the recipient's debt.

The *ovasa* closes as it began, some days after the feast, with a gathering of the agnates and other members of the hamlet, for the 'eating of the pigs' hearts'. The heart of every pig which was slaughtered has been returned to the host's house to be salted. Formerly the ancestors would again be offered tribute from a sacrificial pig, and this was served along with the pigs' hearts to the villagers. If a megalith had been erected a head might be taken as a *binu govasa* ('*ovasa* human sacrifice'). This was placed beneath the stone bench (*dao-dao*) and was said to be the 'clearer up of banana leaves' left by the guests. Thus the closing stage or completion (*fangasiwai*) is a small-scale, comparatively private affair, reinforcing agnatic and community ties.

19 The Meaning of *Ovasa* Exchange

Relationships in Nias tend to be characterized in terms of debt (*ömö*). One elder once told me, simplifying, that there are two kinds of debt: *bövö* (referring to the whole complex of affinal prestations) and *urakha*. The conception of debt in each case is different, but it is interesting that they should be brought together and contrasted under the same heading. As the foregoing description shows, *ovasa* exchanges fall into these two kinds. Table 9.2 summarizes the differences between the two systems of exchange.

The two systems differ in every respect, and in some sense (e.g. content and reckoning) they are opposed and are conceived by

---

[20] Appropriately he was given the title Fadru Samobörö, Lamp-Beginner.

TABLE 9.2 Two types of exchange

Bövö	Urakha
Structural level	
Egocentric	Sociocentric
Partners	
Exchange derives from and maintains prior relation	Independent of prior relation; exchange may create relation
Type of status symbolized	
Ascribed status, enacted in temporary form due to overlapping of roles	Achieved status (rank) valid outside *ovasa* context
Form	
Complementary: unequal exchange of different kinds or differently named prestations between unequal partners	Symmetrical: like for like (in quantity or kind) or status quo is affected
Content	
Mainly live pigs and gold	Pigs for slaughter, and meat
Purpose	
To acquire blessing and good fortune	To acquire prestige, promote or validate status
Reckoning	
No public measurement; exactness not a criterion	Exact measurement, highly public
Sanction on non-return	
Withdrawal of benevolent influence; curse	Loss of esteem and influence; shame

Niasans to be opposed. However, the meaning of each system of exchange does not, in my opinion, derive to any significant extent from this contrast; nor is there a native model in which the systems are exhaustively contrasted. In exchanging pigs there are only a limited number of principles which can be applied to distinguish different economic and symbolic ends, and these I have spelt out in the course of this and preceding chapters. The meaning of prestige payments derives to a much greater extent from an implicit contrast with non-ceremonial forms of exchange than with *bövö*. Both systems are to a degree self-contained and, as can be seen, they operate at different structural levels. In the ritual of the *ovasa* structural levels are occasionally confused, as when the host receives a title from his wife-givers or when his promotion in rank is symbolized by his physical elevation above them. However, for the most part, affinity and rank are separate foci of the *ovasa*. If there are basic similarities between affinal and prestige payments, these are at the level of the universal characteristics of gift-exchange identified by Mauss (1954).

If it is a question of two independent systems of exchange operating on different structural levels, how are we to grasp the moral framework of the *ovasa* in its totality? To pursue this Maussian aim, let us return to the nature of the gifts and their associated sanctions.

Given the declared aims of the exchanges, one would expect that prestige payments depend on social, or temporal, sanctions, and affinal payments depend on supernatural ones; and indeed this expectation is easily confirmed. The social sanctions do not take immediate effect but are no less conspicuous for that. *Urakha* debts can stand for many years but must eventually be repaid. As long as one has the intention of giving an *ovasa*, and thus of discharging one's debts they remain honourable. It is a sign of worth after all that one has received so much pork and run up vast debts over the years. Such good intentions are evident, for example, in the donation of *sulö* at others' feasts, since these are only reclaimable at one's own *ovasa*. But to delay beyond reasonable limits is to risk public exposure and humiliation. A sanction with wider effect is loss of standing and influence, which is discussed in the next chapter.

However, the mystical/temporal contrast is not quite so clear-cut as my schema suggests. Non-return of *urakha* is considered a cardinal sin (*horö*) leading to exclusion from heaven. In this, both the pagan and latter-day Christian eschatologies concur. Until very recently, dying men whose debts were unpaid or who had 'shifted' wealth from its promised end, would lacerate themselves in terror and remorse. (I was always asked by people who had not been present how the late chief of Sifalagö died.) Such debts could deny them a place in Teteholi Ana'a, the abode of chiefly spirits. As Ama Gamböta described it to me—his nostalgia tempered with a proper Christian scepticism—Teteholi Ana'a was conceived as a slightly improved version of the earthly village, but riven by strife and envy all the same. A narrow bridge spans a gulf between the worlds of the living and the dead. Down below is a pool patrolled by vicious dogs (*asu hulandro*, 'Dutch dogs') ready to devour whoever falls off the bridge. Ancestors wait on the other side with hands eagerly outstretched in welcome, not for the deceased, but for the tribute he bears. Should the freshman arrive without either an *urakha* or a human head in his hand, or with his festive debts unpaid, he is pitched into the howling gulf below. The human head shows that his sons have performed the full mortuary rites and sacrifices necessary for his resurrection (*femaoso*); the tribute he brings is merely a token indicating that he has given feasts and made offering to the ancestors.

Last judgement, it appears, is literally a day of reckoning; and damnation is to be weighed in the balance and found wanting. It was with such a prospect that the late chief's father had 'come back from death's door' to order a feast to pay off his debts. That was in the late 1960s when Sifalagö had been Christian for some thirty years. The chief himself, a staunch traditionalist, organized another such feast shortly before dying in 1988. In the same spirit, pious or vociferous Christians often claim that there is a verse in the Bible which states that an ounce of pork unpaid will bar the entrance to heaven. Others cite the biblical commandment against stealing. If a man dies in debt, his sons—whatever their religious persuasion—are always anxious to settle up at the funeral.

Thus, the sanctions on *urakha* and *bövö* relate, ultimately, to two different aspects of the Nias moral universe. *Urakha* are sanctioned by the eventual retribution of God and the patrilineal ancestors, who merge in this function. *Bövö* is sanctioned by the swift retribution of the affines, who invoke the wrath of their ancestors—a punishment in this world. Evidently, the return of the gift is, in each case, divinely sanctioned. Again, what is most striking is the continuity of values in the face of historical and cultural change. The traditional theory has simply been reinterpreted in Christian terms, albeit with a little sophistry.

The religious aspect of feasting achievement is obscured in the ritually poor version that can be witnessed today. The abolition of the ancestor cult and the suppression of traditional cosmological ideas have left the celebration of affinity and its symbolic aspect unduly prominent (the idea of wife-givers' powers seems ineradicable). What one observes in today's *ovasa* is a curiously dual-purpose feast with a sacred ritual (the purchase of affinal blessing) and a mundane unceremonial distribution of meat. If the celebration of rank retains any explicit ritual aspect it is only with the collusion of the affines (in the slaughter of the origin pigs, the host's elevation and entitling). The acquisition of prestige is not ritually manifest in the distribution of *urakha*.

In the earliest reports it was, on the contrary, the religious aspect of the host's promotion which most struck observers. Fries explains the function of the *ovasa* entirely in terms of ancestor worship. At a funeral *ovasa* (*fangasi*) the deceased is resurrected and liberated from the 'field-hut of the ten thousand', which is where men who have not given a feast are condemned to remain. Having attained the heavenly village, the noble spirits, like living men, are engaged in a perpetual struggle, as each tries to win more *sumange* than the next through his descendants' festive offerings (1908: 86). They are prepared to twist the necks of their descendants if tribute is withheld. An *ovasa* pacifies them and simulaneously brings about their promotion with that of the host.

The host's earthly prosperity depends on his ancestors' approval, purchased with tribute, but he also expects a reward in the afterlife for his festive achievements. Fries writes (1908: 83) that by once mounting his litter at a great feast a man becomes a chief and thus guarantees his place in heaven. In central Nias this privilege is extended to all *ovasa* hosts, whether elders or chiefs. The notion of festive merit or prestige thus has a religious dimension, at least in the traditional setting. We can now appreciate Schröder's comment that noblemen 'during their earthly existence are none other than ancestors in the making' (1917: 340).

Placed in this light, the climactic events of the *ovasa* gain a new significance. The host's ritual elevation appears as enactment of his future resurrection.[21] He is united with the lineage spirits on the litter and carried aloft around the village. The slaughter of the origin pigs—explicitly a substitute for the host—then appears as a ritual death and rebirth. Modern Niasans do not make the latter inference, or at any rate do not put it in these baldly heretical terms. But there is no doubt that the sacrifice is still taken to be a divination of salvation: the movement of the pig's head indicates which

---

[21] Hoskins (1986) has described a similar pre-mortem enactment of the journey of the soul in stone-dragging ceremonies of Kodi, West Sumba.

direction its *noso* ('life-breath') has flown and thus divines the host's own destiny.

Niasans today mostly reject the traditional cosmology in favour of the Christian heaven which is open to all. Nevertheless, among senior men there is a widespread opinion that access to heaven is restricted to those who have paid all their debts. Since *ovasa* debts can only be repaid at an *ovasa*, the implication is that only feastgivers go to heaven. But, again, no one would put the matter in quite such heretical or dogmatic terms, and there is no clear or consistent view to be discerned. It is not a question of establishing what people 'really think', since, in differing degrees, many hold to both views. The familiar anthropological appeal to context will go some way towards explaining this paradox, as will the fragmentation of experience in a period of rapid social change. But pagan and Christian world-views are sometimes perceived to be in direct conflict, and if forced to declare one's position—as sometimes happens in debate—there are two common recourses. Leaders, as practical men of action, can be heard to express impatience with or indifference to the details of theological controversy; though it is true that such men may suffer a crisis of doubt when misfortune strikes. Others more inclined to reflect on the problems of cultural change, and perhaps with less to gain from the old ways, sometimes express the opinion that Christianity requires one to believe in what is contrary to reason (given Niasan premises about exchange)—that is its peculiar burden for the faithful. Much soul-searching and moralizing in Nias is given to precisely this question: the obligation to be a good Christian, but the impossibility of achieving that aim, given Niasan premisses.

Doctrinal issues aside, in practical terms the egalitarianism of Christianity has so far made little headway against traditional values, and the indigenous theory that mankind is divided into rulers and ruled, great men and small, is largely unchallenged. With these observations in mind, in the next chapter I look at concepts of status and leadership.

10
Status and Leadership

As with the *ovasa*, the nature of leadership in contemporary Nias is best understood by presenting it first in its traditional context. Again, the purpose is not to reconstruct the past, but to portray those aspects which are relevant to the present in a living tradition; for the imprint of the past is perhaps most powerfully felt in the question of status. No single account could do justice to the complexity of the subject: different generations have different perspectives on status and leadership; there is variation within a generation in the assimilation of 'modern' Indonesian and Christian ideas; and what an individual asserts or thinks may vary with immediate context. But a description must reflect the largely traditional outlook of those in control, as well as of most of the villagers, even if this leaves out of account the youths who will eventually take over but who for the moment have no voice in society.

1 Leadership in Historical Perspective

Early descriptions of Nias emphasize the highly competitive ethos. Thomas (1892: 7) wrote: 'from youth onwards there begins, among the *siulu* [south: nobles] a quest for influence in which intrigues of every kind, even murder, are nothing strange.' Palmer van den Broek (cited in Schröder 1917: 354) wrote: 'under the *siulu* reigns the greatest jealousy, each striving for the greatest power and most following'. Ködding (1868a and b) describes a similar situation in Fagulu (east). Schröder found these accounts 'too black, too generalized and possibly tendentious'; they were incompatible with the rigid class system and autocratic leadership of south Nias, as he saw it. However, they provide a fair approximation, as far as one can tell, of the comparatively fluid and dynamic society of central Nias as it was before about 1920, when Dutch government was consolidated in the area.

The level of political integration in the centre varied greatly. Independent villages might consist of a single descent group (e.g. Böe) or a loose association of lineages belonging to different clans and occupying the same or adjacent hamlets (e.g. Sifalagö). There might also be settler lineages living on borrowed land. Unlike south Nias, where the most senior noble (*balö ziulu*) was the official village head, in central Nias there was no such office until the Dutch introduced it. Leadership of the village was informal and unstable, as the prominent men of each lineage vied for supremacy. In one village, there might be three or four rivals ruling in concert; in another a first among equals; in a third, domination by an outstanding individual.[1]

Besides the leaders (whom we may call chiefs) there were other men of influence who had organized feasts and had superior personal abilities. All such men of rank were called *satua mbanua* ('village elders'); but the leading men might be denoted additionally by rank-titles won in feasting, such as *tuha* ('lord'), or noble epithets such as *se'ulu* (cf. south: *siulu*) or *salawa* ('he who is high'). The latter term, denoting a leader or senior man in the northern dialect, was adopted by Dutch and Indonesian administrations for the office of village headman. The category of elders otherwise remains unchanged, as does that of ordinary villagers (*ono mbanua*, lit. 'child/member of the village'), which is simply the residual category of persons without rank. The words *satua* and *ono* mean parent and child, but it would be a mistake to see the relation between elders and other villagers as modelled on the parent–child relation. *Ono* can denote membership in a class or category, or an element of something, e.g. *ono hörö*, 'pupil of the eye'. Thus the plural of *ono mbanua* is not the collective noun *iraono mbanua* (children of the village), but simply *banua*, village, i.e. the class as a whole.

Despite the competitive ethos, apparently unfavourable to the consolidation of status, there is a tendency for power and wealth to become concentrated in particular descent lines leading to their becoming known as noble or chiefly lines (*nga'ötö zalawa*). It is usually from such groups that the headman is now drawn; and in such cases, where traditional eminence corresponds to offical authority, it seems appropriate to continue to speak of chiefs. The enduring symbols of this pre-eminence are the megaliths, formerly erected at

[1] Nieuwenhuisen and Rosenberg (1863: 86) noted a similar variety on their expedition.

ovasa, and the great houses built by chiefs, which are home to generations of their descendants. Thus, while there is no formally constituted class of rulers or nobles there is a *de facto* aggregation of power and status, more or less stable, and an ideological recognition of the superiority of rulers over ordinary men. This is what I call consolidated rank, as distinct from a hereditary ruling class such as is found in the south.

Consolidated rank is based on the following factors:

1. Feasting. Prestige is attained and maintained through lavish feast-giving. The scale of the feasts—the number of pigs killed, the amount of gold given away, the size of *urakha* payments, the number of guests—wins acclaim and creates indebtedness among the guests which translates indirectly into influence. Feasting in turn legitimizes influence by public recognition of prowess.

2. Superior resources in land and labour. Wealth is an essential basis for leadership.

3. Descent.

4. Achievement in other, potentially rival, systems (local government, church).

A fifth factor applied in former times: warfare. A leading man was a warlord and had to be prepared to attack rivals and to defend lineages subservient to him.

I consider, below, each of these factors in more detail, concentrating on the first.

2 Status and the Politics of Feasting

In the realm of politics, what feasting achieves first of all is influence rather than power. It gives the host a title and reputation (a 'name'); it also silences critics—for the moment—and forces people to take him seriously. It is essential for any young man of ability to kill a few pigs as a start so that he can have a voice in village affairs. I once heard a neighbour planning his political debut in this way with an elder: he was tired of being ignored in disputes of which he was often the cause (he was murdered before his debut could take place). At the debates which accompany any gathering only men with titles won by feasting carry any weight. The same comment from the mouth of an inexperienced man counts for little, so generally he keeps quiet. This does not mean that the content of speech is irrelevant; rather, a titled man is listened to because, as Niasans say, 'he's travelled that path, he's done what he says.'[2] Since most customary speeches concern the exchange of prestations, obviously one cannot lecture others without having first established one's credibility. An elder is qualified to comment and advise others because in giving an *ovasa* he has achieved a practical mastery of the culture, marshalling a wide range of resources and taking on a huge economic commitment (as we should say, putting his money where his mouth is). This could not have been done without organizational abilities, oratorical skills, and the confidence of supporters, who would not lend without hope of return.

Upstart juniors can be silenced by the merest hint of this, the voice of experience, without need of explicit rebuke. A personal confrontation between two men can end angrily, but decisively, when one reminds the other of his greater achievements in *adat*, and, perhaps, to drive home the advantage, reminds him of a still unpaid *ovasa* debt. Generally the junior man avoids this kind of humiliation and submits.

Influence, then, has two sources in the feast: (1) the direct sense of obligation felt by a debtor to a creditor (a consumer to a provider); (2) the renown or status which the host has achieved and which commands public respect. In the literature on exchange systems a failure to separate these two aspects of exchange has sometimes led to misunderstanding.

1. As we have seen, the recipient of generosity at a feast is not crushed, or shamed, but honoured by the prestation. There is no immediate pressure to reciprocate; the sanction on non-return is a very distant worry. Indeed the length of the interval enhances the appearance of loss, the gift aspect, and thus the honour to both parties. Neither does the distribution of *urakha* establish a rank order, which could in any case only subsist until the next *ovasa* rearranged the balance of payments between participants. Such a system would be unworkable given the large number of participants and the two-way flow of prestations in *sulö* and *urakha*. It would be a different matter, perhaps, if groups rather than individuals were the sponsors of feasts.

[2] One elder, quite unprompted, saw the analogy with fieldwork as an initiation into academic debate. 'If you haven't followed the path of suffering will anyone listen to you?'

The exchange of prestige payments is, in essence, symmetrical. There is always the expectation that the return gift will cancel the asymmetry introduced by the first payment. Consequently, at the level of individual debts, the relative status of partners in an exchange is unaffected. This is an important point which, while not of universal relevance, is, I would suggest, often overlooked in the anthropology of exchange, leading to an over-simple equation of gift-credit with domination. In an influential study, C. A. Gregory argues that

gift exchange—the exchange [at intervals] of like-for-like—establishes an unequal relationship of *domination* between the transactors. This comes about because the giver usually is regarded as superior to the receiver (Gregory 1982: 47; original emphasis).

Gregory is generalizing mainly from Melanesian examples in which this does indeed appear to be the case.[3] In Nias, however, the individual *ovasa* debt creates an inequality, that is the subordination of the debtor, only if there is no expectation or possibility of repaying.[4] This subordination, where it occurs, is not publicly recognized: formal status is not involved. It consists merely in the debtor's submission to his creditor's will. He will not contradict him and he will support him if called upon. In this, the *ovasa* debt becomes like any other debt. It ceases to be an exchange of honour and, unrequited, turns into a sort of purchase of influence or patronage. The many poor men who attend *ovasa* with no hope or prospect of repaying find themselves in this humbling condition. But clearly no man of substance would ever accept an *urakha* if it immediately put him in the power of his benefactor. Important men in the village must wait many years before they can repay all their debts, but they do not thereby lose influence.

The host's award of a large *urakha* is a public demonstration of confidence in the recipient's ability to repay. And for his part, the guest at others' feasts shows, by the occasional donation of *sulö* and by 'support loans' of pigs for bridewealth and *ovasa*, that he will

---

[3] See Strathern's discussion of 'alternating disequilibrium' among big-men in the *moka* of Mount Hagen (1971: 10–14, 222–3). The extreme instability of political ascendancy in a setting of egalitarianism marks a crucial difference from the sociology of Southeast Asian feasting.

[4] The sanction on return of *sulö* (as opposed to *urakha*) only comes into consideration when the original donor reclaims it for his own *ovasa*. If he fails to hold a feast it is lost without prejudice to the beneficiary.

eventually repay all his debts in a feast of his own. This is a kind of public 'servicing' of his debts. It keeps them in the realm of honour.

Once influence has outstripped feasting achievement—as frequently happens since influence depends on a variety of factors—a man becomes vulnerable to criticism and is wary of opposing his creditors. Even if the creditor (or benefactor in other forms of help) does not remind him personally, he does not miss the opportunity to mention the debt to others. This is one of the functions of boasting, which is habitual among some leading men. When factions form in a dispute it is sufficient explanation to account for the lines of loyalty to say of someone that 'he has eaten So-and-so's pork'. Thus, influence is exerted between individuals through *ovasa* debts only in so far as they depart from the norm of reciprocity associated with *urakha*. It is non-ceremonial debts which are much more clearly associated with subordination; the extreme case was debt slavery, which derived from inability to pay off a commercial loan (grown huge by extortionate interest). But this type of exchange was at the opposite pole from those of the *ovasa*.

2. In the wider public forum, influence works through reputation and one-upmanship. Here what matters is the tally of pigs killed and the number of feasts, rather than particular portions. These figures are common knowledge in the village. But again, there is no simple equation of feasting achievement with influence or power. It is pointless to eclipse a rival by exhausting one's own stocks and running up huge debts with others. Power is won by the man who is undiminished by his generosity, as in the rhyme quoted earlier. He can still sponsor future projects, solicit the aid of wife-takers with regular gifts, and so on. Power without wealth is impossible. In this respect Sifalagö and neighbouring Orahili provide an instructive contrast. In Orahili the office of headman, since it was introduced, has shifted between different lineages and even different clan-settlements/hamlets as there is no decisive economic advantage among the leading men. In Sifalagö the chief's line, with greatly superior resources, has dominated for generations.

Likewise, one must possess the abilities needed to take advantage of one's feasting renown: ruthlessness, intelligence, and vigour. One elder who saved his greatest feast for what must be the last years of his life has gained little in terms of influence, lacking both the means and the will to dominate. He was begged by his adult sons to be moderate but disregarded them. Now he regrets his policy and the huge debts he will pass on to his sons. People comment not on his greatness but on the greatness of his debt. The late chief, by contrast, killed more pigs than anyone and reaped the full reward of his glory in his thirty-three years' rule.

In Sifalagö at present, the contest for the job of government headman is being fought out in this idiom. Both candidates have attained positions of influence in the village by traditional means—patronage of clan juniors in bridewealth, donations of *sulö*, exploitation of affinal links (the elder candidate has nine ZH in the village, a solid enough economic basis for power). Both also have modern credentials: fluency in Indonesian, middle-school education, a position on the village staff (secretary and deputy). But neither has yet validated his position by feast-giving. The outcome of the struggle for power now rests largely on such validation. Of the senior man, who is an agnate and deputy of the late chief, elders maintain that he must give a feast of at least 20 pigs for the village—this would only be an instalment on his future *ovasa*. The younger man is not given a chance of election unless he can pre-empt the older with a feast of a dozen pigs (he has less *ovasa* debts). But there are doubts about his ability to sustain the losses required of a chief, as well as about personal weaknesses. Moreover, a division according to clan loyalties favours a kinsman of the deceased chief.

If the election is disregarded by the authorities and a successor is appointed by the local government, as sometimes happens, he lacks legitimacy and has no authority in matters of customary law and tradition. The man with traditional pre-eminence may then be called the *salawa hada* (*adat* chief) to distinguish him from the official headman (Indon. *kepala desa*). Sometimes a junior man is elected as a compromise, where two senior men are equally strong, or because he is the only one with an education which qualifies him for the post (since 1987 all headmen are supposed to be educated to middle-school [SMP] level). In such cases, he is no more than a clerk or a puppet in the hands of those with traditional influence. In contrast, where a leading man is appointed headman, as has been the case in Sifalagö since the office was introduced, his eminence is enhanced and his powers of patronage and jurisdiction are increased. In sum, feasting is not the sole means to influence and power, but it plays a key role.

Challenge Feasts

The mechanism of achieving domination by outdoing the other appeared in purer form in the institution of the challenge feast (*fahölu*), no longer practised. This was a trial of strength between individuals in which one side would respond to some insult or political threat by challenging the other to reciprocal feasts. The invitations would go back and forth until one side was exhausted. This could be quite soon, as the series began immediately without preparations. For the same reason, the number of pigs killed might remain in single figures—whatever could be mustered by a quick tour of supporters. Defeat could lead to a political realignment within the village, with the victor and his lineage turning into protector and exploiter of the vanquished rival, sometimes paying off his debts. The name of the challenge feasts is derived from the term for ordeal by oath (*hölu*), and there is clearly an element of trial by ordeal in the contest.

In Sifalagö one such exchange, around the turn of the century, led to the eclipse of Saruruhili, the leading man of Lölömoyo hamlet, when he was crushed by Saefafarongo, an elder in the chiefly line of the dominant hamlet (Sifalagö). Saruruhili had turned up at Saefa's *ovasa* with a sack and challenged him to fill it with *urakha*. Saefa had immediately responded, 'Let's have a trial of strength' (*fahölu ita!*). He sent him away with several pigs. Saruruhili topped this figure but was trounced in the second round. He was said to have 'spoken out of line' (*mo itöraigö bava*, lit. 'his mouth had exceeded'). In defeat he was said to be 'mastered' (*nifatörö*) or to be 'beneath the mouth' of the other. The victor was said to have demonstrated his 'hardness' or warrior's valour, his *lakhömi horö*: a grace or virtue visited on the strong by ancestral warrior spirits. The preternatural aspect to the contest is evident also in the idea of outdoing the rival by killing for him freakish animals. Pigs with some deformity were reared as *bawi fahölusa*, challenge-feast pigs. Sometimes the tail of a piglet would be split to cultivate the appearance of a double tail. It was difficult to match this in a challenge. One had to be particularly wary of provoking the owner of such a beast.

The goal of outdoing the other depends on a like-for-like symmetrical principle (asymmetry constituting defeat), which is of course fundamental to prestige payments in the *ovasa* but lacks there the element of direct competition. Since only two participants are involved in the challenge, the same principle can be used to establish a clear ranking.

Somewhat different was the demand for hospitality, intended to 'measure' the reputation of a chief in another village. This was called *sifa'ora* or *simotome omo zalawa* ('the chief's house entertains'). At short notice, the chief of one village would turn up at another, and expect to be feasted. If the host failed to live up to his reputation he was 'shamed'. A year or so later he would return the visit. Ama Huku, age 78, remembers going with Matanihela, the head of the Upper Susua district, and a party of seventy men to Mazinö in the south, where they demanded hospitality from Mekhönö, who was a remote agnate and similarly a district chief. Such visits are exemplified in many *hoho famaedo zalawa* ('parable of a chief'), which are sometimes recited as a eulogy at an *ovasa*. Marschall (1976: 160) describes the (now obsolete) *fa'ora* reciprocal feasting in south Nias as a contest between villages which was won when the stocks of one side were exhausted, resembling the individual challenge feast described above.

There is no memory in Sifalagö of such challenge feasts between villages or of wars of generosity, though, rarely, *ovasa* could end in bloodshed. Undoubtedly rival chiefs competed for fame through feasting, but as I have shown, neither the gift of *urakha* nor the total tally of kills translates directly into power. The major emphasis of the feast in central Nias has always been, so far as we know, on fulfilling obligations and honouring guests, thereby winning prestige for oneself. Only in the simpler challenge feast was this dimension lacking and competition came to the fore. Prestige payments were formerly spoken of, in polite speech, as *halövö va'omasi* ('the work of kindness/love'), not as the creation or settling of debt.

It is possible that a special form of feasting in Nias was wrongly assumed by early observers to be typical of all *ovasa*. In this respect the ethnography of the *ovasa* resembles that of the potlatch. Among the Northwest Coast Indians, 'competition between two men for a specific status resulted in the rivalry potlatch' but this was a special case (Drucker 1967: 488).[5] It may well be true, however, that in

---

[5] Several authors have, in fact, compared the *ovasa* to the potlatch as 'fighting with property'. Suzuki (1959: 108–9), summarizing the literature, writes: 'We get a general impression of the ovasa as a feast of rivalry, antagonism and combativeness. . . . In fine the ovasa is a battle, the planning of which savors [of] the potlatch.' As with the potlatch (Drucker 1967: 485), it has been wrongly assumed that prestige payments in the *ovasa* incurred interest and thus led to an escalation of gifts.

areas of Nias where there was political federation between villages, feasting did establish a rank order among them. Officers of the *öri* were ranked by several criteria (sequence of settlement, strength of descent group/village), which may have included feasting seniority. In the Susua valley villages were independent and the feast probably did not have this function. However, one cannot be certain on this point. The decline of the descent group as a corporate political unit may have obscured the extent to which, formerly, it had a collective status tied to that of its senior members.

A further point which needs to be kept in mind if we are to understand the nature of the *ovasa* is that the combative aspect of much of the ritual should not simply be equated with competition for rank. It derives partly from the relations of mutual hostility between villages which is overcome in marriage alliance. The confrontation of the host and guest groups represents the bridging of political discontinuity through the bonds of affinity.

Power and Legitimacy

How, then, is the link between feasting and influence conceived? What is the ideological justification of the leader's position?

A chief or leading man did not have constitutional autocratic powers. His authority depended on public support and the network of debts of which he was the centre, besides his own abilities. This still applies, *mutatis mutandis*, to the present-day chief/village head. The nexus between exchange, status, and power is to be found in the concept of *lakhömi* ('glory, spiritual potency'). Feasting legitimizes influence by public acknowledgement of *lakhömi*. This chiefly attribute is both a virtue radiated by the great (it is said to shine visibly) and something which exists in the public eye—a product of acclaim in feasting or valiant warfare. As such it is both won and manifest in the *ovasa*. A roughly equivalent concept would be charisma; but there is the added sense of efficacy or inherent power. However, in many utterances the best translation would simply be 'prestige'.

Previous authors have identified a number of senses of *lakhömi*, some of which indicate a spiritual substance, others a mere attribute. Steinhart (1929) compares it to the Polynesian concept of *mana* (which of course has its own controversial history). Sundermann's dictionary translates it as *Glanz* ('radiance, glory') and *Herrlichkeit*

('grandeur, splendour').[6] In Fries (1908: 85) *lakhömi dua* is given as
noble ancestral spirit. A modern author from north Nias regards
lakhömi as a synonym for *malaika* (Indon. *malaikat*), meaning dead
soul or spirit (Zebua 1984: 404). Chiefs and priests 'possess a more
powerful spirit than ordinary men'. It is this spirit which is associated
with the ancestor image.

In view of these diverse senses of *lakhömi*, let us review some of
the uses of this word in central Nias. From the recollection of
informants and from present-day usage, it appears that *lakhömi*
refers to an attribute or property of certain men and spirits, rather
than to the spirits themselves, which are denoted by other names
(*bekhu*, *malaika*, 'ghost'). Grammatically, *lakhömi* is a noun, and
to describe someone as glorious, *molakhömi*, is to attribute to him
possession of this quality. In one usage it refers to outward and
visible splendour: thus clothes and hair are the 'glory of the body'
(*lakhömi mboto*). Other instances suggest a hidden influence which
may be good or bad. Formerly, at the inauguration of a house, the
wife-givers were given the task of removing the *lakhömi* of the
house. Each part of the building derives from a different species of
tree, and each tree has a spirit (*belada*) whose *lakhömi* remains
attached to the house timber, posing a danger to the occupants. The
wife-givers would address each part and ask the *lakhömi* to vacate
it. The ancestral skulls buried beneath monuments on the square
were described to me as the *lakhömi mbanua* (*lakhömi* of the
village). By this is meant not the dead souls themselves, but
the ghostly radiance they shed and its protective influence over the
village. The head, face, and mouth are particularly associated with
lakhömi and are singled out for special treatment in rites of passage;
but there is no notion that they 'contain' this property as if it were
something substantial.[7]

Contests of strength signified possession of *lakhömi horö*, warrior's
valour. A celebrated mock combat with shield and spear which once
took place at an *ovasa* in Sifalagö many years ago was described in
terms of a competition for this force. The combatants danced round

[6] In the southern dialect it has the additional meaning of fortune or luck
(Sundermann 1905*a*; Laiya *et al.* 1985). *Lakhömi* is not used in this sense in central
Nias, though fortune is possessed by one who is charismatic.
[7] Head-hunting, remembered well by the oldest villagers, is never explained as
the the acquisition of *lakhömi* or of any spiritual element or attribute; it was a
sacrificial substitution and tribute for the dead—the victim dies so that the deceased
may be resurrected.

the square in opposite directions, and when they came face to face one of them fell to the ground before even a blow was struck, defeated by the sudden visitation of *lakhömi* on his adversary. Warrior's valour was personified in the life-size figure of a legendary hero, called *azu horö*, kept in the lineage house. Before going on a raid to plunder or take heads, the raiders would invoke its aid and perform a sacrifice.

Sons of a deceased leading man would compete for his *lakhömi* at his funeral. Here both the inherent and external aspects of *lakhömi* are clearly reflected in the interplay of ascribed and achieved status. The corpse was seated in a throne on the square in full war garb, with weapons reversed left to right. One by one the sons would perform before him the war dance, confronting him as an adversary. The elders watched to see who would receive his father's *lakhömi*, evident in a flash passing between the points of the two spears. If the eldest son was not the 'chosen one' the next son was invited to try. Reception of the father's *lakhömi* was not simply a rite of succession but a divination of ancestral approval, and thus an omen of future success, similar to that indicated in the slaughter of the origin pigs at an *ovasa*. The custom exemplifies several of the qualifications of leadership in central Nias: succession to a father's position (as *de facto* leader, or prominent man) by primogeniture modified by ability; warrior prowess; the approval of the elders, who arbitrate on the spiritual election; the possession of special attributes.

Of these examples, only the last two seem clearly connected with the commonest contemporary sense of 'chiefly prowess'. But no theory can presently be elicited connecting the various meanings and indicating decisively either an abstract quality or something concrete like the Javanese conception of power (Anderson 1972); so we must leave the ambiguity as it is and hope that an approximate understanding will emerge from the following description.

In present-day usage, *lakhömi* is the glory and spiritual virtue possessed by great men and transmissible to their successors. A chief's *lakhömi* exercises a charm on others, bending them to his will, 'softening the hearts' of wife-takers so that they render lavish tribute, defeating rivals in combat. It is both an attribute and a tool of leadership. At the Request for Blessing feast held for the chief of Sifalagö, during the general airing of grievances which was thought to be beneficial to the dying man, one elder commented: 'We are doubtful, we your *talifusö*, about what to do with you. Because of your *lakhömi* we cannot simply give vent to our thoughts.'

Lakhömi is enhanced in both giving and receiving. The essence of an *ovasa* was once explained to me as the 'exchange of *lakhömi*'. To entertain someone formally is to 'endow them with *lakhömi*' (*folakhömi*). But it is principally as a host that one exhibits and wins it. Theoretically, then, this attribute of the great is accessible to others, and in the sense of 'glory' pertains to all honourable exchange. It follows that although chiefs are regarded as superior beings, their superiority derives from achievement more than from birth. It is a superman philosophy rather than a class ideology.

Another chiefly attribute, which again is acquired rather than innate, is *söfu* or *söfu mbava*, denoting 'hardness' or 'authority' (*söfu* also means 'venom' and 'to temper' steel). It is sometimes used as a synonym of *lakhömi*, but particularly relates to the power vested in a superior deriving from his largesse, his decisive speech, etc. *Söfu* can be transmitted, along with other personal qualities, in the breath of the dying man. Matanihela, on his deathbed in 1968, was tricked by his daughter's son into giving him his glory, wisdom, and hardness. He had thought he was blowing into the mouth of his eldest son. As with the 'request for *lakhömi*' of the dead chief in mock combat, the transmission of breath is a spiritual endowment not an official recognition of succession. Since there was no formal office of chief in central Nias, there could be no formal handing over of power.[8] Moreover, as with *lakhömi*, chiefs do not have a monopoly of this attribute. As the above example shows it is not intrinsically connected to patrilineal descent or to heredity; rather, it relates to acquired status. An old man can nominate whom he wishes to give his breath to. One veteran, Ama Huku, has vowed to give it to his infant son who, when fatherless, will need his qualities, rather than to his well-established eldest son.

Kirsch (1973), in a notable essay, has constructed a model of the place of feasts of merit in the social organization of Southeast Asian

---

[8] The situation was perhaps different in the south where the position of leading noble was formally recognized. Modigliani (1890: 479–80) refers to usurpation of chiefship by stealing the last breath. Chiefs in north Nias were thought to possess an extra spiritual element, called *eheha*, which transmitted in the dying breath (Schröder 1917: 558–9). It was the eldest son who rightfully inherited *eheha* but he could be denied it by a stronger brother. Again a principle of primogeniture is modified by competition among heirs.

hill tribes. He suggests that feasts are organized to maximize spiritual force, fertility, or some such religiously defined property (ibid. 3). Political legitimacy rests on possession of this virtue. Power-seeking, which is the motor in Leach's model of oscillating equilibrium in Kachin society (1954), is replaced in Kirsch's analysis by a competition for ritual efficacy and control of ritual rights (1973: 8). Rank and prestige are conceived in religious terms and are linked to a 'theory of unequal souls'. In the 'absence of a radical distinction between the secular and the sacred', promotion in this world is linked to promotion in the next (ibid. 12).

The parallels between highland Burma/Assam and Nias society are very striking. How well can the Nias data be encompassed in Kirsch's model? There are two major difficulties. First, it seems to me that in substituting a religious motive for a political one, or in seeing them as indissociable, Kirsch has obscured a difference between power and rank (or what he calls 'ritual status') which matters very much at the level of individual action. As I have shown, in the case of Nias neither prestige nor rank translates directly into power. Rank has to be consolidated by other means than through feasting, and it is in this gap between rank and power or influence that much of the stuff of village politics is to be found.

Second, the equation of chiefly virtue with fertility is inappropriate to Nias, and possibly to some of Kirsch's own examples as well. Feasting proves that the Highlands feastgiver has 'innate virtue', and the feast may indeed be a quest for fertility; but these goals, though they may be interrelated, are not simply to be equated. The Kachin chief's ritual function, his control of the fertility of his domain, derives from his genealogical link with a sky spirit, not from his possession of 'innate spiritual grace' (*tsam*) (Leach 1954: 129, 262). Of analogous concepts found in other Highland societies (Kirsch 1973: 13, 14), only the Ao *aren* appears to combine fertility and chiefly virtue.

We have seen how, in the *ovasa*, the benefits of feasting are not summed up in a single concept. Fertility and prosperity (*harazaki*) are assigned to the realm of affinity and its associated prestations. They derive from blessing and are purchased with tribute on the analogy of the exchange of bride and bridewealth. *Lakhömi* pertains to a distinct system of exchange. As I have shown, these two types of exchange are distinguished ideologically and operate on entirely different principles: complementary exchange on the one hand, symmetrical on the other.[9]

The division of these concepts of fertility and rank, which appear to be combined in some of Kirsch's examples, relates ultimately to the crucial distinction in Nias sociology between the relative, ego-centric status associated with affinity on the one hand and status in society as a whole on the other. This distinction has important implications for the largely secular nature of leadership in Nias.[10] A man who has won prestige and high rank, who has *lakhömi*, is not considered to have obtained more fertility for himself or his group. Nor does he gain any ritual rights over the fertility of territory such as a Kachin chief controls. Each villager seeks prosperity through offerings to his lineage ancestors (formerly) and through affinal exchange, which in most cases involves links between villages, in other words across political boundaries.

In central Nias, rank and its attributes, including *lakhömi*, are not innate. There is a proverbial sense of the equality of men before the vicissitudes of Fortune, the arbitrary will of God, and the certainty of death. As one verse goes, said with grim humour as a 'cheerer' at funerals.

Ebua niha ö kulö-kulö	Great men are food for the worms
Ebua niha ö deteho	Great men are food for the flies
Famaha-mahalö danö saukha	The cracked earth closes over
Famadou-madou danö soyo.	The red earth swallows up.

The ebb and flow of fortune is a rich source of proverbs. During the waxing phase of the moon certain species of fish move from the deeps to the shallows where they are easily caught. Just so, we are prosperous at one period and poor at the next. The debtor tells his creditor: *so möi namö, so möi hohou* ('some go to the depths, some to the shallows'), i.e. 'Don't press too hard. Reflect on the inconstancy of Fortune.' But differences are built up and consolidated

[9] Hoskins (1986) has also found Bateson's (1958) terms useful to distinguish affinal exchange from prestige payments in West Sumba. These forms of exchange do not lead in Nias to 'schismogenesis', except in the special case of the challenge feast.

[10] Priestly cults, usually centred on a tree of origin, have been reported from the south (Thomas 1892; Hämmerle 1986), east (Ködding 1868a), and centre (Noll 1930). Hereditary priests controlled the fertility of the area, while temporal power was in the hands of chiefs. These regional cults are mostly forgotten.

and these determine one's spiritual destiny. Contrary to the words of comfort above, it is also held that only men who have never given an *ovasa* 'become worms', whereas feastgivers are rewarded in the afterlife.

The Character of a Chief

It is appropriate here to add some general remarks on chiefly qualities, since these, rather than constitutional rights, are what qualify a person to lead. During the last months of my stay in Sifalagö, this subject was very much in the air, as the chief who had ruled for thirty-three years was dying and the search for a successor had begun. A chief or leading man is meant to combine the virtues of generosity, flexibility, decisiveness, and ruthlessness, backed by wealth. He needs to be firm in pressing debts in order to be able to finance feasts and public works such as maintaining the village square. Nothing is done for him without payment. But 'he gives away his wealth', and hence one is anxious to show loyalty. He is quick to offer interest-free loans for bridewealth and lets the loan ride for years. He must be able to satisfy constant demands for hospitality from visiting chiefs and officials. The ability to sustain loss extends into small acts of kindness and tokens of respect. These win him respect and loyalty in turn. A leading role is maintained by constant effort and solicitude for one's followers; it is not simply a question of outdoing rivals. Furthermore, although wealth is frequently tainted with corruption and duplicity, it is also said that prosperity comes with diligence and the good fortune that rewards acts of kindness and care for others.

During the late chief's illness and its aftermath, the leading role in overseeing a transition was taken by his elder brother, Ama Da'o. He had worked in local government since the Japanese occupation and had eventually become *camat* ('government district head') of Lahusa, which then included Gomo, and later *camat* of Lölöwa'u, leaving his younger brother, Ama Wati'asa, to succeed their father as village and *öri* chief. Ama Da'o had achieved great eminence in feasting as well as in the modern bureaucracy and was regarded by all as the very model of a Nias leader. He was frequently contrasted by informants with various possible candidates for the chiefship, usually to their detriment. Indeed, he was begged by several elders to return to the village and take over—as he repeatedly told us in his speeches. The infrequent visitor is welcome and liked. Another favourite son of the village, now head of the Lölöwa'u clinic, commented drily on Ama Da'o's popularity:

Sökhi fagaröu mbambatö	It is good if in-laws are distant
Sökhi fagaröu la'o	Good to be far from your brother-in-law
Ova'ami lövö-lövö	The parcel of food [they bring] tastes sweeter
Ova'ami vegero.	The morsels shared out taste better.

Nevertheless, the long visits by Ama Da'o and other senior men with ties to the village provided an opportunity to observe how judgements were made on leadership qualities in particular cases.

The oratorical style of Ama Da'o was contrasted favourably with that of certain others. It was said of him that he would always return a topic to the floor, rather than lecture the audience. He would seek assent rather than impose it. This canvassing of opinion is expressed in the simile of a wild pig which turns up the soil with its snout (*nifanuagö zökha hili*). In well-ordered, refined speech (*li nihaogö-haogö*) one refers back and defers to others in order to get one's point across. A harangue (*pidato ndava*, 'foreign [Indonesian] speech') does not 'get through' to the listeners, it does not 'go to their hearts'. The important thing is to 'give a place to the people or else what use are they?'

This picture of the ideal chief as a mild-mannered chairman is somewhat misleading. Often the canvassing of opinion is done in private. In public debate there is an impression of resolution and of knowing one's own mind. Pronouncements are delivered in a resounding, authoritative voice, usually from the house platform or some strategically placed chair. There may be little pretence of taking others seriously—as long as the respected elders are given due regard. A common tactic is to get up and leave the room on some pretext when someone else is expressing an opinion, or to turn to one's neighbour to ask for betel. Chiefs cultivate a bullying, aggressive humour which has people laughing but a bit afraid. The humour consists partly in putting someone on the spot, making him speechless, 'like the voice of a duck after its throat is cut'. Frequently the gibe is a sexual innuendo. On one occasion at a public gathering I heard the chief ask a man who had irritated him: 'Did you check your wife's lice last night?' The moment of tense silence following the challenge was broken by his loud ironic bark—'a chief's laugh'. Powerful men like to impose themselves by breaking the rules of

etiquette and flouting the norms of conversation such as the sympathetic head-wagging and grunts of encouragement expected of a
listener. One evening a candidate for the chiefship came to see Ama
Da'o, anxious to secure his approval. We sat on the window seat of
the great house in the gathering gloom. Ama Da'o was disconcert-
ingly hidden in heavy shadow but made no command to light the
lamp. It was a curiously one-sided interview, almost a monologue.
Each of the aspirant's questions and pleas was left trailing in the air,
unrewarded by the merest murmur of assent. Throughout the half-
hour petition Ama Da'o maintained a gravid silence disturbed only
by the occasional rustle of his betel bag, his only discernible
movement. The man's voice, addressed as to a void, grew more and
more diffident until finally cut off by the invisible listener's response,
which was more of an evasion than a reply.

Unpredictability is also part of the armoury. The chief does not
reveal to others—even to his agnates—his next move. Likewise, in
speech he can veer suddenly from anger to laughter. In manner he is
authoritative, even when he has no formal authority. Orders to run
an errand or fetch something may be issued suddenly to a junior
man who is too embarrassed in front of others to disobey, and
unable to outface the senior. Juniors forgive this kind of behaviour
because they can count on patronage when in trouble. The leader
always keeps his achievements in view: he reminds the audience of
his illustrious ancestry, his feasting record, his experience in office,
etc. In short, he boasts shamelessly. This is entirely acceptable so
long as it is true. The speech of a man who has done what he says
'hits the mark'.

The characteristic behaviour of authority on the one hand and
deference on the other is maintained even when a chief has lost
credibility through a failure to maintain his flow of redistributive
payments. But though he is shown respect, he is no longer able to
get anything done without direct and immediate payment.

3   Resources and Social Stratification

Land

Rights in land are obtained in perpetuity by the person who first
clears it and his patrilineal descendants. Direct descendants of the

village founders, who usually comprise a chiefly line, own the most and the best land close to the village. But mere acreage is not a decisive economic indicator, at least not until recently when land became scarce. Primary forest is a free good and it is up to each household to determine the size of its swiddens. The area cleared is limited only by the size of the household and the diligence of its members. The important economic indicator is productivity—the amount of land under cultivation and its yield—not the total land holdings. Some of the poorest households in Sifalagö own large tracts of land (deriving from first clearer's rights) but lack the labour needed to exploit it. It is in labour that a chief has an advantage.

Initial clearing is done by men, sometimes on a co-operative basis. A leading man can expect help from agnates whom he rewards materially in one way or another. The fields are tended by women. A chief with two or three wives and as many sets of daughters can obviously cultivate a relatively larger area. Rich men also employ poor youths to work on their land in exchange for a meal. Formerly slaves performed this work. Women are also largely responsible for keeping the pigs and growing cassava and sweet potatoes as pig fodder and as the domestic staple. With these various sources of labour, and his other sources of income, a chief or leading man does not usually need to perform agricultural work.

Formerly much or even most of the rice harvest would be allocated to feasts, so the stimulus for production derived from the quest for prestige, rather than from economic motives. Feasts did not absorb a surplus over and above subsistence. Rather the feasting system absorbed surplus labour and allocated it to production of a non-staple food. Likewise, pigs were mostly reared for feasts, sacrifices, hospitality, and bridewealth, rather than for private domestic consumption. With some modification these observations still apply. Feasts are less frequent and sacrifices are no longer held, so festive food accounts for a smaller proportion of the diet than formerly. Nowadays most households supplement their tuber diet with rice and an occasional purchase of pork from the market. But no one would slaughter a piglet merely to feed his family unless he were suffering from irresistible 'pork cravings'.

In sum, a chief's superior resources in land and the labour to exploit it are not directed towards the accumulation of wealth but towards its redistribution among his followers for prestige rather than for economic ends.

In recent years land has become scarce due to an expanding population and the conversion of rice fields to cash crops. A shortening of the fallow cycle, for the same reasons, has led to soil depletion and low yields. In the months before harvest, few households have any remaining rice in store. During this period Gomo and Lahusa districts, which once exported rice, now import it expensively at the rate of 200 sacks per week from Sibolga on the Sumatran coast (via a Chinese intermediary in Teluk Dalam, south Nias), two or three of which reach the Sifalagö weekly market.

Where does this new situation leave the land-rich chiefs? It is only now that they begin to recognize the potential economic advantage this newly scarce resource gives them. As yet, in Sifalagö and other remote villages, the unequal distribution of land and the new problem of land scarcity have not led to an increase in wealth differences—not only because of the redistributive function of the feasting system. As I have said, a chief's economic advantage was in labour rather than in mere land holdings. Since the abolition of slavery and the Church's outlawing of polygyny, big landowners lack the labour resources needed to plant on a large scale. Small landowners are still able to supplement their resources by borrowing land or cultivating remote forest plots, as well as by turning to other sources of income such as market peddling or carpentry. Many households have moved on a semi-permanent basis to field huts miles from Sifalagö and make a good living. Probably, though, when roads finally connect the interior with the town and cash crops can be more easily marketed the potential will be realized and big landowners—usually chiefs—will find a new source of wealth in commercial production which has no integral relation to feasting and redistribution. Marschall (1976: 179, 202) writes that in Maenamölö (south) this situation has already arisen and a new stratification is emerging based on land ownership and possession of coconut groves, encroaching on the traditional noble/commoner class system which is constituted in a more complex fashion.

The traditional method of allocating land in the south differed from the democratic free-for-all in the centre. According to Samson (1925b: 41) the leading *siulu* had the authority to allocate land surrounding the village for cultivation each year. Marschall (1976: 164) describes a system where the leading *siulu* had first pick of the land, followed by the other *siulu*, then the *si'ila* (elders), and finally the commoners, the plots forming a pattern of hierarchized concentric circles. Thus there was a symbolic and practical advantage in the nobles' prerogative. This system has now been abandoned in favour of one similar to that of the centre, thus diminishing chiefly privilege.

Slaves

Slavery continued in Nias long after its official abolition. It is difficult to estimate with any conviction the scale of slave-holding in central Nias. It is clear, though, that it was on a much smaller scale than in south Nias, where slaves comprised a sizeable proportion of the population. The chief of Sifalagö until 1924, Mbumbugosali, is said to have had between twelve and twenty-five slaves, but I cannot tell how reliable are these figures. His son, Matanihela, kept at least four servants at a time, slaves in all but name, whose stories are still remembered. Other important men in the village had one or two slaves.

If I could not establish the existence of anyone of slave descent in the central cluster of hamlets, it was not because of secrecy or reticence. No lineage would accept the pretensions to membership of a slave's descendant, and everyone could be fitted into clan genealogies, so there is no reason to doubt this finding. It is known that some of the slaves' descendants settled in other villages. Others died childless or were killed.

The general term for slave is *savuyu* (lit. 'the young'). There were degrees of bondage and different forms of slavery. A man whose debts had risen beyond the point where he could hope to pay them would become, with his entire household, the pawn of his creditor. In most cases a lineage would take collective responsibility to bail out an agnate, but this was not always possible. Once the debt had been paid off by so many years' labour, the man regained his freedom. If he died, his children were required to work off the debt. This kind of inherited but conditional debt-bondage is not the same as a class of hereditary slaves.

Others became slaves through wrongdoing. In the case of capital crimes such as adultery, a rich man could pay a ransom (*höli*) for the life of the offender, who now became his permanent slave. Several of Matanihela's 'servants' were obtained in this way. A third and lower category comprised purchased slaves, usually people who had been sold into bondage by deception. Villagers remember losing relatives in this way as little as fifty years ago. It is said in denigration of the old ways, but with some truth, that driven by debt 'people sold their own relatives; they "ate" their companions'. Some victims were hired ostensibly as wage labourers, with a secret payment made to the go-between who was a relative or friend (*simana gazi*, 'wage labourer', retains for Niasans the connotation of bondage); others were sold for human sacrifice. Either fate awaited fugitives or those who strayed off alone.

The ritual category of *binu*, the victim of human sacrifice or head-hunting, has sometimes been mistakenly translated as 'slave'. As a rule, only slaves captured or purchased outside the village could be sacrificed. One of the senior elders in Sifalagö, Ama Huku, remembers seeing his father's slave, who came from Gomo, sacrificed upon reaching adolescence, having served him for several years.[11]

With the removal of many of the coercive powers of village leaders since Dutch times, and the steady erosion of village independence under national rule, forms of labour exploitation have become less open. Traditional exchange requires every man at some point in his life to raise large sums, and this can give rise to heavy debt and exploitative penalties for default. The introduction of the weekly market and the availability of products from outside, such as building materials and consumer goods, created new opportunities for making and losing money and a similar preying of the strong on the weak. There are credit associations (*arisan*) in which the last person to withdraw credit, therefore the one least in need, makes most profit; and in which members who fail in one of their monthly payments forfeit their principal.

Quick profits can be made by lending at high interest. If the debtor cannot pay up, his property can be confiscated and his agnates may be forced to bail him out. Failing this, violence may follow, or the police are called in as a last resort—a situation in which everyone loses. For the borrower, loans of this kind are high risk and are intended to be short term. For the creditor they are a commercial venture which is regarded as morally dubious. It is invidious to ruin a fellow-villager, so it is better to deal with other villages where one has affines who can help enforce the terms.

---

[11] While slavery finished many years ago, head-hunting occurred sporadically until recent times—perhaps as recently as the 1950s. A man from a Susua village was jailed five years ago for killing a child whose head was to be used to 'strengthen' a concrete bridge.

Other Sources of Labour

A leading man counts among his principal resources his own lineage. In nearly every lineage there are one or two senior men who have married off a number of their junior agnates, paying their bridewealth, and in so doing obtain their allegiance. This is an important aspect of leadership and informal authority in the village. The junior agnates are expected to contribute labour and resources for an *ovasa*, some of which they may never reclaim. It is difficult to see who benefits most from such arrangements. Certainly the senior man is not seeking economic advantage, but loyalty and influence.

I have described the role of polygyny in the domestic economy and the representation of female labour in affinal exchange. Missionaries and administrators noted the increase in polygyny following the enforcement of the abolition of slavery in the Gunung Sitoli region (Lagemann 1893: 304). This suggests a functional equivalence between wives and slaves which was in fact recognized by Niasans themselves in the frequent designation of secondary wives as *sohalöwö* ('workers'). Despite Church disapproval, polygyny continues to be practised by a minority of chiefs, elders, and civil servants.

Wealthy households frequently foster or take in the child of a poor relation as a 'fetcher of wood' or 'worker'. Usually this individual works full-time while the sons of the house go to school or enjoy a more leisurely life. When I made a household survey of the village these exploited dependants were never mentioned—not, I think, out of a desire to conceal the truth, but from a simple disregard of them as members of the house. Civil servants (i.e. teachers and paramedics) usually have living with them a changing population of nieces and nephews who carry out the agricultural work, freeing their uncles to work for money. In return, civil servants act as patrons, often paying for the education of agnates' and affines' children and contributing handsomely to bridewealth and feasts. In this they merely conform to a traditional pattern.

Two further important sources of labour in the household, which I have referred to in Chapter 7, are widows, who generally lead a dog's life, and uxorilocal husbands who work to pay off bridewealth or are fully incorporated as permanent exploited dependants of the householder.

What I have described so far applies to any wealthy or influential man. What follows refers only to dominant persons, that is village or hamlet chiefs. Outside the household, with its wives, children and worker-dependants, and the lineage as a whole, a chief can call on the services of other lineages in preparations for a feast. No specific payment is due, but it is understood that nothing will be done without some ultimate compensation, whether the chief is acting as an individual or in his capacity as headman responsible for maintenance of the village paths and amenities. Traditionally he had no judicial power to enforce co-operation, and nowadays, with government backing, he can only compel participation in government forced labour, such as road building. In everything else, as soon as the flow of payments dries up he fails to obtain any practical help.

Wife-Takers as a Resource

A major source of funds for a feast, and thus the guarantee of a leading man's position, is his wife-takers. As mentioned earlier, one of the characteristics of a chiefly line is its recognition and exploitation of a wide range of wife-takers, who are regarded as a pool of resources. They are potential contributors to feasts, funerals, house-building, bridewealth, or any other customary expenditure. These affinal relationships are kept alive by intermittent small gifts (*so'i-so'i*), where among ordinary villagers they are allowed to lapse. A chief is able to maintain a flow of these gifts partly by redistributing payments due to him as chief in other contexts—fines, marriage payments, tribute and prestige payments at *ovasa*, and so on. His sons and other close agnates inherit this network. Even though they have to maintain it with intermittent gifts, they have a decisive advantage over the ordinary man who has to start from scratch. In many cases the genealogical relation can no longer be traced; it is known only that the ancestor of the *ono alave* ('wife-taker'), traced through the line of maternal affiliation, derives from the chief's clan. In contrast, an ordinary villager has only half a dozen wife-takers to count on: usually his ZS, DH, BDH, FBDH, FBSDH and in turn the wife-takers of these (DDH, ZDH, etc.).

Again it should be emphasized that there is no radical distinction between a chief and others—rather there is a difference of degree. The scope of a man's affinal network is partly a function of his position within the lineage or lineage segment. The closer he is to the chiefly line the easier it is for him to exploit the affinal network centred on the chief. He can claim a share of the tribute or bridewealth due to his senior agnate; and he can activate the affinal relation with *so'i-so'i*. But with increasing genealogical distance from the chief, he has to rely on his own devices. Nevertheless, I heard a few men who do not belong to a chiefly line or even a chief's lineage boast that they live off their wife-takers and never need to do any heavy farming work. This may be an exaggeration but it highlights the fact that it is not only chiefs who are conceived to be in such a privileged position.

4   Warfare

The traditional leader was a warlord—if not the fiercest warrior, at least the strongman of the lineage or settlement whose word carried more weight than his rivals'. In the story of the three brothers—Ndruru, Laia, and Bu'ulölö—the founders of the three main clans of the area, it was the youngest, Bu'ulölö, who was accepted by the others as their superior due to his valour. It was he who avenged the murder of their grandfather in Mazinö by taking the head of the murderer.

A leader commanded the loyalty of his followers by guaranteeing their safety. In litigation he would ransom them; in feuding he would defend them. If he was not capable of crushing all the enemies, he could buy them off with a secret bribe (*sölö*). Settlers or fugitives seeking safety would immediately enter into marriage alliance with the chief. If the settlers took a wife from their protectors the affinal inequality confirmed the political relation. If they gave wives, the gift of a bride appeared as a kind of tribute.

A chief had a sphere of influence (*öhö-öhö*) rather than a traditional domain or region of sovereignty. It extended as far spatially and genealogically as he was able to contest (*fadöni*) or intervene on behalf of clients. The sphere of influence was therefore subject to continual revision, and factions waxed and waned with the fortunes of their leaders. Stories of betrayal and bribery abound. A lineage might stand by while its brother lineage was wiped out if it had been bribed 'not to move'. In a world of greed and duplicity wealth was the key to dominance.

5 Descent and Rank

Clearly descent is involved in some of the factors by which rank is consolidated; but compared to south Nias, its place in social stratification is not easy to define. In the system of prestige payments there is a great emphasis on individual responsibility. *Ovasa* debts, and the prestige which accrues from creating them and paying them off, fall to the individual. The only important exception is in the distribution of *urakha* at a funeral feast, when any remaining debts of the deceased are paid off by his heirs. In this case there is some sharing of the glory between the living and the dead, although the host does not receive a title or new rank unless he sponsors a further distribution in his own right. A general principle seems to be that while *ovasa credit* can be passed on to heirs, everything possible is done to ensure that *ovasa debts* are paid off before death, even if this means organizing a deathbed feast. Not to do so has consequences in the afterlife.

Thus rank and *ovasa* debts are not transferable. One brother cannot reclaim the *sulö* of another, and if he receives an *urakha* on behalf of his brother (who may be absent), it is the brother's debt, not his own. A son cannot inherit his father's rank: he can only achieve it by feast-giving. The feast may be organized by the father in his son's name (or vice versa) but the debt/credit/rank is not shared. Once achieved, this rank is permanent, but public esteem and influence can only be maintained by giving more feasts. Despite these egalitarian principles, the son or other junior agnate of an eminent man starts with considerable advantages, as I have shown.

In conclusion, leadership depends on a variety of qualities and resources, none of which is in principle denied to ordinary men. Fortune comes and goes; war and epidemic change the political and demographic map, and many impoverished families boast of an illustrious past.

6 Status in Other Systems

Leadership has undergone certain formal changes since Dutch colonization introduced the office of village headman, but the nature of authority has, I believe, remained largely unchanged. The introduced ideas either complement the old or exist somewhat awkwardly alongside them. They have not replaced them.

The Susua valley was one of the last regions to be affected by Dutch rule and there are a number of old people whose lives span both eras. Conquest is still the stuff of reminiscence rather than legend. Acquainted with Schröder only through his mandarin prose, in Nias I was personally introduced to the grandson of 'the man who was shot by Si Lauma' (as Schröder was known). Regulations concerning a chief's jurisdiction and powers which had been implemented many years before in other parts of the island came late to the Susua or were simply ignored.

The problem of overseeing government in the centre is one which has not changed under national Indonesian rule. Communications have, if anything, deteriorated. It was in 1937 that the first and last motor vehicle—carrying a Dutch official—came to Sifalagö, for the *tuhenöri*'s feast. The road from Lahusa near the coast was never again used and has now completely disappeared under scrub.

The important administrative centre is at Gomo, the capital of Kecamatan (district) Gomo. It is an office complex grafted on to a former village, a world of rubber stamps, flag parades, and dairy-white safari suits which has little to do with the life of the population. The district head official (*camat*) maintains contact with the villages by summoning the thirty-three headmen to Gomo. The four hours' walk from Sifalagö can only be made during dry spells when the river is low. Fondraköô Raya, the furthest village, is two days away. Policing is also done from Gomo, but visits to outlying villages such as Sifalagö are rare. Police usually accompany any official delegation, but during my stay they came only once to deal with a crime. Other official visits to the village include an annual tax-gathering when each household pays up to Rp.5,000 (£2), and visits to oversee the election of a headman and the performance of *corvée*. In these respects the relations of village and government, and the mediating role of headman, are no different from the colonial situation. In 1987 there was a general election and a group of officials stayed for several days to canvass support for the government party.[12] In general it can be stated with some confidence that most villagers in the interior of Nias—graduates of senior school excepted—have little or no idea of nationhood and virtually no idea of government

---

[12] I was not permitted to continue research during the election and returned to Jakarta to renew my visa.

beyond its local manifestations, which are restricted to these occasional punitive and money-raising forays from the administrative
centre.

All government rulings are mediated through the village headman and his staff of deputy, secretary, and ward heads. The
headman keeps a register of births, marriages, and deaths. He also
deals with the paperwork of legal disputes which cannot be settled
under customary law and go to the *camat* for arbitration. In the
remote villages this rarely happens. Villagers regard any involvement of officials as an expensive and unwarranted interference, and
a headman is highly valued and fulfils the role of a traditional leader
if he can solve disputes himself. Only a weak man without the
backing of village elders needs to apply for outside help, and he is
not likely to remain in office for long. Petty crimes are also dealt
with by the headman but are supposed to be reported to the *camat*,
as is any kind of disorder. Again, this requirement, which conflicts
with strongly held feelings of village solidarity and independence, is
mostly performed in a perfunctory fashion if at all. It is only in the
villages near the administrative centre that government officers
have a real influence in the running of village affairs.[13]

Two or three times a year the village staff meets to appoint new
officers and pass resolutions or regulations, some of which require
the *camat*'s approval to become theoretically binding. For example,
there was a meeting in Sifalagö in 1986 to introduce measures to
improve hygiene in response to a cholera epidemic. An official
came from Gomo and sang a song in which the causes of cholera
were explained. Villagers were instructed to boil water; pigs were to
be corralled instead of roaming free; latrines were to be built
instead of allowing pigs to eat human faeces, etc. There were heavy
fines for offenders. In the event, none of these measures were
carried out by anyone. Fines, to be shared out among the staff, were
also introduced to penalize villagers moving into remote field huts
beyond village supervision; and on another occasion, the staff voted
themselves as beneficiaries of a Rp.50,000 'wedding tax'. None of
these regulations were taken seriously by villagers and there was no
means of enforcing them. Most villagers do not attend the meetings

[13] According to my information the situation is now very different in south Nias
(the most traditional area after the centre) where the easy access to villages from
Teluk Dalam has led to a breakdown of traditional authority and a reliance on
officials to solve even minor disputes.

and have little idea of what is discussed or indeed any interest in them. At all the meetings I attended the pattern was the same: competition for influence and getting one's point accepted against a rival, the foisting of responsibility for action on to villagers, sanctioned by lucrative fines, an airing of minor grievances by junior officials as regards the sharing out of funds. In general there is cynicism about governmental matters at village level and above. In the daily affairs of the village, leadership is almost entirely a matter of customary influence.

Nevertheless, some chiefs successfully combine the roles of traditional leader and government headman, and in such cases each role enhances the strength of the other. The headman's main asset in strengthening his traditional role is in his position as arbiter of disputes and in his control of the village finances—the administering of fines and taxes, registration fees, and the division of the annual village development grant (£300–£400) as he and his staff see fit.

Headmen commonly use their wealth to sponsor their children's education and to obtain for them government jobs; but success in the outside world brings greater obligations at home. The few men of Sifalagö who have become civil servants have held large *ovasa* to convert their status in the modern system into traditional rank. They are expected to contribute substantially to the bridewealth and feasts of relatives, thus redistributing their wealth along traditional lines. This is no mere formality. The head of Lölöwa'u clinic, Ama Osara'ö, a cousin of the late chief of Sifalagö, built a large family house in the village for all his brothers, married them off and sponsored an *ovasa* of 106 pigs. Although he himself does not intend to return to Sifalagö to live, he retains an influential voice as a visitor, and he has guaranteed a strong position for his brothers and their sons for many years to come. As an absentee senior elder, he is owed a huge number of *urakha* which will all be consumed by his brothers over the years. This gives them a regular festive income and a certain reflected glory. Their position in the village as *ono zalawa*, members of a noble line, is reconfirmed by Ama Osara'ö's feast at a time when lineage expansion and fission would have marginalized them. Indeed the job of headman in succession to Ama Wati'asa would be within the grasp of Ama Osara'ö if he wanted it.

Status in the church hierarchy is not clearly at odds with traditional conceptions of rank. It is assumed that any chief or headman is a

Christian—indeed there are probably no avowed pagans left in Nias. But beyond observing the formalities, chiefs are not expected to show a lead in religious matters. In Sifalagö the four or five leading men were among the few residents (as opposed to field-hut denizens) who did not normally attend church. They do not appear to be criticized for this, and I myself, following their lead, was not judged badly for infrequent attendance. Junior men who seek influence, on the other hand, cultivate esteem as good church-goers. The situation in Sifalagö is not necessarily typical. In the adjacent villages of Orahili and Hiliorahua the present chiefs are former church teachers.

The priest, who lives in Sifalagö, ministers to twenty parishes in the region. As a non-native temporary resident usually busy else-where he does not have much knowledge of or say in the conduct of daily affairs; though when he issues prohibitions they are usually followed. Most services and prayers at funerals and weddings are conducted by the church elders (*satua gosali*) and the church teacher (*sinenge*, 'evangelist') who are the regular face of official religion in the village. The church elders are elected, one for every twenty households, and if elected must stand. The position therefore does not denote any special piety or zeal. On the contrary, in administering collections and funds, church elders are criticized for being as venal as secular leaders. They receive official payment, like the priest, from an annual tithe of rice levied on every household.

The conversion movements of the 1920s and 1930s were spear-headed by village elders who became the first generation of church elders. It might be said that they pre-empted the threat of a rival status system by taking it over, and without ever fully realizing what it implied. In retirement they have largely been succeeded in both status systems by their sons, who understand less of the old ways but more of the new. In Sifalagö most church elders are men on the brink of middle age with junior titles and basic literacy; capable and respectable, therefore, but not yet powerful. It is to these potential future leaders that the conflict between Christian values and tradition is most evident; so it seems as they contemplate the vast and forbidding expenditure that faces any man who sets out on the path to fame and power. An intriguing revaluation of tradition is begin-ning, as it did, in different terms, for their parents. But that would be the subject of another book.

Conclusion

I have approached the topic of social organization in Nias through an analysis of exchange. We have seen that there are two systems of ceremonial exchange characterized by two contrasted modes of relation—symmetric and complementary. Symmetric exchange operates in the realm of prestige and rank, and thus articulates position within society as a whole: prestige won in reciprocal feasting is the basis of political ascendancy, but must be consolidated by other means. Complementary exchange, exemplified in bride-wealth and marriage alliance prestations at feasts, operates in the ego-centred realm of kinship and affinity; tribute is given in return for the blessing of wife-giving affines. The two modes of relation, corresponding to different levels of social structure, come together in the ritual of the *ovasa* when the wife-givers confer a title on the host. At the global level, alliance and prestige exchange systems are interrelated in the production of surplus by wife-takers and its redistribution by chiefs. Chiefs maintain their position at the top of the social hierarchy by recognizing and servicing a wide network of affinal relations and by legitimizing their influence through feasting.

This bare summary is, of course, remote from the cut and thrust of village politics and the dense texture of social life. I have tried to convey something of the latter by considering my subject in the round, showing the detail as well as the pattern, placing analytical models of alliance in the context of daily life, and by taking into account the sorts of decisions and concerns which preoccupy the participants in alliance and festive exchange. We have seen, through the example of case histories, how concepts of gift, debt, and credit are manipulated to win advantage, and how ideological and pragmatic concerns are constantly weighed against each other in particular exchanges and in the value system in general. The interplay of precept and practice is especially striking in the field of measurement. And in this, as in exchange generally in Nias, there is a short step from mere techniques to things of ultimate value; for exchange concerns all that is most fundamental to life in Nias: the acquisition of prosperity and fortune, the creation of alliances and networks of support, the promotion of rank and prestige, the assurance of salvation.

A view of a society based on two years' experience is bound to be partial and limited. The village we left in 1988 was a different place from the one we arrived to in 1986. The transfer of leadership, still undecided, marked a passing of generations; the arrival of a new and efficient priest signalled an end to such cherished institutions as the funeral feast, now deprecated as heathenry; a new road, long promised by the government, may soon materialize, bringing profound changes in its wake. But, to take a longer view, what is perhaps most striking about social and cultural change in central Nias is its unevenness. Economic, political, and cultural changes have not moved in step with each other—though none has occurred in isolation—and different aspects of life and thought have shown varying degrees of resistance and adaptability to changes imposed from outside. The people of the Susua valley have been nominally Christian for fifty years or more, and colonial subjects or citizens of a nation state for even longer, but they speak little Indonesian, have little contact with outsiders, receive news of elsewhere by word of mouth, if at all; and their technology and agriculture is hardly changed from pre-colonial times.

Such variability in the pace of change defeats attempts to construct a single model of a society interrelating all analytical levels. Even within a given area of study one finds surprising variation in change and adaptation. As we have seen, sectors of the village economy have been monetized, but market principles have been confined to certain types of relation, and customary modes of exchange are deliberately protected from the procedures and motives of market dealings.

Religious conversion, too, has been uneven in its effects. Although the ancestor cult was vigorously suppressed, and anything perceived as 'religious' was rooted out by missionaries and converts, the ideology of alliance has endured—all the more surprising since its sanctions depend on ancestral powers. Again, church prohibitions and decrees are strictly obeyed, but Christian ethics are poorly understood and have little influence on everyday life; while indigenous moral concepts are mostly unquestioned and have the stability that comes from being taken for granted. Although the pagan cosmology has been for the most part superseded, the residue of associated values has proved more tenacious. No better example of this can be adduced than the continuing centrality and relevance of the *ovasa*. As the details of traditional thinking about world and cosmos, creation and eschatology recede in the public memory, what remains is a pattern of values and ideas concerning exchange, merit, status, retribution and salvation, largely divorced from their traditional cosmological framework and somewhat awkwardly accommodated to the demands of the present. Some of the conceptual links have been suppressed, but the internal consistency and coherence of this pattern underpins the feasting system and ensures its continuation.

APPENDIX 1:
Descent Groups in Sifalagö

1. CLAN PROGENITORS

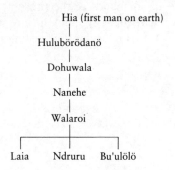

Hia (first man on earth)
|
Hulubörödanö
|
Dohuwala
|
Nanehe
|
Walaroi

Laia   Ndruru   Bu'ulölö

2. CLANS

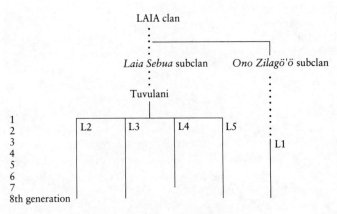

LAIA clan

Laia Sebua subclan   Ono Zilagö'ö subclan

Tuvulani

1
2   L2   L3   L4   L5
3   L1
4
5
6
7
8th generation

L1: a lineage of Ono Zilagö'ö subclan (Sifalagö)
L2: lineage stemming from Bavaulu (Laia Sebua subclan) (Balöhili)
L3: lineage stemming from Afore (Laia Sebua subclan) (Balöhili)
L4: lineage stemming from Samarani (Laia Sebua subclan) (Lölömoyo)
L5: lineage stemming from Baru Alitö (Laia Sebua subclan) (Lölömoyo)

The column on the left of the diagram indicates the number of generations from the apical ancestor of a lineage or lineage segment to the generation of youngest married men. A dotted vertical line shows omission of intervening generations.

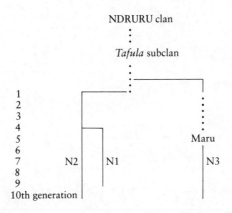

N1 and N2: segments of lineage descended from Sobawiluo (Sifalagö)
N3: segment of lineage descended from Maru (Ono Ndruru and Hilisibohou)

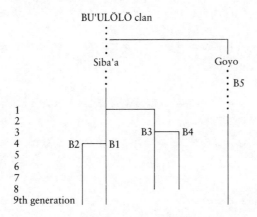

B1 and B2: segments of lineage stemming from Gavölö (Sifalagö)
B3 and B4: segments of lineage stemming from Yawa Idanö (Sifalagö)
B5: lineage stemming from Goyo (other segments have migrated elsewhere)
   (Lölömoyo)

Distribution of descent groups

Lineage segment	Total number of houses	Total number of households	Total number of persons	Households resident in the village	Persons resident in the village	ose households[a]	Persons living in ose	halama households[b]	Persons living in halama	Lower Sifalagö[c]	Upper Sifalagö[c]	Balöhili[c]	Lölömoyo[c]
Bu'ulölö													
B1[d]	8	9	61	8	53	1	8	—	—	67%	33%		
B2	4	5	35	4	27	1	8	—	—	20%	80%		
B3	4	11	53	3	17	4	22	4	14		100%		
B4	3	15	59	6	25	1	3	8	31		100%		
B5	3	3	18	3	18	—	—	—	—				100%
TOTAL	22	43	226	24	140	7	41	12	45				
Laia													
L1	2	7	40	1	5	2	6	4	20		100%		
L2	3	7	37	4	24	1	3	2	10			100%	
L3	6	13	84	8	58	2	17	3	15			100%	
L4	2	3	21	3	21	—	—	—	—				
L5	3	4	21	2	14	2	7	—	—				100%
TOTAL	16	34	203	18	122	7	33	7	45				
Ndruru													
N1	5	10	53	7	30	2	15	2	8		100		
N2	2	10	42	2	6	—	—	8	36		100%		
N3	1	2	11	2	11	—	—	—	—			100%	
TOTAL	8	22	106	11	47	2	15	10	44				
Halawa	2	3	18	2	17	1	1	—	—	100%			
Giawa	1	1	10	2	10	—	—	—	—	100%			
Settlers	12	15	76	11	59	3	15	1	2	67%		7%	26%

[a] Households living in *ose* (temporary huts).
[b] Households living permanently away from the village in huts (*halama*).
[c] Percentage of lineage segment living in hamlet.
[d] For identification of segments, see diagrams above.

APPENDIX 2:
Measurement by Hand

famoto zi 6 saga ('division [in two] of 6 *saga*', i.e. 3 *saga*). The left hand (L.H.) encircles the piglet's girth leaving a gap of three right hand (R.H.) fingers' width (at their tips) between the left (L) thumb tip and the left index finger tip.

famoto zi 7 saga ('division of 7 *saga*', i.e. 3½ *saga*). L.H. as above. The gap is 'four fingers'.

famoto zi 8 saga (i.e. 4 *saga*). The gap is four fingers' width just above the knuckle of the R.H.

famoto zi 9 saga (i.e. 4½ *saga*). A gap of four fingers just below the R.H. knuckle.

famoto zi 10 saga (i.e. 5 *saga*). L.H. as above, L thumb tip against outer side of R thumb top joint. L index finger tip against R palm edge on the life-line.

6 saga. Hands as for 5 *saga*, but with thumb tips together.

7 saga. Both hands encircle the piglet, with thumb tips together, and L first finger tip against R index finger tip.

8 saga. As for 7 *saga*, except that L and R index finger tips join.

9 saga. As for 8 *saga*, with a gap of one R.H. first finger width between the thumbs.

10 saga. As above, with a gap of two finger widths between the thumbs.

11 saga. As above, with a gap of three finger widths between the thumbs.

1 alisi (= 12 *saga*). Two spans of thumb tip to index finger tip (a *lito*) plus four fingers' width (try encircling your bent knee with both hands).

18 saga (i.e. 1½ *alisi*). Two spans plus the distance from edge of one palm to point of its extended thumb (*sagofa*).

2 alisi. Three spans.

2½ alisi. Three spans plus one finger width.

3 alisi. Three spans plus three fingers' width, or two spans plus one thumb-to-first finger span (*ri'i*) plus four fingers at the knuckle.

3½ alisi. Three spans plus *sagofa*.

4 alisi. Four spans.

5 alisi. Four spans plus three fingers' width at their mid-joints.

5½ alisi. Four spans plus four fingers' width at the knuckle.

sazilo (i.e. 6 *alisi*). Four spans plus *sagofa*.

APPENDIX 3:
Types of Non-Ceremonial Pig Exchange

Bawi nira'u ('borrowed pigs')
Pigs are borrowed to pay off a debt, to fund bridewealth, etc. The return must be exactly the same as the loan, size for size and in other respects. A male pig must be returned if a male was borrowed. If a male is replaced with a sow an increment (*fogozi galogo*) must be added, since males do not suffer the damaging effects of pregnancy and are therefore more valuable. If a sterilized sow is returned no increment is added. The like-for-like principle which operates in the measurement and the evaluation of the object is thus purely utilitarian in these types of impersonal exchange. Small pigs are not obtained in this way. In addition to the return, the borrower adds a sort of reward called *fanö'ö* 'so that no interest is charged'. The *fanö'ö* is usually fixed at *sazo'e* of rice (about one sack full) or 6 *saga*, regardless of the size of the loan.

Bawi ni'uri ('raised pigs')
This is a form of capital investment.[1] *A* gives *B* a pig of 1 *alisi* to look after. When it has grown to the size required, *A* reclaims it. If the pig is now 5 *alisi*, *A* and *B* 'divide the growth' between them. The growth is 4 *alisi*, so *A* pays back a pig of 2 *alisi* or other goods of this value. If the loaned pig is a sow, *A* and *B* divide the offspring as follows. If there are 4 offspring, 3 go to the *sanuri* ('raiser') and 1 to the *sobawi* ('pig-owner'); if there are 5 in the litter the ratio is 3/2; if 6: 4/2; if 7: 4/3. If the pig dies, the owner loses.

Bawi ni'owuru ('preserved pig')
A pig which is sick or has been speared while trespassing on fields is killed and butchered. Also pork is occasionally sold in this way in the village as a way of raising money. Since the pork is cheaper than in the market (there is no profit for the owner/butcher) and purchasers are invited to take part, it is a friendly transaction, different from an impersonal market sale. Only the well-off can afford a full share and the salt needed to preserve it (there is too much to eat at once). The number of divisions (*bacu*) depends on the girth. A pig of 5 *alisi* is divided into 5 *bacu* among 5, 10, or 20 men. One *bacu* is therefore the equivalent of 1 *alisi*, and if the live pig is worth 50,000 rupiah in the market, each *bacu* costs 10,000 rupiah; subdivisions are priced pro

---

[1] Vergouwen (1964 [1933]: 325) describes a similar arrangement among the Toba Batak.

rata. Formerly the value of *bacu* was fixed by custom: 1 *bacu* cost *sazo'e* of rice.

There are several ways of subdividing the *bacu*. Portions can be weighed against a stone, in the way that prestige payments are weighed at an *ovasa*.[2] Or they can be equalized by weighing them against one portion, used as a standard. If the division is made by creating equal piles (*nibacuagö*), judged by sight, then no subdivision is made: there are only 5 portions.

The valuation of the portions takes account of the difference between measurement by circumference, which is necessarily an approximation of size, and measurement by volume (e.g. by equalizing piles) or by weight. Oddly, the portions are still spoken of in terms of girth. Thus, if a 5 *alisi* pig is divided into 10 portions, each portion is called 6 *saga* (i.e. ½ *alisi*). In fact, where a figure of 5 *alisi* is given, this reflects an actual girth of 5½. The *ösi* (content) is said to be worth only 5 because ½ has been deducted to allow for waste in the butchering operation.

---

[2] Fries (1915: 129–30) describes a similar practice and notes that 'formerly' rice was used as the counterweight.

APPENDIX 4:
Exchange Rates

The following table shows exchange rates over a period of 140 years. Some figures are approximate, and adjustments have been made to take account of the difference between the northern and southern *so'e*. These figures are only as reliable as the sources, and there remain certain doubts, e.g. over the gold unit recorded by Nieuwenhuisen.

Source	Gold	Pigs	Rice	Money
N & R[a] 1848	1 *tail* (38 g.)	10 *alisi*	37 *so'e*	—
Schröder[b] 1908	*sara* (10 g.)	6 *alisi*	8 *so'e*	fl.10
Korn[c]		6 *saga* (½ *alisi*)	1 *so'e*	
1938	*sara* (10 g.)	5 *alisi*	10 *so'e*	—
A[d] 1925	*sara* (10 g.)	2 *alisi*	—	—
B[e]	1 *huakete* (1 g.)	6 *saga* (½ *alisi*)	1 *so'e*	
1940–	*sara* (= 10 *huakete*)	5 *alisi*	10 *so'e*	—
	(Rp.150,000)	(Rp.50,000)	(Rp.150,000)	
C[f]	*sara* (8 g.) (= 8 *huakete*)	5 *alisi*	8–10 *so'e*	—

[a] Commercial rates recorded by Nieuwenhuisen and Rosenberg (1863) in 1848 in the north. 1 *tumba* = 2 *kati* (3.3 lb.); 30 *tumba* = 1 *so'e* (100 lb.).
[b] Rate recorded by Schröder (1917) in Lahömi (west). The gold is medium quality.
[c] Customary rate in *öri* O'o'u (west Nias) (Korn 475/6).
[d] Customary rate in the Upper Susua around 1925.
[e] Post-1940 customary rate in the Upper Susua for non-commercial (i.e. non-market) exchange; still valid. Approximate market prices in 1986 are given in brackets. The gold is said to be 16-carat.
[f] Upper Susua customary ratio for bridewealth substitutions, still valid.

Nieuwenhuisen and Rosenberg (1863: 48–50) and Schröder (1917: 206) differ over the relative values of the *tail* (*tahil*), *pao* (pound), and *batu* as gold units.

The monetary value of the gold unit at precise dates was something I could not establish, lacking written evidence. Elders say that the rate 'formerly' (i.e. 'in Dutch times') was 10 florins = *sara*. Fries (1915: 149) reports the same figure. Schröder reports a value of fl.10 in the west and fl.12 in the north. In *öri* O'o'u, west Nias, the value of medium-quality gold (*siwalu alogo*) in 1938 is given as *sara* = fl.10 (Korn 475/6). The price seems to have been stable therefore from the beginning of the century until the Dutch departed. A list of the gold units, equivalent weights, and monetary values, as they were at the beginning of the century, is found in Fries (1915: 38, 149).

BIBLIOGRAPHY

MANUSCRIPTS IN THE KORN COLLECTION AT THE KONINKLIJK INSTITUUT VOOR TAAL-, LAND- EN VOLKENKUNDE, LEIDEN

The number 475/6 means 'bundle 475, item 6'. Authors are anonymous unless otherwise indicated.

BOUMAN, M. (1937), 'Nota over het Ori-wezen in Nias', in Korn 475/8.

PIEPER, A. (1921), Letter of 15 Mar. to A. Kruyt on the *adat* of Sa'ua, in Korn 479.

SAMSON, A. L. (1925a), 'Aanteekeningen betreffende het land en volk van öri Moro'ö (onderdistrict Mandrehe)', in Korn 475/2.

—— (1925b), 'Aanteekeningen betreffende het land en volk van het gebied bekend onder den naam Ono Maenamölö', in Korn 475/2.

475/6 (1938), 'Enige adatvragen in het onderdistrict Lölöwa'oe.'

—— 'Rapport pemereksaan asal oesoel kedatangan pendoedoek öri O'o'oe dan keadaan pendirian adatnya.'

475/10 (1938), 'Nota over het öri Lahömi.'

—— 'Keterangan dari mado-mado yang memboeat "fondrakö" di dalam satoe-satoe öri onderdistrict Lölöwa'oe.'

—— 'Onderzoek naar het ontstaan der öri O'o'oe gehouden te Hilinamadzjihönö', 28 Mar. 1938.

475/51 (1937), *Adat* of underdistrict Lahewa. Report (in Dutch) by Controleur of North Nias; with a postscript by M. Bouman, 18 May 1938.

476/28 (1937), Transcript (in Indonesian) of interview held at Hilisimaetanö, with the chiefs of Maenamölö, 17 Apr. 1937.

476/42 (1938), 'Bijlage bij het dagboek van den Controleur van Noord Nias over de maand Mei 1938.'

OTHER WORKS

ANDERSON, B. R. O'G. (1972), 'The Idea of Power in Javanese Culture', in C. Holt, B. Anderson, and J. Siegel (eds.), *Culture and Politics in Indonesia* (Ithaca, NY: Cornell University Press), 1–69.

ARDENER, EDWIN (1975), 'Belief and the Problem of Women', in Shirley Ardener (ed.), *Perceiving Women* (London: J. M. Dent), 1–27.

BARNES, R. H. (1974), *Kédang: A Study of the Collective Thought of an Eastern Indonesian People* (Oxford: Clarendon Press).

—— (1980a), 'Concordance, Structure, and Variation: Considerations of Alliance in Kédang', in Fox (1980a), 68–97.

—— (1980b), 'Marriage, Exchange and the Meaning of Corporations in Eastern Indonesia', in J. L. Comaroff (ed.), *The Meaning of Marriage Payments* (London: Academic Press), 93–122.

BARRAUD, CÉCILE (1979), *Tanebar-Evav: Une société de maisons tournée vers le large* (Cambridge: CUP).

BATESON, GREGORY (1958), *Naven*, 2nd edn. (Stanford, Calif.: Basic Books).

CHATELIN, L. N. (1881), 'Godsdienst en bijgeloof der Niassers', *Tijdschrift voor Indische Taal-, Land- en Volkenkunde*, 26: 109–67, 573–9.

DEMPWOLFF, O. (1938), *Austronesisches Wörterverzeichnis* (Berlin: Reimer).

DRUCKER, PHILIP (1967), 'The Potlatch', in George Dalton (ed.), *Tribal and Peasant Economies* (New York: Natural History Press), 481–93.

DUMONT, LOUIS (1961), Letter to *Man*, 24–5.

ENDICOTT, KIRK MICHAEL (1970), *An Analysis of Malay Magic* (Oxford: Clarendon Press).

FELDMAN, JEROME (1979), 'The House as World in Bawömataluo, South Nias', in E. M. Bruner and J. O. Becker (eds.), *Art, Ritual, and Society in Indonesia* (Papers in International Studies, Southeast Asia Series, 53; Athens, Oh.), 127–89.

FISCHER, H. TH. (1932), 'Der magische Charakter des Brautpreises', *Der Weltkreis*, 3(3): 65–8.

FORTES, MEYER (1959), 'Descent, Filiation and Affinity: A Rejoinder to Dr. Leach', Part I, *Man*, 193–7; Part II, *Man*, 206–12.

FORTH, GREGORY L. (1981), *Rindi: An Ethnographic Study of a Traditional Domain in Eastern Sumba* (KITLV Verhandelingen, 93; The Hague: Nijhoff).

FOX, JAMES J. (1971), 'Sister's Child as Plant: Metaphors in an Idiom of Consanguinity', in R. Needham (ed.), *Rethinking Kinship and Marriage* (ASA Monograph, 11; London: Tavistock), 219–52.

—— (1980a) (ed.), *The Flow of Life: Essays on Eastern Indonesia* (Cambridge, Mass.: Harvard University Press).

—— (1980b), 'Introduction', in Fox (1980a), 1–18.

—— (1980c), 'Obligation and Alliance: State Structure and Moiety Organization in Thie, Roti', in Fox (1980a), 98–133.

FRIES, E. (1908), 'Das "Koppensnellen" auf Nias', *Allgemeine Missions-Zeitschrift*, 35: 73–88.

—— (1915), *Leitfaden zur Erlernung der Niassischen Sprache* (Ombölata: Missionsdruckerei).

GOODY, JACK (1961), 'The Classification of Double Descent Systems', *Current Anthropology*, 2(1): 3–25.

GREGORY, C. A. (1982), *Gifts and Commodities* (London: Academic Press).

HALAWA, T., HAREFA, A., and SILITONGA, M. (1983), *Struktur Bahasa Nias* (Jakarta: Pusat Pembinaan dan Pengembangan Bahasa dan Kebudayaan Jakarta).

HALLPIKE, C. R. (1979), *The Foundations of Primitive Thought* (Oxford: Clarendon Press).

HÄMMERLE, JOHANNES M. (1982), *Nias: 'Land der Menschen'. Ein Beitrag aus Zentral Nias* (Münster: Missionsprokur der Kapuziner).

—— (1984), 'Die Megalithkultur im Susua-Gomo Gebiet, Nias', *Anthropos*, 79: 587–625.

—— (1986), *Famatö Harimao: Pesta Harimao-Fondrakö-Börönadu dan Kebudayaan lainnya di Wilayah Maenamölö- Nias Selatan* (Medan: Abidin).

HEINE-GELDERN, R. (1972 [1935]), 'The Archeology and Art of Sumatra', in Edwin M. Loeb, *Sumatra, Its History and People* (Singapore: Oxford University Press), 305–31.

HERTZ, ROBERT (1922), 'Le Péché et l'expiation dans les sociétés primitives', *Revue de l'histoire des religions*, 86: 1–60.

HOSKINS, JANET A. (1986), 'So My Name Shall Live: Stone-dragging and Grave-building in Kodi, West Sumba', *Bijdragen tot de Taal-, Land- en Volkenkunde*, 142: 31–51.

KAYSER, HELGA (1976), *Aspekte des sozio-kulturellen Wandels auf Nias: Schul- und Gesundheitswesen der Rheinischen Mission 1865–1940* (Munich: Renner).

KELLY, RAYMOND C. (1974), *Etoro Social Structure: A Study in Structural Contradiction* (Ann Arbor: University of Michigan Press).

KIRSCH, THOMAS (1973), *Feasting and Social Oscillation: A Working Paper on Religion and Society in Upland Southeast Asia* (Data Paper No. 52; Ithaca, NY: Cornell University Southest Asia Program).

KÖDDING, W. (1868a), 'Die zweite Station auf Nias', *Berichte der Rheinischen Missions-Gesellschaft*, 274–83.

—— (1868b), 'Prüfungszeiten auf Nias', *Berichte der Rheinischen Missions-Gesellschaft*, 359–76.

KRAMER, F. (1890), 'Der Götzendienst der Niasser', *Tijdschrift voor Indische Taal-, Land- en Volkenkunde*, 33: 473–500.

KRUYT, A. C. (1923), 'Koopen in Midden Celebes', *Mededeelingen der Koninklijke Akademie van Wetenschappen*, 56, Series B, No. 5: 149–78.

LAGEMANN, H. (1893), 'Das Niassische Mädchen von seiner Geburt bis zu seiner Verheiratung', *Tijdschrift voor Indische Taal-, Land- en Volkenkunde*, 36: 296–324.

—— (1906), 'Ein Heldensang der Niasser', *Tijdschrift voor Indische Taal-, Land- en Volkenkunde*, 48: 341–407.

LA'IYA, BAMBÖWÖ (1980), *Solidaritas Kekeluargaan dalam Salah Satu Masyarakat Desa di Nias, Indonesia* (Jakarta: Gadjah Mada University Press).

LAIYA, SITASI Z. *et al.* (1985), *Kamus Nias–Indonesia* (Jakarta: Pusat Pembinaan dan Pengembangan Bahasa).

LEACH, E. R. (1954), *Political Systems of Highland Burma: A Study of Kachin Social Structure* (London: Bell).

—— (1960), Letter to *Man*, 9–10.

—— (1961), *Rethinking Anthropology* (London: Athlone Press).

—— (1967), 'The Language of Kachin Kinship: Reflections on a Tikopia Model', in M. Freedman (ed.), *Social Organisation: Essays Presented to Raymond Firth* (London: Cass), 125–52.

LOMBARD, DENYS (1967), *Le Sultanat d'Atjeh au temps d'Iskandar Muda* (Publications de l'École Française d'Extrême-Orient, 61).

MALINOWSKI, B. (1922), *Argonauts of the Western Pacific* (London: Routledge).

MARSCHALL, WOLFGANG (1976), *Der Berg des Herrn der Erde* (Munich: Deutscher Taschenbuch Verlag).

MAUSS, MARCEL (1954), *The Gift*, trans. Ian Cunnison (London: Cohen and West).

MODIGLIANI, E. (1890), *Un viaggio a Nias* (Milan).

MOOR, J. H. (1837), 'Slave Trade at the Island of Nias', in *Notices of the Indian Archipelago and adjacent countries* (Singapore), 185–8.

MOORE, HENRIETTA L. (1988), *Feminism and Anthropology* (Cambridge: Polity Press).

MOYER, DAVID S. (1984), 'South Sumatra in the Indonesian Field of Anthropological Study', in P. E. de Josselin de Jong (ed.), *Unity in Diversity: Indonesia as a Field of Anthropological Study* (Dordrecht: Foris), 88–99.

MÜLLER, T. (1931), *Die 'grosse Reue' auf Nias. Geschichte und Gestalt einer Erweckung auf dem Missionsfelde* (Gütersloh: C. Bertelsmann).

MÜLLER-KRÜGER, THEODOR (1968), *Der Protestantismus in Indonesien: Geschichte und Gestalt* (Stuttgart: Evangelisches Verlagswerk).

MURDOCK, GEORGE PETER (1949), *Social Structure* (New York: Free Press).

NEEDHAM, RODNEY (1957), 'Circulating Connubium in Eastern Sumba: A Literary Analysis', *Bijdragen tot de Taal-, Land- en Volkenkunde*, 113: 168–78.

—— (1962), *Structure and Sentiment* (Chicago: Chicago University Press).

—— (1967), 'Terminology and Alliance, II: Mapuche, Conclusions', *Sociologus*, 17: 39–53.

—— (1970), 'Endeh, II: Test and Confirmation', *Bijdragen tot de Taal-, Land- en Volkenkunde*, 126: 246–58.

—— (1971), 'Remarks on the Analysis of Kinship and Marriage', in id. (ed.), *Rethinking Kinship and Marriage* (ASA Monograph, 11; London: Tavistock), 1–34.

—— (1973), 'Prescription', *Oceania*, 43: 166–81.

—— (1974), 'Age, Category and Descent', in id., *Remarks and Inventions: Skeptical Essays about Kinship* (London: Tavistock), 72–108.

—— (1980), 'Principles and Variations in the Structure of Sumbanese Society', in Fox (1980*a*), 21–47.

NIEUWENHUISEN, J. T., and ROSENBERG, H. C. B. VON (1863), *Verslag omtrent het eiland Nias en deszelfs bewoners* (Verhandelingen van het Koninklijk Bataviaasch Genootschap van Kunsten en Wetenschappen, 30; Batavia).

NOLL, J. (1930), 'Die ersten Heidentaufen an der ehemaligen Stätte der Entstehung des niassischen Götzendienst', *Berichte der Rheinischen Missions-Gesellschaft*, 299–304.

NOTHOFER, B. (1984), 'The Barrier Island Languages in the Austronesian Language Family', unpub. paper given at the Fourth International conference on Austronesian Linguistics in Suva, Fiji.

RADCLIFFE-BROWN, A. R. (1950), 'Introduction', in A. R. Radcliffe-Brown and Daryll Forde (eds.), *African Systems of Kinship and Marriage* (London: Oxford University Press), 1–85.

RAPPARD, T. C. (1909), 'Het eiland Nias en zijne Bewoners', *Bijdragen tot de Taal-, Land- en Volkenkunde*, 62: 477–648.

RICKLEFS, M. C. (1981), *A History of Modern Indonesia c.1300 to the Present* (London: Macmillan).

ROTH, ROLF B. (1985), 'Simeuluë-Nias-Mentawai-Enggano. Eine bibliographische Ergänzung und Erweiterung (1959–1984) zu Suzukis "Critical Survey" ', *Anthropos*, 80: 421–70.

SAHLINS, MARSHALL D. (1965), 'On the Ideology and Composition of Descent Groups', *Man*, 65: 104–7.

SCHEFOLD, REIMAR (1986), 'The Unequal Brothers-in-Law; Indonesia as a "Field of Anthropological Study" and the Case of Mentawai', *Bijdragen tot de Taal-, Land- en Volkenkunde*, 142: 69–86.

SCHEKATZ, HERBERT (1969), 'Der Einfluss der Häuptlinge in der Nias-Kirche (BNKP)', *Evangelische Missionszeitschrift* (Stuttgart), NF 26: 230–9.

SCHNEPEL, BURKHARD (1987), 'Max Weber's Theory of Charisma and its Applicability to Anthropological Research', *Journal of the Anthropological Society of Oxford*, 18(1): 26–48.

SCHNITGER, F. M. (1939), *Forgotten Kingdoms of Sumatra* (Leiden: Brill).

SCHRÖDER, E. E. W. GS. (1917), *Nias, ethnographische, geographische en historische aanteekeningen en studien* (Leiden: Brill).

SCHULTE NORDHOLT, H. G. (1971), *The Political System of the Atoni of Timor* (KITLV Verhandelingen, 60; The Hague: Nijhoff).

SINGARIMBUN, M. (1975), *Kinship, Descent and Alliance among the Karo Batak* (Berkeley: University of California Press).

STEINHART, W. L. (1929), 'De Christianiseering van het Niassche begrip "heilig" ', *De Opwekker*, 74: 47–58.

—— (1934), 'Niassche teksten', *Tijdschrift voor Indische Taal-, Land- en Volkenkunde*, 74: 326–75, 391–440.

—— (1937), 'Niassche teksten', *Verhandelingen van het Koninklijk Bataviaasch Genootshap van Kunsten en Wetenschappen*, Vol. lxxiii (Batavia).

—— (1954), *Niasse teksten* (The Hague: Martinus Nijhoff).

STRATHERN, ANDREW (1971), *The Rope of Moka* (Cambridge: CUP).

SUNDERMANN, H. (1892), 'Kleine Niassische Chrestomathie mit Wörterverzeischniss', *Bijdragen tot de Taal-, Land- en Volkenkunde*, 41: 335–446.

—— (1905*a*), *Niassisch–deutsches Wörterbuch* (Barmen).

—— (1905*b*), *Die Insel Nias und die Mission daselbst* (Barmen: Verlag des Missionshauses).

SUZUKI, PETER T. (1958), *Critical Survey of Studies on the Anthropology of Nias, Mentawai and Enggano* (The Hague: Martinus Nijhoff).

—— (1959), *The Religious System and Culture of Nias, Indonesia* (The Hague: Excelsior).

THOMAS, J. W. (1892), *Drei Jahre in Südnias, Erlebnisse* (Barmen: Verlag des Missionshauses).

THOMSEN, MARTIN G. TH. (1976), *Famareso Ngawalö Huku Föna Awö Gowe Nifasindro ba Danö Niha* (Gunung Sitoli: BNKP).

—— (1979), 'Die Sage vom Stammvater Hija. Ein Gesang aus Mittelnias', *Zeitschrift für Ethnologie*, 104 (2): 209–77.

TIBBETTS, G. R. (1979), *A Study of the Arabic Texts containing Material on South-east Asia* (Leiden and London: Brill).

VERGOUWEN, J. C. (1964), *The Social Organization and Customary Law of the Toba-Batak of Northern Sumatra* (KITLV Translation Series, 7; The Hague: Nijhoff).

VIARO, ALAIN M. (1980), *Urbanisme et architecture traditionnels du sud de l'île de Nias* (UNESCO, Établissements humains et environnement socio-culturel, 21).

WATERSON, H. ROXANA (1986), 'The Ideology and Terminology of Kinship among the Sa'dan Toraja', *Bijdragen tot de Taal-, Land- en Volkenkunde*, 142: 87–112.

WATSON, C. W. (1984), 'Comments on David S. Moyer's Paper', in P. E. de

Josselin de Jong (ed.), *Unity in Diversity: Indonesia as a Field of Anthropological Study* (Dordrecht: Foris), 100–5.

WILKINSON, R. J. (1932), *A Malay–English Dictionary* (Mytilene: Salavopoulos and Kinderlis).

WOUDEN, F. A. E. VAN (1977), 'Local Groups and Double Descent in Kodi, West Sumba', in P. E. de Josselin de Jong (ed.), *Structural Anthropology in the Netherlands* (The Hague: Martinus Nijhoff), 184–222.

ZEBUA, S. (1984), *Sejarah Kebudayaan Ono Niha, Seri 2* (Gunung Sitoli: By the author).

GLOSSARY

adat: (Indon.) custom, tradition
afore: measuring stick for pigs
alave: female
alisi: girth, unit of pig measurement
ama: father
ana'a: gold
ana'iwa: tributary gift
azu: idol (north: *adu*)
banua: village
batu: unit of gold
bawi: pig
behu: unhewn vertical memorial monument
böli: price
böli niha: bridewealth
bö'ö: other, unrelated
bosi: step, grade
bövö: wife-givers' prestations
eheha: spiritual element possessed by northern chiefs
ere: priest or specialist
evali: paved village square
fanö'ö: payment to creditor in lieu of interest
fo'omo: spouse
halama: substantial field house
harazaki: good fortune, prosperity
horö: sin, transgression, state of war
ina: mother
lakha: widow
lakhömi: glory, lustre, prestige, chiefly virtue
lauru: large rice-measure
löfö: fortune
Lovalangi: God
mado: clan
maso-maso: bridewealth portion to bride's mother's agnates
matua: male, wife's father and his group
naekhu-naekhu: support loan
nafulu: local descent group, (south) work squad
nga'ötö: genealogical line
niha: person, Niasan (adj.)

nira'u: friendly loan
omo: house
omo sebua: chief's house
ona: market place
ono: child, wife-taker
ono mbanua: villager
ono niha: Niasan
ono yomo: uxorilocal son-in-law
öri: federation of villages
osali: village temple, church
ose: field hut
ovasa: feast of merit
salakha: cursed or prohibited
salawa: chief, leading man
sara: one, one unit of gold
satua mbanua: village elder
sibaya: mother's male agnate
siulu: (south) noble
so'i-so'i: solicitory gifts from wife-givers
sovatö: host
sulö: donation of live pig for slaughter as *urakha*
sumange: tribute, respect
tanö: land
tome: guest
tumba: rice-measure
urakha: weighed portion of meat, prestige payment

INDEX

Aceh 3–4, 187, 204
adat 116, 236, 248
adoption 29, 39–40, 172, 173, 175
adultery 143, 176–9, 213
affinal prestations 116–19, 126–7, 130–42, 248–51, 202, 225, 228, 259–61
see also *bövö*; bridewealth; *ovasa*; wife-givers; wife-takers
affines:
    antagonism between 75, 138, 144, 150, 231–3, 236
    distinction from marriage parties 111–15
    inequality of 64–5, 95, 103, 118, 132, 145, 150, 171, 246–7; see also reversal
    see also alliance groups; wife-givers; wife-takers
afore pig-measure 190, 194–8, 201, 212
afterlife, see eschatology
age, see relative age
agnates 31, 32, 33, 35, 36, 40, 50–3, 160, 168, 219, 234–5, 257, 259, 287
    see also lineage
alliance 55–80
    categories 73–6, 91, 94–6, 227
    and class 64–5
    groups 53, 56–65, 68, 69, 74, 80, 91, 94–5, 112
    ideology 63, 69–73, 148, 172, 219–20, 223, 246–7
    idioms of 59–69
    initiating of 112–13, 119–25
    and local exogamy 65–9
    native models 62–3, 66, 74
    renewal 67, 76–9, 84, 103, 108, 130
    and status 57, 61–3, 67, 107–8, 171–2
Amoroa 14, 15, 46
ancestors 31, 34, 36, 73, 122–3, 218–20, 228–9, 230, 243, 245–7, 262–3, 275
ancestor figures 19, 33–4, 43, 68, 133, 162, 187, 243
ancestor worship 31, 33–6, 54, 71, 123, 124, 148, 154, 216, 218–20, 228
Anderson, B. R. O'G. 276

anomalous unions 30, 34, 67 n., 68–9, 74, 76, 91, 105–6, 176–9
Aramö 13, 25, 111
architecture 11
Ardener, E. 99
asymmetric alliance, see alliance
asymmetry 96–7
atavism 105–6
Atoni 29 n.
avoidance 148 n., 172 n.

background, in conception of person 69, 105–6, 110
    see also origin
Balöhili 13, 14, 16, 22–4, 26, 255, 300
Banua Bahili 13
Barnes, R. H. vii, 22, 29 n., 63 n., 64 n., 70 n., 95 n.
Barraud, Cécile 187 n.
barter 201, 202–3
Batak 3, 19, 55, 84
    see also Karo Batak; Toba Batak
Bateson, Gregory 279 n.
batu 125, 193, 203
    see also gold unit
Batu Islands 2, 7, 185 n., 190
betel 52, 121, 125, 185, 233, 242
betrothal 110, 121–5, 132
Bible 7, 42, 170, 209, 214, 220, 263
blessing 42, 63, 72, 76, 93, 98, 123, 124, 140, 148, 150, 208, 219, 223, 228, 243, 246, 278
    Request for Blessing feast 36, 202, 276
Böe 17, 24, 30
Börönövö 23
Botohili 7
boundary 47, 178–9
bövö 116, 129, 154–5, 189, 244, 248–50, 259–60, 262
breath 42, 184, 277
bride 117
    incorporation in husband's lineage 37, 96, 153–4
    rights in 124, 132, 140, 155, 168
    song of 153
bride service 29, 172–3